THE **2007**

COMPENSATION
HANDBOOK
FOR CHURCH
STAFF

A CHURCH LAW & TAX RESOURCE

James F. Cobble, Jr., D.Min., Ed.D. &
Richard R. Hammar, J.D., LL.M., CPA

YOUR
CHURCH

Christianity Today International
www.churchlawtoday.com

YOUR CHURCH

The 2007 Compensation Handbook for Church Staff

Copyright © 2006 Church Law & Tax Report/Christianity Today International

For any other use, including for tuition-based classroom use, advance permission must be obtained from the copyright holder. For information, contact:

Church Law & Tax Permissions
Christianity Today International
Resources Dept.
465 Gundersen Dr.
Carol Stream, IL 60188
Phone: (877) 247-4787
E-mail: **cltodaycustserv@christianitytoday.com**

Visit our Web site: **www.churchlawtoday.com**

CREDITS

Authors: James F. Cobble, Jr., D.Min., Ed.D. & Richard R. Hammar, J.D., LL.M., CPA

Editor: Janine Petry

Executive Editor: Amy Simpson

Designer: Mary Bellus and Ragont Design

Cover Designer: Dean H. Renninger

Cover image © 2006 Jupiterimages Corporation

0-917463-29-3

978-0-917463-29-7

10 9 8 7 6 5 4 3 2 1   08 07 06

Printed in the United States of America

TABLE OF CONTENTS

1

BEFORE YOU BEGIN

If you've ever had questions or needed guidance when it comes to compensation planning for your church staff, you've picked up the right resource. Welcome to *The 2007 Compensation Handbook for Church Staff*. As you read through this introductory chapter, you'll learn about the many ways you can maximize the use of this book to meet your compensation planning needs.

The *Compensation Handbook* was developed to provide church leaders and employees with a current and reliable picture of compensation practices across a broad spectrum of American churches. It presents survey data from nearly 1,300 churches representing approximately 6,600 staff members. The survey data was obtained between January 2006 and May 2006 from churches that subscribe to one or more of the following: *Church Law & Tax Report, Church Treasurer Alert!, Church Secretary Today, Leadership Journal,* various Christianity Today International e-newsletters. The information included can play an important role in determining equitable compensation packages for church staff members. More specifically, the *Compensation Handbook* can help you to:

- **determine appropriate compensation levels for eleven key pastoral, professional, and support staff positions (Note: Nine of these positions have information for both full-time and part-time individuals. Two of these positions are unique: part-time organist, and part-time pastor, which includes both part-time senior pastors and part-time solo pastors in one grouping.)**

- **develop effective compensation packages—guidelines are given in the Special Section of this handbook to help you create a package which will maximize net income while remaining in compliance with federal tax laws.**

- **provide church workers with a statistical framework for evaluating their present compensation package—comparisons can be made regarding church size, budget, setting, and other important variables.**

- **develop an objective standard for evaluating requests for raises and changes in benefits.**

- **assist denominational offices and other ecclesiastical organizations in promoting equitable and fair compensation practices within their churches.**

- **better understand the nature of church compensation planning.**

How to Make the Best Use of this Book

Compensation planning is a multi-faceted process. This book is one tool that you can use to guide you in measuring appropriate levels of compensation, but it is not a complete guide. Many factors go into determining compensation planning, and this book attempts to help you explore those aspects knowledgeably.

A key feature that this book uses is the many informative tables found throughout the book. The background information you need in order to use the data in these tables with ease and accuracy is found in Chapter 2: *Using the Compensation Tables*. Included in this chapter is an example that illustrates how to determine the compensation range for a senior pastor. You can use the same process to examine all of the staff positions.

Chapter 3 provides comparisons between the national averages of the eleven staff positions included in this study. Table 3-1 provides a comparative ranking of each position.

Chapters 4 through 14 provide detailed information on each individual staff position. Each chapter begins by providing an employment profile of the staff position. Natural curiosity will pull most church staff members immediately to the chapter which presents data about their position. Remember, though, understanding chapters 2 and 3 is critical to using this book effectively.

Chapter 17 provides a statistical abstract of the churches participating in this study. This data is useful for learning more about the churches that are contributing information. This chapter can also help you to examine: 1) trends in church attendance and income; 2) the percentage of church budgets devoted to salaries; 3) the percentage of churches that contribute to Social Security; and 4) the percentage of churches that reimburse professional expenses.

The Special Section: *Tax Law & Compensation Planning*, found toward the end of the book, provides critical information for completing the compensation planning process. Anyone engaged in this type of planning for church staff members must become familiar with some basic federal tax laws, since the structure of a compensation package can either help or hurt a church staff member. This special section explores in detail the major—and often hard-to-understand—laws that affect compensation planning. It also provides tax saving tips that can benefit everyone. Additional resources are also listed in this section.

Background Information

The results in the charts to follow represent the churches that participated in the survey. The sampling population used was a fair representation of American churches, but certain church sizes, budget sizes, and denominations have a stronger representation than others. To the extent possible, we have attempted to organize the data in ways that avoid small samples. At times, however, small samples simply reflect a reality such as rural churches with an attendance over 1,000, or churches smaller than 100 with a full-time business administrator. Nevertheless, sample size should be taken into account when considering the value of any particular finding.

Here are a few additional facts to help clarify the data analyses which follow.

- **Averages and quartiles ("Lowest 25%" and "Highest 25%") are based on individuals receiving one or more items in the compensation and/or benefit packages. Zeros are included in calculations.**

- **A footnote that says *"Not enough responses to provide meaningful data"* means either one or both of these:**
  - **There are less than eight people responding.**
  - **There are relatively few responses (maybe more than eight) with a very wide gap between the lowest and highest values that throws off the quartile values.**

- ⮑ **Blanks (no response) and zeros are treated similarly and are part of the compensation quartiles and averages calculations.**

- ⮑ **Figures that appeared unrealistic or way outside the normal distribution were eliminated to avoid skewing the results.**

- ⮑ **Some percentages may add up to more than 100% due to rounding. This particularly refers to the data found at the beginning of each section titled, "Employment Profile."**

- ⮑ **Data for part-time senior pastors and part-time solo pastors are combined under the heading "Part-time Pastor," since there was not enough data to separate them out.**

Explanation of Average Compensation Package Tables

At the end of several chapters, you will find an additional table with the title, "Average Compensation Package." This extra table shows the breakdown of compensation components, which includes base salary, parsonage allowance, and housing allowance. For six of the eleven positions, total compensation averages varied greatly by the differing combinations of these components. The six positions are Solo Pastors, Youth Pastors, Adult Ministry Directors, Children's/Preschool Directors, Music/Choir Directors, and Administrators. For these positions, data is provided in the following five groups to illustrate the differences in compensation depending on the combination of components:

1. **Those who receive base salary only**

2. **Those who do not receive base salary but receive parsonage and housing allowances**

3. **Those who receive base salary and parsonage allowance but not housing allowance**

4. **Those who receive base salary and housing allowance but no parsonage allowance**

5. **Those who receive base salary, parsonage allowance, and housing allowance**

This data serves as a guideline for compensation planning, depending on the combination of compensation components being offered at your church.

Explanation of the Use of Quartiles

In the charts that follow, quartiles, noted as "Lowest 25%" and "Highest 25%" are used to represent survey findings. A quartile is one of four segments of a distribution that has been divided into quarters. A particular quartile is the border between two neighboring quarters of the distribution. So that, for example in showing "base salary," the 25% quartile (*Lowest 25%*) actually means that the number shown represents a number that exceeds the base salary of 1-25% of the people in the population represented in the report.

The same thing is true with the 75% quartile (*Highest 25%*), which actually means that the number shown represents a number that exceeds the base salary of 1-75% of the people in the population represented in the report.

The *Average,* also called the *mean,* is a value that depends equally on all of the data, and may include outliers. It is calculated by taking the sum of all the data values, dividing by the total number of data values. Please keep in mind that the averages, as presented, are not the averages of the highest and lowest quartiles, but an overall average of the data.

To illustrate:

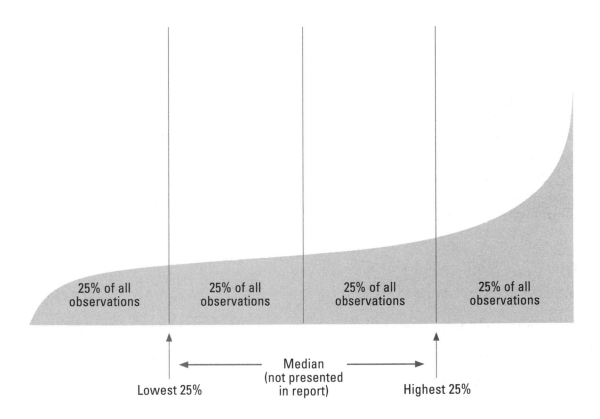

2

USING THE COMPENSATION TABLES

The following chapters present compensation patterns for eleven major positions within the local church. These profiles are the statistical heart of the *Compensation Handbook*. This chapter is designed to help you interpret the tables and maximize your use of the information in this book.

Each staff position has its own chapter, including both compensation tables and a discussion of the findings. The tables are for full-time staff members, except for the last two tables in each chapter which provides data for part-time staff members. Note, however, that due to the low incidence of part-time Solo and Senior Pastors, their data have been combined. Chapter 6 focuses on this unique situation. A comparative summary of all the positions is presented in Chapter 3.

Interpreting the Tables

Each chapter contains tables that portray compensation averages according to several key variables. The variables include the following:

- **Worship attendance (Sunday morning)**
- **Church income (from all sources)**
- **Church setting and size[1]**
- **Gender**
- **Education**
- **Years employed (in current position)**
- **Region**
- **Denomination**

Each table provides key characteristics that include:

- **Average Sun AM worship attendance**
- **Average church income**
- **Average # of years employed**
- **Average # of weeks of paid vacation**
- **% College graduate or higher**
- **% Who receive auto reimbursement**

---

[1] Five church size groupings are used: 250 & Under, 251-500, 501-750, 751-1,000, and Over 1,000.

⊃ **% Ordained**

⊃ **Average % salary increase this year**

In addition, each table provides several columns of averages for these compensation and benefit items (Compensation and Benefits are listed separately):

⊃ **Base Salary—annual base salary**

⊃ **Housing—amount of housing allowance provided for the purchase or rent of a home and its up-keep and furnishings[2]**

⊃ **Parsonage—rental value of parsonage plus other housing expenses[2]**

⊃ **Retirement—money church provides for retirement, not including social security payments**

⊃ **Life Insurance—cost of life insurance provided for staff member as a benefit**

⊃ **Health Insurance—cost of health insurance provided for staff member as a benefit**

⊃ **Continuing Education—amount of funds provided for continuing education**

Immediately following each listed compensation and benefits item are three categories: *Highest 25%, Average,* and *Lowest 25%.* The number listed after *Lowest 25%* represents a number that exceeds the base salary of 1-25% of the people in the population represented in the report. Similarly, the number following *Highest 25%* represents a number that exceeds the base salary of 1-75% of the people in the population represented in the report (for more information, please see section titled, "Explanation of the Use of Quartiles" in the first chapter.)

---

[2] In gathering data, we allowed respondents to use their own judgment in determining the definitions of housing, benefits, and parsonages.

To illustrate, consider this example:

TABLE: ANNUAL COMPENSATION OF
SENIOR PASTOR BY CHURCH SETTING & SIZE

ATTENDANCE 250 & UNDER		Church Setting			
		Metropolitan city	Suburb of large city	Small town or rural city	Farming area
COMPENSATION					
Base Salary:	Highest 25%	$43,001	$44,330	$41,000	$44,164
	Average	$34,525	$37,661	$34,054	$38,521
	Lowest 25%	$24,768	$28,838	$26,002	$27,499
Housing:	Highest 25%	$25,204	$29,994	$24,005	$18,436
	Average	$16,869	$20,757	$15,910	$10,902
	Lowest 25%	$3,996	$9,500	$3,000	–
Parsonage:	Highest 25%	–	–	–	$7,201
	Average	$1,843	$3,902	$2,521	$3,631
	Lowest 25%	–	–	–	–
Total Compensation	Highest 25%	$68,666	$69,999	$60,469	$56,001
	Average	$53,237	$62,320	$52,485	$53,054
	Lowest 25%	$42,351	$52,001	$42,614	$39,999
Number of Respondents		49	94	130	13

– Not enough responses to provide meaningful data

Notice that within the heading *Base Salary,* figures are shown in three categories: *Highest 25%, Average,* and *Lowest 25%.* After *Highest 25%,* the number $43,001 appears. This means that 25% of all Senior Pastors serving a church in the Metropolitan city setting, and with a church attendance of 250 and under make $43,001 or more. Another way to say this is that 75% of pastors in the Metropolitan city make less than $43,001.

After the category *Average,* the number $34,525 is listed. This number represents the average amount of the salaries for all respondents.

Following the category *Lowest 25%* the number $24,768 appears, which indicates that 25% of all Senior Pastors in the same Metropolitan City setting and church size make $24,768 or less. Again, another way to say this is that 75% of pastors in the Metropolitan city make more than $24,768.

Also, all calculated figures, including the sub-categories *Highest 25%, Average,* and *Lowest 25%* are based on individuals receiving one or more items in the Compensation chart (the same is true of the Benefits chart). Zeros are included in calculations.

Total Compensation plus Benefits Comparisons

At the bottom of each Compensation chart is a category that lists *Total Compensation*. These numbers include the averages of the base salary, housing allowance, and parsonage allowance. Likewise, at the bottom of each Benefits chart is a category that lists *Total Benefits*. These numbers include the averages of the Retirement, Life Insurance, Health Insurance, and Continuing Education benefits. A separate box in the table, titled *Total Compensation and Benefit* includes the averages of all of the Compensation and Benefits items. Note: *Totals are the key figures for compensation analysis.*

ROUNDING ERRORS

Rounding errors may exist in some of the data in this study. They do not, however, impact the final results in any significant way.

Using the Tables to Plan Compensation

The most important use of this handbook is for compensation planning. The following example illustrates one approach of how this book can be used.

EXAMPLE: PLANNING THE COMPENSATION OF A SENIOR PASTOR

Pastor West has served as senior pastor of Maywood Church for the past nine years. Maywood Church is a suburban congregation with an average Sunday worship attendance of 395, and an annual budget of $775,000. Pastor West has a Master of Divinity degree.

The above example provides us with relevant data that can be used in coordination with the tables in this book. Church income and attendance are the two most important variables we looked at in predicting compensation. Other factors that we will look at include the geographical setting of the church (in this case suburban), plus the pastor's length of service (nine years) and educational background (Master of Divinity degree).

KEY POINT

The goal is not to come up with a single compensation number, but rather to identify a *compensation range*. Once that range is determined, a variety of factors will affect the final choice of a specific level of compensation.

STEP 1

The first step is to use the Tables in Chapter 6 to identify the *average compensation range* for senior pastors in settings comparable to those of Pastor West. We begin by examining *worship attendance* (Table 4-1), *church income* (Table 4-2), and *church setting and size* (which for this example is Table 4-4: a church set in the suburb of a large city with an attendance between 251-500). The main data we are interested in is found at the bottom of each table in the box labeled *Total Compensation + Benefit*. There we find data that summarizes the average church attendance, income, years employed, and compensation for the participants detailed in each column of each table. Also, we can examine the range of the middle 50% of respondents by looking at the *Lowest 25%* and the *Highest 25%* numbers. The relevant data from these tables are summarized below.

1. Data for Example	2. Average Sun AM worship attendance	3. Average church income	4. Average compensation + benefits	5. Range of middle 50% of respondents
Maywood Church	395	$775,000	To be determined	N/A
Table 4-1 [Worship attendance] 301-500	407	$803,997	$90,156	$74,397–$104,164
Table 4-2 [Church Income] $751K-$1M	475	$883,747	$89,096	$74,214–$102,636
Table 4-4 Suburb of large city with attendance of 251-500	384	$821,598	$90,022	$74,400–$102,854

The above table enables us to establish a compensation and benefits range. This is based on the average compensation + benefits (column 4). The data from Tables 4-1, 4-2, and 4-4 provide us with a range of *average compensation + benefits* between $89,096 on the low end to $90,156 on the high end. These figures serve as an *average compensation range.*

Since church income is one of the most important factors in determining compensation, let's begin by focusing on column 3. First, we see that the average church income for Maywood Church is slightly lower than the amounts for Table 4-1, Table 4-2, and Table 4-4. As a result, church income may be a factor in making an adjustment to the base compensation + benefits range.

Also, we note that Maywood Church's attendance, found in column 1, is similar to the average attendance found in the other three tables. Overall, we can conclude that Maywood church is quite similar in most respects to the data found in the three tables.

These conclusions suggest that the base compensation + benefits range of $89,096 to $90,156 fits the profile of Maywood Church fairly well, though it doesn't take into account other factors not measured in this study. Next, let's look at two variations of our example and consider the resulting implications for the base compensation range.

Variation 1

First, let's change Maywood Church's income from $775,000 to $950,000. This produces a per capita giving of $2,405. The income and giving would then be higher than the averages from Tables 4-1, 4-2 and 4-4. That suggests that Pastor West's *average compensation range* might be increased beyond the upper limit of $90,156. How much beyond will depend on the factors that we examine in Steps 2 and 3 below.

Variation 2

Next, suppose that Maywood Church's income drops to $650,000. That results in a per capita income of $1,646. Both the income and the per capita giving would be below the national averages presented above. That suggests that Pastor West's compensation may be lower than the average range taken from column five. The final determination would depend on several of the factors that we examine below.

After establishing a base compensation+ benefit range, the next step is to determine if Pastor West's final compensation + benefit should fit within that range, and if so where, or if the compensation + benefit should go beyond or below that range based upon other key factors such as education, length of service, and congregational values, and if so, how much above or below.

In making the final determination, the quartiles provide us with some working boundaries on both the upper and lower limits. Since, on initial observation, there is nothing extraordinary about Maywood Church's profile, in all likelihood, Pastor West's compensation + benefit will fall within the middle 50% range of respondents, as described in column 5 on our chart above (using the *Lowest 25%* and *Highest 25%* numbers).

STEP 2

The second step is to examine additional factors that might impact compensation + benefit such as *education* and *years of service*. This requires an examination of Table 5-9: *Annual Compensation of Senior Pastors by Education,* and Table 5-10: *Annual Compensation of Senior Pastors by Years Employed.* These factors do not have as strong a correlation with compensation and benefits as do church income and attendance. As such, they are less useful in establishing a compensation + benefit range, but are helpful in deciding whether an individual is in the upper or lower parts of the range identified in Step 1.

1. Profile of Pastor West M.Div. 9 years exp.	2. Average Sun AM worship attendance	3. Average # of years employed	4. Average Church income	5. Average compen-sation + benefits	6. Range of middle 50% of respondents
Maywood Church	395	9	$775,000	To be determined	N/A
Table 4-9 Master's Degree	575	11	$1,005,953	$85,631	$65,800–$101,558
Table 4-10 6–10 year service	509	8	$920,367	$83,983	$64,600–$98,800

In column 5 above, we find that the average compensation for pastors with a master's degree is very close to the national average ($85,631 compared to $87,284). Similarly, those with 6-10 years of service, such as Pastor West, receive an annual compensation similar to the national average ($83,983 compared to $87,284). So, based on the data for Pastor West, education and years of service will not be factors in making adjustments to compensation plus benefits.

Variation 1

Suppose Pastor West has a doctoral degree. On average, senior pastors with a doctorate earn approximately $15,186 above the national average (see Table 5-10 in Chapter 5). In part this is because they serve in higher income churches. The average compensation + benefit for those with a doctorate is $102,470. This falls with the range we identified from Step 1 ($89,096 to $90,156). The average church attendance for those with doctorates is 664, which is higher than Maywood Church's average of 395, and the average church income of $1,480,481 is well above that of Maywood's $775,000. So all things considered, the compensation range from Step 1 would still serve us fairly well even if Pastor West had a doctoral degree. Nevertheless, a doctoral degree is a relevant factor that suggests higher levels of compensation are normal. How much higher will vary from one situation to another. In this case it would be a positive factor that might suggest moving toward or above the higher end of the range from Step 1 rather than the lower end of the range.

Variation 2

What if Pastor West's educational level is lower than a Master of Divinity degree? It would probably have little impact. The reason is that Maywood Church has an average income and attendance that is well above that of most churches with pastors that have less education, and church income and attendance are the strongest factors that correlate with pastoral compensation. As a result, even with less education (or years of service), the compensation range established in Step 1 still applies.

STEP 3

The third step is to take into account the unique circumstances that define each individual situation. One factor is the cost of living for your area. Is it higher or lower than the national average? Your local Chamber of Commerce or a real estate agency can help you obtain that information. Other factors such as denominational affiliation (see Table 4-12), theological beliefs, pastoral performance, financial needs, goodwill, the local economy, personal motivation, congregational goals, internal church politics, and many other considerations will also contribute to the final decision. For some churches that may mean a final compensation package much lower or much higher than the projected range listed in Step 1. How that compensation will be divided up will vary greatly from one church to another, and even from one individual staff member to another. Care should be given, however, to avoid gender discrimination. This is a widespread problem involving many churches (see Table 4-8). In addition, a large disparity between the pastor's compensation, and that of other staff members, can have an impact on the rate of increase that the pastor may experience in future years. Often, once a staff member has reached the upper limits of his or her compensation range, future raises may be somewhat smaller in order to better compensate other staff members.

The final determination of compensation + benefit is unique to every congregation. It would not be surprising to see a range of compensation for Pastor West somewhere between $70,000 - $95,000. Higher compensation levels are possible, and could be argued to be reasonable. It would be unlikely, however, for Pastor West to exceed $110,000, which would fall outside the limits of the *Highest 25%* range for churches similar to Maywood Church. Such a compensation level would require independent justification to avoid the possibility of intermediate sanctions (see the Special Section for a discussion of intermediate sanctions). Also, remember that a crucial step in this decision-making process must involve an awareness of tax law found in the Special Section.

The detailed process above can be used for each of the eleven staff positions found in this handbook. This same process can be used for each of the nine staff positions found in this handbook.

3

COMPENSATION PROFILES: GENERAL COMPARISONS

This chapter provides comparisons of the average compensations for the eleven staff positions included in this study. A summary table exists for each of the variables examined. More detailed analysis can be found in the individual chapter for each staff position.

As expected, Senior pastors consistently rank first in total compensation for church staff members. Adult Ministry Directors and Associate pastors received the next highest compensation amount followed generally by Music/Choir Directors and Solo pastors. The tables presented later in this chapter provide compensation comparisons according to the national averages for each position.

What Factors Determine Compensation and Benefits?

In general, church income, attendance, education, gender, geographical setting and years of service play some role in almost every church. Among the variables we looked at, church income and attendance proved to play a big role in affecting compensation and benefits for each of the positions examined in this study. Yet, the correlation between these variables and employee compensation accounts for only part of the variation in compensation figures by position. These factors, while important, must be viewed in the context of other factors, the combination of which ultimately determine compensation and benefits.

As an example, theology may play a significant role in some churches in the determination of compensation. The compensation of a Catholic priest who has taken a vow of poverty will be low regardless of church size or income. In churches that promote financial prosperity as a sign of God's blessing, the pastor may receive a disproportionate amount of the church's total income. Politics and power may prove the decisive factors in determining compensation in a church embroiled in conflict. A building program may be the controlling factor somewhere else. In general, education, geographical setting, and years of service play some role in almost every church.

Please note this about gender differences: female staff members consistently received significantly lower compensation than did their male counterparts in all positions except Solo Pastor, Associate Pastor, and Secretary. Some of the difference can be explained on the basis of demographic factors such as education. The position with the largest gap between men and women as well as having a sufficient sample size was Administrator—on average, for this position, females earned approximately 65% of the compensation of males. Or, in other words, males earned 55% more than females.

Benefits vary significantly from one position to the next. This was especially true for the more important health insurance and retirement programs. Fifty to eighty percent of church staff have health insurance and 37 to 70 percent have retirement benefits. Part-time staff members receive fewer fringe benefits.

General Trends

This study examined the "rate of increase" with respect to compensation and church attendance, and compensation and church income. In this context, "rate of increase" refers to the percent change in compensation with respect to church attendance or size of church budget.

For most staff positions, the rate of increase for total compensation was the highest for churches with an attendance between 301-500. Youth Pastors, Children's/Preschool Directors, Secretaries, and Custodians experienced modest compensation change, as the church size increased. Like the other positions, compensation increase rate is lower in churches with an attendance between 501-1,000.

Similar trends could be seen based upon church income. For most staff positions, the rate of increase for total compensation was the highest for churches with an income between $251-$500K. Youth Pastors and Children's/Preschool Directors showed modest compensation rate increase as the church income increased. Music Director and Administrator showed higher rate increases as income increased.

The tables below provide comparisons of compensation and benefits packages (please note that some position titles and benefit listings have been abbreviated).

TABLE 3-1: PERCENTAGE OF FULL-TIME STAFF RECEIVING COMPENSATION AND BENEFITS

	SOLO PASTOR	SENIOR PASTOR	ASSOCIATE PASTOR	YOUTH PASTOR	ADULT MINISTRY DIRECTOR	CHILDREN'S/ PRESCHOOL DIRECTOR
BASE SALARY	97%	99%	98%	98%	99%	99%
PARSONAGE	35%	14%	8%	7%	5%	2%
HOUSING	71	84%	81%	66%	67%	31%
RETIREMENT	65%	70%	62%	52%	58%	47%
LIFE INSURANCE	27%	36%	31%	30%	35%	28%
HEALTH INSURANCE	65%	75%	74%	73%	80%	56%
VACATION	97%	95%	94%	94%	94%	92%
AUTO REIMBURSEMENT	73%	75%	71%	66%	63%	53%
EDUCATION	48%	43%	43%	39%	39%	32%
RECEIVED SALARY INCREASE	58%	69%	69%	69%	72%	68%
NUMBER OF RESPONDENTS	375	773	459	493	171	276

	MUSIC/ CHOIR DIRECTOR	ADMIN- ISTRATOR	BOOKKEEPER	SECRETARY	CUSTODIAN
BASE SALARY	99%	100%	99%	99%	99%
PARSONAGE	3%	1%	0%	0%	1%
HOUSING	57%	21%	1%	0%	1%
RETIREMENT	61%	49%	46%	37%	38%
LIFE INSURANCE	35%	32%	33%	25%	29%
HEALTH INSURANCE	74%	64%	65%	50%	60%
VACATION	93%	91%	94%	90%	88%
AUTO REIMBURSEMENT	54%	51%	38%	35%	34%
EDUCATION	34%	28%	15%	12%	4%
RECEIVED SALARY INCREASE	69%	74%	72%	72%	70%
NUMBER OF RESPONDENTS	297	330	178	460	342

TABLE 3-2: PERCENTAGE OF PART-TIME STAFF RECEIVING COMPENSATION AND BENEFITS

	PASTOR	ASSOCIATE PASTOR	YOUTH PASTOR	ADULT MINISTRY DIRECTOR	CHILDREN'S/ PRESCHOOL DIRECTOR	MUSIC/ CHOIR DIRECTOR
BASE SALARY	85%	74%	94%	91%	99%	97%
PARSONAGE	22%	6%	4%	4%	0%	0%
HOUSING	61%	52%	8%	14%	2%	5%
RETIREMENT	33%	20%	5%	13%	7%	3%
LIFE INSURANCE	9%	4%	3%	7%	2%	1%
HEALTH INSURANCE	26%	11%	8%	5%	6%	4%
VACATION	70%	59%	51%	50%	48%	44%
AUTO REIMBURSEMENT	43%	52%	36%	39%	26%	16%
EDUCATION	39%	24%	23%	32%	23%	10%
RECEIVED SALARY INCREASE	39%	50%	43%	70%	63%	54%
NUMBER OF RESPONDENTS	46	82	171	56	204	331

	ADMINISTRATOR	BOOK-KEEPER	SECETARY	CUSTODIAN	ORGANIST
BASE SALARY	99%	97%	96%	98%	99%
PARSONAGE	0%	0%	0%	1%	0%
HOUSING	2%	1%	0%	0%	0%
RETIREMENT	10%	5%	7%	2%	1%
LIFE INSURANCE	0%	3%	2%	0%	0%
HEALTH INSURANCE	14%	5%	5%	2%	3%
VACATION	56%	38%	46%	25%	35%
AUTO REIMBURSEMENT	24%	19%	13%	9%	4%
EDUCATION	3%	5%	5%	0%	1%
RECEIVED SALARY INCREASE	60%	55%	52%	45%	55%
NUMBER OF RESPONDENTS	106	237	469	447	78

Note: the following tables are for comparative purposes only.
For a full analysis of each staff position, consult chapters 4-14.

TABLE 3-3: NATIONAL FULL-TIME CHURCH STAFF COMPENSATION AND BENEFITS AVERAGE

	AVERAGE COMPENSATION	RANGE AS DETERMINED BY LOWEST 25% QUARTILE– HIGHEST 25% QUARTILE (50%)
SOLO PASTOR	59,852	43,750 - 73,880
SENIOR PASTOR	87,284	65,324 - 103,951
ASSOCIATE PASTOR	66,310	51,541 - 77,000
YOUTH PASTOR	51,640	40,300 - 62,208
ADULT MINISTRY DIRECTOR	67,711	48,542 - 77,050
CHILDREN'S/PRE-SCHOOL DIRECTOR	46,361	34,895 - 56,616
MUSIC/CHOIR DIRECTOR	64,075	48,600 - 74,304
ADMINISTRATOR	52,036	36,500 - 64,435
BOOKKEEPER	36,122	29,765 - 42,241
SECRETARY	29,551	23,000 - 35,264
CUSTODIAN	32,884	26,000 - 38,360
ORGANIST	N/A	N/A

TABLE 3-4: ANNUAL FULL-TIME CHURCH STAFF COMPENSATION AND BENEFITS AVERAGES BY WORSHIP ATTENDANCE

	WORSHIP ATTENDANCE					
	100 or less	101-300	301-500	501-750	751-1000	Over 1000
SOLO PASTOR	$51,115	$65,370	$78,646	–	–	–
SENIOR PASTOR	$54,598	$69,896	$90,156	$95,031	$108,709	$127,449
ASSOCIATE PASTOR	–	$51,906	$64,890	$67,074	$73,113	$81,287
YOUTH PASTOR	–	$41,804	$50,830	$53,105	$56,309	$61,295
ADULT MINISTRY DIRECTOR	–	$44,476	$65,253	$60,717	$73,542	$72,255
CHILDREN'S/PRE-SCHOOL DIRECTOR	–	$37,147	$40,999	$46,353	$46,747	$53,540
MUSIC/CHOIR DIRECTOR	–	$43,198	$57,606	$61,719	$67,206	$77,364
ADMINISTRATOR	–	$37,429	$44,144	$47,615	$58,166	$68,042
BOOKKEEPER	–	$27,665	$32,613	$34,456	$34,081	$41,403
SECRETARY	–	$24,305	$28,986	$29,243	$31,521	$35,281
CUSTODIAN	–	$26,742	$30,346	$32,924	$36,272	$35,829

– Not enough responses to provide meaningful data

TABLE 3-5: ANNUAL FULL-TIME CHURCH STAFF COMPENSATION AND BENEFITS AVERAGES BY CHURCH INCOME

	CHURCH INCOME				
	$250K & Under	$251K-$500K	$501K-$750K	$751K-$1M	Over $1 Million
SOLO PASTOR	$53,325	$73,026	$78,435	$72,010	–
SENIOR PASTOR	$56,788	$74,068	$81,602	$89,096	$115,829
ASSOCIATE PASTOR	$39,683	$53,101	$58,911	$65,373	$76,862
YOUTH PASTOR	$39,624	$43,452	$47,696	$51,013	$57,284
ADULT MINISTRY DIRECTOR	–	$38,719	$52,066	$54,830	$72,802
CHILDREN'S/PRE-SCHOOL DIRECTOR	$36,048	$35,331	$36,351	$39,285	$51,070
MUSIC/CHOIR DIRECTOR	–	$42,200	$46,683	$54,492	$71,338
ADMINISTRATOR	$38,819	$37,391	$34,373	$43,808	$61,063
BOOKKEEPER	–	$27,338	$30,022	$33,184	$38,559
SECRETARY	$20,132	$25,811	$26,748	$26,961	$32,718
CUSTODIAN	–	$24,213	$31,574	$32,777	$34,610

– Not enough responses to provide meaningful data

TABLE 3-6: ANNUAL FULL-TIME CHURCH STAFF COMPENSATION AND BENEFITS AVERAGES BY CHURCH SETTING & SIZE

ATTENDANCE 250 & UNDER	CHURCH SETTING			
	Metropolitan city	Suburb of large city	Small town or rural city	Farming area
SOLO PASTOR	$65,865	$59,260	$57,149	$43,158
SENIOR PASTOR	$64,766	$72,929	$62,023	$63,252
ASSOCIATE PASTOR	$44,010	$57,372	$44,561	–
YOUTH PASTOR	$43,016	$42,052	$40,206	–
ADULT MINISTRY DIRECTOR	–	–	–	–
CHILDREN'S/PRE-SCHOOL DIRECTOR	–	$39,506	$34,422	–
MUSIC/CHOIR DIRECTOR	–	–	$35,104	–
ADMINISTRATOR	$33,257	$39,201	$36,299	–
BOOKKEEPER	–	–	–	–
SECRETARY	$22,107	$25,202	$22,580	–
CUSTODIAN	–	$23,779	$22,855	–

– Not enough responses to provide meaningful data

TABLE 3-7: ANNUAL FULL-TIME CHURCH STAFF COMPENSATION AND BENEFITS AVERAGES BY CHURCH SETTING & SIZE

ATTENDANCE 251-500	CHURCH SETTING			
	Metropolitan city	Suburb of large city	Small town or rural city	Farming area
SOLO PASTOR	$80,713	$86,376	$78,818	–
SENIOR PASTOR	$98,836	$90,022	$80,522	–
ASSOCIATE PASTOR	$66,932	$66,093	$59,452	–
YOUTH PASTOR	$48,020	$51,705	$46,953	–
ADULT MINISTRY DIRECTOR	–	$63,219	$65,358	–
CHILDREN'S/PRE-SCHOOL DIRECTOR	$47,716	$41,871	$31,591	–
MUSIC/CHOIR DIRECTOR	$56,329	$59,686	$50,198	–
ADMINISTRATOR	$47,942	$43,469	$41,088	–
BOOKKEEPER	$32,697	$34,836	$29,371	–
SECRETARY	$29,792	$30,670	$26,106	–
CUSTODIAN	$28,682	$31,799	$28,884	–

– Not enough responses to provide meaningful data

TABLE 3-8: ANNUAL FULL-TIME CHURCH STAFF COMPENSATION AND BENEFITS AVERAGES BY CHURCH SETTING & SIZE

ATTENDANCE 751-1,000	CHURCH SETTING			
	Metropolitan city	Suburb of large city	Small town or rural city	Farming area
SOLO PASTOR	–	–	–	–
SENIOR PASTOR	$112,461	$114,086	$99,283	–
ASSOCIATE PASTOR	$77,203	$77,044	$64,784	–
YOUTH PASTOR	$54,326	$60,817	$53,018	–
ADULT MINISTRY DIRECTOR	$60,454	–	$94,820	–
CHILDREN'S/PRE-SCHOOL DIRECTOR	$50,801	$48,778	$39,437	–
MUSIC/CHOIR DIRECTOR	$69,689	$72,323	$57,235	–
ADMINISTRATOR	$61,317	$56,100	–	–
BOOKKEEPER	$39,024	$34,590	$29,988	–
SECRETARY	$30,855	$33,511	$29,959	–
CUSTODIAN	$36,754	$39,252	$33,994	–

– Not enough responses to provide meaningful data

TABLE 3-9: ANNUAL FULL-TIME CHURCH STAFF COMPENSATION AND BENEFITS AVERAGES BY CHURCH SETTING & SIZE

ATTENDANCE 501-750	CHURCH SETTING			
	Metropolitan city	Suburb of large city	Small town or rural city	Farming area
SOLO PASTOR	–	–	–	–
SENIOR PASTOR	$106,923	$96,276	$90,219	–
ASSOCIATE PASTOR	$70,725	$68,261	$63,726	–
YOUTH PASTOR	$49,000	$54,348	$51,262	–
ADULT MINISTRY DIRECTOR	–	$62,487	–	–
CHILDREN'S/PRE-SCHOOL DIRECTOR	$48,141	$45,268	$45,899	–
MUSIC/CHOIR DIRECTOR	$56,772	$64,307	$62,217	–
ADMINISTRATOR	$53,114	$44,278	$49,907	–
BOOKKEEPER	–	$36,213	$34,716	–
SECRETARY	$30,363	$30,046	$27,541	–
CUSTODIAN	$33,762	$33,137	$31,611	–

– Not enough responses to provide meaningful data

TABLE 3-10: ANNUAL FULL-TIME CHURCH STAFF COMPENSATION AND BENEFITS AVERAGES BY CHURCH SETTING & SIZE

ATTENDANCE OVER 1,000	CHURCH SETTING			
	Metropolitan city	Suburb of large city	Small town or rural city	Farming area
SOLO PASTOR	–	–	–	–
SENIOR PASTOR	$133,801	$135,777	$107,557	–
ASSOCIATE PASTOR	$88,641	$84,288	$70,376	–
YOUTH PASTOR	$67,472	$63,512	$53,631	–
ADULT MINISTRY DIRECTOR	$80,440	$76,568	$61,580	–
CHILDREN'S / PRE-SCHOOL DIRECTOR	$54,370	$54,356	$51,175	–
MUSIC / CHOIR DIRECTOR	$84,540	$79,364	$68,343	–
ADMINISTRATOR	$73,945	$68,941	$62,128	–
BOOKKEEPER	$42,166	$42,257	$38,657	–
SECRETARY	$36,486	$35,592	$33,583	–
CUSTODIAN	$36,906	$34,779	$36,046	–

– Not enough responses to provide meaningful data

TABLE 3-11: ANNUAL FULL-TIME CHURCH STAFF COMPENSATION AND BENEFITS AVERAGES BY GENDER

	GENDER	
	Male	Female
SOLO PASTOR	$59,893	$61,611
SENIOR PASTOR	$87,702	$51,877
ASSOCIATE PASTOR	$67,023	$61,952
YOUTH PASTOR	$52,601	$40,818
ADULT MINISTRY DIRECTOR	$71,494	$55,593
CHILDREN'S/PRE-SCHOOL DIRECTOR	$55,029	$43,352
MUSIC/CHOIR DIRECTOR	$66,644	$47,000
ADMINISTRATOR	$63,105	$41,299
BOOKKEEPER	$43,822	$35,362
SECRETARY	$29,121	$29,608
CUSTODIAN	$34,247	$27,427

TABLE 3-12: ANNUAL FULL-TIME CHURCH STAFF COMPENSATION AND BENEFITS AVERAGES BY EDUCATION

	EDUCATION			
	< than Bachelor	Bachelor	Master	Doctorate
SOLO PASTOR	$55,824	$52,336	$60,561	$69,900
SENIOR PASTOR	$77,628	$77,481	$85,631	$102,470
ASSOCIATE PASTOR	$58,171	$60,507	$69,797	$78,625
YOUTH PASTOR	$48,503	$49,538	$59,223	–
ADULT MINISTRY DIRECTOR	$52,410	$67,737	$69,387	$78,525
CHILDREN'S/PRE-SCHOOL DIRECTOR	$35,859	$47,985	$52,167	–
MUSIC/CHOIR DIRECTOR	$54,001	$64,793	$65,233	$72,763
ADMINISTRATOR	$39,056	$52,622	$65,891	–
BOOKKEEPER	$34,251	$38,469	–	–
SECRETARY	$28,995	$30,575	–	–
CUSTODIAN	$32,503	$34,576	–	–

– Not enough responses to provide meaningful data

TABLE 3-13: ANNUAL FULL-TIME CHURCH STAFF COMPENSATION AND BENEFITS AVERAGES BY YEARS EMPLOYED

	YEARS EMPLOYED			
	< 6 years	6-10 years	11-15 years	Over 15 years
SOLO PASTOR	$58,313	$58,200	$62,860	$64,749
SENIOR PASTOR	$85,408	$83,983	$87,812	$93,124
ASSOCIATE PASTOR	$62,295	$70,056	$71,450	$76,559
YOUTH PASTOR	$49,693	$55,711	$63,326	–
ADULT MINISTRY DIRECTOR	$65,769	$73,004	$66,875	$66,779
CHILDREN'S/PRE-SCHOOL DIRECTOR	$44,806	$49,064	$48,502	$54,936
MUSIC/CHOIR DIRECTOR	$59,640	$61,143	$75,865	$74,782
ADMINISTRATOR	$49,467	$51,622	$58,034	$56,172
BOOKKEEPER	$35,495	$35,585	$40,333	$36,662
SECRETARY	$27,588	$30,002	$31,446	$33,369
CUSTODIAN	$31,677	$33,816	$32,153	$37,287

– Not enough responses to provide meaningful data

TABLE 3-14: ANNUAL FULL-TIME CHURCH STAFF
COMPENSATION AND BENEFITS AVERAGES BY DENOMINATION

	DENOMINATION					
	Assemblies of God	Baptist	Independent / Non-denom	Lutheran	Methodist	Presbyterian
SOLO PASTOR	$45,629	$61,638	$58,987	$76,258	$62,425	$62,647
SENIOR PASTOR	$74,389	$89,051	$86,730	$89,058	$90,318	$107,769
ASSOCIATE PASTOR	$54,268	$67,777	$66,953	$61,645	$60,119	$77,175
YOUTH PASTOR	$47,237	$56,392	$52,922	$48,616	$39,952	$46,112
ADULT MINISTRY DIRECTOR	$58,169	$77,820	$58,302	$66,164	$47,710	$77,496
CHILDREN'S/PRE-SCHOOL DIRECTOR	$42,525	$47,915	$47,539	$40,157	$39,942	$44,084
MUSIC/CHOIR DIRECTOR	$56,395	$68,133	$65,590	$57,595	$52,646	$57,958
ADMINISTRATOR	$58,210	$58,219	$50,876	$39,353	$41,523	$50,162
BOOKKEEPER	$35,039	$36,294	$36,680	–	$35,162	$35,736
SECRETARY	$24,888	$28,637	$30,734	$27,760	$28,436	$33,793
CUSTODIAN	$30,151	$33,777	$32,402	$35,840	$29,252	$35,559

– Not enough responses to provide meaningful data

TABLE 3-15: ANNUAL FULL-TIME CHURCH STAFF COMPENSATION AND BENEFITS AVERAGES BY REGION

	REGION								
	New England	Middle Atlantic	South Atlantic	E-N Central	E-S Central	W-N Central	W-S Central	Mountain	Pacific
SOLO PASTOR	$63,410	$62,466	$59,633	$57,252	71,561	$54,014	$59,988	$60,232	$61,801
SENIOR PASTOR	$84,509	$75,175	$91,597	$85,804	$103,143	$77,597	$96,860	$83,960	$87,194
ASSOCIATE PASTOR	–	$58,598	$67,092	$67,061	$75,264	$61,783	$72,172	$58,918	$69,805
YOUTH PASTOR	–	$48,875	$54,751	$53,390	$47,187	$47,687	$51,683	$46,725	$53,608
ADULT MINISTRY DIRECTOR	–	$57,426	$61,510	$65,803	$58,015	$65,009	$116,625	$59,083	$66,330
CHILDREN'S/PRE-SCHOOL DIRECTOR	–	$41,281	$45,522	$48,589	$46,786	$45,133	$46,320	$39,946	$49,919
MUSIC/CHOIR DIRECTOR	–	$51,548	$60,265	$63,782	$68,564	$55,259	$69,529	$62,348	$73,950
ADMINISTRATOR	–	$40,722	$47,577	$54,442	$57,093	$52,407	$52,418	$53,598	$58,488
BOOKKEEPER	–	$26,146	$35,277	$39,203	$36,218	$34,583	$39,200	$37,952	$35,169
SECRETARY	–	$27,895	$31,043	$28,885	$28,974	$29,364	$28,476	$25,929	$33,081
CUSTODIAN	–	$34,090	$33,834	$35,702	$31,216	$31,058	$29,027	$29,349	$37,899

– Not enough responses to provide meaningful data

TABLE 3-16: ANNUAL PART-TIME CHURCH STAFF COMPENSATION AND BENEFITS AVERAGES BY WORSHIP ATTENDANCE

	WORSHIP ATTENDANCE					
	100 or less	101-300	301-500	501-750	751-1000	Over 1000
PASTOR	$23,253	$42,563	–	–	–	–
ASSOCIATE PASTOR	$9,228	$19,705	$25,031	–	–	–
YOUTH PASTOR	$9,865	$12,441	$17,167	–	–	–
ADULT MINISTRY DIRECTOR	–	$11,530	$18,005	–	–	–
CHILDREN'S/PRE-SCHOOL DIRECTOR	$8,568	$11,295	$15,031	$19,880	$24,394	$20,262
MUSIC/CHOIR DIRECTOR	$6,700	$12,039	$15,575	$16,659	–	$24,667
ADMINISTRATOR	$8,728	$17,481	$18,893	$26,373	–	–
BOOKKEEPER	$3,997	$8,483	$12,847	$16,669	$14,401	$25,755
SECRETARY	$7,319	$11,634	$14,352	$17,629	$16,546	$14,429
CUSTODIAN	$4,285	$8,815	$11,664	$12,809	$14,471	$11,746
ORGANIST	$3,776	$7,237	$13,531	–	–	–

– Not enough responses to provide meaningful data

37

TABLE 3-17: ANNUAL PART-TIME CHURCH STAFF COMPENSATION AND BENEFITS AVERAGES BY CHURCH INCOME

	CHURCH INCOME				
	$250K & Under	$251-$500K	$501-$750K	$751K-$1M	Over $1 Million
PASTOR	$24,526	–	–	–	–
ASSOCIATE PASTOR	$13,106	$20,788	$17,391	–	$23,351
YOUTH PASTOR	$10,360	$13,233	$16,830	$17,956	$24,246
ADULT MINISTRY DIRECTOR	–	$14,615	$19,068	$13,848	$21,057
CHILDREN'S/PRE-SCHOOL DIRECTOR	$11,052	$10,340	$14,408	$20,676	$19,524
MUSIC/CHOIR DIRECTOR	$8,153	$11,984	$15,580	$15,627	$19,245
ADMINISTRATOR	$10,135	$17,802	$18,677	$21,578	$28,921
BOOKKEEPER	$5,360	$8,503	$11,064	$15,096	$20,072
SECRETARY	$8,535	$12,781	$14,215	$15,650	$16,806
CUSTODIAN	$5,591	$9,276	$11,295	$13,327	$13,231
ORGANIST	$4,454	$7,935	–	–	$12,986

– Not enough responses to provide meaningful data

4

SENIOR PASTORS

Employment Profile

With 773 positions reported, senior pastors provided a significant number of responses to this survey. As can be expected, this group is quite diverse. All of the pastors in this chapter serve full-time. The senior pastor is the most highly paid position in the local church, and receiving the most comprehensive benefit packages. The following statistical features profile this sample:

Ordained	99%
Average years employed	11
Male	99%
Female	1%
Self-employed (receives 1099)	7%
Church employee (receives W-2)	93%
High school diploma	4%
Associate's degree	1%
Bachelor's degree	24%
Master's degree	45%
Doctorate	26%
Number of respondents	*773*

Total Compensation plus Benefits Package Analysis

The analyses below are based upon the data in the tables that you will find in the remainder of the chapter. The tables present compensation plus benefit data for senior pastors who serve full-time according to church attendance, church income, combinations of size and setting, region, education, years employed, and denomination. In this way, the senior pastor's compensation plus benefit can be analyzed and compared from a variety of useful perspectives. The total compensation plus benefit amount includes the base salary, housing and/or parsonage amount, retirement contribution, life and health insurance payments, and educational funds.

As far as a full-time staff member is concerned, three-fourths of pastors receive health insurance and 70% have retirement benefits. Consider the information below.

COMPENSATION & BENEFITS SUMMARY

Base salary	99%
Housing	84%
Parsonage	14%
Retirement	70%
Life insurance	36%
Health insurance	75%
Paid vacation	95%
Auto reimbursement	75%
Continuing education	43%

KEY POINTS

⮑ **Church worship attendance affects pastoral compensation.** Of the senior pastors' data received, approximately 44% worked in churches with an average attendance under 300 people. The compensation of these senior pastors was below the national average (National average = $87,284). The average number of years served tends to be longer on larger church sizes. *See Table 4-1.*

⮑ **Church income has the strongest correlation with compensation and benefits.** While the correlation is a fairly strong one, it should be considered as only one of many factors that determined a senior pastor's complete package. In general, as church income increases, compensation goes up. In most cases, senior pastors in churches with budgets over $750,000 tend to be at or above the national average compensation. Senior pastors serving churches with incomes over $1,000,000 receive on average about twice the compensation of a pastor in a church with a budget under $250,000. *See Table 4-2.*

⮑ **A church's geographical setting affects pastoral compensation.** Generally, senior pastors of metropolitan and suburban churches have higher compensation consistent with their larger church attendance and income compared to senior pastors in small town or farming areas. Historically, senior pastors from the metropolitan city have the highest levels of compensation for larger churches. In general, churches located in metropolitan and suburban cities tend to provide higher housing allowances, retirement contributions, and insurance payments. *See Tables 4-3, 4-4, 4-5, 4-6 and 4-7.*

⮑ **A relationship exists between educational achievement and income for senior pastors.** Senior pastors with only a high school diploma earned approximately $8,000 less than senior pastors with a master's degree. There is little difference in compensation among senior pastors who do not have a Bachelor's degree versus those who do. In general, only those groups with doctorate degrees exceeded the national average. A significant increase in compensation occurs for senior pastors with a doctoral degree. These individuals are more likely to serve larger metropolitan or suburban churches which provide the highest levels of compensation. Average years employed tends to be similar regardless of educational background. Over 90% of the respondents are college graduates and 71% have graduate degrees. The most common is a master's degree held by 45% of reported senior pastor positions; 26% held doctoral degrees. *See Table 4-9.*

⮑ **Years of service has an impact on compensation.** Those serving for five years or less in their current position (32% of the respondents) received about $7,700 a year less in total compensation than those who had served over 15 years. The difference, however, appears to be more dependent on church income than on years served. Those serving the longest tended to be in bigger churches with significantly higher incomes. *See Table 4-10.*

⮑ **Gender disparities exist concerning pastoral compensation.** Though data shows they do exist, given the relatively small number of female senior pastor positions reported, it is difficult to quantify the disparity. The average congregational size that men serve is about three times higher than women serve. The difference in congregational size represents a considerable difference in church income which impacts the overall compensation. *See Table 4-11.*

Ten Year Compensation & Benefits Trend: National Averages for Pastors*

	Senior Pastor data only	Combined Solo and Senior Pastor data
1997		$56,172
1998		$59,067
1999		$62,869
2000		$66,096
2001		$69,543
2002		$71,232
2003		$73,230
2004		$74,969
2005		$77,096
2006	$87,284	$78,339

National averages for Senior Pastor from 1997-2005 include data for both Senior and Solo Pastors. In 2006, we are able to provide detailed data for each position. Refer to Chapter 5 for Solo Pastor's data.

43

TABLE 4-1: ANNUAL COMPENSATION OF SENIOR PASTOR BY WORSHIP ATTENDANCE

CHARACTERISTICS		WORSHIP ATTENDANCE					
		100 or less	101-300	301-500	501-750	751-1000	Over 1000
AVERAGE SUNDAY AM WORSHIP ATTENDANCE		79	200	407	615	888	2,143
AVERAGE CHURCH INCOME		$149,980	$387,457	$803,997	$1,245,155	$1,799,598	$3,600,446
AVERAGE # of YEARS EMPLOYED		9	10	11	12	12	14
AVERAGE # of WEEKS OF PAID VACATION		3	4	4	4	4	4
% COLLEGE GRADUATE OR HIGHER		91%	94%	97%	95%	95%	96%
% WHO RECEIVE AUTO REIMBURSEMENT		78%	77%	85%	77%	78%	67%
% ORDAINED		96%	99%	100%	100%	100%	99%
AVERAGE % SALARY INCREASE THIS YEAR		4%	5%	5%	4%	5%	6%

COMPENSATION		100 or less	101-300	301-500	501-750	751-1000	Over 1000
BASE SALARY:	Highest 25%	$37,000	$46,364	$60,000	$66,848	$82,000	$90,982
	Average	$30,608	$37,961	$50,884	$55,564	$66,344	$78,007
	Lowest 25%	$22,849	$28,140	$39,412	$41,888	$48,580	$55,798
HOUSING:	Highest 25%	$24,500	$26,400	$31,100	$34,368	$36,100	$44,350
	Average	$14,882	$18,300	$22,386	$22,894	$24,764	$31,615
	Lowest 25%	$500	$9,000	$12,000	$14,061	$12,000	$20,800
PARSONAGE:	Highest 25%	–	–	–	–	–	–
	Average	$1,943	$2,716	$2,501	$1,003	$3,295	$1,430
	Lowest 25%	–	–	–	–	–	–
TOTAL COMPENSATION	Highest 25%	$53,800	$67,645	$87,701	$88,907	$113,411	$129,335
	Average	$47,434	$58,978	$75,771	$79,461	$94,403	$111,052
	Lowest 25%	$37,325	$48,000	$61,000	$66,066	$70,000	$85,000

– Not enough responses to provide meaningful data

TABLE 4-1: ANNUAL COMPENSATION OF SENIOR PASTOR BY WORSHIP ATTENDANCE

BENEFITS		WORSHIP ATTENDANCE					
		100 or less	101-300	301-500	501-750	751-1000	Over 1000
RETIREMENT:	Highest 25%	$3,700	$5,040	$8,000	$8,415	$10,462	$9,548
	Average	$1,840	$3,298	$5,161	$5,074	$6,270	$6,601
	Lowest 25%	–	–	–	$1,040	–	–
LIFE INSURANCE:	Highest 25%	–	–	–	$600	–	$505
	Average	$233	$365	$337	$386	$376	$488
	Lowest 25%	–	–	–	–	–	–
HEALTH INSURANCE:	Highest 25%	$7,965	$11,000	$12,066	$12,840	$11,200	$12,307
	Average	$4,689	$6,625	$7,699	$9,096	$6,953	$8,151
	Lowest 25%	–	–	–	$5,000	–	$3,400
CONTINUING EDUCATION	Highest 25%	$500	$1,000	$1,413	$1,500	$1,500	$1,150
	Average	$404	$630	$945	$1,013	$708	$1,018
	Lowest 25%	–	–	–	–	–	–
TOTAL BENEFITS	Highest 25%	$10,500	$15,332	$20,486	$21,346	$18,873	$20,106
	Average	$7,165	$10,918	$14,142	$15,570	$14,306	$16,258
	Lowest 25%	$1,510	$4,640	$7,282	$9,550	$8,648	$9,254
TOTAL COMPENSATION AND BENEFIT		100 or less	101-300	301-500	501-750	751-1000	Over 1000
	Highest 25%	$64,121	$81,000	$104,164	$107,418	$127,625	$146,992
	Average	$54,598	$69,896	$90,156	$95,031	$108,709	$127,449
	Lowest 25%	$42,435	$58,200	$74,397	$81,172	$84,999	$98,460
NUMBER OF RESPONDENTS		56	279	148	104	59	108

– Not enough responses to provide meaningful data

TABLE 4-2: ANNUAL COMPENSATION OF SENIOR PASTOR BY CHURCH INCOME

CHARACTERISTICS		$250K & under	$251K-$500K	$501K-$750K	$751K-$1M	Over $1 Million
AVERAGE SUNDAY AM WORSHIP ATTENDANCE		144	236	396	475	1,278
AVERAGE CHURCH INCOME		$166,699	$375,655	$620,779	$883,747	$2,425,724
AVERAGE # of YEARS EMPLOYED		9	11	13	9	13
AVERAGE # of WEEKS OF PAID VACATION		4	4	4	4	4
% COLLEGE GRADUATE OR HIGHER		93%	94%	94%	99%	96%
% WHO RECEIVE AUTO REIMBURSEMENT		77%	79%	75%	83%	75%
% ORDAINED		99%	98%	100%	100%	99%
AVERAGE % SALARY INCREASE THIS YEAR		5%	4%	6%	4%	5%
COMPENSATION		$250K & under	$251K-$500K	$501K-$750K	$751K-$1M	Over 1 Million
BASE SALARY:	Highest 25%	$38,350	$48,000	$57,000	$60,000	$82,000
	Average	$30,816	$40,932	$48,723	$49,039	$68,800
	Lowest 25%	$23,255	$30,888	$38,859	$37,688	$48,072
HOUSING:	Highest 25%	$25,000	$26,213	$28,000	$34,881	$40,000
	Average	$15,427	$18,544	$18,097	$25,681	$28,524
	Lowest 25%	$2,450	$11,000	$3,750	$18,600	$18,000
PARSONAGE:	Highest 25%	–	–	–	–	–
	Average	$2,267	$2,990	$1,485	$874	$1,906
	Lowest 25%	–	–	–	–	–
TOTAL COMPENSATION	Highest 25%	$56,000	$70,000	$78,925	$85,000	$113,411
	Average	$48,510	$62,466	$68,305	$75,595	$99,230
	Lowest 25%	$38,840	$52,140	$57,660	$65,000	$76,000

– Not enough responses to provide meaningful data

TABLE 4-2: ANNUAL COMPENSATION OF SENIOR PASTOR BY CHURCH INCOME

BENEFITS		CHURCH INCOME				
		$250K & under	$251K-$500K	$501K-$750K	$751K-$1M	Over $1 Million
RETIREMENT:	Highest 25%	$3,671	$5,200	$6,935	$7,500	$9,399
	Average	$2,351	$3,258	$4,336	$4,788	$6,370
	Lowest 25%	–	–	–	$1,312	$750
LIFE INSURANCE:	Highest 25%	–	–	–	$500	–
	Average	$301	$370	$248	$369	$466
	Lowest 25%	–	–	–	–	–
HEALTH INSURANCE:	Highest 25%	$8,199	$11,900	$13,000	$11,700	$12,560
	Average	$5,008	$7,235	$7,888	$7,312	$8,585
	Lowest 25%	–	$1,690	$287	–	$3,819
CONTINUING EDUCATION	Highest 25%	$1,000	$1,000	$1,050	$1,500	$1,500
	Average	$617	$616	$826	$892	$1,019
	Lowest 25%	–	–	–	–	–
TOTAL BENEFITS	Highest 25%	$12,250	$16,305	$20,312	$18,851	$21,935
	Average	$8,278	$11,479	$13,297	$13,361	$16,441
	Lowest 25%	$3,000	$6,000	$5,100	$7,264	$10,212
TOTAL COMPENSATION AND BENEFIT		$250K & under	$251K-$500K	$501K-$750K	$751K-$1M	Over 1 Million
	Highest 25%	$66,224	$84,250	$93,674	$102,636	$129,800
	Average	$56,788	$74,068	$81,602	$89,096	$115,829
	Lowest 25%	$44,825	$63,748	$69,772	$74,214	$90,107
NUMBER OF RESPONDENTS		120	194	84	78	253

– Not enough responses to provide meaningful data

TABLE 4-3: ANNUAL COMPENSATION OF SENIOR PASTOR
BY CHURCH SETTING & SIZE

ATTENDANCE 250 & UNDER		CHURCH SETTING			
		Metropoli-tan city	Suburb of large city	Small town or rural city	Farming area
AVERAGE SUNDAY AM WORSHIP ATTENDANCE		156	175	157	169
AVERAGE CHURCH INCOME		$356,092	$377,461	$271,479	$240,860
AVERAGE # of YEARS EMPLOYED		13	10	9	9
AVERAGE # of WEEKS OF PAID VACATION		4	4	4	4
% COLLEGE GRADUATE OR HIGHER		92%	97%	93%	77%
% WHO RECEIVE AUTO REIMBURSEMENT		79%	67%	81%	77%
% ORDAINED		100%	99%	98%	100%
AVERAGE % SALARY INCREASE THIS YEAR		4%	4%	4%	4%

COMPENSATION		Metropoli-tan city	Suburb of large city	Small town or rural city	Farming area
BASE SALARY:	Highest 25%	$43,001	$44,330	$41,000	$44,164
	Average	$34,525	$37,661	$34,054	$38,521
	Lowest 25%	$24,768	$28,838	$26,002	$27,499
HOUSING:	Highest 25%	$25,204	$29,994	$24,005	$18,436
	Average	$16,869	$20,757	$15,910	$10,902
	Lowest 25%	$3,996	$9,500	$3,000	–
PARSONAGE:	Highest 25%	–	–	–	$7,201
	Average	$1,843	$3,902	$2,521	$3,631
	Lowest 25%	–	–	–	–
TOTAL COMPENSATION	Highest 25%	$68,666	$69,999	$60,469	$56,001
	Average	$53,237	$62,320	$52,485	$53,054
	Lowest 25%	$42,351	$52,001	$42,614	$39,999

– Not enough responses to provide meaningful data

TABLE 4-3: ANNUAL COMPENSATION OF SENIOR PASTOR
BY CHURCH SETTING & SIZE

BENEFITS		CHURCH SETTING			
		Metropoli-tan city	Suburb of large city	Small town or rural city	Farming area
RETIREMENT:	Highest 25%	$5,761	$4,150	$4,325	$4,752
	Average	$3,693	$2,946	$2,938	$2,643
	Lowest 25%	–	–	–	$1,199
LIFE INSURANCE:	Highest 25%	–	–	–	–
	Average	$319	$344	$317	$487
	Lowest 25%	–	–	–	–
HEALTH INSURANCE:	Highest 25%	$11,999	$11,652	$9,601	$8,601
	Average	$6,554	$6,819	$5,808	$6,709
	Lowest 25%	–	–	–	$2,500
CONTINUING EDUCATION	Highest 25%	$1,601	$750	$501	$601
	Average	$963	$500	$475	$359
	Lowest 25%	–	–	–	–
TOTAL BENEFITS	Highest 25%	$16,305	$15,800	$13,984	$12,600
	Average	$11,529	$10,609	$9,538	$10,198
	Lowest 25%	$5,000	$3,500	$4,100	$7,200
TOTAL COMPENSATION AND BENEFIT		Metropoli-tan city	Suburb of large city	Small town or rural city	Farming area
	Highest 25%	$85,869	$84,222	$71,230	$65,325
	Average	$64,766	$72,929	$62,023	$63,252
	Lowest 25%	$47,700	$61,800	$51,600	$42,700
NUMBER OF RESPONDENTS		49	94	130	13

– Not enough responses to provide meaningful data

TABLE 4-4: ANNUAL COMPENSATION OF SENIOR PASTOR
BY CHURCH SETTING & SIZE

ATTENDANCE 251 - 500		CHURCH SETTING			
		Metropoli- tan city	Suburb of large city	Small town or rural city	Farming area
AVERAGE SUNDAY AM WORSHIP ATTENDANCE		396	384	368	–
AVERAGE CHURCH INCOME		$868,767	$821,598	$637,813	–
AVERAGE # of YEARS EMPLOYED		9	12	10	–
AVERAGE # of WEEKS OF PAID VACATION		4	4	4	–
% COLLEGE GRADUATE OR HIGHER		92%	97%	96%	–
% WHO RECEIVE AUTO REIMBURSEMENT		88%	80%	88%	–
% ORDAINED		100%	99%	99%	–
AVERAGE % SALARY INCREASE THIS YEAR		4%	5%	6%	–

COMPENSATION		Metropoli- tan city	Suburb of large city	Small town or rural city	Farming area
BASE SALARY:	Highest 25%	$60,004	$59,449	$59,000	–
	Average	$55,710	$47,795	$48,349	–
	Lowest 25%	$42,907	$36,003	$35,580	–
HOUSING:	Highest 25%	$30,003	$36,001	$25,998	–
	Average	$24,327	$25,822	$17,851	–
	Lowest 25%	$15,000	$15,003	$9,597	–
PARSONAGE:	Highest 25%	–	–	–	–
	Average	$769	$2,901	$1,720	–
	Lowest 25%	–	–	–	–
TOTAL COMPENSATION	Highest 25%	$90,000	$86,998	$77,199	–
	Average	$80,806	$76,518	$67,921	–
	Lowest 25%	$65,001	$64,999	$56,000	–

– Not enough responses to provide meaningful data

TABLE 4-4: ANNUAL COMPENSATION OF SENIOR PASTOR
BY CHURCH SETTING & SIZE

BENEFITS		CHURCH SETTING			
		Metropoli-tan city	Suburb of large city	Small town or rural city	Farming area
RETIREMENT:	Highest 25%	$8,195	$8,000	$7,136	–
	Average	$6,111	$4,697	$4,416	–
	Lowest 25%	–	–	–	–
LIFE INSURANCE:	Highest 25%	–	–	–	–
	Average	$352	$417	$316	–
	Lowest 25%	–	–	–	–
HEALTH INSURANCE:	Highest 25%	$15,000	$12,000	$11,164	–
	Average	$9,373	$7,520	$6,908	–
	Lowest 25%	$6,000	$0	$0	–
CONTINUING EDUCATION	Highest 25%	$1,500	$1,005	$1,125	–
	Average	$811	$870	$961	–
	Lowest 25%	–	–	–	–
TOTAL BENEFITS	Highest 25%	$23,273	$19,436	$18,950	–
	Average	$16,646	$13,504	$12,601	–
	Lowest 25%	$11,219	$7,200	$4,691	–
TOTAL COMPENSATION AND BENEFIT		Metropoli-tan city	Suburb of large city	Small town or rural city	Farming area
	Highest 25%	$107,250	$102,854	$93,627	–
	Average	$98,836	$90,022	$80,522	–
	Lowest 25%	$81,474	$74,400	$67,400	–
NUMBER OF RESPONDENTS		26	75	86	4

– Not enough responses to provide meaningful data

TABLE 4-5: ANNUAL COMPENSATION OF SENIOR PASTOR BY CHURCH SETTING & SIZE

ATTENDANCE 501 - 750		CHURCH SETTING			
		Metropolitan city	Suburb of large city	Small town or rural city	Farming area
AVERAGE SUNDAY AM WORSHIP ATTENDANCE		610	623	600	–
AVERAGE CHURCH INCOME		$1,405,336	$1,238,995	$1,252,177	–
AVERAGE # of YEARS EMPLOYED		10	12	11	–
AVERAGE # of WEEKS OF PAID VACATION		4	4	4	–
% COLLEGE GRADUATE OR HIGHER		100%	95%	91%	–
% WHO RECEIVE AUTO REIMBURSEMENT		69%	72%	84%	–
% ORDAINED		100%	100%	100%	–
AVERAGE % SALARY INCREASE THIS YEAR		5%	4%	4%	–

COMPENSATION		Metropolitan city	Suburb of large city	Small town or rural city	Farming area
BASE SALARY:	Highest 25%	$67,980	$64,951	$69,000	–
	Average	$61,460	$52,985	$56,291	–
	Lowest 25%	$41,410	$39,896	$43,500	–
HOUSING:	Highest 25%	$37,513	$34,988	$30,006	–
	Average	$28,313	$25,967	$20,522	–
	Lowest 25%	$24,188	$20,000	$5,013	–
PARSONAGE:	Highest 25%	–	–	–	–
	Average	–	–	$1,049	–
	Lowest 25%	–	–	–	–
TOTAL COMPENSATION	Highest 25%	$93,601	$88,300	$90,599	–
	Average	$89,774	$78,952	$77,863	–
	Lowest 25%	$77,999	$68,000	$62,237	–

– Not enough responses to provide meaningful data

TABLE 4-5: ANNUAL COMPENSATION OF SENIOR PASTOR
BY CHURCH SETTING & SIZE

BENEFITS		CHURCH SETTING			
		Metropoli-tan city	Suburb of large city	Small town or rural city	Farming area
RETIREMENT:	Highest 25%	$9,797	$9,197	$5,219	–
	Average	$5,377	$6,064	$3,321	–
	Lowest 25%	–	$2,568	–	–
LIFE INSURANCE:	Highest 25%	$574	$637	$599	–
	Average	$383	$441	$310	–
	Lowest 25%	–	–	–	–
HEALTH INSURANCE:	Highest 25%	$15,277	$13,000	$11,520	–
	Average	$10,836	$9,533	$7,878	–
	Lowest 25%	$9,024	$5,748	$2,881	–
CONTINUING EDUCATION	Highest 25%	$994	$1,983	$1,506	–
	Average	$554	$1,286	$846	–
	Lowest 25%	–	–	–	–
TOTAL BENEFITS	Highest 25%	$24,947	$23,828	$16,176	–
	Average	$17,149	$17,324	$12,356	–
	Lowest 25%	$11,795	$12,388	$6,439	–
TOTAL COMPENSATION AND BENEFIT		Metropoli-tan city	Suburb of large city	Small town or rural city	Farming area
	Highest 25%	$119,936	$106,920	$106,775	–
	Average	$106,923	$96,276	$90,219	–
	Lowest 25%	$83,282	$85,200	$72,401	–
NUMBER OF RESPONDENTS		13	46	39	5

– Not enough responses to provide meaningful data

53

TABLE 4-6: ANNUAL COMPENSATION OF SENIOR PASTOR
BY CHURCH SETTING & SIZE

ATTENDANCE 751 - 1,000	Metropolitan city	Suburb of large city	Small town or rural city	Farming area
AVERAGE SUNDAY AM WORSHIP ATTENDANCE	915	853	893	–
AVERAGE CHURCH INCOME	$2,083,309	$1,687,251	$1,632,543	–
AVERAGE # of YEARS EMPLOYED	14	10	11	–
AVERAGE # of WEEKS OF PAID VACATION	4	4	4	–
% COLLEGE GRADUATE OR HIGHER	95%	100%	87%	–
% WHO RECEIVE AUTO REIMBURSEMENT	76%	74%	80%	–
% ORDAINED	100%	100%	100%	–
AVERAGE % SALARY INCREASE THIS YEAR	4%	5%	5%	–

COMPENSATION		Metropolitan city	Suburb of large city	Small town or rural city	Farming area
BASE SALARY:	Highest 25%	$89,014	$80,998	$72,881	–
	Average	$72,584	$66,151	$62,417	–
	Lowest 25%	$54,987	$48,086	$48,870	–
HOUSING:	Highest 25%	$29,309	$57,191	$28,000	–
	Average	$19,552	$30,511	$24,209	–
	Lowest 25%	–	$4,809	$18,792	–
PARSONAGE:	Highest 25%	–	–	–	–
	Average	$4,224	$2,650	–	–
	Lowest 25%	–	–	–	–
TOTAL COMPENSATION	Highest 25%	$125,019	$113,393	$100,893	–
	Average	$96,361	$99,312	$86,626	–
	Lowest 25%	$68,982	$76,019	$68,580	–

– Not enough responses to provide meaningful data

TABLE 4-6: ANNUAL COMPENSATION OF SENIOR PASTOR
BY CHURCH SETTING & SIZE

BENEFITS		CHURCH SETTING			
		Metropoli-tan city	Suburb of large city	Small town or rural city	Farming area
RETIREMENT:	Highest 25%	$11,584	$10,585	$9,304	–
	Average	$7,754	$5,551	$5,563	–
	Lowest 25%	$1,982	–	–	–
LIFE INSURANCE:	Highest 25%	–	$343	–	–
	Average	$424	$332	$349	–
	Lowest 25%	–	–	–	–
HEALTH INSURANCE:	Highest 25%	$11,202	$12,001	$11,023	–
	Average	$7,308	$8,013	$6,089	–
	Lowest 25%	$3,599	$1,986	–	–
CONTINUING EDUCATION	Highest 25%	$1,506	$1,498	$1,000	–
	Average	$614	$878	$656	–
	Lowest 25%	–	–	–	–
TOTAL BENEFITS	Highest 25%	$22,321	$17,932	$18,271	–
	Average	$16,100	$14,773	$12,657	–
	Lowest 25%	$9,999	$8,649	$9,215	–
TOTAL COMPENSATION AND BENEFIT		Metropoli-tan city	Suburb of large city	Small town or rural city	Farming area
	Highest 25%	$139,626	$130,636	$112,610	–
	Average	$112,461	$114,086	$99,283	–
	Lowest 25%	$84,998	$87,570	$76,856	–
NUMBER OF RESPONDENTS		21	19	16	1

– Not enough responses to provide meaningful data

TABLE 4-7: ANNUAL COMPENSATION OF SENIOR PASTOR
BY CHURCH SETTING & SIZE

ATTENDANCE OVER 1,000	CHURCH SETTING			
	Metropolitan city	Suburb of large city	Small town or rural city	Farming area
AVERAGE SUNDAY AM WORSHIP ATTENDANCE	2,246	2,347	1,702	–
AVERAGE CHURCH INCOME	$4,740,593	$3,604,874	$2,886,109	–
AVERAGE # of YEARS EMPLOYED	14	15	13	–
AVERAGE # of WEEKS OF PAID VACATION	4	4	4	–
% COLLEGE GRADUATE OR HIGHER	94%	95%	100%	–
% WHO RECEIVE AUTO REIMBURSEMENT	63%	69%	63%	–
% ORDAINED	100%	98%	100%	–
AVERAGE % SALARY INCREASE THIS YEAR	6%	6%	6%	–

COMPENSATION		Metropolitan city	Suburb of large city	Small town or rural city	Farming area
BASE SALARY:	Highest 25%	$96,890	$96,000	$68,820	–
	Average	$85,676	$82,148	$65,137	–
	Lowest 25%	$64,011	$62,750	$47,814	–
HOUSING:	Highest 25%	$39,999	$45,000	$40,001	–
	Average	$32,625	$33,392	$27,794	–
	Lowest 25%	$25,501	$24,999	$14,401	–
PARSONAGE:	Highest 25%	–	–	$2,317	–
	Average	–	$2,517	$280	–
	Lowest 25%	–	–	–	–
TOTAL COMPENSATION	Highest 25%	$132,995	$135,000	$93,500	–
	Average	$118,301	$118,058	$93,211	–
	Lowest 25%	$90,005	$93,150	$75,000	–

– *Not enough responses to provide meaningful data*

TABLE 4-7: ANNUAL COMPENSATION OF SENIOR PASTOR
BY CHURCH SETTING & SIZE

BENEFITS		CHURCH SETTING			
		Metropoli-tan city	Suburb of large city	Small town or rural city	Farming area
RETIREMENT:	Highest 25%	$9,063	$11,000	$8,174	–
	Average	$6,518	$7,241	$5,299	–
	Lowest 25%	–	–	$621	–
LIFE INSURANCE:	Highest 25%	–	$720	–	–
	Average	$642	$504	$362	–
	Lowest 25%	–	–	–	–
HEALTH INSURANCE:	Highest 25%	$9,500	$15,150	$11,676	–
	Average	$7,140	$8,550	$8,036	–
	Lowest 25%	$4,543	$2,300	$4,400	–
CONTINUING EDUCATION	Highest 25%	–	$1,489	$1,200	–
	Average	$1,200	$1,166	$650	–
	Lowest 25%	–	–	–	–
TOTAL BENEFITS	Highest 25%	$18,997	$26,408	$19,594	–
	Average	$15,500	$17,461	$14,346	–
	Lowest 25%	$10,366	$8,836	$8,885	–
TOTAL COMPENSATION AND BENEFIT		Metropoli-tan city	Suburb of large city	Small town or rural city	Farming area
	Highest 25%	$155,182	$154,257	$110,457	–
	Average	$133,801	$135,777	$107,557	–
	Lowest 25%	$98,052	$108,042	$90,107	–
NUMBER OF RESPONDENTS		19	58	30	–

– Not enough responses to provide meaningful data

TABLE 4-8: ANNUAL COMPENSATION OF SENIOR PASTOR BY REGION

CHARACTERISTICS	New England	Middle Atlantic	South Atlantic	E-N Central	E-S Central	W-N Central	W-S Central	Mountain	Pacific
AVERAGE SUNDAY AM WORSHIP ATTENDANCE	373	396	719	699	728	480	773	692	534
AVERAGE CHURCH INCOME	$556,462	$680,089	$1,240,996	$1,101,705	$1,782,559	$918,441	$1,725,696	$1,148,162	$983,817
AVERAGE # of YEARS EMPLOYED	13	11	11	12	9	12	11	12	12
AVERAGE # of WEEKS OF PAID VACATION	4	4	4	4	4	4	4	4	4
% COLLEGE GRADUATE OR HIGHER	100%	95%	95%	96%	3%	99%	95%	93%	93%
% WHO RECEIVE AUTO REIMBURSEMENT	89%	83%	77%	83%	75%	79%	63%	79%	73%
% ORDAINED	100%	100%	99%	98%	100%	100%	99%	98%	98%
AVERAGE % SALARY INCREASE THIS YEAR	6%	5%	6%	4%	5%	4%	5%	4%	5%

COMPENSATION		New England	Middle Atlantic	South Atlantic	E-N Central	E-S Central	W-N Central	W-S Central	Mountain	Pacific
BASE SALARY:	Highest 25%	$60,250	$52,944	$64,360	$61,199	$81,297	$57,700	$75,000	$60,000	$55,240
	Average	$47,768	$44,383	$52,589	$50,449	$63,612	$45,113	$57,974	$46,813	$46,573
	Lowest 25%	$36,125	$35,580	$35,000	$31,668	$36,997	$31,500	$37,688	$30,000	$30,142
HOUSING:	Highest 25%	$26,400	$23,400	$32,400	$30,000	$33,643	$24,000	$34,700	$35,000	$36,000
	Average	$16,912	$14,512	$23,305	$20,690	$20,949	$18,323	$23,065	$24,122	$26,830
	Lowest 25%	–	–	$13,735	$7,500	$4,000	$11,000	$11,140	$12,000	$18,000
PARSONAGE:	Highest 25%	$6,240	$300	–	–	–	–	–	–	–
	Average	$3,713	$3,890	$1,707	$1,967	$4,899	$1,021	$2,220	$905	$2,019
	Lowest 25%	–	–	–	–	–	–	–	–	–
TOTAL COMPENSATION	Highest 25%	$97,850	$71,944	$93,960	$86,199	$100,987	$71,250	$101,494	$85,006	$84,316
	Average	$68,393	$62,786	$77,600	$73,105	$89,460	$64,456	$83,258	$71,841	$75,422
	Lowest 25%	$52,125	$57,149	$57,600	$51,000	$61,900	$48,643	$54,600	$55,000	$56,805

– Not enough responses to provide meaningful data

TABLE 4-8: ANNUAL COMPENSATION OF SENIOR PASTOR BY REGION

BENEFITS		REGION								
		New England	Middle Atlantic	South Atlantic	E-N Central	E-S Central	W-N Central	W-S Central	Mountain	Pacific
RETIREMENT:	Highest 25%	$9,500	$7,046	$8,220	$6,736	$7,690	$6,438	$8,500	$7,017	$5,880
	Average	$4,793	$4,367	$5,289	$3,997	$5,244	$4,116	$4,820	$4,032	$4,110
	Lowest 25%	–	$500	–	–	–	–	–	–	–
LIFE INSURANCE:	Highest 25%	$350	–	–	–	$555	–	–	–	–
	Average	$177	$500	$412	$358	$375	$539	$302	$439	$219
	Lowest 25%	–	–	–	–	–	–	–	–	–
HEALTH INSURANCE:	Highest 25%	$16,190	$10,740	$11,160	$12,403	$9,513	$12,247	$12,000	$10,884	$10,716
	Average	$10,260	$6,649	$7,181	$7,596	$6,391	$7,834	$7,668	$7,027	$6,639
	Lowest 25%	$3,800	–	–	–	$1,279	–	$2,940	–	$250
CONTINUING EDUCATION	Highest 25%	$1,001	$1,001	$1,499	$1,001	$1,600	$1,000	$1,499	$1,000	$962
	Average	$886	$874	$869	$748	$1,128	$653	$813	$621	$686
	Lowest 25%	–	–	–	–	–	–	–	–	–
TOTAL BENEFITS	Highest 25%	$22,117	$16,226	$20,300	$18,851	$17,826	$16,798	$18,669	$16,974	$15,979
	Average	$16,116	$12,390	$13,751	$12,699	$13,138	$13,141	$13,603	$12,120	$11,655
	Lowest 25%	$11,964	$7,906	$7,600	$6,000	$6,700	$6,500	$6,747	$5,000	$4,605
TOTAL COMPENSATION AND BENEFIT		New England	Middle Atlantic	South Atlantic	E-N Central	E-S Central	W-N Central	W-S Central	Mountain	Pacific
	Highest 25%	$115,980	$87,000	$108,000	$101,045	$116,863	$91,000	$118,100	$100,441	$98,736
	Average	$84,509	$75,175	$91,597	$85,804	$103,143	$77,597	$96,860	$83,960	$87,194
	Lowest 25%	$64,089	$62,600	$69,160	$64,300	$70,891	$59,143	$67,332	$64,000	$66,573
NUMBER OF RESPONDENTS		18	79	146	139	44	79	79	57	128

– Not enough responses to provide meaningful data

TABLE 4-9: ANNUAL COMPENSATION OF SENIOR PASTOR BY GENDER

CHARACTERISTICS	GENDER	
	Male	Female
AVERAGE SUNDAY AM WORSHIP ATTENDANCE	626	225
AVERAGE CHURCH INCOME	$1,142,860	–
AVERAGE # of YEARS EMPLOYED	11	11
AVERAGE # of WEEKS OF PAID VACATION	4	3
% COLLEGE GRADUATE OR HIGHER	95%	100%
% WHO RECEIVE AUTO REIMBURSEMENT	77%	63%
% ORDAINED	99%	88%
AVERAGE % SALARY INCREASE THIS YEAR	5%	–

COMPENSATION		Male	Female
BASE SALARY:	Highest 25%	$62,725	$49,000
	Average	$50,422	$32,858
	Lowest 25%	$33,902	$22,000
HOUSING:	Highest 25%	$30,889	$18,000
	Average	$21,938	$11,589
	Lowest 25%	$11,450	–
PARSONAGE:	Highest 25%	–	–
	Average	$2,243	$500
	Lowest 25%	–	–
TOTAL COMPENSATION	Highest 25%	$88,000	$52,000
	Average	$74,604	$44,947
	Lowest 25%	$55,000	$36,000

– Not enough responses to provide meaningful data

TABLE 4-9: ANNUAL COMPENSATION OF SENIOR PASTOR BY GENDER

BENEFITS		GENDER	
		Male	Female
RETIREMENT:	Highest 25%	$7,177	–
	Average	$4,528	$1,432
	Lowest 25%	–	–
LIFE INSURANCE:	Highest 25%	–	–
	Average	$378	$56
	Lowest 25%	–	–
HEALTH INSURANCE:	Highest 25%	$11,895	$6,282
	Average	$7,306	$4,420
	Lowest 25%	$795	–
CONTINUING EDUCATION	Highest 25%	$1,001	$1,501
	Average	$787	$1,022
	Lowest 25%	–	–
TOTAL BENEFITS	Highest 25%	$18,045	$12,570
	Average	$13,000	$6,930
	Lowest 25%	$6,724	$0
TOTAL COMPENSATION AND BENEFIT		Male	Female
	Highest 25%	$104,063	$52,000
	Average	$87,702	$51,877
	Lowest 25%	$65,917	$36,000
NUMBER OF RESPONDENTS		764	9

– Not enough responses to provide meaningful data

61

TABLE 4-10: ANNUAL COMPENSATION OF SENIOR PASTOR BY EDUCATION

CHARACTERISTICS	EDUCATION			
	< than Bachelor	Bachelor	Master	Doctorate
AVERAGE SUNDAY AM WORSHIP ATTENDANCE	453	686	575	664
AVERAGE CHURCH INCOME	$815,377	$994,733	$1,005,953	$1,480,481
AVERAGE # of YEARS EMPLOYED	14	12	11	12
AVERAGE # of WEEKS OF PAID VACATION	3	4	4	4
% COLLEGE GRADUATE OR HIGHER	–	100%	100%	100%
% WHO RECEIVE AUTO REIMBURSEMENT	73%	73%	82%	75%
% ORDAINED	97%	98%	99%	100%
AVERAGE % SALARY INCREASE THIS YEAR	10%	5%	4%	4%

COMPENSATION		< than Bachelor	Bachelor	Master	Doctorate
BASE SALARY:	Highest 25%	$55,000	$58,900	$60,000	$72,000
	Average	$45,122	$45,332	$48,179	$58,990
	Lowest 25%	$27,170	$30,000	$33,940	$40,327
HOUSING:	Highest 25%	$30,000	$30,000	$30,000	$35,000
	Average	$22,187	$19,820	$21,546	$24,838
	Lowest 25%	$13,500	$4,000	$12,000	$14,400
PARSONAGE:	Highest 25%	–	–	–	–
	Average	$687	$1,715	$2,051	$3,453
	Lowest 25%	–	–	–	–
TOTAL COMPENSATION	Highest 25%	$82,000	$79,918	$83,615	$100,291
	Average	$67,996	$66,866	$71,775	$87,281
	Lowest 25%	$49,400	$49,200	$54,100	$64,214

– Not enough responses to provide meaningful data

TABLE 4-10: ANNUAL COMPENSATION OF SENIOR PASTOR BY EDUCATION

BENEFITS		EDUCATION			
		< than Bachelor	Bachelor	Master	Doctorate
RETIREMENT:	Highest 25%	$6,000	$4,200	$7,684	$9,200
	Average	$3,028	$2,841	$4,910	$5,887
	Lowest 25%	–	–	–	$1,380
LIFE INSURANCE:	Highest 25%	–	–	–	–
	Average	$559	$323	$347	$420
	Lowest 25%	–	–	–	–
HEALTH INSURANCE:	Highest 25%	$10,000	$11,164	$12,000	$12,000
	Average	$5,825	$6,800	$7,658	$7,682
	Lowest 25%	$573	$0	$1,973	$0
CONTINUING EDUCATION	Highest 25%	–	$999	$1,251	$1,499
	Average	$221	$651	$894	$885
	Lowest 25%	–	–	–	–
TOTAL BENEFITS	Highest 25%	$14,400	$15,312	$18,997	$20,300
	Average	$9,633	$10,615	$13,810	$14,873
	Lowest 25%	$1,550	$4,176	$7,500	$8,620
TOTAL COMPENSATION AND BENEFIT		< than Bachelor	Bachelor	Master	Doctorate
	Highest 25%	$89,700	$97,148	$101,558	$118,626
	Average	$77,628	$77,481	$85,631	$102,470
	Lowest 25%	$57,500	$58,000	$65,800	$77,000
NUMBER OF RESPONDENTS		38	175	330	190

– Not enough responses to provide meaningful data

TABLE 4-11: ANNUAL COMPENSATION OF SENIOR PASTOR BY YEARS EMPLOYED

CHARACTERISTICS		YEARS EMPLOYED			
		< 6 years	6-10 years	11-15 years	Over 15 years
AVERAGE SUNDAY AM WORSHIP ATTENDANCE		510	509	683	810
AVERAGE CHURCH INCOME		$984,448	$920,367	$1,175,821	$1,488,046
AVERAGE # of YEARS EMPLOYED		3	8	13	23
AVERAGE # of WEEKS OF PAID VACATION		4	4	4	4
% COLLEGE GRADUATE OR HIGHER		97%	93%	96%	92%
% WHO RECEIVE AUTO REIMBURSEMENT		77%	73%	74%	82%
% ORDAINED		98%	99%	99%	100%
AVERAGE % SALARY INCREASE THIS YEAR		5%	5%	5%	4%

COMPENSATION		< 6 years	6-10 years	11-15 years	Over 15 years
BASE SALARY:	Highest 25%	$61,000	$58,500	$62,750	$68,000
	Average	$48,537	$46,077	$50,153	$55,974
	Lowest 25%	$31,529	$32,500	$33,940	$37,960
HOUSING:	Highest 25%	$31,000	$30,000	$35,000	$30,000
	Average	$21,894	$22,658	$22,681	$20,880
	Lowest 25%	$10,000	$12,000	$12,000	$11,000
PARSONAGE:	Highest 25%	–	–	–	–
	Average	$2,263	$1,984	$2,652	$2,258
	Lowest 25%	–	–	–	–
TOTAL COMPENSATION	Highest 25%	$86,000	$83,864	$89,500	$93,960
	Average	$72,694	$70,718	$75,486	$79,112
	Lowest 25%	$54,100	$53,000	$56,000	$55,566

– Not enough responses to provide meaningful data

TABLE 4-11: ANNUAL COMPENSATION OF SENIOR PASTOR BY YEARS EMPLOYED

BENEFITS		YEARS EMPLOYED			
		< 6 years	6-10 years	11-15 years	Over 15 years
RETIREMENT:	Highest 25%	$7,073	$7,988	$6,112	$7,496
	Average	$4,283	$4,733	$4,229	$4,926
	Lowest 25%	–	–	–	–
LIFE INSURANCE:	Highest 25%	–	–	–	–
	Average	$371	$388	$319	$417
	Lowest 25%	–	–	–	–
HEALTH INSURANCE:	Highest 25%	$11,400	$11,281	$12,000	$12,377
	Average	$7,176	$7,315	$7,024	$7,655
	Lowest 25%	–	$1,680	$750	$1,080
CONTINUING EDUCATION	Highest 25%	$1,100	$1,200	$999	$1,001
	Average	$838	$829	$574	$819
	Lowest 25%	–	–	–	–
TOTAL BENEFITS	Highest 25%	$17,568	$19,000	$17,263	$19,400
	Average	$12,668	$13,265	$12,146	$13,818
	Lowest 25%	$6,500	$6,900	$5,000	$7,441
TOTAL COMPENSATION AND BENEFIT		< 6 years	6-10 years	11-15 years	Over 15 years
	Highest 25%	$104,084	$98.800	$102,700	$106,287
	Average	$85,408	$83,983	$87,812	$93,124
	Lowest 25%	$64,100	$64,600	$65,800	$68,938
NUMBER OF RESPONDENTS		242	175	139	201

– Not enough responses to provide meaningful data

65

TABLE 4-12: ANNUAL COMPENSATION OF SENIOR PASTOR BY DENOMINATION

CHARACTERISTICS	DENOMINATION					
	Assemblies of God	Baptist	Independent/ Nondenom	Lutheran	Methodist	Presbyterian
AVERAGE SUNDAY AM WORSHIP ATTENDANCE	412	599	846	402	628	530
AVERAGE CHURCH INCOME	$776,973	$1,311,459	$1,210,149	$830,084	$1,059,989	$1,353,579
AVERAGE # of YEARS EMPLOYED	11	12	12	12	9	10
AVERAGE # of WEEKS OF PAID VACATION	4	4	4	4	4	4
% COLLEGE GRADUATE OR HIGHER	90%	98%	90%	100%	95%	100%
% WHO RECEIVE AUTO REIMBURSEMENT	74%	77%	70%	87%	80%	87%
% ORDAINED	100%	99%	99%	100%	100%	100%
AVERAGE % SALARY INCREASE THIS YEAR	5%	5%	5%	3%	5%	5%

COMPENSATION		Assemblies of God	Baptist	Independent/ Nondenom	Lutheran	Methodist	Presbyterian
BASE SALARY:	Highest 25%	$50,000	$64,667	$62,150	$68,600	$79,717	$63,935
	Average	$42,046	$51,154	$51,182	$52,319	$59,176	$54,435
	Lowest 25%	$30,000	$35,000	$32,777	$40,000	$36,000	$38,936
HOUSING:	Highest 25%	$31,800	$30,000	$32,000	$34,300	$24,000	$40,000
	Average	$20,723	$22,654	$22,940	$19,979	$13,778	$28,489
	Lowest 25%	$11,400	$13,500	$13,000	$600	–	$19,000
PARSONAGE:	Highest 25%	–	–	–	–	$10,600	–
	Average	$1,768	$2,041	$1,278	$650	$5,556	$3,754
	Lowest 25%	–	–	–	–	–	–
TOTAL COMPENSATION	Highest 25%	$81,735	$90,000	$88,000	$89,500	$92,826	$94,459
	Average	$64,537	$75,848	$75,400	$72,948	$78,511	$86,678
	Lowest 25%	$50,000	$55,727	$55,100	$60,159	$54,000	$66,200

– Not enough responses to provide meaningful data

TABLE 4-12: ANNUAL COMPENSATION OF SENIOR PASTOR BY DENOMINATION

BENEFITS		DENOMINATION					
		Assemblies of God	Baptist	Independent/ Nondenom	Lutheran	Methodist	Presbyte-rian
RETIREMENT:	Highest 25%	$4,000	$7,725	$4,000	$8,050	$6,600	$10,462
	Average	$2,866	$5,182	$2,819	$4,447	$4,115	$7,555
	Lowest 25%	–	$1,200	–	–	–	$3,000
LIFE INSURANCE:	Highest 25%	$180	–	–	–	–	$746
	Average	$164	$510	$470	$288	$94	$562
	Lowest 25%	–	–	–	–	–	–
HEALTH INSURANCE:	Highest 25%	$10,008	$10,815	$12,000	$15,276	$11,300	$15,957
	Average	$6,295	$6,779	$7,246	$10,196	$6,926	$10,979
	Lowest 25%	$954	$750	$946	$5,000	$4,000	$7,680
CONTINUING EDUCATION	Highest 25%	–	$1,000	$1,000	$1,500	$1,001	$2,000
	Average	$527	$614	$795	$1,179	$673	$1,592
	Lowest 25%	–	–	–	–	–	–
TOTAL BENEFITS	Highest 25%	$14,534	$18,200	$16,176	$23,800	$16,560	$26,488
	Average	$9,851	$13,085	$11,331	$16,110	$11,808	$20,688
	Lowest 25%	$4,000	$7,704	$4,888	$9,000	$7,206	$14,086
TOTAL COMPENSATION AND BENEFIT		Assemblies of God	Baptist	Independent/ Nondenom	Lutheran	Methodist	Presbyte-rian
	Highest 25%	$93,621	$106,287	$100,570	$110,192	$107,900	$118,048
	Average	$74,389	$89,051	$86,730	$89,058	$90,318	$107,769
	Lowest 25%	$52,335	$65,270	$65,294	$70,150	$64,600	$79,800
NUMBER OF RESPONDENTS		53	205	173	31	42	62

– Not enough responses to provide meaningful data

5

SOLO PASTORS

Employment Profile

Solo pastors are a unique group of church staff members. They are set apart from the previous group of Senior pastors in that they are the only ordained employee of their church. In this way, they oversee no other clergy, though they may oversee other staff members, such as a church secretary or a custodian. With 375 positions reported, this group of individuals provided significant information for study in this survey. Solo pastors most likely serve in smaller churches with a worship attendance of 300 or less and an income of $500,000 or less. Nearly all solo pastors (97%) have college degrees and about three-quarters have graduate degrees. The most common was a master's degree held by 62% of those reported in this survey. Only 14% held doctoral degrees.

Ordained	**98%**
Average years employed	**9**
Male	**95%**
Female	**5%**
Self-employed (receives 1099)	**10%**
Church employee (receives W-2)	**90%**
High school diploma	**2%**
Associate's degree	**1%**
Bachelor's degree	**21%**
Master's degree	**62%**
Doctorate	**14%**
Number of respondents	*375*

Total Compensation plus Benefits Package Analysis

The analyses on the next page are based upon the data in the tables that you will find in the remainder of the chapter. The tables present compensation plus benefits data for solo pastors who serve full-time according to church attendance, church income, combinations of size and setting, region, gender, education, years employed, and denomination. In this way, the solo pastor's compensation plus benefit can be analyzed and compared from a variety of useful perspectives. The total compensation plus benefit amount includes the base salary, housing and/or parsonage amount, retirement contribution, life and health insurance payments, and educational funds.

The average compensation for a full-time solo pastor is about two-thirds lower than that of a full-time senior pastor, yet the benefits remain comparable for both. The compensation difference is most likely related to the fact that solo pastors serve in smaller churches. 65% of solo pastors receive health insurance, and the same percentage also had retirement benefits.

COMPENSATION PLUS BENEFITS

Base salary	97%
Housing	71%
Parsonage	35%
Retirement	65%
Life insurance	27%
Health insurance	65%
Paid vacation	97%
Auto reimbursement	73%
Continuing education	48%

KEY POINTS

⊃ **Church income affects the compensation and benefits of solo pastors.** In general, as church income increases, compensation and benefits go up. Three-quarters of the reported solo pastors positions serve in a church with income of $250,000 and under receive compensation plus benefit packages that are slightly lower than the national average of $59,852. Those who serve in churches with an income of $251,000-$500,000 receive approximately $20,000 more in compensation plus benefits than those who are in churches with lower income. *See Table 5-1.*

⊃ **Church worship attendance affects the compensation and benefits of the solo pastor.** Of the solo pastors surveyed, approximately 90% worked in churches with an average worship attendance of 300 people and under. The compensation of solo pastors who serve in churches with an attendance of 100 or less was slightly below the national average. Compensation increases significantly as attendance moves between 101 to 300 and 301 to 500. *See Table 5-2.*

⊃ **A church's geographical setting affects the compensation and benefits of the solo pastor.** Generally, solo pastors serving churches set in a metropolitan city or a suburban setting have the highest compensation and benefits packages compared to those who serve in small town or farming areas. Church income in these settings is also higher, which greatly impacts overall compensation. Churches located in metropolitan cities and suburbs of large cities tend to provide higher housing allowances. *See Tables 5-3 and 5-4.*

⊃ **A relationship exists between educational achievement and income for solo pastors.** Solo pastors with less than a master's degree earned approximately $8,000 less than solo pastors with a master's degree. Solo pastors with doctorate degrees earned approximately $9,000 more than those with master's degrees. In general, only those groups with graduate degrees reached the national average. *See Table 5-10.*

⊃ **Years of service impact the compensation and benefits package of the solo pastor.** Those serving for five years or less in their current position (40% of reported positions) received about $6,400 a year less in total compensation than those who had served over 15 years. The difference, however, appears to also be dependent on church income not just years served. Those serving the longest tended to be in bigger churches with significantly higher incomes. *See Table 5-11.*

Ten Year Compensation & Benefits Trend: National Averages for Solo Pastors*

FULL TIME

2006	$59,852

* No historical data available

TABLE 5-1: ANNUAL COMPENSATION OF SOLO PASTOR BY CHURCH INCOME

CHARACTERISTICS	CHURCH INCOME				
	$250K & under	$251K-$500K	$501K-$750K	$751K-$1M	Over $1 Million
AVERAGE SUNDAY AM WORSHIP ATTENDANCE	96	217	516	373	–
AVERAGE CHURCH INCOME	$130,281	$350,957	$607,653	$878,793	–
AVERAGE # of YEARS EMPLOYED	9	9	10	14	–
AVERAGE # of WEEKS OF PAID VACATION	3	4	3	4	–
% COLLEGE GRADUATE OR HIGHER	97%	98%	93%	100%	–
% WHO RECEIVE AUTO REIMBURSEMENT	73%	76%	87%	56%	–
% ORDAINED	98%	98%	100%	100%	–
AVERAGE % SALARY INCREASE THIS YEAR	5%	4%	6%	–	–

COMPENSATION		$250K & under	$251K-$500K	$501K-$750K	$751K-$1M	Over 1 Million
BASE SALARY:	Highest 25%	$38,001	$50,224	$55,999	$46,001	–
	Average	$30,017	$41,706	$45,678	$33,034	–
	Lowest 25%	$22,220	$32,701	$35,001	$23,305	–
HOUSING:	Highest 25%	$17,998	$24,001	$29,932	$32,005	–
	Average	$10,571	$15,541	$17,805	$25,710	–
	Lowest 25%	–	$1,505	$4,005	$18,995	–
PARSONAGE:	Highest 25%	$6,605	–	$11,495	–	–
	Average	$3,848	$3,107	$4,460	–	–
	Lowest 25%	–	–	–	–	–
TOTAL COMPENSATION	Highest 25%	$53,000	$65,000	$78,000	$75,000	–
	Average	$44,437	$60,353	$67,943	$58,744	–
	Lowest 25%	$35,000	$50,655	$63,000	$44,087	–

– Not enough responses to provide meaningful data

TABLE 5-1: ANNUAL COMPENSATION OF SOLO PASTOR BY CHURCH INCOME

BENEFITS		CHURCH INCOME				
		$250K & under	$251K-$500K	$501K-$750K	$751K-$1M	Over $1 Million
RETIREMENT:	Highest 25%	$4,800	$7,211	$5,395	$6,000	–
	Average	$2,802	$5,207	$3,626	$3,275	–
	Lowest 25%	–	$727	–	–	–
LIFE INSURANCE:	Highest 25%	–	–	$200	–	–
	Average	$221	$196	$161	$136	–
	Lowest 25%	–	–	–	–	–
HEALTH INSURANCE:	Highest 25%	$9,001	$11,417	$9,321	$13,718	–
	Average	$5,009	$6,004	$5,432	$9,077	–
	Lowest 25%	–	–	$1,201	$1,249	–
CONTINUING EDUCATION	Highest 25%	$790	$1,202	–	$1,502	–
	Average	$592	$885	$1,273	$778	–
	Lowest 25%	–	–	–	–	–
TOTAL BENEFITS	Highest 25%	$13,372	$19,050	$15,781	$18,800	–
	Average	$8,624	$12,292	$10,492	$13,266	–
	Lowest 25%	$2,620	$5,172	$5,710	$2,250	–
TOTAL COMPENSATION AND BENEFIT		$250K & under	$251K-$500K	$501K-$750K	$751K-$1M	Over 1 Million
	Highest 25%	$65,243	$85,200	$87,800	$91,837	–
	Average	$53,325	$73,026	$78,435	$72,010	–
	Lowest 25%	$40,406	$62,280	$73,900	$50,000	–
NUMBER OF RESPONDENTS		261	63	15	9	5

– Not enough responses to provide meaningful data

73

TABLE 5-2: ANNUAL COMPENSATION OF SOLO PASTOR BY WORSHIP ATTENDANCE

CHARACTERISTICS	WORSHIP ATTENDANCE					
	100 or less	101-300	301-500	501-750	751-1000	Over 1000
AVERAGE SUNDAY AM WORSHIP ATTENDANCE	68	167	403	–	–	–
AVERAGE CHURCH INCOME	$115,882	$254,539	$593,088	–	–	–
AVERAGE # of YEARS EMPLOYED	9	9	12	–	–	–
AVERAGE # of WEEKS OF PAID VACATION	3	4	4	–	–	–
% COLLEGE GRADUATE OR HIGHER	98%	97%	96%	–	–	–
% WHO RECEIVE AUTO REIMBURSEMENT	72%	74%	83%	–	–	–
% ORDAINED	99%	97%	100%	–	–	–
AVERAGE % SALARY INCREASE THIS YEAR	5%	5%	4%	–	–	–

COMPENSATION		100 or less	101-300	301-500	501-750	751-1000	Over 1000
BASE SALARY:	Highest 25%	$37,399	$44,999	$54,868	–	–	–
	Average	$28,201	$37,715	$44,983	–	–	–
	Lowest 25%	$19,801	$29,930	$40,332	–	–	–
HOUSING:	Highest 25%	$17,991	$22,002	$23,350	–	–	–
	Average	$10,482	$13,457	$16,191	–	–	–
	Lowest 25%	–	–	$4,500	–	–	–
PARSONAGE:	Highest 25%	$6,595	–	–	–	–	–
	Average	$4,072	$3,522	$2,730	–	–	–
	Lowest 25%	–	–	–	–	–	–
TOTAL COMPENSATION	Highest 25%	$50,900	$62,000	$71,910	–	–	–
	Average	$42,755	$54,693	$63,904	–	–	–
	Lowest 25%	$31,000	$43,800	$57,150	–	–	–

– Not enough responses to provide meaningful data

TABLE 5-2: ANNUAL COMPENSATION OF SOLO PASTOR BY WORSHIP ATTENDANCE

BENEFITS		WORSHIP ATTENDANCE					
		100 or less	101-300	301-500	501-750	751-1000	Over 1000
RETIREMENT:	Highest 25%	$4,300	$6,000	$7,497	–	–	–
	Average	$2,659	$3,933	$4,699	–	–	–
	Lowest 25%	–	–	$925	–	–	–
LIFE INSURANCE:	Highest 25%	–	–	–	–	–	–
	Average	$215	$251	$304	–	–	–
	Lowest 25%	–	–	–	–	–	–
HEALTH INSURANCE:	Highest 25%	$8,401	$10,501	$12,777	–	–	–
	Average	$4,605	$5,627	$8,015	–	–	–
	Lowest 25%	–	–	$3,038	–	–	–
CONTINUING EDUCATION	Highest 25%	$501	$1,003	$1,500	–	–	–
	Average	$468	$867	$1,099	–	–	–
	Lowest 25%	–	–	$450	–	–	–
TOTAL BENEFITS	Highest 25%	$12,280	$16,626	$19,012	–	–	–
	Average	$7,947	$10,677	$14,117	–	–	–
	Lowest 25%	$1,200	$4,000	$9,800	–	–	–
TOTAL COMPENSATION AND BENEFIT		100 or less	101-300	301-500	501-750	751-1000	Over 1000
	Highest 25%	$64,000	$76,000	$87,740	–	–	–
	Average	$51,115	$65,370	$78,646	–	–	–
	Lowest 25%	$37,700	$52,700	$72,505	–	–	–
NUMBER OF RESPONDENTS		183	153	24	3	2	4

– Not enough responses to provide meaningful data

75

TABLE 5-3: ANNUAL COMPENSATION OF SOLO PASTOR BY CHURCH SETTING & SIZE

ATTENDANCE 250 & UNDER		CHURCH SETTING			
		Metropoli-tan city	Suburb of large city	Small town or rural city	Farming area
AVERAGE SUNDAY AM WORSHIP ATTENDANCE		94	104	112	93
AVERAGE CHURCH INCOME		$202,567	$187,515	$165,211	$121,744
AVERAGE # of YEARS EMPLOYED		9	9	9	7
AVERAGE # of WEEKS OF PAID VACATION		3	4	4	3
% COLLEGE GRADUATE OR HIGHER		100%	99%	97%	95%
% WHO RECEIVE AUTO REIMBURSEMENT		65%	74%	75%	75%
% ORDAINED		97%	99%	97%	98%
AVERAGE % SALARY INCREASE THIS YEAR		6%	4%	5%	5%

COMPENSATION		Metropoli-tan city	Suburb of large city	Small town or rural city	Farming area
BASE SALARY:	Highest 25%	$43,999	$41,001	$42,001	$33,500
	Average	$35,643	$31,667	$32,783	$26,044
	Lowest 25%	$22,999	$22,002	$25,000	$17,700
HOUSING:	Highest 25%	$22,805	$23,998	$19,005	$10,000
	Average	$15,122	$14,360	$10,711	$6,262
	Lowest 25%	$3,992	–	–	–
PARSONAGE:	Highest 25%	–	–	$7,202	$7,350
	Average	$4,798	$3,857	$3,672	$3,811
	Lowest 25%	–	–	–	–
TOTAL COMPENSATION	Highest 25%	$65,000	$62,000	$56,300	$43,350
	Average	$55,563	$49,884	$47,165	$36,116
	Lowest 25%	$43,000	$38,500	$37,851	$28,790

– Not enough responses to provide meaningful data

TABLE 5-3: ANNUAL COMPENSATION OF SOLO PASTOR BY CHURCH SETTING & SIZE

BENEFITS		CHURCH SETTING			
		Metropoli-tan city	Suburb of large city	Small town or rural city	Farming area
RETIREMENT:	Highest 25%	$4,001	$5,999	$5,514	$3,860
	Average	$2,701	$3,626	$3,413	$2,012
	Lowest 25%	–	–	–	–
LIFE INSURANCE:	Highest 25%	–	–	–	–
	Average	$186	$298	$232	$197
	Lowest 25%	–	–	–	–
HEALTH INSURANCE:	Highest 25%	$7,502	$9,498	$9,999	$9,376
	Average	$4,722	$4,937	$5,525	$4,371
	Lowest 25%	–	–	–	–
CONTINUING EDUCATION	Highest 25%	$1,000	$802	$997	$500
	Average	$912	$514	$662	$463
	Lowest 25%	–	–	–	–
TOTAL BENEFITS	Highest 25%	$12,100	$14,900	$15,500	$11,693
	Average	$8,521	$9,375	$9,832	$7,042
	Lowest 25%	$3,700	$2,842	$3,000	$1,039
TOTAL COMPENSATION AND BENEFIT		Metropoli-tan city	Suburb of large city	Small town or rural city	Farming area
	Highest 25%	$80,701	$76,000	$67,770	$55,597
	Average	$65,865	$59,260	$57,149	$43,158
	Lowest 25%	$49,672	$45,500	$43,160	$30,139
NUMBER OF RESPONDENTS		37	79	161	44

– Not enough responses to provide meaningful data

77

TABLE 5-4: ANNUAL COMPENSATION OF SOLO PASTOR BY CHURCH SETTING & SIZE

ATTENDANCE 251 - 500	CHURCH SETTING			
	Metropoli-tan city	Suburb of large city	Small town or rural city	Farming area
AVERAGE SUNDAY AM WORSHIP ATTENDANCE	345	393	368	–
AVERAGE CHURCH INCOME	$486,551	$709,161	$522,974	–
AVERAGE # of YEARS EMPLOYED	11	13	10	–
AVERAGE # of WEEKS OF PAID VACATION	4	4	4	–
% COLLEGE GRADUATE OR HIGHER	100%	100%	92%	–
% WHO RECEIVE AUTO REIMBURSEMENT	70%	64%	85%	–
% ORDAINED	100%	100%	100%	–
AVERAGE % SALARY INCREASE THIS YEAR	–	4%	5%	–

COMPENSATION		Metropoli-tan city	Suburb of large city	Small town or rural city	Farming area
BASE SALARY:	Highest 25%	$56,830	$64,984	$51,943	–
	Average	$47,159	$47,866	$46,450	–
	Lowest 25%	$35,000	$23,322	$40,647	–
HOUSING:	Highest 25%	$31,254	$31,989	$22,011	–
	Average	$17,625	$23,349	$16,667	–
	Lowest 25%	–	$18,011	$11,984	–
PARSONAGE:	Highest 25%	–	–	–	–
	Average	$3,190	$1,000	$1,740	–
	Lowest 25%	–	–	–	–
TOTAL COMPENSATION	Highest 25%	$78,000	$87,793	$70,587	–
	Average	$67,974	$72,215	$64,856	–
	Lowest 25%	$55,919	$57,007	$57,293	–

– Not enough responses to provide meaningful data

TABLE 5-4: ANNUAL COMPENSATION OF SOLO PASTOR BY CHURCH SETTING & SIZE

BENEFITS		CHURCH SETTING			
		Metropoli-tan city	Suburb of large city	Small town or rural city	Farming area
RETIREMENT:	Highest 25%	$8,699	$9,597	$5,893	–
	Average	$6,002	$5,396	$4,025	–
	Lowest 25%	–	–	$1,825	–
LIFE INSURANCE:	Highest 25%	–	–	–	–
	Average	$482	–	$173	–
	Lowest 25%	–	–	–	–
HEALTH INSURANCE:	Highest 25%	–	$11,823	$13,993	–
	Average	$4,236	$7,360	$8,214	–
	Lowest 25%	$2,000	–	$2,662	–
CONTINUING EDUCATION	Highest 25%	$1,000	$1,999	–	–
	Average	$520	$1,314	$1,549	–
	Lowest 25%	–	–	$499	–
TOTAL BENEFITS	Highest 25%	$19,225	$18,800	$18,285	–
	Average	$11,239	$14,161	$13,961	–
	Lowest 25%	$4,000	$9,900	$9,929	–
TOTAL COMPENSATION AND BENEFIT		Metropoli-tan city	Suburb of large city	Small town or rural city	Farming area
	Highest 25%	$82,225	$93,772	$87,709	–
	Average	$80,713	$86,376	$78,818	–
	Lowest 25%	$69,000	$74,853	$72,772	–
NUMBER OF RESPONDENTS		10	11	13	4

– Not enough responses to provide meaningful data

TABLE 5-5: ANNUAL COMPENSATION OF SOLO PASTOR BY REGION

CHARACTERISTICS	New England	Middle Atlantic	South Atlantic	E-N Central	E-S Central	W-N Central	W-S Central	Mountain	Pacific
AVERAGE SUNDAY AM WORSHIP ATTENDANCE	84	185	175	167	271	144	161	159	126
AVERAGE CHURCH INCOME	$141,659	$208,667	$287,330	$249,834	$441,746	$199,741	$284,867	$228,066	$218,326
AVERAGE # of YEARS EMPLOYED	11	10	8	10	10	8	8	8	8
AVERAGE # of WEEKS OF PAID VACATION	4	4	3	4	3	3	3	4	4
% COLLEGE GRADUATE OR HIGHER	100%	98%	98%	96%	100%	95%	100%	100%	94%
% WHO RECEIVE AUTO REIMBURSEMENT	79%	87%	74%	75%	58%	83%	48%	65%	70%
% ORDAINED	94%	98%	100%	97%	95%	98%	96%	100%	100%
AVERAGE % SALARY INCREASE THIS YEAR	–	5%	4%	4%	5%	4%	7%	5%	5%

COMPENSATION		New England	Middle Atlantic	South Atlantic	E-N Central	E-S Central	W-N Central	W-S Central	Mountain	Pacific
BASE SALARY:	Highest 25%	$41,999	$45,000	$44,617	$43,350	$43,868	$38,799	$48,500	$39,300	$44,999
	Average	$34,830	$35,065	$33,443	$32,475	$40,248	$31,354	$38,191	$30,464	$34,593
	Lowest 25%	$29,001	$23,427	$24,579	$20,270	$28,001	$24,501	$26,340	$24,999	$22,601
HOUSING:	Highest 25%	$16,995	$20,008	$26,003	$19,100	$19,995	$17,993	$18,000	$22,700	$24,005
	Average	$9,360	$10,412	$15,259	$10,707	$12,817	$11,112	$12,421	$13,349	$15,490
	Lowest 25%	–	–	–	–	–	$1,998	$2,400	–	–
PARSONAGE:	Highest 25%	$15,006	$6,605	–	$8,500	$9,055	$5,996	–	$6,360	–
	Average	$8,487	$4,053	$1,830	$3,973	$6,345	$2,612	$2,438	$3,334	$3,770
	Lowest 25%	–	–	–	–	–	–	–	–	–
TOTAL COMPENSATION	Highest 25%	$64,800	$56,000	$63,640	$58,559	$64,917	$54,500	$63,500	$64,200	$66,295
	Average	$52,677	$49,530	$50,532	$47,115	$59,410	$45,079	$53,050	$47,147	$53,854
	Lowest 25%	$43,200	$39,600	$40,498	$32,250	$48,000	$37,200	$38,400	$35,600	$35,000

– Not enough responses to provide meaningful data

TABLE 5-5: ANNUAL COMPENSATION OF SOLO PASTOR BY REGION

BENEFITS		REGION								
		New England	Middle Atlantic	South Atlantic	E-N Central	E-S Central	W-N Central	W-S Central	Moun-tain	Pacific
RETIREMENT:	Highest 25%	$6,000	$8,500	$5,988	$5,215	$5,568	$5,233	–	$6,710	$5,000
	Average	$3,805	$4,895	$3,202	$3,388	$2,905	$3,206	$2,313	$3,199	$3,173
	Lowest 25%	–	–	–	–	–	–	–	–	–
LIFE INSURANCE:	Highest 25%	–	–	$591	–	$800	–	–	–	–
	Average	$170	$100	$494	$198	$503	$133	$425	$356	$186
	Lowest 25%	–	–	–	–	–	–	–	–	–
HEALTH INSURANCE:	Highest 25%	$13,599	$11,821	$8,097	$10,000	$10,209	$8,999	$7,400	$11,837	$7,399
	Average	$6,218	$7,051	$4,723	$5,330	$6,003	$5,012	$3,819	$6,692	$3,986
	Lowest 25%	–	–	–	–	–	–	–	–	–
CONTINUING EDUCATION	Highest 25%	$999	$752	$998	–	$749	$1,000	$750	$800	$1,000
	Average	$541	$546	$681	$1,062	$371	$585	$381	$522	$601
	Lowest 25%	–	–	–	–	–	–	–	–	–
TOTAL BENEFITS	Highest 25%	$18,493	$18,556	$15,050	$15,971	$15,200	$13,295	$11,500	$19,629	$13,420
	Average	$10,734	$12,592	$9,101	$9,978	$9,783	$8,935	$6,938	$10,768	$7,947
	Lowest 25%	$2,620	$7,700	$3,450	$3,050	$3,000	$3,530	$1,200	$2,700	$2,300
TOTAL COMPENSATION AND BENEFIT		New England	Middle Atlantic	South Atlantic	E-N Central	E-S Central	W-N Central	W-S Central	Moun-tain	Pacific
	Highest 25%	$74,833	$71,650	$75,050	$68,980	$85,200	$64,099	$72,800	$77,820	$75,381
	Average	$63,410	$62,466	$59,633	$57,252	$71,561	$54,014	$59,988	$60,232	$61,801
	Lowest 25%	$43,200	$48,800	$45,700	$39,622	$51,000	$43,650	$46,706	$47,429	$40,700
NUMBER OF RESPONDENTS		19	45	51	76	19	55	26	26	55

– Not enough responses to provide meaningful data

TABLE 5-6: ANNUAL COMPENSATION OF SOLO PASTOR BY GENDER

CHARACTERISTICS	GENDER	
	Male	Female
AVERAGE SUNDAY AM WORSHIP ATTENDANCE	164	104
AVERAGE CHURCH INCOME	$246,665	$191,536
AVERAGE # of YEARS EMPLOYED	9	7
AVERAGE # of WEEKS OF PAID VACATION	4	4
% COLLEGE GRADUATE OR HIGHER	97%	100%
% WHO RECEIVE AUTO REIMBURSEMENT	73%	75%
% ORDAINED	98%	100%
AVERAGE % SALARY INCREASE THIS YEAR	5%	5%

COMPENSATION		Male	Female
BASE SALARY:	Highest 25%	$43,999	$35,149
	Average	$34,260	$28,742
	Lowest 25%	$24,361	$24,500
HOUSING:	Highest 25%	$20,004	$27,950
	Average	$12,198	$17,041
	Lowest 25%	–	–
PARSONAGE:	Highest 25%	$5,999	$7,600
	Average	$3,592	$4,141
	Lowest 25%	–	–
TOTAL COMPENSATION	Highest 25%	$61,200	$61,209
	Average	$50,050	$49,924
	Lowest 25%	$37,500	$40,925

– Not enough responses to provide meaningful data

TABLE 5-6: ANNUAL COMPENSATION OF SOLO PASTOR BY GENDER

BENEFITS		GENDER	
		Male	Female
RETIREMENT:	Highest 25%	$5,233	$8,873
	Average	$3,250	$5,852
	Lowest 25%	–	$615
LIFE INSURANCE:	Highest 25%	–	$569
	Average	$246	$425
	Lowest 25%	–	–
HEALTH INSURANCE:	Highest 25%	$9,999	$7,120
	Average	$5,329	$4,601
	Lowest 25%	–	–
CONTINUING EDUCATION	Highest 25%	$998	$1,100
	Average	$650	$810
	Lowest 25%	–	–
TOTAL BENEFITS	Highest 25%	$15,337	$16,824
	Average	$9,474	$11,687
	Lowest 25%	$3,000	$2,977
TOTAL COMPENSATION AND BENEFIT		Male	Female
	Highest 25%	$72,800	$77,910
	Average	$59,893	$61,611
	Lowest 25%	$43,160	$49,561
NUMBER OF RESPONDENTS		351	20

– Not enough responses to provide meaningful data

TABLE 5-7: ANNUAL COMPENSATION OF SOLO PASTOR BY EDUCATION

CHARACTERISTICS	EDUCATION			
	< than Bachelor	Bachelor	Master	Doctorate
AVERAGE SUNDAY AM WORSHIP ATTENDANCE	216	129	148	240
AVERAGE CHURCH INCOME	$288,706	$192,344	$210,772	$451,943
AVERAGE # of YEARS EMPLOYED	8	9	9	8
AVERAGE # of WEEKS OF PAID VACATION	3	3	4	4
% COLLEGE GRADUATE OR HIGHER	–	100%	100%	100%
% WHO RECEIVE AUTO REIMBURSEMENT	60%	55%	80%	79%
% ORDAINED	100%	94%	99%	100%
AVERAGE % SALARY INCREASE THIS YEAR	–	6%	4%	4%

COMPENSATION		< than Bachelor	Bachelor	Master	Doctorate
BASE SALARY:	Highest 25%	$44,374	$39,999	$43,999	$46,650
	Average	$31,358	$31,863	$33,969	$37,413
	Lowest 25%	$20,801	$23,001	$24,701	$25,000
HOUSING:	Highest 25%	$23,995	$17,991	$20,993	$25,250
	Average	$16,364	$10,194	$12,150	$17,707
	Lowest 25%	$8,325	–	–	–
PARSONAGE:	Highest 25%	–	$4,805	$7,196	$6,600
	Average	$93	$2,590	$3,999	$3,876
	Lowest 25%	–	–	–	–
TOTAL COMPENSATION	Highest 25%	$66,559	$50,928	$61,418	$66,486
	Average	$47,815	$44,647	$50,118	$58,996
	Lowest 25%	$33,500	$34,000	$38,500	$42,250

— Not enough responses to provide meaningful data

TABLE 5-7: ANNUAL COMPENSATION OF SOLO PASTOR BY EDUCATION

BENEFITS		EDUCATION			
		< than Bachelor	Bachelor	Master	Doctorate
RETIREMENT:	Highest 25%	$4,750	$3,035	$5,996	$5,956
	Average	$2,468	$2,131	$3,650	$4,100
	Lowest 25%	–	–	–	–
LIFE INSURANCE:	Highest 25%	–	–	–	–
	Average	–	–	$285	$428
	Lowest 25%	–	–	–	–
HEALTH INSURANCE:	Highest 25%	$9,583	$8,399	$10,002	$10,105
	Average	$5,012	$4,071	$5,577	$5,738
	Lowest 25%	–	–	–	–
CONTINUING EDUCATION	Highest 25%	$499	–	$999	$1,198
	Average	$482	$516	$730	$638
	Lowest 25%	–	–	–	–
TOTAL BENEFITS	Highest 25%	$15,800	$10,000	$16,000	$16,857
	Average	$8,009	$6,791	$10,242	$10,904
	Lowest 25%	$2,300	$948	$4,000	$3,600
TOTAL COMPENSATION AND BENEFIT		< than Bachelor	Bachelor	Master	Doctorate
	Highest 25%	$77,559	$58,882	$74,200	$80,090
	Average	$55,824	$52,336	$60,561	$69,900
	Lowest 25%	$36,100	$39,548	$46,000	$47,369
NUMBER OF RESPONDENTS		11	75	227	52

– Not enough responses to provide meaningful data

TABLE 5-8: ANNUAL COMPENSATION OF SOLO PASTOR BY YEARS EMPLOYED

CHARACTERISTICS	YEARS EMPLOYED			
	< 6 years	6-10 years	11-15 years	Over 15 years
AVERAGE SUNDAY AM WORSHIP ATTENDANCE	139	125	223	205
AVERAGE CHURCH INCOME	$191,376	$209,284	$358,464	$302,306
AVERAGE # of YEARS EMPLOYED	3	8	13	22
AVERAGE # of WEEKS OF PAID VACATION	3	4	4	4
% COLLEGE GRADUATE OR HIGHER	96%	99%	95%	98%
% WHO RECEIVE AUTO REIMBURSEMENT	69%	75%	80%	78%
% ORDAINED	98%	99%	97%	98%
AVERAGE % SALARY INCREASE THIS YEAR	5%	5%	4%	4%

COMPENSATION		< 6 years	6-10 years	11-15 years	Over 15 years
BASE SALARY:	Highest 25%	$42,000	$40,999	$44,950	$46,001
	Average	$33,482	$33,213	$35,424	$34,812
	Lowest 25%	$24,000	$23,307	$26,808	$25,000
HOUSING:	Highest 25%	$22,800	$18,995	$20,003	$20,005
	Average	$12,552	$11,671	$13,657	$12,515
	Lowest 25%	–	–	–	–
PARSONAGE:	Highest 25%	$5,400	$7,993	$3,850	–
	Average	$3,394	$4,034	$3,550	$3,536
	Lowest 25%	–	–	–	–
TOTAL COMPENSATION	Highest 25%	$60,529	$60,000	$62,000	$62,047
	Average	$49,428	$48,918	$52,631	$50,863
	Lowest 25%	$37,600	$35,775	$43,000	$38,629

– Not enough responses to provide meaningful data

TABLE 5-8: ANNUAL COMPENSATION OF SOLO PASTOR BY YEARS EMPLOYED

BENEFITS		YEARS EMPLOYED			
		< 6 years	6-10 years	11-15 years	Over 15 years
RETIREMENT:	Highest 25%	$4,850	$5,160	$5,285	$8,000
	Average	$2,805	$3,213	$3,695	$4,975
	Lowest 25%	–	–	$844	$1,200
LIFE INSURANCE:	Highest 25%	–	–	–	–
	Average	$230	$225	$394	$226
	Lowest 25%	–	–	–	–
HEALTH INSURANCE:	Highest 25%	$10,000	$9,998	$8,885	$11,001
	Average	$5,197	$5,088	$5,487	$5,952
	Lowest 25%	–	–	$557	–
CONTINUING EDUCATION	Highest 25%	$999	$787	$700	$1,000
	Average	$592	$756	$654	$679
	Lowest 25%	–	–	–	–
TOTAL BENEFITS	Highest 25%	$15,075	$13,250	$15,669	$17,048
	Average	$8,824	$9,282	$10,230	$11,832
	Lowest 25%	$1,040	$2,700	$5,186	$5,040
TOTAL COMPENSATION AND BENEFIT		< 6 years	6-10 years	11-15 years	Over 15 years
	Highest 25%	$74,125	$68,479	$74,195	$77,658
	Average	$58,313	$58,200	$62,860	$64,749
	Lowest 25%	$40,942	$42,650	$49,729	$47,321
NUMBER OF RESPONDENTS		148	99	64	61

– Not enough responses to provide meaningful data

TABLE 5-9: ANNUAL COMPENSATION OF SOLO PASTOR BY DENOMINATION

CHARACTERISTICS	Assemblies of God	Baptist	Independent/ Nondenom	Lutheran	Methodist	Presbyte- rian
AVERAGE SUNDAY AM WORSHIP ATTENDANCE	76	203	178	180	169	158
AVERAGE CHURCH INCOME	$161,045	$331,735	$259,659	$334,412	$262,420	$244,106
AVERAGE # of YEARS EMPLOYED	7	10	11	9	8	9
AVERAGE # of WEEKS OF PAID VACATION	3	3	3	4	4	4
% COLLEGE GRADUATE OR HIGHER	91%	99%	90%	97%	100%	100%
% WHO RECEIVE AUTO REIMBURSEMENT	55%	65%	64%	86%	79%	98%
% ORDAINED	100%	99%	98%	100%	100%	100%
AVERAGE % SALARY INCREASE THIS YEAR	–	4%	5%	3%	5%	54

COMPENSATION		Assemblies of God	Baptist	Independent/ Nondenom	Lutheran	Methodist	Presbyte- rian
BASE SALARY:	Highest 25%	$36,000	$43,999	$42,001	$53,999	$48,000	$40,000
	Average	$26,127	$36,110	$31,663	$42,727	$39,081	$32,542
	Lowest 25%	$16,650	$25,999	$22,501	$30,301	$33,999	$26,000
HOUSING:	Highest 25%	$24,000	$19,993	$22,695	$25,995	$4,007	$22,700
	Average	$12,192	$12,327	$15,272	$18,890	$3,118	$13,120
	Lowest 25%	$1,100	–	$2,505	$12,008	–	–
PARSONAGE:	Highest 25%	–	$7,795	–	–	$9,900	$8,000
	Average	$2,656	$4,118	$2,591	$1,314	$6,139	$3,985
	Lowest 25%	–	–	–	–	–	–
TOTAL COMPENSATION	Highest 25%	$62,150	$61,300	$62,047	$71,660	$58,193	$61,418
	Average	$40,975	$52,555	$49,527	$62,932	$48,337	$49,647
	Lowest 25%	$25,738	$38,500	$37,950	$50,500	$38,330	$42,000

– Not enough responses to provide meaningful data

TABLE 5-9: ANNUAL COMPENSATION OF SOLO PASTOR BY DENOMINATION

		DENOMINATION					
		Assemblies of God	Baptist	Independent/ Nondenom	Lutheran	Methodist	Presbyterian
BENEFITS							
RETIREMENT:	Highest 25%	$2,400	$4,926	$4,200	$7,100	$7,783	$7,211
	Average	$1,128	$2,681	$2,913	$4,450	$4,132	$5,590
	Lowest 25%	–	–	–	–	–	$1,500
LIFE INSURANCE:	Highest 25%	–	–	–	–	–	$400
	Average	–	$474	$206	$156	$184	$253
	Lowest 25%	–	–	–	–	–	–
HEALTH INSURANCE:	Highest 25%	$6,000	$10,000	$9,583	$12,001	$12,001	$11,000
	Average	$3,343	$4,825	$4,739	$7,624	$8,368	$6,248
	Lowest 25%	–	–	–	–	$4,900	–
CONTINUING EDUCATION	Highest 25%	–	$749	$500	$999	–	$1,198
	Average	$183	$561	$445	$653	$1,404	$910
	Lowest 25%	–	–	–	–	–	$500
TOTAL BENEFITS	Highest 25%	$7,230	$15,196	$14,000	$18,493	$17,700	$18,600
	Average	$4,654	$8,541	$8,303	$12,884	$14,088	$13,000
	Lowest 25%	$1,300	$2,250	$2,250	$6,396	$11,400	$8,465
TOTAL COMPENSATION AND BENEFIT		Assemblies of God	Baptist	Independent/ Nondenom	Lutheran	Methodist	Presbyterian
	Highest 25%	$70,328	$72,300	$76,000	$87,800	$74,824	$74,050
	Average	$45,629	$61,638	$58,987	$76,258	$62,425	$62,647
	Lowest 25%	$29,150	$42,650	$43,750	$65,000	$52,318	$48,180
NUMBER OF RESPONDENTS		12	83	51	35	34	42

– Not enough responses to provide meaningful data

TABLE 5-10: AVERAGE COMPENSATION PACKAGE FOR SOLO PASTOR*

		PASTORS WHO RECIEVE...				
	Overall	Base Salary Only	No Base Salary	Base Salary and Parsonage	Base Salary and Housing	Base Salary and Parsonage and Housing
BASE SALARY	$33,826	$43,824		$34,093	$34,761	$31,887
PARSONAGE**	$3,628		$9,455	$9,304		$11,137
HOUSING ALLOWANCE	$12,446		$14,689		$19,295	$8,184
TOTAL COMPENSATION PACKAGE	$49,900	$43,824	$24,144	$43,397	$54,056	$51,208
NUMBER OF RESPONDENTS	375	24	11	80	214	46

*All $ values are annual averages
**Parsonage = Rental value of parsonage plus allowance

For an explanation of the Average Compensation Table, please refer to Chapter 1.

6

PART-TIME PASTORS

Employment Profile

This section combines data for part-time senior and solo pastors, as there are few individuals who serve the church as part-time pastor. Those that do are more likely than full-time pastors to be in churches with attendance less than 100 and income less than $250,000. The churches with part-time pastors are also more likely to be located in a metropolitan city.

The statistical profile of part-time pastors was as follows:

Ordained	98%
Average years employed	6
Male	91%
Female	9%
Self-employed (receives 1099)	26%
Church employee (receives W-2)	74%
High school diploma	14%
Associate's degree	5%
Bachelor's degree	21%
Master's degree	56%
Doctorate	5%
Number of respondents	*46*

Total Compensation plus Benefits Package Analysis

The analysis below is based upon the table found later in this chapter. The table presents compensation data for part-time pastors who serve part-time according to worship attendance and church income. In this way, the part-time pastor's compensation can be analyzed and compared from a variety of useful perspectives. The total compensation plus benefits amount includes the base salary, housing and/or parsonage allowance, retirement contribution, life and health insurance payments, and educational funds. Note that base salary is shown both hourly and annually, while annual amounts are shown for the rest of the compensation package.

About 4% percent of the pastors participating in this survey worked at their church on a part-time basis.

COMPENSATION PLUS BENEFITS

Base salary	85%
Housing	61%
Parsonage	22%
Retirement	33%
Life insurance	9%
Health insurance	26%
Paid vacation	70%
Auto reimbursement	43%
Continuing education	39%

KEY POINTS

⮕ **Church worship attendance has a direct influence upon the compensation and benefits package of the part-time pastor.** Given the relatively low percentage of part-time pastors, we are unable to present the data in much detail. However, consistent with what we have seen with other positions, as church attendance increases, average part-time pastor compensation and benefit package increases. *See Table 6-1.*

Compensation & Benefits: National Average for Part-Time Pastors**

2006	$26,591

*** No historical data available*

TABLE 6-1: COMPENSATION OF PART-TIME PASTOR BY WORSHIP ATTENDANCE & CHURCH INCOME

CHARACTERISTICS	WORSHIP ATTENDANCE		CHURCH INCOME**	
	100 or less	101-500*	$250K & Under	$251- $1M
AVERAGE SUNDAY AM WORSHIP ATTENDANCE	50	211	62	–
AVERAGE CHURCH INCOME	$63,403	–	$73,176	–
AVERAGE # of YEARS EMPLOYED	6	9	7	–
AVERAGE # of WEEKS OF PAID VACATION	3	–	3	–
% COLLEGE GRADUATE OR HIGHER	79%	89%	77%	–
% WHO RECEIVE AUTO REIMBURSEMENT	37%	67%	38%	–
% ORDAINED	97%	100%	97%	–
AVERAGE % SALARY INCREASE THIS YEAR	7%	–	7%	–
HOURLY RATES				
AVERAGE BASE RATE	$10.20	$25.93	$11.15	–
ANNUAL COMPENSATION				
AVERAGE BASE SALARY:	$12,537	$24,080	$13,670	–
AVERAGE HOUSING:	$6,826	$9,719	$6,845	–
AVERAGE PARSONAGE:	$1,399	$5,700	$1,562	–
AVERAGE TOTAL COMPENSATION	$20,762	$39,499	$22,077	–
ANNUAL BENEFITS	100 or less	101-500*	$250K & Under	$251- $1M
AVERAGE RETIREMENT	$752	$527	$791	–
AVERAGE LIFE INSURANCE	$81	$344	$79	–
AVERAGE HEALTH INSURANCE	$1,489	$1,498	$1,411	–
AVERAGE CONTINUING EDUCATION	$169	$694	$167	–
AVERAGE TOTAL BENEFITS	$2,492	$3,064	$2,449	–
ANNUAL COMPENSATION & BENEFIT				
AVERAGE	$23,253	$42,563	$24,526	–
NUMBER OF RESPONDENTS	36	9	38	3

– Not enough responses to provide meaningful data
* No part-time pastors in churches over 500 in worship attendance were reported
** No part-time pastors in churches with income over $1M were reported

TABLE 6-2: AVERAGE COMPENSATION PACKAGE FOR PART-TIME PASTORS*

	Overall	PASTORS WHO RECIEVE...				
		Base Salary Only	No Base Salary	Base Salary and Parsonage	Base Salary and Housing	Base Salary and Parsonage and Housing
BASE SALARY	$14,523	$17,592		–	$14,220	–
PARSONAGE**	$2,210		–	–		–
HOUSING ALLOWANCE	$7,276		–		$12,419	–
TOTAL COMPENSATION PACKAGE	$24,009	$17,592	–	–	$26,639	–
NUMBER OF RESPONDENTS	46	13	7	4	17	5

*All $ values are annual averages
**Parsonage = Rental value of parsonage plus allowance
– Not enough responses to provide meaningful data

For an explanation of the Average Compensation Table, please refer to Chapter 1.

7

ASSOCIATE PASTORS

Employment Profile

The roles and duties of the associate pastor are quite diverse depending upon the church. Three-quarters of reported associate pastors are in churches with income higher than $500,000. The statistical profile of associate pastors was as follows:

	FULL-TIME	PART-TIME
Ordained	93%	88%
Average years employed	7	6
Male	88%	83%
Female	12%	17%
Self-employed (receives 1099)	5%	9%
Church employee (receives W-2)	95%	91%
High school diploma	7%	17%
Associate's degree	3%	0%
Bachelor's degree	33%	41%
Master's degree	49%	36%
Doctorate	8%	6%
Number of respondents	*459*	*82*

Total Compensation plus Benefits Package Analysis

The analyses following are based upon the tables found later in this chapter. The tables present compensation and benefits data for associate pastors who serve full-time according to worship attendance, church income, combinations of size and setting, region, gender, education, years employed, and denomination. The final table provides data for part-time associate pastors based upon worship attendance and church income. In this way, the associate pastor's compensation and benefits can be analyzed and compared from a variety of useful perspectives. The total compensation plus benefits amount includes the base salary, housing and/or parsonage allowance, retirement contribution, life and health insurance payments, and educational funds.

Full-time staff members. Associate pastors receive approximately the same benefits as senior or solo pastors, except senior and solo pastors were more likely to live in a church-owned parsonage. On average, associate pastors tend to receive a compensation of about 75% of that of senior pastors, but 10% higher than that of solo pastors. The compensation gap between associate and senior pastors widens steadily as church attendance and church income increase, with the most dramatic gap being among those in churches with attendance over 1,000 and income over $1,000,000. For a comparative analysis of all staff positions, see Table 3-1 in Chapter 3.

Part-time staff members. About 15% percent of the associate pastors participating in this survey worked at their church on a part-time basis.

COMPENSATION PLUS BENEFITS	FULL TIME	PART TIME
Base salary	98%	74%
Housing	81%	52%
Parsonage	8%	6%
Retirement	62%	20%
Life insurance	31%	4%
Health insurance	74%	11%
Paid vacation	94%	59%
Auto reimbursement	71%	52%
Continuing education	43%	24%

KEY POINTS

⮑ **Church income impacts the compensation of associate pastors.** Church income is one of the most important factors affecting total compensation and benefits. About 50% of the associate pastors served in churches with an average annual budget over $1,000,000. Housing allowance amount increased with church income. Total compensation and benefits exceed the national average of $66,310 for church with a reported annual income over $1,000,000 per year. *See Table 7-1.*

⮑ **Church worship attendance has a direct influence on the compensation of the associate pastor.** In general, associate pastors in churches with an average attendance of 500 or less receive compensation and benefit packages below the national average. Associate pastors from churches with attendance above 500 receive compensation and benefit packages higher than the national average. *See Table 7-2.*

⮑ **A church's geographic setting impacts the compensation of associate pastors.** In general, associate pastors serving churches located in metropolitan and suburban settings receive the highest average compensation and benefits compared to small town or farming areas. This is probably influenced by the fact that metropolitan and suburban churches tend to have the highest church income. *See Tables 7-3, 7-4, 7-5, 7-6, and 7-7.*

⮑ **The region of the country in which the associate pastor's church is set partially influences their package.** Associate pastors from the south central region (east and west) tend to receive higher compensation and benefit packages than those from the other parts of the country. In general, the largest churches are found in these regions, which impacts compensation greatly. *See Table 7-8.*

⮑ **Female associate pastors received slightly lower levels of compensation than did their male counterparts.** The gap, however, is closing. On average, females earn 92% of the compensation of their male counterparts, up from 75% last year, bringing it to the same percentage it was three years ago (88% in 2005 and 92% in 2004). Men tend to serve in larger churches with income averaging more than those churches in which females serve. *See Table 7-9.*

⮑ **The highest compensation levels are found with those having graduate degrees.** All Associate pastor positions reported in this study have Bachelor's degrees. 57% have graduate degrees. These individuals receive higher levels of compensations than those with less education. Associate pastors who have less than a Master's degree receive compensation and benefit packages that are lower than the national average. *See Table 7-10.*

⮑ **Total compensation is partially tied to length of service.** Compensation tends to increase with length of service. Those serving the longest (from 6 years and longer) tend to serve in churches with average annual incomes of about 1.8 to over 2 million dollar range. In this sample, those with more than 15 years of service earned $14,000 more than those with 5 or less years of service. *See Table 7-11.*

⮑ **Most part-time associate pastors work at smaller size churches.** More than 80% of part-time Associate pastor positions reported serve in churches with worship attendance of 500 or less and church income of $750,000 or less. *See Tables 7-13 and 7-14.*

Compensation & Benefits:
National Averages for Associate Pastors

FULL TIME

1997	$45,042
1998	$47,076
1999	$49,827
2000	$51,973
2001	$54,729
2002	$58,072
2003	$59,742
2004	$61,263
2005	$64,034
2006	$66,310

TABLE 7-1: ANNUAL COMPENSATION OF ASSOCIATE PASTOR BY CHURCH INCOME

CHARACTERISTICS	CHURCH INCOME				
	$250K & under	$251K-$500K	$501K-$750K	$751K-$1M	Over $1 Million
AVERAGE SUNDAY AM WORSHIP ATTENDANCE	205	263	447	481	1,273
AVERAGE CHURCH INCOME	$166,226	$388,155	$620,120	$892,586	$2,483,129
AVERAGE # of YEARS EMPLOYED	5	5	5	6	8
AVERAGE # of WEEKS OF PAID VACATION	3	3	3	3	4
% COLLEGE GRADUATE OR HIGHER	86%	85%	88%	94%	92%
% WHO RECEIVE AUTO REIMBURSEMENT	64%	79%	81%	76%	71%
% ORDAINED	86%	90%	91%	96%	95%
AVERAGE % SALARY INCREASE THIS YEAR	4%	4%	5%	5%	6%

COMPENSATION		$250K & under	$251K-$500K	$501K-$750K	$751K-$1M	Over 1 Million
BASE SALARY:	Highest 25%	$30,000	$36,858	$42,000	$43,500	$54,600
	Average	$21,052	$29,466	$32,878	$34,591	$43,279
	Lowest 25%	$14,000	$22,000	$22,000	$25,068	$30,900
HOUSING:	Highest 25%	$18,002	$19,998	$24,997	$25,500	$30,000
	Average	$13,008	$13,096	$16,474	$19,033	$21,447
	Lowest 25%	$9,000	–	$8,602	$12,500	$14,900
PARSONAGE:	Highest 25%	–	–	–	–	–
	Average	$709	$2,561	$664	$504	$1,330
	Lowest 25%	–	–	–	–	–
TOTAL COMPENSATION	Highest 25%	$44,554	$49,803	$56,600	$59,749	$75,534
	Average	$34,769	$45,123	$50,016	$54,128	$66,056
	Lowest 25%	$25,000	$35,700	$41,107	$47,813	$51,000

– Not enough responses to provide meaningful data

TABLE 7-1: ANNUAL COMPENSATION OF ASSOCIATE PASTOR BY CHURCH INCOME

BENEFITS		CHURCH INCOME				
		$250K & under	$251K-$500K	$501K-$750K	$751K-$1M	Over $1 Million
RETIREMENT:	Highest 25%	$1,500	$3,256	$4,330	$4,988	$5,774
	Average	$1,017	$1,886	$2,222	$3,213	$3,247
	Lowest 25%	–	–	–	–	–
LIFE INSURANCE:	Highest 25%	–	–	–	$215	–
	Average	–	$138	–	$210	$231
	Lowest 25%	–	–	–	–	–
HEALTH INSURANCE:	Highest 25%	$5,700	$8,640	$10,600	$11,325	$10,466
	Average	$3,520	$5,401	$5,986	$7,117	$6,494
	Lowest 25%	–	–	–	$960	–
CONTINUING EDUCATION	Highest 25%	$600	$997	$1,002	$1,100	$1,103
	Average	$364	$553	$621	$705	$742
	Lowest 25%	–	–	–	–	–
TOTAL BENEFITS	Highest 25%	$9,100	$12,500	$14,531	$15,051	$16,142
	Average	$4,915	$7,978	$8,895	$11,245	$10,714
	Lowest 25%	$500	$3,000	$3,000	$6,170	$4,400
TOTAL COMPENSATION AND BENEFIT		$250K & under	$251K-$500K	$501K-$750K	$751K-$1M	Over 1 Million
	Highest 25%	$51,298	$60,000	$68,300	$73,899	$92,100
	Average	$39,683	$53,101	$58,911	$65,373	$76,862
	Lowest 25%	$25,000	$43,250	$49,550	$55,816	$60,178
NUMBER OF RESPONDENTS		22	82	55	56	218

– Not enough responses to provide meaningful data

TABLE 7-2: ANNUAL COMPENSATION OF ASSOCIATE PASTOR BY WORSHIP ATTENDANCE

CHARACTERISTICS		WORSHIP ATTENDANCE					
		100 or less	101-300	301-500	501-750	751-1000	Over 1000
AVERAGE SUNDAY AM WORSHIP ATTENDANCE		–	208	412	618	874	2,067
AVERAGE CHURCH INCOME		–	$448,929	$809,484	$1,237,863	$1,808,995	$3,651,353
AVERAGE # of YEARS EMPLOYED		–	5	6	7	8	8
AVERAGE # of WEEKS OF PAID VACATION		–	3	3	3	3	4
% COLLEGE GRADUATE OR HIGHER		–	84%	93%	91%	91%	94%
% WHO RECEIVE AUTO REIMBURSEMENT		–	74%	83%	73%	70%	67%
% ORDAINED		–	89%	93%	96%	93%	95%
AVERAGE % SALARY INCREASE THIS YEAR		–	5%	4%	5%	5%	6%
COMPENSATION		100 or less	101-300	301-500	501-750	751-1000	Over 1000
BASE SALARY:	Highest 25%	–	$35,500	$42,750	$45,118	$54,989	$57,000
	Average	–	$28,137	$34,325	$37,949	$42,129	$46,630
	Lowest 25%	–	$20,000	$24,525	$29,504	$30,150	$32,000
HOUSING:	Highest 25%	–	$20,003	$26,000	$25,001	$26,350	$32,000
	Average	–	$14,327	$18,034	$17,666	$18,847	$23,275
	Lowest 25%	–	–	$10,771	$9,900	$4,250	$16,706
PARSONAGE:	Highest 25%	–	–	–	–	–	–
	Average	–	$2,277	$1,632	$581	$1,875	$1,095
	Lowest 25%	–	–	–	–	–	–
TOTAL COMPENSATION	Highest 25%	–	$52,260	$60,017	$64,607	$72,180	$84,000
	Average	–	$44,741	$53,990	$56,196	$62,851	$71,000
	Lowest 25%	–	$34,000	$43,686	$47,462	$49,000	$53,000

– Not enough responses to provide meaningful data

TABLE 7-2: ANNUAL COMPENSATION OF ASSOCIATE PASTOR BY WORSHIP ATTENDANCE

BENEFITS		WORSHIP ATTENDANCE					
		100 or less	101-300	301-500	501-750	751-1000	Over 1000
RETIREMENT:	Highest 25%	–	$3,000	$5,040	$5,166	$5,980	$5,885
	Average	–	$1,631	$3,345	$2,896	$3,325	$3,144
	Lowest 25%	–	–	–	–	–	–
LIFE INSURANCE:	Highest 25%	–	–	–	–	–	–
	Average	–	$132	$177	$257	$137	$178
	Lowest 25%	–	–	–	–	–	–
HEALTH INSURANCE:	Highest 25%	–	$8,500	$10,900	$11,019	$10,492	$10,116
	Average	–	$4,930	$6,542	$6,989	$5,936	$6,275
	Lowest 25%	–	–	–	$2,400	–	–
CONTINUING EDUCATION	Highest 25%	–	$671	$1,004	$1,150	$1,494	$1,004
	Average	–	$473	$643	$735	$864	$690
	Lowest 25%	–	–	–	–	–	–
TOTAL BENEFITS	Highest 25%	–	$11,592	$16,495	$15,390	$15,310	$15,625
	Average	–	$7,166	$10,708	$10,878	$10,262	$10,288
	Lowest 25%	–	$2,087	$4,088	$5,270	$4,000	$3,380
TOTAL COMPENSATION AND BENEFIT		100 or less	101-300	301-500	501-750	751-1000	Over 1000
	Highest 25%	–	$61,059	$73,306	$76,520	$87,603	$95,500
	Average	–	$51,906	$64,890	$67,074	$73,113	$81,287
	Lowest 25%	–	$41,054	$52,350	$54,690	$56,587	$60,629
NUMBER OF RESPONDENTS		5	103	104	80	60	95

– Not enough responses to provide meaningful data

TABLE 7-3: ANNUAL COMPENSATION OF ASSOCIATE PASTOR BY CHURCH SETTING & SIZE

ATTENDANCE 250 & UNDER		Metropolitan city	Suburb of large city	Small town or rural city	Farming area
AVERAGE SUNDAY AM WORSHIP ATTENDANCE		165	192	172	–
AVERAGE CHURCH INCOME		$363,111	$470,343	$346,724	–
AVERAGE # of YEARS EMPLOYED		5	4	5	–
AVERAGE # of WEEKS OF PAID VACATION		3	3	3	–
% COLLEGE GRADUATE OR HIGHER		87%	86%	80%	–
% WHO RECEIVE AUTO REIMBURSEMENT		67%	73%	74%	–
% ORDAINED		87%	92%	85%	–
AVERAGE % SALARY INCREASE THIS YEAR		–	5%	5%	–

COMPENSATION		Metropolitan city	Suburb of large city	Small town or rural city	Farming area
BASE SALARY:	Highest 25%	$29,997	$37,412	$30,597	–
	Average	$24,618	$30,388	$23,575	–
	Lowest 25%	$17,999	$24,703	$17,605	–
HOUSING:	Highest 25%	$17,994	$21,603	$16,794	–
	Average	$10,500	$17,437	$11,047	–
	Lowest 25%	–	$13,206	–	–
PARSONAGE:	Highest 25%	–	–	$8,100	–
	Average	$1,147	$1,964	$4,559	–
	Lowest 25%	–	–	–	–
TOTAL COMPENSATION	Highest 25%	$44,993	$56,410	$45,995	–
	Average	$36,264	$49,789	$39,182	–
	Lowest 25%	$27,205	$40,605	$25,008	–

– Not enough responses to provide meaningful data

TABLE 7-3: ANNUAL COMPENSATION OF ASSOCIATE PASTOR BY CHURCH SETTING & SIZE

BENEFITS		CHURCH SETTING			
		Metropoli-tan city	Suburb of large city	Small town or rural city	Farming area
RETIREMENT:	Highest 25%	$1,499	$3,418	$2,499	–
	Average	$1,050	$2,001	$1,397	–
	Lowest 25%	–	–	–	–
LIFE INSURANCE:	Highest 25%	–	–	–	–
	Average	$92	$129	$201	–
	Lowest 25%	–	–	–	–
HEALTH INSURANCE:	Highest 25%	$11,498	$8,498	$6,598	–
	Average	$6,113	$4,817	$3,664	–
	Lowest 25%	–	–	–	–
CONTINUING EDUCATION	Highest 25%	$988	$1,008	–	–
	Average	$490	$636	$118	–
	Lowest 25%	–	–	–	–
TOTAL BENEFITS	Highest 25%	$13,500	$11,704	$8,892	–
	Average	$7,745	$7,583	$5,379	–
	Lowest 25%	$1,501	$3,601	–	–
TOTAL COMPENSATION AND BENEFIT		Metropoli-tan city	Suburb of large city	Small town or rural city	Farming area
	Highest 25%	$55,597	$64,429	$56,933	–
	Average	$44,010	$57,372	$44,561	–
	Lowest 25%	$27,203	$47,003	$31,203	–
NUMBER OF RESPONDENTS		15	39	27	2

– Not enough responses to provide meaningful data

TABLE 7-4: ANNUAL COMPENSATION OF ASSOCIATE PASTOR BY CHURCH SETTING & SIZE

ATTENDANCE 251 - 500	CHURCH SETTING			
	Metropoli-tan city	Suburb of large city	Small town or rural city	Farming area
AVERAGE SUNDAY AM WORSHIP ATTENDANCE	404	394	378	–
AVERAGE CHURCH INCOME	$893,976	$868,188	$636,765	–
AVERAGE # of YEARS EMPLOYED	6	5	6	–
AVERAGE # of WEEKS OF PAID VACATION	3	4	3	–
% COLLEGE GRADUATE OR HIGHER	94%	91%	89%	–
% WHO RECEIVE AUTO REIMBURSEMENT	80%	76%	86%	–
% ORDAINED	94%	96%	91%	–
AVERAGE % SALARY INCREASE THIS YEAR	4%	5%	5%	–

COMPENSATION		Metropoli-tan city	Suburb of large city	Small town or rural city	Farming area
BASE SALARY:	Highest 25%	$39,205	$42,000	$42,000	–
	Average	$35,994	$33,883	$32,677	–
	Lowest 25%	$24,056	$25,568	$22,000	–
HOUSING:	Highest 25%	$25,008	$28,000	$22,295	–
	Average	$19,079	$18,684	$16,138	–
	Lowest 25%	$17,733	$4,800	$8,305	–
PARSONAGE:	Highest 25%	–	–	–	–
	Average	–	$2,621	$1,042	–
	Lowest 25%	–	–	–	–
TOTAL COMPENSATION	Highest 25%	$56,942	$63,134	$56,238	–
	Average	$55,074	$55,188	$49,857	–
	Lowest 25%	$43,740	$43,846	$41,609	–

– Not enough responses to provide meaningful data

TABLE 7-4: ANNUAL COMPENSATION OF ASSOCIATE PASTOR BY CHURCH SETTING & SIZE

BENEFITS		CHURCH SETTING			
		Metropolitan city	Suburb of large city	Small town or rural city	Farming area
RETIREMENT:	Highest 25%	$5,080	$5,728	$4,800	–
	Average	$3,527	$2,899	$2,998	–
	Lowest 25%	–	–	–	–
LIFE INSURANCE:	Highest 25%	–	–	–	–
	Average	$108	$256	$101	–
	Lowest 25%	–	–	–	–
HEALTH INSURANCE:	Highest 25%	$8,774	$12,465	$9,971	–
	Average	$6,344	$7,010	$5,994	–
	Lowest 25%	$3,141	–	–	–
CONTINUING EDUCATION	Highest 25%	$1,263	$1,006	$977	–
	Average	$703	$741	$501	–
	Lowest 25%	–	–	–	–
TOTAL BENEFITS	Highest 25%	$15,701	$17,074	$14,999	–
	Average	$10,682	$10,905	$9,594	–
	Lowest 25%	$5,999	$4,900	$3,201	–
TOTAL COMPENSATION AND BENEFIT		Metropolitan city	Suburb of large city	Small town or rural city	Farming area
	Highest 25%	$73,492	$77,704	$68,439	–
	Average	$66,932	$66,093	$59,452	–
	Lowest 25%	$50,935	$52,290	$49,888	–
NUMBER OF RESPONDENTS		17	48	59	2

– Not enough responses to provide meaningful data

107

TABLE 7-5: ANNUAL COMPENSATION OF ASSOCIATE PASTOR BY CHURCH SETTING & SIZE

ATTENDANCE 501 - 750	CHURCH SETTING			
	Metropoli-tan city	Suburb of large city	Small town or rural city	Farming area
AVERAGE SUNDAY AM WORSHIP ATTENDANCE	600	627	611	–
AVERAGE CHURCH INCOME	$1,663,553	$1,217,588	$1,133,077	–
AVERAGE # of YEARS EMPLOYED	6	9	6	–
AVERAGE # of WEEKS OF PAID VACATION	4	3	3	–
% COLLEGE GRADUATE OR HIGHER	100%	97%	78%	–
% WHO RECEIVE AUTO REIMBURSEMENT	69%	70%	75%	–
% ORDAINED	92%	94%	100%	–
AVERAGE % SALARY INCREASE THIS YEAR	5%	7%	4%	–

COMPENSATION		Metropoli-tan city	Suburb of large city	Small town or rural city	Farming area
BASE SALARY:	Highest 25%	$57,365	$42,121	$50,005	–
	Average	$41,655	$36,381	$38,509	–
	Lowest 25%	$30,899	$29,999	$28,479	–
HOUSING:	Highest 25%	$28,505	$25,008	$24,690	–
	Average	$19,384	$20,341	$15,114	–
	Lowest 25%	$13,195	$17,675	$5,495	–
PARSONAGE:	Highest 25%	–	–	$830	–
	Average	–	–	$310	–
	Lowest 25%	–	–	–	–
TOTAL COMPENSATION	Highest 25%	$70,565	$63,433	$56,601	–
	Average	$61,040	$56,722	$53,934	–
	Lowest 25%	$51,195	$47,999	$46,496	–

– Not enough responses to provide meaningful data

TABLE 7-5: ANNUAL COMPENSATION OF ASSOCIATE PASTOR BY CHURCH SETTING & SIZE

BENEFITS		CHURCH SETTING			
		Metropolitan city	Suburb of large city	Small town or rural city	Farming area
RETIREMENT:	Highest 25%	$4,404	$5,530	$3,065	–
	Average	$2,077	$3,410	$2,422	–
	Lowest 25%	–	–	–	–
LIFE INSURANCE:	Highest 25%	$179	$401	$349	–
	Average	$107	$309	$293	–
	Lowest 25%	–	–	–	–
HEALTH INSURANCE:	Highest 25%	$12,002	$10,596	$10,516	–
	Average	$7,056	$6,773	$6,581	–
	Lowest 25%	$3,899	$2,399	$2,401	–
CONTINUING EDUCATION	Highest 25%	$988	$1,613	$1,113	–
	Average	$446	$1,048	$497	–
	Lowest 25%	–	–	–	–
TOTAL BENEFITS	Highest 25%	$17,934	$15,502	$14,202	–
	Average	$9,686	$11,539	$9,792	–
	Lowest 25%	$4,999	$7,025	$4,199	–
TOTAL COMPENSATION AND BENEFIT		Metropolitan city	Suburb of large city	Small town or rural city	Farming area
	Highest 25%	$82,414	$77,697	$70,101	–
	Average	$70,725	$68,261	$63,726	–
	Lowest 25%	$63,785	$57,611	$54,052	–
NUMBER OF RESPONDENTS		13	33	29	5

– Not enough responses to provide meaningful data

TABLE 7-6: ANNUAL COMPENSATION OF ASSOCIATE PASTOR BY CHURCH SETTING & SIZE

ATTENDANCE 751 - 1,000	CHURCH SETTING			
	Metropolitan city	Suburb of large city	Small town or rural city	Farming area
AVERAGE SUNDAY AM WORSHIP ATTENDANCE	906	844	880	–
AVERAGE CHURCH INCOME	$2,041,404	$1,749,882	$1,683,403	–
AVERAGE # of YEARS EMPLOYED	8	8	7	–
AVERAGE # of WEEKS OF PAID VACATION	3	4	3	–
% COLLEGE GRADUATE OR HIGHER	94%	95%	79%	–
% WHO RECEIVE AUTO REIMBURSEMENT	61%	82%	57%	–
% ORDAINED	100%	82%	100%	–
AVERAGE % SALARY INCREASE THIS YEAR	5%	5%	8%	–

COMPENSATION		Metropolitan city	Suburb of large city	Small town or rural city	Farming area
BASE SALARY:	Highest 25%	$61,643	$62,148	$40,000	–
	Average	$46,667	$42,909	$35,465	–
	Lowest 25%	$33,750	$26,600	$30,730	–
HOUSING:	Highest 25%	$29,000	$26,700	$23,500	–
	Average	$18,007	$18,467	$21,338	–
	Lowest 25%	–	$3,500	$19,994	–
PARSONAGE:	Highest 25%	–	–	–	–
	Average	$3,105	$2,291	–	–
	Lowest 25%	–	–	–	–
TOTAL COMPENSATION	Highest 25%	$89,542	$82,478	$60,769	–
	Average	$67,779	$63,666	$56,803	–
	Lowest 25%	$50,000	$44,766	$50,775	–

– Not enough responses to provide meaningful data

TABLE 7-6: ANNUAL COMPENSATION OF ASSOCIATE PASTOR BY CHURCH SETTING & SIZE

		CHURCH SETTING			
BENEFITS		Metropoli-tan city	Suburb of large city	Small town or rural city	Farming area
RETIREMENT:	Highest 25%	$5,610	$7,175	$3,477	–
	Average	$3,580	$4,249	$1,926	–
	Lowest 25%	–	$1,721	–	–
LIFE INSURANCE:	Highest 25%	–	$350	–	–
	Average	–	$244	$138	–
	Lowest 25%	–	–	–	–
HEALTH INSURANCE:	Highest 25%	$8,750	$12,004	$10,154	–
	Average	$5,293	$7,453	$5,395	–
	Lowest 25%	–	$3,885	–	–
CONTINUING EDUCATION	Highest 25%	$1,000	$2,500	$1,250	–
	Average	$525	$1,431	$522	–
	Lowest 25%	–	–	–	–
TOTAL BENEFITS	Highest 25%	$13,687	$16,221	$12,762	–
	Average	$9,424	$13,377	$7,981	–
	Lowest 25%	$4,409	$9,143	$2,997	–
TOTAL COMPENSATION AND BENEFIT		Metropoli-tan city	Suburb of large city	Small town or rural city	Farming area
	Highest 25%	$93,923	$92,100	$73,251	–
	Average	$77,203	$77,044	$64,784	–
	Lowest 25%	$56,300	$56,674	$60,361	–
NUMBER OF RESPONDENTS		20	22	16	1

– Not enough responses to provide meaningful data

TABLE 7-7: ANNUAL COMPENSATION OF ASSOCIATE PASTOR BY CHURCH SETTING & SIZE

ATTENDANCE OVER 1,000		CHURCH SETTING			
		Metropolitan city	Suburb of large city	Small town or rural city	Farming area
AVERAGE SUNDAY AM WORSHIP ATTENDANCE		2,407	2,077	1,827	–
AVERAGE CHURCH INCOME		$4,421,555	$3,726,327	$3,009,101	–
AVERAGE # of YEARS EMPLOYED		8	8	9	–
AVERAGE # of WEEKS OF PAID VACATION		4	4	3	–
% COLLEGE GRADUATE OR HIGHER		94%	93%	96%	–
% WHO RECEIVE AUTO REIMBURSEMENT		58%	70%	67%	–
% ORDAINED		100%	100%	81%	–
AVERAGE % SALARY INCREASE THIS YEAR		5%	6%	6%	–

COMPENSATION		Metropolitan city	Suburb of large city	Small town or rural city	Farming area
BASE SALARY:	Highest 25%	$68,525	$58,246	$51,995	–
	Average	$54,335	$46,550	$41,079	–
	Lowest 25%	$37,964	$31,933	$28,005	–
HOUSING:	Highest 25%	$33,996	$32,850	$24,996	–
	Average	$22,696	$25,652	$19,577	–
	Lowest 25%	$8,404	$19,723	$3,604	–
PARSONAGE:	Highest 25%	$672	–	–	–
	Average	$263	$1,216	$1,508	–
	Lowest 25%	–	–	–	–
TOTAL COMPENSATION	Highest 25%	$100,012	$86,887	$73,789	–
	Average	$77,294	$73,418	$62,164	–
	Lowest 25%	$51,001	$53,038	$54,001	–

– Not enough responses to provide meaningful data

TABLE 7-7: ANNUAL COMPENSATION OF ASSOCIATE PASTOR BY CHURCH SETTING & SIZE

		CHURCH SETTING			
BENEFITS		Metropoli-tan city	Suburb of large city	Small town or rural city	Farming area
RETIREMENT:	Highest 25%	$4,111	$6,969	$4,211	–
	Average	$3,224	$3,248	$2,747	–
	Lowest 25%	–	–	–	–
LIFE INSURANCE:	Highest 25%	$306	–	$121	–
	Average	$257	$193	–	–
	Lowest 25%	–	–	–	–
HEALTH INSURANCE:	Highest 25%	$10,000	$10,875	$10,000	–
	Average	$7,140	$6,622	$4,893	–
	Lowest 25%	$4,001	$1,235	–	–
CONTINUING EDUCATION	Highest 25%	$1,003	$1,100	$1,006	–
	Average	$726	$806	$483	–
	Lowest 25%	–	–	–	–
TOTAL BENEFITS	Highest 25%	$15,186	$17,546	$12,980	–
	Average	$11,347	$10,870	$8,212	–
	Lowest 25%	$5,500	$3,000	$3,000	–
TOTAL COMPENSATION AND BENEFIT		Metropoli-tan city	Suburb of large city	Small town or rural city	Farming area
	Highest 25%	$113,042	$98,146	$82,998	–
	Average	$88,641	$84,288	$70,376	–
	Lowest 25%	$57,776	$62,235	$60,001	–
NUMBER OF RESPONDENTS		19	48	27	0

– Not enough responses to provide meaningful data

TABLE 7-8: ANNUAL COMPENSATION OF ASSOCIATE PASTOR BY REGION

CHARACTERISTICS	REGION								
	New England	Middle Atlantic	South Atlantic	E-N Central	E-S Central	W-N Central	W-S Central	Mountain	Pacific
AVERAGE SUNDAY AM WORSHIP ATTENDANCE	–	560	708	1,051	896	657	1,027	1,005	751
AVERAGE CHURCH INCOME	–	$907,794	$1,500,147	$1,643,846	$2,456,265	$1,425,017	$2,444,658	$1,442,481	$1,286,675
AVERAGE # of YEARS EMPLOYED	–	6	6	6	7	6	7	7	7
AVERAGE # of WEEKS OF PAID VACATION	–	3	3	3	3	3	3	3	3
% COLLEGE GRADUATE OR HIGHER	–	81%	94%	96%	86%	84%	95%	91%	86%
% WHO RECEIVE AUTO REIMBURSEMENT	–	78%	76%	80%	75%	73%	56%	73%	68%
% ORDAINED	–	86%	93%	94%	100%	93%	100%	92%	95%
AVERAGE % SALARY INCREASE THIS YEAR	–	5%	5%	5%	3%	4%	5%	6%	7%

COMPENSATION		New England	Middle Atlantic	South Atlantic	E-N Central	E-S Central	W-N Central	W-S Central	Mountain	Pacific
BASE SALARY:	Highest 25%	–	$37,800	$44,373	$43,995	$59,008	$43,800	$50,820	$45,000	$50,000
	Average	–	$31,382	$36,413	$36,895	$45,483	$33,680	$42,427	$34,496	$38,394
	Lowest 25%	–	$24,700	$26,009	$26,200	$30,950	$21,528	$30,450	$22,954	$27,492
HOUSING:	Highest 25%	–	$24,002	$25,002	$26,002	$30,150	$22,002	$26,000	$24,998	$30,002
	Average	–	$15,898	$18,287	$18,147	$18,727	$15,830	$18,521	$17,051	$21,257
	Lowest 25%	–	–	$12,003	$11,997	$7,250	$9,494	$9,600	$8,402	$10,000
PARSONAGE:	Highest 25%	–	–	–	–	–	–	–	–	–
	Average	–	$1,536	$1,449	$1,558	$2,732	$1,694	$705	$977	$1,549
	Lowest 25%	–	–	–	–	–	–	–	–	–
TOTAL COMPENSATION	Highest 25%	–	$56,416	$65,000	$65,000	$79,688	$58,620	$74,249	$57,450	$70,672
	Average	–	$48,816	$56,149	$56,600	$66,942	$51,203	$61,653	$52,524	$61,199
	Lowest 25%	–	$37,820	$42,000	$45,000	$46,870	$37,564	$46,680	$42,000	$46,725

– Not enough responses to provide meaningful data

TABLE 7-8: ANNUAL COMPENSATION OF ASSOCIATE PASTOR BY REGION

BENEFITS		REGION								
		New England	Middle Atlantic	South Atlantic	E-N Central	E-S Central	W-N Central	W-S Central	Mountain	Pacific
RETIREMENT:	Highest 25%	–	$4,995	$6,723	$3,975	$3,000	$4,960	$6,212	$2,736	$3,442
	Average	–	$2,729	$3,768	$2,401	$2,748	$2,907	$3,331	$1,435	$2,469
	Lowest 25%	–	–	–	–	–	–	–	–	–
LIFE INSURANCE:	Highest 25%	–	–	–	$155	$205	–	–	–	–
	Average	–	$153	$188	$126	$170	$334	$245	$158	$111
	Lowest 25%	–	–	–	–	–	–	–	–	–
HEALTH INSURANCE:	Highest 25%	–	$9,778	$10,200	$12,000	$8,670	$10,600	$10,075	$7,443	$9,000
	Average	–	$6,108	$5,930	$7,338	$4,649	$6,683	$6,251	$4,302	$5,606
	Lowest 25%	–	–	–	–	–	$2,765	$1,061	–	$1,625
CONTINUING EDUCATION	Highest 25%	–	$1,008	$1,499	$1,000	$1,005	$1,000	$1,200	$996	$625
	Average	–	$793	$827	$596	$754	$655	$693	$499	$419
	Lowest 25%	–	–	–	–	–	–	–	–	–
TOTAL BENEFITS	Highest 25%	–	$14,200	$17,939	$15,500	13,110	$14,459	$14,648	$11,310	$13,500
	Average	–	$9,783	$10,713	$10,461	$8,322	$10,580	$10,520	$6,394	$8,605
	Lowest 25%	–	$6,500	$3,800	$3,680	$2,800	$6,418	$4,607	$2,200	$3,000
TOTAL COMPENSATION AND BENEFIT		New England	Middle Atlantic	South Atlantic	E-N Central	E-S Central	W-N Central	W-S Central	Mountain	Pacific
	Highest 25%	–	$69,453	$82,020	$77,613	$93,648	$74,593	$91,050	$63,000	$79,493
	Average	–	$58,598	$67,092	$67,061	$75,264	$61,783	$72,172	$58,918	$69,805
	Lowest 25%	–	$45,500	$51,541	$55,018	$50,047	$44,430	$55,403	$51,298	$52,600
NUMBER OF RESPONDENTS		7	50	87	82	24	46	40	39	78

– Not enough responses to provide meaningful data

TABLE 7-9: ANNUAL COMPENSATION OF SOLO PASTOR BY GENDER

CHARACTERISTICS	GENDER	
	Male	Female
AVERAGE SUNDAY AM WORSHIP ATTENDANCE	846	564
AVERAGE CHURCH INCOME	$1,578,808	$1,147,131
AVERAGE # of YEARS EMPLOYED	7	6
AVERAGE # of WEEKS OF PAID VACATION	3	4
% COLLEGE GRADUATE OR HIGHER	90%	94%
% WHO RECEIVE AUTO REIMBURSEMENT	73%	77%
% ORDAINED	93%	91%
AVERAGE % SALARY INCREASE THIS YEAR	5%	6%

COMPENSATION		Male	Female
BASE SALARY:	Highest 25%	$45,000	$41,000
	Average	$37,304	$33,442
	Lowest 25%	$26,000	$23,142
HOUSING:	Highest 25%	$26,003	$22,398
	Average	$18,654	$15,587
	Lowest 25%	$9,917	$8,234
PARSONAGE:	Highest 25%	–	–
	Average	$1,503	$1,334
	Lowest 25%	–	–
TOTAL COMPENSATION	Highest 25%	$67,113	$56,300
	Average	$57,462	$50,362
	Lowest 25%	$44,766	$40,000

– Not enough responses to provide meaningful data

TABLE 7-9: ANNUAL COMPENSATION OF SOLO PASTOR BY GENDER

		GENDER	
BENEFITS		Male	Female
RETIREMENT:	Highest 25%	$4,113	$6,500
	Average	$2,596	$4,328
	Lowest 25%	–	$1,241
LIFE INSURANCE:	Highest 25%	–	$180
	Average	$173	$177
	Lowest 25%	–	–
HEALTH INSURANCE:	Highest 25%	$10,128	$10,000
	Average	$6,114	$6,268
	Lowest 25%	–	$2,384
CONTINUING EDUCATION	Highest 25%	$1,003	$1,093
	Average	$628	$816
	Lowest 25%	–	–
TOTAL BENEFITS	Highest 25%	$14,268	$16,549
	Average	$9,512	$11,590
	Lowest 25%	$3,450	$5,314
TOTAL COMPENSATION AND BENEFIT		Male	Female
	Highest 25%	$77,696	$73,121
	Average	$67,023	$61,952
	Lowest 25%	$52,300	$48,900
NUMBER OF RESPONDENTS		401	55

– Not enough responses to provide meaningful data

TABLE 7-10: ANNUAL COMPENSATION OF ASSOCIATE PASTOR BY EDUCATION

CHARACTERISTICS	EDUCATION			
	< than Bachelor	Bachelor	Master	Doctorate
AVERAGE SUNDAY AM WORSHIP ATTENDANCE	668	805	819	681
AVERAGE CHURCH INCOME	$1,276,924	$1,344,425	$1,526,900	$1,668,176
AVERAGE # of YEARS EMPLOYED	7	6	6	8
AVERAGE # of WEEKS OF PAID VACATION	3	3	4	4
% COLLEGE GRADUATE OR HIGHER	–	100%	100%	100%
% WHO RECEIVE AUTO REIMBURSEMENT	65%	68%	77%	84%
% ORDAINED	95%	89%	95%	97%
AVERAGE % SALARY INCREASE THIS YEAR	6%	5%	5%	4%

COMPENSATION		< than Bachelor	Bachelor	Master	Doctorate
BASE SALARY:	Highest 25%	$39,300	$41,000	$46,837	$57,736
	Average	$29,962	$34,388	$38,695	$43,633
	Lowest 25%	$18,620	$24,850	$28,301	$25,941
HOUSING:	Highest 25%	$25,400	$25,001	$25,000	$30,003
	Average	$19,670	$16,657	$18,074	$21,825
	Lowest 25%	$11,400	$5,139	$11,100	$14,974
PARSONAGE:	Highest 25%	–	–	–	–
	Average	$2,352	$1,517	$1,137	$2,932
	Lowest 25%	–	–	–	–
TOTAL COMPENSATION	Highest 25%	$63,000	$60,000	$67,836	$78,051
	Average	$51,984	$52,562	$57,906	$68,390
	Lowest 25%	$34,000	$41,000	$45,268	$48,142

– Not enough responses to provide meaningful data

TABLE 7-10: ANNUAL COMPENSATION OF ASSOCIATE PASTOR BY EDUCATION

BENEFITS		EDUCATION			
		< than Bachelor	Bachelor	Master	Doctorate
RETIREMENT:	Highest 25%	$2,000	$3,001	$5,913	$5,631
	Average	$1,146	$1,894	$3,754	$3,331
	Lowest 25%	–	–	$175	–
LIFE INSURANCE:	Highest 25%	–	–	–	–
	Average	$148	$139	$223	$189
	Lowest 25%	–	–	–	–
HEALTH INSURANCE:	Highest 25%	$8,000	$9,232	$10,492	$9,731
	Average	$4,762	$5,460	$7,025	$5,411
	Lowest 25%	–	$316	$1,563	–
CONTINUING EDUCATION	Highest 25%	–	$800	$1,388	$1,495
	Average	$131	$453	$888	$698
	Lowest 25%	–	–	–	–
TOTAL BENEFITS	Highest 25%	$10,514	$12,539	$17,936	$13,927
	Average	$6,187	$7,945	$11,891	$9,628
	Lowest 25%	$573	$2,703	$5,490	$4,227
TOTAL COMPENSATION AND BENEFIT		< than Bachelor	Bachelor	Master	Doctorate
	Highest 25%	$69,202	$70,024	$82,137	$94,085
	Average	$58,171	$60,507	$69,797	$78,625
	Lowest 25%	$41,479	$46,650	$55,667	$60,100
NUMBER OF RESPONDENTS		42	140	208	33

– Not enough responses to provide meaningful data

119

TABLE 7-11: ANNUAL COMPENSATION OF ASSOCIATE PASTOR BY YEARS EMPLOYED

CHARACTERISTICS	YEARS EMPLOYED			
	< 6 years	6-10 years	11-15 years	Over 15 years
AVERAGE SUNDAY AM WORSHIP ATTENDANCE	672	976	1,040	991
AVERAGE CHURCH INCOME	$1,250,666	$1,782,506	$1,845,163	$2,267,780
AVERAGE # of YEARS EMPLOYED	3	8	13	19
AVERAGE # of WEEKS OF PAID VACATION	3	4	4	4
% COLLEGE GRADUATE OR HIGHER	91%	90%	82%	94%
% WHO RECEIVE AUTO REIMBURSEMENT	73%	71%	78%	72%
% ORDAINED	91%	95%	96%	97%
AVERAGE % SALARY INCREASE THIS YEAR	5%	5%	4%	5%

COMPENSATION		< 6 years	6-10 years	11-15 years	Over 15 years
BASE SALARY:	Highest 25%	$41,942	$50,000	$49,000	$45,000
	Average	$34,866	$39,536	$39,395	$37,655
	Lowest 25%	$25,000	$28,000	$30,546	$23,817
HOUSING:	Highest 25%	$24,498	$25,320	$27,998	$31,002
	Average	$16,517	$19,057	$20,009	$25,649
	Lowest 25%	$5,502	$11,998	$8,402	$20,002
PARSONAGE:	Highest 25%	–	–	–	–
	Average	$1,637	$1,442	$1,945	–
	Lowest 25%	–	–	–	–
TOTAL COMPENSATION	Highest 25%	$61,045	$68,917	$73,904	$70,372
	Average	$53,020	$60,034	$61,349	$63,595
	Lowest 25%	$40,719	$46,725	$47,232	$53,549

– Not enough responses to provide meaningful data

TABLE 7-11: ANNUAL COMPENSATION OF ASSOCIATE PASTOR BY YEARS EMPLOYED

BENEFITS		YEARS EMPLOYED			
		< 6 years	6-10 years	11-15 years	Over 15 years
RETIREMENT:	Highest 25%	$4,379	$5,686	$4,176	$7,071
	Average	$2,498	$3,191	$2,815	$4,022
	Lowest 25%	–	–	–	–
LIFE INSURANCE:	Highest 25%	–	–	$186	$600
	Average	$138	$196	$159	$438
	Lowest 25%	–	–	–	–
HEALTH INSURANCE:	Highest 25%	$9,887	$10,128	$10,802	$11,600
	Average	$6,006	$5,809	$6,527	$7,807
	Lowest 25%	$573	–	–	$3,819
CONTINUING EDUCATION	Highest 25%	$1,004	$1,003	$996	$1,005
	Average	$634	$651	$601	$697
	Lowest 25%	–	–	–	–
TOTAL BENEFITS	Highest 25%	$13,821	$15,186	$15,700	$18,821
	Average	$9,275	$9,846	$10,102	$12,964
	Lowest 25%	$3,600	$3,500	$4,176	$6,100
TOTAL COMPENSATION AND BENEFIT		< 6 years	6-10 years	11-15 years	Over 15 years
	Highest 25%	$72,000	$83,593	$84,289	$92,133
	Average	$62,295	$70,056	$71,450	$76,559
	Lowest 25%	$48,000	$52,800	$57,543	$60,577
NUMBER OF RESPONDENTS		251	114	47	33

– Not enough responses to provide meaningful data

121

TABLE 7-12: ANNUAL COMPENSATION OF ASSOCIATE PASTOR BY DENOMINATION

CHARACTERISTICS	DENOMINATION					
	Assemblies of God	Baptist	Independent/ Nondenom	Lutheran	Methodist	Presbyterian
AVERAGE SUNDAY AM WORSHIP ATTENDANCE	480	759	974	443	873	656
AVERAGE CHURCH INCOME	$911,600	$1,753,814	$1,538,346	$919,968	$1,518,821	$1,678,197
AVERAGE # of YEARS EMPLOYED	6	7	6	4	5	6
AVERAGE # of WEEKS OF PAID VACATION	3	3	3	4	3	4
% COLLEGE GRADUATE OR HIGHER	50%	94%	87%	100%	95%	100%
% WHO RECEIVE AUTO REIMBURSEMENT	63%	70%	68%	84%	76%	83%
% ORDAINED	85%	95%	93%	95%	88%	96%
AVERAGE % SALARY INCREASE THIS YEAR	6%	6%	6%	4%	6%	5%

COMPENSATION		Assemblies of God	Baptist	Independent/ Nondenom	Lutheran	Methodist	Presbyterian
BASE SALARY:	Highest 25%	$43,078	$50,000	$42,000	$47,000	$45,000	$45,000
	Average	$28,473	$39,723	$36,711	$36,092	$38,022	$37,209
	Lowest 25%	$18,125	$26,550	$26,640	$24,192	$30,000	$26,746
HOUSING:	Highest 25%	$25,424	$24,843	$29,998	$22,498	$21,000	$27,000
	Average	$18,358	$16,273	$21,022	$12,866	$11,746	$21,399
	Lowest 25%	$12,500	$4,800	$14,582	–	–	$17,840
PARSONAGE:	Highest 25%	–	–	–	–	–	–
	Average	$1,100	$1,456	$923	$837	$1,362	$2,984
	Lowest 25%	–	–	–	–	–	–
TOTAL COMPENSATION	Highest 25%	$62,973	$70,522	$68,917	$56,942	$61,480	$65,000
	Average	$47,931	$57,452	$58,656	$49,794	$51,130	$61,593
	Lowest 25%	$31,462	$43,540	$45,000	$41,588	$36,000	$48,711

– Not enough responses to provide meaningful data

TABLE 7-12: ANNUAL COMPENSATION OF ASSOCIATE PASTOR BY DENOMINATION

BENEFITS		DENOMINATION					
		Assemblies of God	Baptist	Independent/ Nondenom	Lutheran	Methodist	Presbyte-rian
RETIREMENT:	Highest 25%	$2,032	$4,927	$2,500	$5,900	$6,649	$6,982
	Average	$1,124	$3,065	$1,597	$3,619	$3,506	$5,090
	Lowest 25%	–	–	–	–	–	$159
LIFE INSURANCE:	Highest 25%	–	–	–	–	–	–
	Average	$153	$277	$140	–	–	$335
	Lowest 25%	–	–	–	–	–	–
HEALTH INSURANCE:	Highest 25%	$10,302	$10,477	$9,624	$12,012	$9,000	$12,616
	Average	$5,060	$6,532	$5,861	$6,963	$5,011	$8,347
	Lowest 25%	–	$1,350	$573	$3,418	–	–
CONTINUING EDUCATION	Highest 25%	–	$550	$1,009	$1,495	$993	$1,997
	Average	–	$452	$699	$1,179	$412	$1,393
	Lowest 25%	–	–	–	–	–	$150
TOTAL BENEFITS	Highest 25%	$11,538	$15,693	$12,980	$17,147	$14,100	$20,588
	Average	$6,337	$10,325	$8,298	$11,850	$8,989	$15,166
	Lowest 25%	$1,644	$4,148	$2,400	$6,000	$4,800	$8,618
TOTAL COMPENSATION AND BENEFIT		Assemblies of God	Baptist	Independent/ Nondenom	Lutheran	Methodist	Presbyte-rian
	Highest 25%	$68,445	$81,725	$76,200	$73,491	$72,000	$86,744
	Average	$54,268	$67,777	$66,953	$61,645	$60,119	$77,175
	Lowest 25%	$36,115	$52,840	$53,200	$52,300	$46,700	$61,246
NUMBER OF RESPONDENTS		20	100	123	19	26	48

– Not enough responses to provide meaningful data

123

TABLE 7-13: COMPENSATION OF PART-TIME ASSOCIATE PASTOR BY WORSHIP ATTENDANCE

CHARACTERISTICS	WORSHIP ATTENDANCE					
	100 or less	101-300	301-500	501-750	751-1000	Over 1000
AVERAGE SUNDAY AM WORSHIP ATTENDANCE	81	204	400	–	–	–
AVERAGE CHURCH INCOME	$132,467	$395,516	$694,638	–	–	–
AVERAGE # of YEARS EMPLOYED	8	5	5	–	–	–
AVERAGE # of WEEKS OF PAID VACATION	3	3	3	–	–	–
% COLLEGE GRADUATE OR HIGHER	93%	84%	93%	–	–	–
% WHO RECEIVE AUTO REIMBURSEMENT	62%	61%	60%	–	–	–
% ORDAINED	88%	89%	87%	–	–	–
AVERAGE % SALARY INCREASE THIS YEAR	–	5%	4%	–	–	–
HOURLY RATES	100 or less	101-300	301-500	501-750	751-1000	Over 1000
AVERAGE BASE RATE	$8.87	$7.60	$8.42	–	–	

– Not enough responses to provide meaningful data

TABLE 7-13: COMPENSATION OF PART-TIME ASSOCIATE PASTOR BY WORSHIP ATTENDANCE

	WORSHIP ATTENDANCE					
ANNUAL COMPENSATION	100 or less	101-300	301-500	501-750	751-1000	Over 1000
AVERAGE BASE SALARY	$6,251	$11,425	$16,369	–	–	–
AVERAGE HOUSING	$2,595	$6,567	$5,507	–	–	–
AVERAGE PARSONAGE	–	–	–	–	–	–
AVERAGE TOTAL COMPENSATION	$8,905	$18,669	$22,676	–	–	–
ANNUAL BENEFITS	100 or less	101-300	301-500	501-750	751-1000	Over 1000
AVERAGE RETIREMENT	–	$418	$745	–	–	–
AVERAGE LIFE INSURANCE	–	–	–	–	–	–
AVERAGE HEALTH INSURANCE	$256	$413	$1,387	–	–	–
AVERAGE CONTINUING EDUCATION	–	$187	$224	–	–	–
AVERAGE TOTAL BENEFITS	$323	$1,037	$2,356	–	–	–
TOTAL COMPENSATION AND BENEFIT	100 or less	101-300	301-500	501-750	751-1000	Over 1000
AVERAGE	$9,228	$19,705	$25,031	–	–	–
NUMBER OF RESPONDENTS	17	39	15	5	2	3

– Not enough responses to provide meaningful data

125

TABLE 7-14: COMPENSATION OF PART-TIME ASSOCIATE PASTOR BY CHURCH INCOME

CHARACTERISTICS	CHURCH INCOME				
	$250K & under	$251K-$500K	$501K-$750K	$751K-$1M	Over 1 Million
AVERAGE SUNDAY AM WORSHIP ATTENDANCE	109	221	426	–	920
AVERAGE CHURCH INCOME	$151,441	$387,944	$634,581	–	$2,025,963
AVERAGE # of YEARS EMPLOYED	5	5	6	–	11
AVERAGE # of WEEKS OF PAID VACATION	3	3	–	–	–
% COLLEGE GRADUATE OR HIGHER	89%	89%	89%	–	78%
% WHO RECEIVE AUTO REIMBURSEMENT	65%	59%	44%	–	–
% ORDAINED	91%	84%	91%	–	89%
AVERAGE % SALARY INCREASE THIS YEAR	–	5%	–	–	–
HOURLY RATES	$250K & under	$251K-$500K	$501K-$750K	$751K-$1M	Over 1 Million
AVERAGE BASE RATE	$6.90	$8.34	$7.40	–	11.28

— *Not enough responses to provide meaningful data*

ASSOCIATE PASTORS—TABLE 7-14

TABLE 7-14: COMPENSATION OF PART-TIMEASSOCIATE PASTOR BY CHURCH INCOME

	CHURCH INCOME				
ANNUAL COMPENSATION	$250K & under	$251K-$500K	$501K-$750K	$751K-$1M	Over 1 Million
AVERAGE BASE SALARY	$7,840	$12,199	$12,083	–	$17,079
AVERAGE HOUSING	$4,587	$6,460	$3,293	–	$6,095
AVERAGE PARSONAGE	–	–	–	–	–
AVERAGE TOTAL COMPENSATION	$12,576	$19,409	$15,377	–	$23,173
ANNUAL BENEFITS	$250K & under	$251K-$500K	$501K-$750K	$751K-$1M	Over 1 Million
AVERAGE RETIREMENT	$153	$455	$595	–	–
AVERAGE LIFE INSURANCE	–	–	–	–	–
AVERAGE HEALTH INSURANCE	$334	$674	$1,182	–	–
AVERAGE CONTINUING EDUCATION	–	$244	$237	–	$178
AVERAGE TOTAL BENEFITS	$531	$1,379	$2,014	–	$178
TOTAL COMPENSATION AND BENEFIT	$250K & under	$251K-$500K	$501K-$750K	$751K-$1M	Over 1 Million
AVERAGE	$13,106	$20,788	$17,391	–	$23,351
NUMBER OF RESPONDENTS	23	32	11	4	9

– Not enough responses to provide meaningful data

127

TABLE 7-15: AVERAGE COMPENSATION PACKAGE FOR PART-TIME ASSOCIATE PASTORS*

		PASTORS WHO RECIEVE...				
	Overall	Base Salary Only	No Base Salary	Base Salary and Parsonage	Base Salary and Housing	Base Salary and Parsonage and Housing
BASE SALARY	$11,735	$16,604		–	$14,979	–
PARSONAGE**	$480		$571	–		–
HOUSING ALLOWANCE	$5,515		$7,839		$12,981	–
TOTAL COMPENSATION PACKAGE	$17,730	$16,604	$8,410	–	$27,960	–
NUMBER OF RESPONDENTS	82	36	21	1	21	3

*All $ values are annual averages
**Parsonage = Rental value of parsonage plus allowance
– Not enough responses to provide meaningful data

**For an explanation of the Average Compensation Table,
please refer to Chapter 1.**

8

ADULT MINISTRY DIRECTORS

Employment Profile

The majority of full-time Adult Ministry Directors positions reported in this study serve in their positions as ordained ministers. The vast majority of Adult Ministry Directors are college graduates, and 51% have graduate degrees and serve in churches located in the suburbs or small town/rural areas. Approximately three-quarters serve in churches with an income greater than $1,000,000. Adult Ministry Directors reflected the following profile:

	FULL-TIME	PART-TIME
Ordained	72%	45%
Average years employed	7	5
Male	78%	45%
Female	22%	55%
Self-employed (receives 1099)	2%	2%
Church employee (receives W-2)	98%	98%
High school diploma	5%	10%
Associate's degree	2%	2%
Bachelor's degree	41%	46%
Master's degree	44%	36%
Doctorate	7%	6%
Number of respondents	*171*	*56*

Total Compensation plus Benefits Package Analysis

The analysis below is based upon the tables found later in this chapter. The tables present compensation plus benefits data according to worship attendance, church income, combinations of size and setting, region, gender, education, years employed, and denomination for Adult Ministry Directors who serve full-time. The final table provides data for part-time Adult Ministry Directors based upon worship attendance and church income. In this way, the Director's compensation can be viewed from a variety of useful perspectives. The total compensation plus benefits amount found in a separate box at the bottom of each page includes the base salary, housing and/or parsonage amount, life and health insurance payments, retirement contribution, and educational funds.

Full-time staff members. Full-time Adult Ministry Directors receive benefit packages comparable to those of other professional and ministerial staff members within the church. Of the benefits included, the majority receive housing, health insurance, paid vacation, and auto allowance.

Part-time staff members. 55% of part-time Adult Ministry Directors are female. Ninety-eight percent of part-time Directors are church employees, receiving W-2s for their tax form. Part-time Adult Ministry Directors receive few benefits, with the most common being a paid vacation, an auto allowance and adult education funds.

COMPENSATION PLUS BENEFITS	FULL TIME	PART TIME
Base salary	99%	91%
Housing	67%	14%
Parsonage	5%	4%
Retirement	58%	13%
Life insurance	35%	7%
Health insurance	80%	5%
Paid vacation	94%	50%
Auto reimbursement	63%	39%
Continuing education	39%	32%

KEY POINTS

⮑ **Church income is highly correlated with compensation.** Average compensation among full-time Adult Ministry Directors increases steadily as church income increases with the most significant jumps being from $251-$500,000 to $501 to $750,000 and then from $751 to $1,000,000 to over $1,000,000. There is little difference in compensation from $501 to $1,000,000 in church income. From the standpoint of compensation, Adult Ministry Directors are more closely aligned with Music/Choir Directors than any other position per year. *See Table 8-1.*

⮑ **Church attendance impacts Adult Ministry Directors' compensation and benefit package.** Most full-time Adult Ministry Directors serve in churches with an attendance over 750, with close to one-half in congregations over 1,000. Overall compensation remains below the national average until a position is secured in a larger church with an average attendance over 750. *See Table 8-2.*

⮑ **Significant gender differences exists among Adult Ministry Directors.** Women earn approximately 25% (or $15,000) lower than their male counterparts, on average. Some of the difference is due to the fact that women work in smaller churches from a church income and worship attendance standpoint. The disparity in compensation and benefit package, where women receive significantly less than men, are mainly in the areas of housing, retirement, and health insurance. *See Table 8-9.*

➲ **Educational achievement has a relationship to compensation.** Overall compensation increases steadily with education. College graduates tend to be just at the national average. Fifty-one percent of the full-time Adult Ministry Directors surveyed had either a master's degree or a doctorate. Those with doctoral degrees earn on average $10,000 more than the typical Adult Ministry Director with a bachelor's or master's degree. The difference in compensation across education levels has little to do with church income and attendance, as income and attendance are similar across the three highest levels of education (Bachelor's degree and higher). *See Table 8-10.*

➲ **Approximately one-quarter of Adult Ministry Directors work part-time.** The majority of part-time Adult Ministry Directors serve in churches with a worship attendance of 300 or more and a church income of $500,000 or more. *See Tables 8-14 and 8-15.*

Compensation & Benefits: National Average for Adult Ministry Directors*

FULL TIME

| 2006 | $67,711 |

* No historical data available

TABLE 8-1: ANNUAL COMPENSATION OF ADULT MINISTRY DIRECTOR BY CHURCH INCOME

CHARACTERISTICS	CHURCH INCOME				
	$250K & under	$251K-$500K	$501K-$750K	$751K-$1M	Over $1 Million
AVERAGE SUNDAY AM WORSHIP ATTENDANCE	–	267	378	493	1,490
AVERAGE CHURCH INCOME	–	$420,560	$608,462	$883,294	$2,902,925
AVERAGE # of YEARS EMPLOYED	–	6	6	8	7
AVERAGE # of WEEKS OF PAID VACATION	–	–	3	3	3
% COLLEGE GRADUATE OR HIGHER	–	75%	100%	86%	94%
% WHO RECEIVE AUTO REIMBURSEMENT	–	–	67%	75%	70%
% ORDAINED	–	38%	64%	59%	76%
AVERAGE % SALARY INCREASE THIS YEAR	–	–	–	3%	4%

COMPENSATION		$250K & under	$251K-$500K	$501K-$750K	$751K-$1M	Over 1 Million
BASE SALARY:	Highest 25%	–	$37,673	$39,264	$40,691	$49,596
	Average	–	$30,701	$34,138	$30,344	$43,484
	Lowest 25%	–	$22,519	$28,001	$21,913	$26,000
HOUSING:	Highest 25%	–	–	$16,156	$20,002	$29,538
	Average	–	$2,250	$10,102	$12,427	$18,719
	Lowest 25%	–	–	–	–	–
PARSONAGE:	Highest 25%	–	–	–	–	–
	Average	–	$1,200	–	$2,706	$613
	Lowest 25%	–	–	–	–	–
TOTAL COMPENSATION	Highest 25%	–	$37,673	$54,207	$51,000	$66,520
	Average	–	$34,151	$44,240	$45,476	$62,816
	Lowest 25%	–	$28,200	$33,601	$42,000	$45,772

– Not enough responses to provide meaningful data

TABLE 8-1: ANNUAL COMPENSATION OF ADULT MINISTRY DIRECTOR BY CHURCH INCOME

BENEFITS		CHURCH INCOME				
		$250K & under	$251K-$500K	$501K-$750K	$751K-$1M	Over $1 Million
RETIREMENT:	Highest 25%	–	$1,700	$3,089	$1,972	$4,747
	Average	–	$945	$1,392	$1,425	$2,525
	Lowest 25%	–	–	–	–	–
LIFE INSURANCE:	Highest 25%	–	–	–	–	–
	Average	–	–	–	$168	$200
	Lowest 25%	–	–	–	–	–
HEALTH INSURANCE:	Highest 25%	–	–	$6,422	$9,999	$10,114
	Average	–	$2,585	$5,953	$7,045	$6,688
	Lowest 25%	–	–	–	$5,255	$3,330
CONTINUING EDUCATION	Highest 25%	–	–	$994	$992	$1,004
	Average	–	$1,038	$464	$715	$575
	Lowest 25%	–	–	–	–	–
TOTAL BENEFITS	Highest 25%	–	–	$9,277	$13,001	$13,752
	Average	–	$4,568	$7,826	$9,353	$9,986
	Lowest 25%	–	$300	$1,001	$6,808	$6,020
TOTAL COMPENSATION AND BENEFIT		$250K & under	$251K-$500K	$501K-$750K	$751K-$1M	Over 1 Million
	Highest 25%	–	$39,623	$77,258	$64,000	$79,809
	Average	–	$38,719	$52,066	$54,830	$72,802
	Lowest 25%	–	$30,216	$37,776	$47,600	$53,612
NUMBER OF RESPONDENTS		0	8	11	17	124

– Not enough responses to provide meaningful data

TABLE 8-2: ANNUAL COMPENSATION OF ADULT MINISTRY DIRECTOR BY WORSHIP ATTENDANCE

CHARACTERISTICS	WORSHIP ATTENDANCE					
	100 or less	101-300	301-500	501-750	751-1000	Over 1000
AVERAGE SUNDAY AM WORSHIP ATTENDANCE	–	259	413	631	906	1,998
AVERAGE CHURCH INCOME	–	$520,352	$968,290	$1,454,619	$2,009,483	$3,685,367
AVERAGE # of YEARS EMPLOYED	–	7	5	6	7	7
AVERAGE # of WEEKS OF PAID VACATION	–	3	3	3	3	3
% COLLEGE GRADUATE OR HIGHER	–	75%	91%	93%	96%	94%
% WHO RECEIVE AUTO REIMBURSEMENT	–	75%	71%	75%	50%	73%
% ORDAINED	–	33%	67%	78%	68%	79%
AVERAGE % SALARY INCREASE THIS YEAR	–	6%	3%	3%	4%	5%

COMPENSATION		100 or less	101-300	301-500	501-750	751-1000	Over 1000
BASE SALARY:	Highest 25%	–	$38,051	$42,841	$47,000	–	$55,000
	Average	–	$31,809	$41,824	$32,587	$47,141	$41,617
	Lowest 25%	–	$20,000	$26,651	$21,914	$24,543	$27,908
HOUSING:	Highest 25%	–	$14,402	$21,999	$26,906	$22,300	$29,998
	Average	–	$6,062	$12,304	$17,582	$14,669	$19,957
	Lowest 25%	–	–	–	–	–	$999
PARSONAGE:	Highest 25%	–	–	–	–	–	–
	Average	–	$1,067	$2,667	$556	$1,511	$987
	Lowest 25%	–	–	–	–	–	–
TOTAL COMPENSATION	Highest 25%	–	$44,001	–	$53,000	–	$72,101
	Average	–	$38,938	$56,795	$50,725	$63,321	$62,561
	Lowest 25%	–	$33,600	$38,001	$44,940	$39,290	$48,996

– Not enough responses to provide meaningful data

TABLE 8-2: ANNUAL COMPENSATION OF ADULT MINISTRY DIRECTOR BY WORSHIP ATTENDANCE

BENEFITS		WORSHIP ATTENDANCE					
		100 or less	101-300	301-500	501-750	751-1000	Over 1000
RETIREMENT:	Highest 25%	–	$2,355	$2,700	$5,740	$4,058	$3,879
	Average	–	$1,102	$1,409	$2,667	$2,516	$2,426
	Lowest 25%	–	–	–	–	$367	–
LIFE INSURANCE:	Highest 25%	–	–	–	$472	–	$153
	Average	–	–	$312	$375	–	$153
	Lowest 25%	–	–	–	–	–	–
HEALTH INSURANCE:	Highest 25%	–	$4,177	$9,993	$9,599	$11,082	$10,167
	Average	–	$3,536	$6,321	$6,024	$7,253	$6,600
	Lowest 25%	–	–	$3,361	$3,266	$3,910	$1,499
CONTINUING EDUCATION	Highest 25%	–	–	$989	$1,094	$950	$756
	Average	–	$900	$416	$926	$402	$534
	Lowest 25%	–	–	–	–	–	–
TOTAL BENEFITS	Highest 25%	–	–	$11,836	$14,099	$14,911	$13,911
	Average	–	$5,538	$8,458	$9,992	$10,221	$9,694
	Lowest 25%	–	$2,039	$4,499	$4,180	$6,395	$4,519
TOTAL COMPENSATION AND BENEFIT		100 or less	101-300	301-500	501-750	751-1000	Over 1000
	Highest 25%	–	$48,542	$70,100	$71,926	$74,501	$83,018
	Average	–	$44,476	$65,253	$60,717	$73,542	$72,255
	Lowest 25%	–	$37,560	$43,496	$50,200	$46,360	$55,588
NUMBER OF RESPONDENTS		0	9	27	27	28	77

– Not enough responses to provide meaningful data

137

TABLE 8-3: ANNUAL COMPENSATION OF ADULT MINISTRY DIRECTOR BY CHURCH SETTING & SIZE

ATTENDANCE 251 - 500		CHURCH SETTING			
		Metropoli-tan city	Suburb of large city	Small town or rural city	Farming area
AVERAGE SUNDAY AM WORSHIP ATTENDANCE		–	422	369	–
AVERAGE CHURCH INCOME		–	$1,034,414	$765,988	–
AVERAGE # of YEARS EMPLOYED		–	6	4	–
AVERAGE # of WEEKS OF PAID VACATION		–	3	3	–
% COLLEGE GRADUATE OR HIGHER		–	82%	92%	–
% WHO RECEIVE AUTO REIMBURSEMENT		–	67%	70%	–
% ORDAINED		–	60%	67%	–
AVERAGE % SALARY INCREASE THIS YEAR		–	3%	3%	–

COMPENSATION		Metropoli-tan city	Suburb of large city	Small town or rural city	Farming area
BASE SALARY:	Highest 25%	–	$44,317	–	–
	Average	–	$34,301	$48,069	–
	Lowest 25%	–	$27,010	$21,348	–
HOUSING:	Highest 25%	–	$28,614	$19,000	–
	Average	–	$15,880	$11,381	–
	Lowest 25%	–	–	–	–
PARSONAGE:	Highest 25%	–	–	–	–
	Average	–	$4,000	–	–
	Lowest 25%	–	–	–	–
TOTAL COMPENSATION	Highest 25%	–	$58,573	–	–
	Average	–	$54,181	$59,449	–
	Lowest 25%	–	$44,021	$31,100	–

– Not enough responses to provide meaningful data

TABLE 8-3: ANNUAL COMPENSATION OF ADULT MINISTRY DIRECTOR BY CHURCH SETTING & SIZE

BENEFITS		CHURCH SETTING			
		Metropoli-tan city	Suburb of large city	Small town or rural city	Farming area
RETIREMENT:	Highest 25%	–	$1,344	$4,208	–
	Average	–	$833	$1,493	–
	Lowest 25%	–	–	–	–
LIFE INSURANCE:	Highest 25%	–	–	–	–
	Average	–	$524	–	–
	Lowest 25%	–	–	–	–
HEALTH INSURANCE:	Highest 25%	–	$10,799	$6,272	–
	Average	–	$7,182	$4,077	–
	Lowest 25%	–	$3,602	–	–
CONTINUING EDUCATION	Highest 25%	–	$1,002	$650	–
	Average	–	$500	$304	–
	Lowest 25%	–	–	–	–
TOTAL BENEFITS	Highest 25%	–	$12,096	$10,667	–
	Average	–	$9,039	$5,908	–
	Lowest 25%	–	$4,502	$2,177	–
TOTAL COMPENSATION AND BENEFIT		Metropoli-tan city	Suburb of large city	Small town or rural city	Farming area
	Highest 25%	–	$78,915	–	–
	Average	–	$63,219	$65,358	–
	Lowest 25%	–	$48,910	$32,846	–
NUMBER OF RESPONDENTS		6	15	12	1

– Not enough responses to provide meaningful data

TABLE 8-4: ANNUAL COMPENSATION OF ADULT MINISTRY DIRECTOR BY CHURCH SETTING & SIZE

ATTENDANCE 501 - 750		CHURCH SETTING			
		Metropoli-tan city	Suburb of large city	Small town or rural city	Farming area
AVERAGE SUNDAY AM WORSHIP ATTENDANCE		–	650	–	–
AVERAGE CHURCH INCOME		–	$1,400,305	–	–
AVERAGE # of YEARS EMPLOYED		–	7	–	–
AVERAGE # of WEEKS OF PAID VACATION		–	3	–	–
% COLLEGE GRADUATE OR HIGHER		–	94%	–	–
% WHO RECEIVE AUTO REIMBURSEMENT		–	75%	–	–
% ORDAINED		–	78%	–	–
AVERAGE % SALARY INCREASE THIS YEAR		–	3%	–	–

COMPENSATION		Metropoli-tan city	Suburb of large city	Small town or rural city	Farming area
BASE SALARY:	Highest 25%	–	$45,000	–	–
	Average	–	$31,097	–	–
	Lowest 25%	–	$21,913	–	–
HOUSING:	Highest 25%	–	$30,000	–	–
	Average	–	$19,900	–	–
	Lowest 25%	–	$17,000	–	–
PARSONAGE:	Highest 25%	–	–	–	–
	Average	–	–	–	–
	Lowest 25%	–	–	–	–
TOTAL COMPENSATION	Highest 25%	–	$53,583	–	–
	Average	–	$50,997	–	–
	Lowest 25%	–	$45,000	–	–

– *Not enough responses to provide meaningful data*

TABLE 8-4: ANNUAL COMPENSATION OF ADULT MINISTRY DIRECTOR BY CHURCH SETTING & SIZE

BENEFITS		CHURCH SETTING			
		Metropolitan city	Suburb of large city	Small town or rural city	Farming area
RETIREMENT:	Highest 25%	–	$5,924	–	–
	Average	–	$3,372	–	–
	Lowest 25%	–	–	–	–
LIFE INSURANCE:	Highest 25%	–	$472	–	–
	Average	–	$261	–	–
	Lowest 25%	–	–	–	–
HEALTH INSURANCE:	Highest 25%	–	$9,600	–	–
	Average	–	$6,634	–	–
	Lowest 25%	–	$4,800	–	–
CONTINUING EDUCATION	Highest 25%	–	$1,500	–	–
	Average	–	$1,222	–	–
	Lowest 25%	–	$40	–	–
TOTAL BENEFITS	Highest 25%	–	$15,535	–	–
	Average	–	$11,490	–	–
	Lowest 25%	–	$7,728	–	–
TOTAL COMPENSATION AND BENEFIT		Metropolitan city	Suburb of large city	Small town or rural city	Farming area
	Highest 25%	–	$74,096	–	–
	Average	–	$62,487	–	–
	Lowest 25%	–	$54,086	–	–
NUMBER OF RESPONDENTS		2	18	6	1

– Not enough responses to provide meaningful data

TABLE 8-5: ANNUAL COMPENSATION OF ADULT MINISTRY DIRECTOR BY CHURCH SETTING & SIZE

ATTENDANCE 751 - 1,000		Metropolitan city	Suburb of large city	Small town or rural city	Farming area
AVERAGE SUNDAY AM WORSHIP ATTENDANCE		911	–	890	–
AVERAGE CHURCH INCOME		$2,327,654	–	$1,761,372	–
AVERAGE # of YEARS EMPLOYED		8	–	9	–
AVERAGE # of WEEKS OF PAID VACATION		3	–	3	–
% COLLEGE GRADUATE OR HIGHER		100%	–	89%	–
% WHO RECEIVE AUTO REIMBURSEMENT		40%	–	50%	–
% ORDAINED		55%	–	100%	–
AVERAGE % SALARY INCREASE THIS YEAR		4%	–	4%	–

COMPENSATION		Metropolitan city	Suburb of large city	Small town or rural city	Farming area
BASE SALARY:	Highest 25%	$45,997	–	–	–
	Average	$36,563	–	$69,397	–
	Lowest 25%	$26,004	–	$23,997	–
HOUSING:	Highest 25%	$29,405	–	$20,095	–
	Average	$14,745	–	$17,247	–
	Lowest 25%	–	–	$12,305	–
PARSONAGE:	Highest 25%	–	–	–	–
	Average	–	–	–	–
	Lowest 25%	–	–	–	–
TOTAL COMPENSATION	Highest 25%	$63,086	–	–	–
	Average	$51,308	–	$86,643	–
	Lowest 25%	$38,047	–	$39,533	–

– Not enough responses to provide meaningful data

TABLE 8-5: ANNUAL COMPENSATION OF ADULT MINISTRY DIRECTOR BY CHURCH SETTING & SIZE

BENEFITS		CHURCH SETTING			
		Metropoli-tan city	Suburb of large city	Small town or rural city	Farming area
RETIREMENT:	Highest 25%	$3,591	–	$4,124	–
	Average	$2,347	–	$2,184	–
	Lowest 25%	–	–	$376	–
LIFE INSURANCE:	Highest 25%	–	–	–	–
	Average	–	–	–	–
	Lowest 25%	–	–	–	–
HEALTH INSURANCE:	Highest 25%	$12,259	–	$8,322	–
	Average	$6,330	–	$5,609	–
	Lowest 25%	–	–	$3,476	–
CONTINUING EDUCATION	Highest 25%	$975	–	$775	–
	Average	$445	–	$383	–
	Lowest 25%	–	–	–	–
TOTAL BENEFITS	Highest 25%	$13,447	–	$11,017	–
	Average	$9,146	–	$8,177	–
	Lowest 25%	$5,977	–	$5,464	–
TOTAL COMPENSATION AND BENEFIT		Metropoli-tan city	Suburb of large city	Small town or rural city	Farming area
	Highest 25%	$77,574	–	–	–
	Average	$60,454	–	$94,820	–
	Lowest 25%	$46,025	–	$43,636	–
NUMBER OF RESPONDENTS		11	7	9	0

– *Not enough responses to provide meaningful data*

TABLE 8-6: ANNUAL COMPENSATION OF ADULT MINISTRY DIRECTOR BY CHURCH SETTING & SIZE

ATTENDANCE OVER 1,000	**CHURCH SETTING**			
	Metropoli-tan city	Suburb of large city	Small town or rural city	Farming area
AVERAGE SUNDAY AM WORSHIP ATTENDANCE	2,127	2,051	1,856	–
AVERAGE CHURCH INCOME	$4,485,450	$3,776,993	$3,151,337	–
AVERAGE # of YEARS EMPLOYED	11	7	6	–
AVERAGE # of WEEKS OF PAID VACATION	3	4	3	–
% COLLEGE GRADUATE OR HIGHER	100%	97%	86%	–
% WHO RECEIVE AUTO REIMBURSEMENT	64%	77%	71%	–
% ORDAINED	82%	82%	72%	–
AVERAGE % SALARY INCREASE THIS YEAR	4%	6%	4%	–

COMPENSATION		Metropoli-tan city	Suburb of large city	Small town or rural city	Farming area
BASE SALARY:	Highest 25%	$65,372	$55,005	$40,003	–
	Average	$47,696	$45,890	$31,935	–
	Lowest 25%	$27,911	$33,401	$19,277	–
HOUSING:	Highest 25%	$29,983	$30,029	$27,350	–
	Average	$20,704	$18,994	$21,207	–
	Lowest 25%	$15,858	–	$15,735	–
PARSONAGE:	Highest 25%	–	$2,150	–	–
	Average	$3,091	$1,024	–	–
	Lowest 25%	–	–	–	–
TOTAL COMPENSATION	Highest 25%	$89,998	$72,259	$60,749	–
	Average	$71,491	$65,908	$53,143	–
	Lowest 25%	$50,002	$54,079	$45,318	–

– Not enough responses to provide meaningful data

TABLE 8-6: ANNUAL COMPENSATION OF ADULT MINISTRY DIRECTOR BY CHURCH SETTING & SIZE

		CHURCH SETTING			
BENEFITS		Metropolitan city	Suburb of large city	Small town or rural city	Farming area
RETIREMENT:	Highest 25%	$5,039	$5,202	$3,482	–
	Average	$2,357	$2,438	$2,437	–
	Lowest 25%	–	–	–	–
LIFE INSURANCE:	Highest 25%	–	–	$154	–
	Average	–	$167	–	–
	Lowest 25%	–	–	–	–
HEALTH INSURANCE:	Highest 25%	$8,814	$11,823	$9,229	–
	Average	$6,115	$7,536	$5,278	–
	Lowest 25%	$2,401	$3,499	$25	–
CONTINUING EDUCATION	Highest 25%	–	$775	$1,525	–
	Average	$364	$518	$635	–
	Lowest 25%	–	–	–	–
TOTAL BENEFITS	Highest 25%	$13,153	$14,724	$11,940	–
	Average	$8,950	$10,659	$8,437	–
	Lowest 25%	$3,901	$6,111	$3,516	–
TOTAL COMPENSATION AND BENEFIT		Metropolitan city	Suburb of large city	Small town or rural city	Farming area
	Highest 25%	$98,848	$83,027	$72,449	–
	Average	$80,440	$76,568	$61,580	–
	Lowest 25%	$53,395	$61,291	$49,925	–
NUMBER OF RESPONDENTS		11	41	25	0

– *Not enough responses to provide meaningful data*

145

TABLE 8-7: ANNUAL COMPENSATION OF ADULT MINISTRY DIRECTOR BY REGION

CHARACTERISTICS	New England	Middle Atlantic	South Atlantic	E-N Central	E-S Central	W-N Central	W-S Central	Mountain	Pacific
AVERAGE SUNDAY AM WORSHIP ATTENDANCE	–	849	938	1,408	1,236	1,002	1,714	1,532	1,265
AVERAGE CHURCH INCOME	–	$1,296,661	$1,990,416	$2,519,539	$3,312,791	$2,343,080	$3,645,571	$2,330,069	$2,295,407
AVERAGE # of YEARS EMPLOYED	–	4	7	6	6	6	6	7	7
AVERAGE # of WEEKS OF PAID VACATION	–	3	3	3	3	3	3	4	3
% COLLEGE GRADUATE OR HIGHER	–	80%	92%	96%	100%	100%	100%	88%	88%
% WHO RECEIVE AUTO REIMBURSEMENT	–	63%	61%	92%	54%	67%	59%	71%	73%
% ORDAINED	–	40%	63%	81%	64%	90%	82%	74%	72%
AVERAGE % SALARY INCREASE THIS YEAR	–	9%	4%	4%	3%	4%	5%	3%	4%

COMPENSATION		New England	Middle Atlantic	South Atlantic	E-N Central	E-S Central	W-N Central	W-S Central	Mountain	Pacific
BASE SALARY:	Highest 25%	–	$49,934	$44,327	$47,800	$48,498	$41,149	–	$48,501	$44,410
	Average	–	$36,385	$36,047	$36,809	$37,445	$33,385	$84,631	$35,225	$33,979
	Lowest 25%	–	$26,650	$28,000	$25,001	$30,000	$20,500	$40,000	$21,913	$19,200
HOUSING:	Highest 25%	–	$20,000	$28,002	$29,999	$20,000	$26,764	$24,146	$26,802	$36,999
	Average	–	$11,430	$14,749	$18,306	$9,713	$19,266	$19,157	$14,077	$22,064
	Lowest 25%	–	–	–	$3,002	–	$14,560	$16,873	–	–
PARSONAGE:	Highest 25%	–	–	–	–	–	–	–	–	–
	Average	–	$1,500	$1,122	$704	$3,022	–	–	$2,000	$1,745
	Lowest 25%	–	–	–	–	–	–	–	–	–
TOTAL COMPENSATION	Highest 25%	–	$55,000	$58,801	$60,747	$60,825	$61,300	–	$52,799	$63,307
	Average	–	$49,315	$51,919	$55,819	$50,181	$52,651	$103,788	$51,302	$57,789
	Lowest 25%	–	$43,000	$41,523	$42,001	$40,800	$38,500	$60,000	$44,500	$42,841

– Not enough responses to provide meaningful data

TABLE 8-7: ANNUAL COMPENSATION OF ADULT MINISTRY DIRECTOR BY REGION

BENEFITS		REGION								
		New England	Middle Atlantic	South Atlantic	E-N Central	E-S Central	W-N Central	W-S Central	Mountain	Pacific
RETIREMENT:	Highest 25%	–	$2,800	$5,400	$2,000	$5,800	$5,040	$8,070	$1,440	$2,430
	Average	–	$1,027	$2,990	$1,170	$2,955	$2,901	$4,252	$1,010	$1,808
	Lowest 25%	–	–	–	–	–	–	$536	–	–
LIFE INSURANCE:	Highest 25%	–	$240	–	$160	–	–	–	–	–
	Average	–	$114	$145	$122	$360	$633	–	$218	–
	Lowest 25%	–	–	–	–	–	–	–	–	–
HEALTH INSURANCE:	Highest 25%	–	$9,600	$9,434	$12,731	$5,000	$12,042	$10,129	$11,428	$9,001
	Average	–	$6,335	$6,011	$8,059	$4,048	$8,164	$8,045	$5,658	$6,057
	Lowest 25%	–	$3,480	$1,499	$4,001	–	$4,191	$6,311	$271	$3,499
CONTINUING EDUCATION	Highest 25%	–	$994	$586	$991	$756	$1,000	$997	$1,106	$1,494
	Average	–	$635	$446	$633	$471	$660	$465	$895	$588
	Lowest 25%	–	–	–	–	–	–	–	–	–
TOTAL BENEFITS	Highest 25%	–	$11,939	$14,581	$14,436	$9,825	$19,317	$15,258	$11,838	$13,464
	Average	–	$8,112	$9,591	$9,985	$7,834	$12,357	$12,837	$7,781	$8,542
	Lowest 25%	–	$4,080	$4,178	$6,501	$4,160	$7,934	$9,166	$3,599	$3,599
TOTAL COMPENSATION AND BENEFIT		New England	Middle Atlantic	South Atlantic	E-N Central	E-S Central	W-N Central	W-S Central	Mountain	Pacific
	Highest 25%	–	$64,000	$76,127	$78,971	$75,924	$78,072	–	$68,813	$74,096
	Average	–	$57,426	$61,510	$65,803	$58,015	$65,009	$116,625	$59,083	$66,330
	Lowest 25%	–	$49,934	$44,046	$48,714	$46,760	$55,317	$68,600	$47,951	$48,542
NUMBER OF RESPONDENTS		1	10	41	27	14	10	17	21	29

– Not enough responses to provide meaningful data

TABLE 8-8: ANNUAL COMPENSATION OF ADULT MINISTRY DIRECTOR BY GENDER

CHARACTERISTICS	GENDER	
	Male	Female
AVERAGE SUNDAY AM WORSHIP ATTENDANCE	1,364	838
AVERAGE CHURCH INCOME	$2,672,799	$1,568,242
AVERAGE # of YEARS EMPLOYED	7	7
AVERAGE # of WEEKS OF PAID VACATION	3	3
% COLLEGE GRADUATE OR HIGHER	94%	88%
% WHO RECEIVE AUTO REIMBURSEMENT	70%	67%
% ORDAINED	82%	34%
AVERAGE % SALARY INCREASE THIS YEAR	4%	4%

COMPENSATION		Male	Female
BASE SALARY:	Highest 25%	$49,220	$44,409
	Average	$39,997	$41,962
	Lowest 25%	$23,881	$26,765
HOUSING:	Highest 25%	$29,998	$12,000
	Average	$19,847	$5,881
	Lowest 25%	$10,602	–
PARSONAGE:	Highest 25%	–	–
	Average	$1,289	$1,211
	Lowest 25%	–	–
TOTAL COMPENSATION	Highest 25%	$67,220	–
	Average	$61,134	$49,054
	Lowest 25%	$46,001	$33,600

– Not enough responses to provide meaningful data

TABLE 8-8: ANNUAL COMPENSATION OF ADULT MINISTRY DIRECTOR BY GENDER

BENEFITS		GENDER	
		Male	Female
RETIREMENT:	Highest 25%	$4,800	$2,355
	Average	$2,541	$1,395
	Lowest 25%	–	–
LIFE INSURANCE:	Highest 25%	–	–
	Average	$156	$256
	Lowest 25%	–	–
HEALTH INSURANCE:	Highest 25%	$11,123	$6,900
	Average	$7,068	$4,342
	Lowest 25%	$3,266	$26
CONTINUING EDUCATION	Highest 25%	$999	$753
	Average	$595	$546
	Lowest 25%	–	–
TOTAL BENEFITS	Highest 25%	$14,579	$9,278
	Average	$10,360	$6,539
	Lowest 25%	$5,481	$3,899
TOTAL COMPENSATION AND BENEFIT		Male	Female
	Highest 25%	$79,500	$56,739
	Average	$71,494	$55,593
	Lowest 25%	$54,600	$37,800
NUMBER OF RESPONDENTS		131	38

– *Not enough responses to provide meaningful data*

TABLE 8-9: ANNUAL COMPENSATION OF ADULT MINISTRY DIRECTOR BY EDUCATION

CHARACTERISTICS	EDUCATION			
	< than Bachelor	Bachelor	Master	Doctorate
AVERAGE SUNDAY AM WORSHIP ATTENDANCE	1,106	1,234	1,205	1,209
AVERAGE CHURCH INCOME	$1,903,173	$2,320,482	$2,367,372	$2,440,228
AVERAGE # of YEARS EMPLOYED	7	8	5	7
AVERAGE # of WEEKS OF PAID VACATION	3	3	3	3
% COLLEGE GRADUATE OR HIGHER	–	100%	100%	100%
% WHO RECEIVE AUTO REIMBURSEMENT	70%	63%	73%	90%
% ORDAINED	64%	68%	75%	91%
AVERAGE % SALARY INCREASE THIS YEAR	5%	4%	5%	3%

COMPENSATION		< than Bachelor	Bachelor	Master	Doctorate
BASE SALARY:	Highest 25%	$42,841	$50,943	$46,725	$60,000
	Average	$33,184	$42,371	$39,839	$42,511
	Lowest 25%	$21,741	$24,001	$25,001	$31,421
HOUSING:	Highest 25%	$21,599	$26,906	$27,499	$31,199
	Average	$13,630	$15,336	$17,153	$20,917
	Lowest 25%	–	–	–	$12,402
PARSONAGE:	Highest 25%	–	–	–	–
	Average	$873	$651	$1,313	$6,937
	Lowest 25%	–	–	–	–
TOTAL COMPENSATION	Highest 25%	$58,000	$60,747	$61,800	$93,804
	Average	$47,687	$58,358	$58,306	$70,365
	Lowest 25%	$39,581	$42,099	$44,327	$53,550

– Not enough responses to provide meaningful data

TABLE 8-9: ANNUAL COMPENSATION OF ADULT MINISTRY DIRECTOR BY EDUCATION

BENEFITS		EDUCATION			
		< than Bachelor	Bachelor	Master	Doctorate
RETIREMENT:	Highest 25%	$1,700	$3,600	$5,050	$5,919
	Average	$778	$2,129	$2,780	$3,045
	Lowest 25%	–	–	–	–
LIFE INSURANCE:	Highest 25%	$121	–	–	–
	Average	–	$185	$247	–
	Lowest 25%	–	–	–	–
HEALTH INSURANCE:	Highest 25%	$5,951	$9,599	$10,127	$7,199
	Average	$3,337	$6,569	$7,342	$4,663
	Lowest 25%	–	$1,501	$4,055	–
CONTINUING EDUCATION	Highest 25%	$994	$989	$999	$894
	Average	$555	$496	$712	$400
	Lowest 25%	–	–	–	–
TOTAL BENEFITS	Highest 25%	$6,808	$13,685	$14,583	$9,166
	Average	$4,723	$9,379	$11,081	$8,160
	Lowest 25%	$601	$5,201	$6,631	$3,628
TOTAL COMPENSATION AND BENEFIT		< than Bachelor	Bachelor	Master	Doctorate
	Highest 25%	$70,100	$76,840	$77,258	$93,900
	Average	$52,410	$67,737	$69,387	$78,525
	Lowest 25%	$41,523	$47,000	$51,201	$61,483
NUMBER OF RESPONDENTS		11	63	67	11

— Not enough responses to provide meaningful data

TABLE 8-10: ANNUAL COMPENSATION OF ADULT MINISTRY DIRECTOR BY YEARS EMPLOYED

CHARACTERISTICS	YEARS EMPLOYED			
	< 6 years	6-10 years	11-15 years	Over 15 years
AVERAGE SUNDAY AM WORSHIP ATTENDANCE	1,135	1,256	1,770	1,280
AVERAGE CHURCH INCOME	$2,203,133	$2,282,447	$3,406,613	$3,241,973
AVERAGE # of YEARS EMPLOYED	2	8	13	24
AVERAGE # of WEEKS OF PAID VACATION	3	4	4	4
% COLLEGE GRADUATE OR HIGHER	92%	100%	70%	93%
% WHO RECEIVE AUTO REIMBURSEMENT	65%	77%	73%	62%
% ORDAINED	71%	77%	73%	69%
AVERAGE % SALARY INCREASE THIS YEAR	5%	3%	6%	3%

COMPENSATION		< 6 years	6-10 years	11-15 years	Over 15 years
BASE SALARY:	Highest 25%	$48,500	$45,000	$47,533	$55,613
	Average	$38,658	$41,772	$42,094	$44,473
	Lowest 25%	$23,881	$23,488	$33,245	$34,754
HOUSING:	Highest 25%	$27,331	$30,001	$29,574	$23,200
	Average	$16,744	$18,472	$16,712	$12,822
	Lowest 25%	–	–	–	–
PARSONAGE:	Highest 25%	–	–	–	–
	Average	$891	$3,030	–	–
	Lowest 25%	–	–	–	–
TOTAL COMPENSATION	Highest 25%	$61,300	$61,928	$63,306	$63,634
	Average	$56,292	$63,274	$58,806	$57,295
	Lowest 25%	$40,801	$45,088	$46,001	$42,473

— *Not enough responses to provide meaningful data*

TABLE 8-10: ANNUAL COMPENSATION OF ADULT MINISTRY DIRECTOR BY YEARS EMPLOYED

		YEARS EMPLOYED			
BENEFITS		< 6 years	6-10 years	11-15 years	Over 15 years
RETIREMENT:	Highest 25%	$3,554	$5,400	$3,400	$5,459
	Average	$2,004	$2,815	$2,610	$2,640
	Lowest 25%	–	–	$300	–
LIFE INSURANCE:	Highest 25%	–	$154	$397	–
	Average	$206	$149	$180	$136
	Lowest 25%	–	–	–	–
HEALTH INSURANCE:	Highest 25%	$9,601	$9,900	$9,748	$11,690
	Average	$6,659	$6,123	$4,688	$6,448
	Lowest 25%	$2,041	$927	$273	$1,910
CONTINUING EDUCATION	Highest 25%	$997	$1,094	$994	–
	Average	$607	$642	$591	$259
	Lowest 25%	–	–	–	–
TOTAL BENEFITS	Highest 25%	$13,685	$14,366	$12,450	$13,687
	Average	$9,477	$9,730	$8,069	$9.484
	Lowest 25%	$4,177	$4,499	$3,901	$3,972
TOTAL COMPENSATION AND BENEFIT		< 6 years	6-10 years	11-15 years	Over 15 years
	Highest 25%	$76,840	$76,108	$76,895	$78,877
	Average	$65,769	$73,004	$66,875	$66,779
	Lowest 25%	$47,130	$52,188	$47,951	$46,445
NUMBER OF RESPONDENTS		95	43	11	16

— Not enough responses to provide meaningful data

153

TABLE 8-11: ANNUAL COMPENSATION OF ADULT MINISTRY DIRECTOR BY DENOMINATION

CHARACTERISTICS	DENOMINATION					
	Assemblies of God	Baptist	Independent/ Nondenom	Lutheran	Methodist	Presbyterian
AVERAGE SUNDAY AM WORSHIP ATTENDANCE	1,165	1,267	1,271	549	917	871
AVERAGE CHURCH INCOME	$1,995,931	$2,922,590	$1,959,153	$1,583,698	$1,547,091	$2,249,410
AVERAGE # of YEARS EMPLOYED	9	7	6	9	8	5
AVERAGE # of WEEKS OF PAID VACATION	3	3	3	–	3	3
% COLLEGE GRADUATE OR HIGHER	88%	98%	86%	–	100%	94%
% WHO RECEIVE AUTO REIMBURSEMENT	75%	71%	53%	–	60%	76%
% ORDAINED	100%	83%	83%	38%	33%	44%
AVERAGE % SALARY INCREASE THIS YEAR	4%	4%	6%	–	3%	4%

COMPENSATION		Assemblies of God	Baptist	Independent/ Nondenom	Lutheran	Methodist	Presbyterian
BASE SALARY:	Highest 25%	$36,442	$50,400	$44,789	$46,863	$42,598	–
	Average	$24,563	$46,028	$33,161	$37,882	$37,191	$56,506
	Lowest 25%	$17,294	$26,524	$21,050	$26,464	$28,500	$31,000
HOUSING:	Highest 25%	$31,760	$29,998	$24,759	$27,275	$3,600	$20,000
	Average	$24,378	$21,032	$16,624	$16,869	$3,017	$8,387
	Lowest 25%	$20,200	$15,002	–	–	–	–
PARSONAGE:	Highest 25%	–	–	–	–	–	–
	Average	$1,200	$900	–	–	$1,000	–
	Lowest 25%	–	–	–	–	–	–
TOTAL COMPENSATION	Highest 25%	$57,794	$72,250	$58,971	$69,739	$52,541	–
	Average	$50,140	$67,961	$49,785	$54,751	$41,207	$64,893
	Lowest 25%	$45,794	$48,001	$39,290	$41,016	$31,310	$44,326

– Not enough responses to provide meaningful data

TABLE 8-11: ANNUAL COMPENSATION OF ADULT MINISTRY DIRECTOR BY DENOMINATION

BENEFITS		DENOMINATION					
		Assemblies of God	Baptist	Independent/ Nondenom	Lutheran	Methodist	Presbyterian
RETIREMENT:	Highest 25%	$3,091	$5,919	$1,365	$4,023	$2,678	$4,000
	Average	$1,846	$3,577	$951	$2,103	$2,258	$2,383
	Lowest 25%	–	–	–	–	$193	–
LIFE INSURANCE:	Highest 25%	–	–	$120	–	–	–
	Average	–	$296	–	–	–	$474
	Lowest 25%	–	–	–	–	–	–
HEALTH INSURANCE:	Highest 25%	$10,632	$8,776	$10,962	$14,294	$6,368	$12,308
	Average	$5,639	$5,587	$6,805	$8,000	$3,941	$9,049
	Lowest 25%	$1,028	$848	$3,240	$3,263	–	$6,000
CONTINUING EDUCATION	Highest 25%	$1,000	$744	$1,008	$1,800	$504	$1,008
	Average	$500	$399	$686	$1,300	$304	$696
	Lowest 25%	–	–	–	–	–	–
TOTAL BENEFITS	Highest 25%	$11,628	$14,099	$14,092	$17,544	$9,223	$17,840
	Average	$8,028	$9,859	$8,517	$11,412	$6,503	$12,603
	Lowest 25%	$2,834	$4,801	$3,600	$4,808	$2,250	$7,862
TOTAL COMPENSATION AND BENEFIT		Assemblies of God	Baptist	Independent/ Nondenom	Lutheran	Methodist	Presbyterian
	Highest 25%	$67,736	$86,271	$71,965	$83,948	$59,874	–
	Average	$58,169	$77,820	$58,302	$66,164	$47,710	$77,496
	Lowest 25%	$52,151	$55,075	$47,250	$45,823	$35,210	$52,188
NUMBER OF RESPONDENTS		8	47	44	8	12	18

– Not enough responses to provide meaningful data

155

TABLE 8-12: AVERAGE COMPENSATION PACKAGE FOR ADULT MINISTRY DIRECTOR*

	Overall	Base Salary Only	No Base Salary	Base Salary and Parsonage	Base Salary and Housing	Base Salary and Parsonage and Housing
	ADULT MINISTRY DIRECTORS WHO RECIEVE...					
BASE SALARY	$40,511	$49,701		–	$37,332	–
PARSONAGE**	$1,257		–	–		–
HOUSING ALLOWANCE	$16,512		–		$24,799	–
TOTAL COMPENSATION PACKAGE	$58,280	$49,701	–	–	$62,131	–
NUMBER OF RESPONDENTS	171	53	2	3	109	4

*All $ values are annual averages
**Parsonage = Rental value of parsonage plus allowance
– Not enough responses to provide meaningful data

For an explanation of the Average Compensation Table, please refer to Chapter 1.

TABLE 8-13: COMPENSATION OF PART-TIME ADULT MINISTRY DIRECTOR BY WORSHIP ATTENDANCE

CHARACTERISTICS	WORSHIP ATTENDANCE					
	100 or less	101 - 300	301 - 500	501 - 750	751 - 1,000	Over 1,000
AVERAGE SUNDAY AM WORSHIP ATTENDANCE	–	227	433	–	–	–
AVERAGE CHURCH INCOME	–	$544,980	$968,281	–	–	–
AVERAGE # of YEARS EMPLOYED	–	5	6	–	–	–
AVERAGE # of WEEKS OF PAID VACATION	–	–	3	–	–	–
% COLLEGE GRADUATE OR HIGHER	–	77%	91%	–	–	–
% WHO RECEIVE AUTO REIMBURSEMENT	–	56%	54%	–	–	–
% ORDAINED	–	33%	50%	–	–	–
AVERAGE % SALARY INCREASE THIS YEAR	–	6%	5%	–	–	–
HOURLY RATES						
AVERAGE BASE RATE		$9.44	$8.65			
ANNUAL COMPENSATION						
AVERAGE BASE SALARY:	–	$10,331	$15,433	–	–	–
AVERAGE HOUSING:	–	–	$1,250	–	–	–
AVERAGE PARSONAGE:	–	–	$833	–	–	–
AVERAGE TOTAL COMPENSATION	–	$10,362	$17,517	–	–	–
ANNUAL BENEFITS						
AVERAGE RETIREMENT	–	–	$212	–	–	–
AVERAGE LIFE INSURANCE	–	–	–	–	–	–
AVERAGE HEALTH INSURANCE	–	–	–	–	–	–
AVERAGE CONTINUING EDUCATION	–	$196	$254	–	–	–
AVERAGE TOTAL BENEFITS	–	$281	$489	–	–	–
ANNUAL COMPENSATION & BENEFIT						
AVERAGE	–	$11,530	$18,005	–	–	–
NUMBER OF RESPONDENTS	0	13	24	5	6	6

– Not enough responses to provide meaningful data

TABLE 8-14: COMPENSATION OF PART-TIME ADULT MINISTRY DIRECTOR BY CHURCH INCOME

CHARACTERISTICS	CHURCH INCOME				
	$250 K & Under	$251 - $500K	$501 - $750K	$751K - $1M	Over $1 Million
AVERAGE SUNDAY AM WORSHIP ATTENDANCE	–	269	468	443	886
AVERAGE CHURCH INCOME	–	$395,907	$640,148	$903,480	$1,914,953
AVERAGE # of YEARS EMPLOYED	–	5	7	6	4
AVERAGE # of WEEKS OF PAID VACATION	–	–	–	–	3
% COLLEGE GRADUATE OR HIGHER	–	90%	89%	82%	–
% WHO RECEIVE AUTO REIMBURSEMENT	–	–	–	–	65%
% ORDAINED	–	30%	75%	55%	47%
AVERAGE % SALARY INCREASE THIS YEAR	–	8%	–	–	5%
HOURLY RATES					
AVERAGE BASE RATE		$10.23	–	$13.51	$6.86
ANNUAL COMPENSATION	$250 K & Under	$251 - $500K	$501 - $750K	$751K - $1M	Over $1 Million
AVERAGE BASE SALARY:	–	$13,360	$13,144	$12,895	$15,748
AVERAGE HOUSING:	–	$1,000	$3,102	–	$3,495
AVERAGE PARSONAGE:	–	–	$2,222	–	–
AVERAGE TOTAL COMPENSATION	–	$14,400	$18,468	$12,895	$19,243
ANNUAL BENEFITS					
AVERAGE RETIREMENT	–	–	$516	–	$1,193
AVERAGE LIFE INSURANCE	–	–	–	–	–
AVERAGE HEALTH INSURANCE	–	–	–	$708	$310
AVERAGE CONTINUING EDUCATION	–	$215	–	$208	$275
AVERAGE TOTAL BENEFITS	–	$215	$600	$953	$1,815
ANNUAL COMPENSATION & BENEFIT					
AVERAGE	–	$14,615	$19,068	$13,848	$21,057
NUMBER OF RESPONDENTS	1	10	9	12	20

– Not enough responses to provide meaningful data

158

9

YOUTH PASTORS

Employment Profile

On average, youth pastors are employed for a shorter period than other staff members. Few congregations under 100 in attendance have a youth pastor. However, a church is more likely to have a full-time youth pastor than any other church staff with the exception of the senior pastor The typical youth pastor is an ordained, male college graduate. The youth pastors surveyed provided the following statistical profile:

	FULL-TIME	PART-TIME
Ordained	68%	21%
Average years employed	4	3
Male	93%	71%
Female	7%	29%
Self-employed (receives 1099)	3%	7%
Church employee (receives W-2)	97%	93%
High school diploma	7%	26%
Associate's degree	4%	4%
Bachelor's degree	65%	59%
Master's degree	24%	12%
Doctorate	1%	0%
Number of respondents	*493*	*171*

Total Compensation plus Benefits Package Analysis

The analysis below is based upon the tables found later in this chapter. The tables present compensation data according to worship attendance, church income, combinations of size and setting, region, gender, education, years employed, and denomination for youth pastors who serve full-time. The final two tables provide data for part-time youth pastors by worship attendance and church income. In this way, the youth pastor's compensation can be viewed from a variety of useful perspectives. The total compensation plus benefits amount found in a separate box at the bottom of each page includes the base salary, housing and/or parsonage amount, life and health insurance payments, retirement contribution, and educational funds.

Full-time staff members. Full-time youth pastors receive benefits quite similar to an Associate pastor and Adult Ministry director but are less likely than the Associate pastors to receive housing or retirement.

Part-time staff members. Approximately 25% of the youth pastors in this sample work part-time. Of this group, 29% were female compared to 7% for full-time youth pastors. Part-time workers often serve in smaller churches (attendance less than 300 and income less than $500,000). Part-time workers receive only a small fraction of the benefits of full-time staff.

COMPENSATION PLUS BENEFITS	FULL TIME	PART TIME
Base salary	98%	94%
Housing	66%	8%
Parsonage	7%	4%
Retirement	52%	5%
Life insurance	30%	3%
Health insurance	73%	8%
Paid vacation	94%	51%
Auto reimbursement	66%	36%
Continuing education	39%	23%

KEY POINTS

➲ **Church attendance impacts the compensation and benefits of youth pastors.** Compensation increases somewhat as church attendance increases. The largest jump in youth pastor compensation and benefit packages is from 101 to 300 and 301 to 500. Those serving in congregations with an attendance less than 500 are below the national average; those in congregations above 500 are generally above the national average. *See Table 9-1.*

➲ **Church income impacts total compensation and benefits.** Compensation increases as church income increases. However, the rate of increase is more slowly for youth pastors than senior or solo pastors and adult ministry or music/choir directors. *See Table 9-2.*

⮥ **Church setting across attendance levels influences compensation of youth pastors.**
Metropolitan churches, representing 16% of youth pastors, provide the best compensation
for youth pastors in congregations with attendance less than 250 and attendance over 1,000.
Suburban churches, representing 45% of youth pastors, provide the best compensation for
them in mid-sized congregations (attendance of 251-1,000). Compensation for youth pastors
in small town or rural areas, making up 39% of those reported, are consistently lower than
those in suburban churches, regardless of attendance. *See Tables 9-3, 9-4, 9-5, 9-6, and 9-7.*

⮥ **The region in which a church is located has some effect on the compensation and
benefits of a youth pastor.** In general, youth pastors in the Pacific or South Atlantic earn
more than those in the other areas. It is interesting to point out that although the youth
pastors in the Pacific region earn the highest compensation, they serve in smaller churches
than five out of the eight regions we looked at. *See Table 9-8.*

⮥ **On average, total compensation and benefits packages are significantly lower
for female youth pastors and than male youth pastors.** Female youth pastors, making
up 7% of all youth pastors, earn less than their male counterparts; however, some of the
difference is because women work in significantly smaller churches than men. The disparity
in compensation and benefit package, where women receive significantly less than men, are
mainly in the areas of housing and health insurance. *See Table 9-9.*

⮥ **Educational achievement impacts compensation levels of youth pastors, especially
for those with a graduate degree.** Church size is playing a part in the compensation
and benefit packages of youth pastors across education levels. In general, the higher the
education level, the larger the church (both in attendance and income), resulting in larger
compensation.89% of the youth pastors have a bachelor's degree or higher. Yet, average
compensation for those with a bachelor's degree is below the national average and similar
to youth pastors who do not have a bachelor's degree. Having a graduate degree results in
significant increases in compensation. *See Table 9-10.*

⮥ **Tenure impacts compensation levels of youth pastors.** Compensation for youth
pastors consistently increases as years employed increases. Over 94% of youth pastors serve
for less than ten years with 74% serving less than five years. There is also some relationship
with tenure and church size where less experienced youth pastors serve in generally smaller
churches than more experienced youth pastors. *See Table 9-11.*

⮥ **The church's denominational affiliation has partial effect on the compensation
and benefits package of the youth pastor.** The compensation and benefits packages of all
but two denominations were below the national average. 68% of youth pastors belonged to
Baptist and Independent/Nondenominational churches, whose youth pastors made just above
the national average. *See Table 9-12.*

⊃ **In general, part-time youth pastors receive compensation closely aligned with part-time adult ministry directors.** Most serve in congregations with an attendance under 300 people and less than $500,000 in church income. Similar to full-time youth pastors, part-time youth pastors serving in larger churches earn more than those serving in smaller churches. However, not surprisingly, part-time youth pastors receive fewer fringe benefits than full-time youth pastors. *See Tables 9-14 and 9-15.*

Ten Year Compensation & Benefits Trend: National Average for Youth Pastors

FULL TIME

1997	$36,968
1998	$37,918
1999	$39,691
2000	$42,561
2001	$43,288
2002	$45,043
2003	$47,058
2004	$47,302
2005	$50,371
2006	$51,640

TABLE 9-1: ANNUAL COMPENSATION OF YOUTH PASTOR BY WORSHIP ATTENDANCE

CHARACTERISTICS		WORSHIP ATTENDANCE					
		100 or less	101-300	301-500	501-750	751-1000	Over 1000
AVERAGE SUNDAY AM WORSHIP ATTENDANCE		–	217	416	616	890	1,936
AVERAGE CHURCH INCOME		–	$434,255	$810,942	$1,255,467	$1,838,197	$3,606,486
AVERAGE # of YEARS EMPLOYED		–	4	4	4	5	5
AVERAGE # of WEEKS OF PAID VACATION		–	2	3	3	3	3
% COLLEGE GRADUATE OR HIGHER		–	85%	89%	89%	91%	94%
% WHO RECEIVE AUTO REIMBURSEMENT		–	69%	75%	72%	74%	64%
% ORDAINED		–	59%	69%	68%	65%	80%
AVERAGE % SALARY INCREASE THIS YEAR		–	5%	4%	4%	4%	5%
COMPENSATION		100 or less	101-300	301-500	501-750	751-1000	Over 1000
BASE SALARY:	Highest 25%	–	$32,108	$35,000	$38,978	$42,000	$42,000
	Average	–	$26,000	$29,041	$31,474	$34,997	$34,108
	Lowest 25%	–	$18,757	$22,550	$22,224	$29,449	$24,863
HOUSING:	Highest 25%	–	$16,000	$20,514	$20,630	$20,000	$25,000
	Average	–	$8,141	$13,168	$11,769	$12,044	$17,509
	Lowest 25%	–	–	–	–	–	$4,000
PARSONAGE:	Highest 25%	–	–	–	–	–	–
	Average	–	$1,599	$1,661	$1,002	$1,686	$266
	Lowest 25%	–	–	–	–	–	–
TOTAL COMPENSATION	Highest 25%	–	$40,085	$52,000	$51,450	$55,000	$58,448
	Average	–	$35,740	$43,871	$44,245	$48,727	$51,884
	Lowest 25%	–	$30,000	$33,279	$36,900	$36,006	$41,640

– Not enough responses to provide meaningful data

TABLE 9-1: ANNUAL COMPENSATION OF YOUTH PASTOR BY WORSHIP ATTENDANCE

BENEFITS		WORSHIP ATTENDANCE					
		100 or less	101-300	301-500	501-750	751-1000	Over 1000
RETIREMENT:	Highest 25%	–	$1,715	$2,600	$3,000	$2,400	$3,000
	Average	–	$991	$1,440	$1,898	$1,713	$1,805
	Lowest 25%	–	–	–	–	–	–
LIFE INSURANCE:	Highest 25%	–	–	–	$190	–	$166
	Average	–	–	–	$163	$118	$155
	Lowest 25%	–	–	–	–	–	–
HEALTH INSURANCE:	Highest 25%	–	$8,000	$8,000	$9,822	$9,000	$10,114
	Average	–	$4,638	$4,758	$6,167	$5,309	$6,781
	Lowest 25%	–	–	–	$2,400	–	$3,000
CONTINUING EDUCATION	Highest 25%	–	$502	$804	$1,001	$998	$998
	Average	–	$386	$502	$632	$442	$669
	Lowest 25%	–	–	–	–	–	–
TOTAL BENEFITS	Highest 25%	–	$9,995	$10,109	$12,397	$11,200	$13,617
	Average	–	$6,064	$6,751	$8,861	$7,582	$9,411
	Lowest 25%	–	$650	$1,742	$5,062	$2,691	$5,584
TOTAL COMPENSATION AND BENEFIT		100 or less	101-300	301-500	501-750	751-1000	Over 1000
	Highest 25%	–	$47,290	$60,361	$59,686	$67,703	$71,000
	Average	–	$41,804	$50,830	$53,105	$56,309	$61,295
	Lowest 25%	–	$32,861	$40,270	$43,830	$42,120	$47,514
NUMBER OF RESPONDENTS		6	116	106	92	53	106

– Not enough responses to provide meaningful data

165

TABLE 9-2: ANNUAL COMPENSATION OF YOUTH PASTOR BY CHURCH INCOME

CHARACTERISTICS		CHURCH INCOME				
		$250K & under	$251K-$500K	$501K-$750K	$751K-$1M	Over $1 Million
AVERAGE SUNDAY AM WORSHIP ATTENDANCE		228	240	409	472	1,238
AVERAGE CHURCH INCOME		$191,481	$372,850	$617,779	$886,414	$2,480,977
AVERAGE # of YEARS EMPLOYED		3	4	5	4	5
AVERAGE # of WEEKS OF PAID VACATION		3	2	3	3	3
% COLLEGE GRADUATE OR HIGHER		81%	86%	95%	86%	91%
% WHO RECEIVE AUTO REIMBURSEMENT		70%	70%	65%	78%	69%
% ORDAINED		48%	64%	57%	65%	75%
AVERAGE % SALARY INCREASE THIS YEAR		5%	4%	4%	4%	4%

COMPENSATION		$250K & under	$251K-$500K	$501K-$750K	$751K-$1M	Over 1 Million
BASE SALARY:	Highest 25%	$30,000	$32,216	$34,880	$40,000	$40,000
	Average	$26,317	$26,877	$29,472	$30,618	$32,449
	Lowest 25%	$19,068	$20,500	$22,000	$22,622	$23,503
HOUSING:	Highest 25%	$10,001	$15,001	$18,000	$20,056	$24,000
	Average	$6,371	$8,990	$10,156	$11,937	$15,130
	Lowest 25%	–	–	–	–	–
PARSONAGE:	Highest 25%	–	$34	$29	$33	–
	Average	$884	$1,240	$821	$1,664	$803
	Lowest 25%	–	–	–	–	–
TOTAL COMPENSATION	Highest 25%	$38,808	$42,200	$49,000	$52,113	$56,197
	Average	$33,572	$37,107	$40,449	$44,220	$48,382
	Lowest 25%	$25,800	$31,000	$32,560	$33,059	$38,126

– Not enough responses to provide meaningful data

TABLE 9-2: ANNUAL COMPENSATION OF YOUTH PASTOR BY CHURCH INCOME

BENEFITS		CHURCH INCOME				
		$250K & under	$251K-$500K	$501K-$750K	$751K-$1M	Over $1 Million
RETIREMENT:	Highest 25%	$1,200	$1,630	$2,630	$2,199	$3,233
	Average	$702	$938	$1,471	$1,144	$1,931
	Lowest 25%	–	–	–	–	–
LIFE INSURANCE:	Highest 25%	–	–	–	–	$138
	Average	–	–	–	–	$130
	Lowest 25%	–	–	–	–	–
HEALTH INSURANCE:	Highest 25%	$8,400	$8,000	$10,000	$8,983	$9,741
	Average	$4,886	$4,857	$5,390	$4,721	$6,207
	Lowest 25%	–	–	–	–	$2,348
CONTINUING EDUCATION	Highest 25%	$599	$698	$702	$775	$1,000
	Average	$424	$497	$348	$489	$635
	Lowest 25%	–	–	–	–	–
TOTAL BENEFITS	Highest 25%	$11,500	$10,000	$10,905	$10,050	$12,388
	Average	$6,052	$6,344	$7,247	$6,449	$8,902
	Lowest 25%	$1,200	$500	$1,300	$2,325	$5,000
TOTAL COMPENSATION AND BENEFIT		$250K & under	$251K-$500K	$501K-$750K	$751K-$1M	Over 1 Million
	Highest 25%	$46,489	$49,500	$57,896	$60,099	$67,873
	Average	$39,624	$43,452	$47,696	$51,013	$57,284
	Lowest 25%	$29,700	$36,000	$37,250	$39.140	$44,768
NUMBER OF RESPONDENTS		29	82	58	64	236

– Not enough responses to provide meaningful data

167

TABLE 9-3: ANNUAL COMPENSATION OF YOUTH PASTOR BY CHURCH SETTING & SIZE

ATTENDANCE 250 & UNDER		Metropolitan city	Suburb of large city	Small town or rural city	Farming area
AVERAGE SUNDAY AM WORSHIP ATTENDANCE		200	194	184	–
AVERAGE CHURCH INCOME		$348,213	$473,998	$291,412	–
AVERAGE # of YEARS EMPLOYED		4	3	4	–
AVERAGE # of WEEKS OF PAID VACATION		2	2	3	–
% COLLEGE GRADUATE OR HIGHER		70%	94%	83%	–
% WHO RECEIVE AUTO REIMBURSEMENT		80%	62%	59%	–
% ORDAINED		56%	56%	58%	–
AVERAGE % SALARY INCREASE THIS YEAR		4%	5%	5%	–

COMPENSATION		Metropolitan city	Suburb of large city	Small town or rural city	Farming area
BASE SALARY:	Highest 25%	$30,200	$35,500	$29,852	–
	Average	$24,678	$26,837	$24,739	–
	Lowest 25%	$18,000	$20,250	$18,001	–
HOUSING:	Highest 25%	$18,000	$12,336	$16,008	–
	Average	$11,712	$5,495	$8,181	–
	Lowest 25%	–	–	–	–
PARSONAGE:	Highest 25%	–	–	–	–
	Average	–	$3,125	$1,377	–
	Lowest 25%	–	–	–	–
TOTAL COMPENSATION	Highest 25%	$40,000	$40,950	$39,999	–
	Average	$36,991	$35,457	$34,297	–
	Lowest 25%	$30,200	$29,998	$28,919	–

– Not enough responses to provide meaningful data

TABLE 9-3: ANNUAL COMPENSATION OF YOUTH PASTOR BY CHURCH SETTING & SIZE

BENEFITS		CHURCH SETTING			
		Metropoli-tan city	Suburb of large city	Small town or rural city	Farming area
RETIREMENT:	Highest 25%	$1,200	$1,500	$2,100	–
	Average	$764	$905	$981	–
	Lowest 25%	–	–	–	–
LIFE INSURANCE:	Highest 25%	–	–	–	–
	Average	–	–	–	–
	Lowest 25%	–	–	–	–
HEALTH INSURANCE:	Highest 25%	$8,000	$8,381	$8,003	–
	Average	$5,022	$4,963	$4,635	–
	Lowest 25%	–	–	–	–
CONTINUING EDUCATION	Highest 25%	$494	–	$498	–
	Average	$220	$613	$281	–
	Lowest 25%	–	–	–	–
TOTAL BENEFITS	Highest 25%	$9,760	$10,775	$10,304	–
	Average	$6,025	$6,595	$5,909	–
	Lowest 25%	$1,200	–	$996	–
TOTAL COMPENSATION AND BENEFIT		Metropoli-tan city	Suburb of large city	Small town or rural city	Farming area
	Highest 25%	$49,500	$49,575	$47,002	–
	Average	$43,016	$42,052	$40,206	–
	Lowest 25%	$32,583	$30,001	$31,498	–
NUMBER OF RESPONDENTS		10	36	45	2

– Not enough responses to provide meaningful data

169

TABLE 9-4: ANNUAL COMPENSATION OF YOUTH PASTOR BY CHURCH SETTING & SIZE

ATTENDANCE 251 - 500	CHURCH SETTING			
	Metropoli-tan city	Suburb of large city	Small town or rural city	Farming area
AVERAGE SUNDAY AM WORSHIP ATTENDANCE	411	388	381	–
AVERAGE CHURCH INCOME	$943,106	$817,784	$658,847	–
AVERAGE # of YEARS EMPLOYED	4	4	4	–
AVERAGE # of WEEKS OF PAID VACATION	3	3	3	–
% COLLEGE GRADUATE OR HIGHER	88%	86%	88%	–
% WHO RECEIVE AUTO REIMBURSEMENT	81%	68%	84%	–
% ORDAINED	71%	75%	59%	–
AVERAGE % SALARY INCREASE THIS YEAR	5%	4%	4%	–

COMPENSATION		Metropoli-tan city	Suburb of large city	Small town or rural city	Farming area
BASE SALARY:	Highest 25%	$34,996	$35,006	$34,184	–
	Average	$30,203	$26,971	$29,189	–
	Lowest 25%	$25,004	$18,856	$20,531	–
HOUSING:	Highest 25%	$24,000	$24,001	$17,750	–
	Average	$10,531	$15,432	$10,271	–
	Lowest 25%	–	–	–	–
PARSONAGE:	Highest 25%	–	–	–	–
	Average	–	$3,011	$358	–
	Lowest 25%	–	$0	$0	–
TOTAL COMPENSATION	Highest 25%	$46,000	$55,000	$45,987	–
	Average	$40,734	$45,414	$39,818	–
	Lowest 25%	$28,000	$35,700	$32,750	–

— Not enough responses to provide meaningful data

TABLE 9-4: ANNUAL COMPENSATION OF YOUTH PASTOR BY CHURCH SETTING & SIZE

BENEFITS		CHURCH SETTING			
		Metropolitan city	Suburb of large city	Small town or rural city	Farming area
RETIREMENT:	Highest 25%	$2,600	$1,443	$3,018	–
	Average	$1,374	$1,034	$1,759	–
	Lowest 25%	–	–	–	–
LIFE INSURANCE:	Highest 25%	–	–	–	–
	Average	–	–	–	–
	Lowest 25%	–	–	–	–
HEALTH INSURANCE:	Highest 25%	$6,000	$8,271	$8,176	–
	Average	$4,077	$4,669	$4,947	–
	Lowest 25%	–	–	–	–
CONTINUING EDUCATION	Highest 25%	$1,183	$863	$700	–
	Average	$593	$509	$401	–
	Lowest 25%	–	–	–	–
TOTAL BENEFITS	Highest 25%	$9,500	$10,057	$11,287	–
	Average	$6,064	$6,292	$7,135	–
	Lowest 25%	$2,251	$1,000	$1,710	–
TOTAL COMPENSATION AND BENEFIT		Metropolitan city	Suburb of large city	Small town or rural city	Farming area
	Highest 25%	$61,718	$60,362	$54,475	–
	Average	$48,020	$51,705	$46,953	–
	Lowest 25%	$33,020	$41,699	$38,201	–
NUMBER OF RESPONDENTS		18	53	60	1

– Not enough responses to provide meaningful data

171

TABLE 9-5: ANNUAL COMPENSATION OF YOUTH PASTOR BY CHURCH SETTING & SIZE

ATTENDANCE 501 - 750	CHURCH SETTING			
	Metropolitan city	Suburb of large city	Small town or rural city	Farming area
AVERAGE SUNDAY AM WORSHIP ATTENDANCE	619	626	595	–
AVERAGE CHURCH INCOME	$1,327,047	$1,242,260	$1,322,391	–
AVERAGE # of YEARS EMPLOYED	3	5	4	–
AVERAGE # of WEEKS OF PAID VACATION	3	3	3	–
% COLLEGE GRADUATE OR HIGHER	–	98%	73%	–
% WHO RECEIVE AUTO REIMBURSEMENT	63%	65%	79%	–
% ORDAINED	63%	66%	74%	–
AVERAGE % SALARY INCREASE THIS YEAR	–	4%	5%	–

COMPENSATION		Metropolitan city	Suburb of large city	Small town or rural city	Farming area
BASE SALARY:	Highest 25%	$33,610	$39,000	$38,536	–
	Average	$25,762	$31,322	$32,112	–
	Lowest 25%	$16,762	$21,995	$27,863	–
HOUSING:	Highest 25%	$20,550	$23,981	$18,500	–
	Average	$15,422	$12,288	$11,361	–
	Lowest 25%	$8,750	$14	$12	–
PARSONAGE:	Highest 25%	–	–	–	–
	Average	–	$972	$422	–
	Lowest 25%	–	–	–	–
TOTAL COMPENSATION	Highest 25%	$46,926	$51,599	$51,150	–
	Average	$41,184	$44,582	$43,895	–
	Lowest 25%	$35,562	$38,136	$36,080	–

– Not enough responses to provide meaningful data

TABLE 9-5: ANNUAL COMPENSATION OF YOUTH PASTOR BY CHURCH SETTING & SIZE

BENEFITS		CHURCH SETTING			
		Metropoli-tan city	Suburb of large city	Small town or rural city	Farming area
RETIREMENT:	Highest 25%	$3,890	$3,000	$2,833	–
	Average	$2,169	$1,918	$1,601	–
	Lowest 25%	–	–	–	–
LIFE INSURANCE:	Highest 25%	$160	$200	–	–
	Average	$115	$160	$175	–
	Lowest 25%	–	–	–	–
HEALTH INSURANCE:	Highest 25%	$7,837	$10,631	$9,318	–
	Average	$5,052	$6,929	$5,114	–
	Lowest 25%	$482	$3,025	$1,125	–
CONTINUING EDUCATION	Highest 25%	$921	$1,008	$875	–
	Average	$480	$759	$477	–
	Lowest 25%	–	–	–	–
TOTAL BENEFITS	Highest 25%	$9,567	$13,632	$11,425	–
	Average	$7,816	$9,765	$7,367	–
	Lowest 25%	$4,186	$5,693	$3,588	
TOTAL COMPENSATION AND BENEFIT		Metropoli-tan city	Suburb of large city	Small town or rural city	Farming area
	Highest 25%	$51,111	$62,455	$57,421	–
	Average	$49,000	$54,348	$51,262	–
	Lowest 25%	$42,378	$46,811	$42,204	–
NUMBER OF RESPONDENTS		8	47	32	4

– Not enough responses to provide meaningful data

TABLE 9-6: ANNUAL COMPENSATION OF YOUTH PASTOR BY CHURCH SETTING & SIZE

ATTENDANCE 751 - 1,000		CHURCH SETTING			
		Metropoli-tan city	Suburb of large city	Small town or rural city	Farming area
AVERAGE SUNDAY AM WORSHIP ATTENDANCE		907	857	898	–
AVERAGE CHURCH INCOME		$1,950,485	$1,688,619	$1,895,046	–
AVERAGE # of YEARS EMPLOYED		5	6	5	–
AVERAGE # of WEEKS OF PAID VACATION		3	3	3	–
% COLLEGE GRADUATE OR HIGHER		88%	94%	91%	–
% WHO RECEIVE AUTO REIMBURSEMENT		72%	65%	91%	–
% ORDAINED		60%	67%	75%	–
AVERAGE % SALARY INCREASE THIS YEAR		4%	4%	4%	–

COMPENSATION		Metropoli-tan city	Suburb of large city	Small town or rural city	Farming area
BASE SALARY:	Highest 25%	$40,000	$50,960	$37,906	–
	Average	$33,311	$41,304	$32,855	–
	Lowest 25%	$24,472	$35,048	$28,999	–
HOUSING:	Highest 25%	$26,720	$19,000	$17,802	–
	Average	$14,858	$8,894	$11,410	–
	Lowest 25%	–	–	$7,998	–
PARSONAGE:	Highest 25%	–	–	–	–
	Average	–	$2,222	–	–
	Lowest 25%	–	–	–	–
TOTAL COMPENSATION	Highest 25%	$62,328	$66,014	$49,142	–
	Average	$48,174	$52,420	$44,266	–
	Lowest 25%	$33,753	$39,999	$37,903	–

– Not enough responses to provide meaningful data

TABLE 9-6: ANNUAL COMPENSATION OF YOUTH PASTOR BY CHURCH SETTING & SIZE

BENEFITS		CHURCH SETTING			
		Metropoli-tan city	Suburb of large city	Small town or rural city	Farming area
RETIREMENT:	Highest 25%	$2,150	$2,400	$4,500	–
	Average	$1,432	$1,738	$1,996	–
	Lowest 25%	–	–	–	–
LIFE INSURANCE:	Highest 25%	–	$240	–	–
	Average	–	$159	$182	–
	Lowest 25%	–	–	–	–
HEALTH INSURANCE:	Highest 25%	$6,004	$10,500	$10,692	–
	Average	$4,258	$6,093	$6,078	–
	Lowest 25%	$1,326	–	–	–
CONTINUING EDUCATION	Highest 25%	$800	$992	$1,002	–
	Average	$438	$407	$496	–
	Lowest 25%	–	–	–	–
TOTAL BENEFITS	Highest 25%	$8,724	$11,500	$12,080	–
	Average	$6,152	$8,397	$8,752	–
	Lowest 25%	$3,096	$2,100	$3,750	–
TOTAL COMPENSATION AND BENEFIT		Metropoli-tan city	Suburb of large city	Small town or rural city	Farming area
	Highest 25%	$72,440	$74,800	$62,409	–
	Average	$54,326	$60,817	$53,018	–
	Lowest 25%	$38,806	$48,400	$42,111	–
NUMBER OF RESPONDENTS		20	18	13	0

– Not enough responses to provide meaningful data

175

TABLE 9-7: ANNUAL COMPENSATION OF YOUTH PASTOR BY CHURCH SETTING & SIZE

ATTENDANCE OVER 1,000	CHURCH SETTING			
	Metropolitan city	Suburb of large city	Small town or rural city	Farming area
AVERAGE SUNDAY AM WORSHIP ATTENDANCE	2,326	1,948	1,687	–
AVERAGE CHURCH INCOME	$4,836,000	$3,640,882	$2,832,658	–
AVERAGE # of YEARS EMPLOYED	4	4	6	–
AVERAGE # of WEEKS OF PAID VACATION	3	3	3	–
% COLLEGE GRADUATE OR HIGHER	88%	96%	93%	–
% WHO RECEIVE AUTO REIMBURSEMENT	67%	63%	65%	–
% ORDAINED	72%	82%	81%	–
AVERAGE % SALARY INCREASE THIS YEAR	3%	5%	5%	–

COMPENSATION		Metropolitan city	Suburb of large city	Small town or rural city	Farming area
BASE SALARY:	Highest 25%	$51,095	$42,001	$33,797	–
	Average	$40,461	$35,684	$27,522	–
	Lowest 25%	$31,920	$26,900	$19,409	–
HOUSING:	Highest 25%	$24,950	$25,274	$24,298	–
	Average	$17,291	$18,250	$16,275	–
	Lowest 25%	–	$9,998	$4,002	–
PARSONAGE:	Highest 25%	–	–	$2,474	–
	Average	–	–	$910	–
	Lowest 25%	–	–	–	–
TOTAL COMPENSATION	Highest 25%	$64,000	$59,999	$48,839	–
	Average	$57,752	$53,934	$44,707	–
	Lowest 25%	$42,000	$44,169	$39,999	–

– Not enough responses to provide meaningful data

TABLE 9-7: ANNUAL COMPENSATION OF YOUTH PASTOR BY CHURCH SETTING & SIZE

BENEFITS		CHURCH SETTING			
		Metropolitan city	Suburb of large city	Small town or rural city	Farming area
RETIREMENT:	Highest 25%	$2,890	$3,001	$3,765	–
	Average	$1,955	$1,670	$1,966	–
	Lowest 25%	–	–	–	–
LIFE INSURANCE:	Highest 25%	$204	–	$144	–
	Average	$124	$208	–	–
	Lowest 25%	–	–	–	–
HEALTH INSURANCE:	Highest 25%	$9,500	$10,750	$9,891	–
	Average	$7,236	$6,907	$6,285	–
	Lowest 25%	$4,542	$3,001	$2,297	–
CONTINUING EDUCATION	Highest 25%	$983	–	$1,088	–
	Average	$406	$793	$596	–
	Lowest 25%	–	–	–	–
TOTAL BENEFITS	Highest 25%	$12,377	$13,782	$13,483	–
	Average	$9,721	$9,578	$8,924	–
	Lowest 25%	$7,458	$4,916	$5,124	–
TOTAL COMPENSATION AND BENEFIT		Metropolitan city	Suburb of large city	Small town or rural city	Farming area
	Highest 25%	$76,882	$72,151	$64,314	–
	Average	$67,472	$63,512	$53,631	–
	Lowest 25%	$55,769	$46,899	$44,301	–
NUMBER OF RESPONDENTS		18	57	31	0

– Not enough responses to provide meaningful data

TABLE 9-8: ANNUAL COMPENSATION OF YOUTH PASTOR BY REGION

CHARACTERISTICS		REGION								
		New England	Middle Atlantic	South Atlantic	E-N Central	E-S Central	W-N Central	W-S Central	Moun-tain	Pacific
AVERAGE SUNDAY AM WORSHIP ATTENDANCE		–	565	734	965	810	630	931	972	685
AVERAGE CHURCH INCOME		–	$1,019,715	$1,590,198	$1,555,646	$2,008,258	$1,227,727	$2,093,631	$1,562,459	$1,290,032
AVERAGE # of YEARS EMPLOYED		–	5	4	4	3	5	4	4	4
AVERAGE # of WEEKS OF PAID VACATION		–	3	3	3	2	3	2	3	3
% COLLEGE GRADUATE OR HIGHER		–	92%	93%	88%	97%	84%	87%	90%	88%
% WHO RECEIVE AUTO REIMBURSEMENT		–	77%	75%	83%	61%	75%	49%	70%	61%
% ORDAINED		–	61%	71%	69%	59%	56%	73%	72%	74%
AVERAGE % SALARY INCREASE THIS YEAR		–	4%	4%	5%	4%	4%	5%	5%	5%

COMPENSATION		New England	Middle Atlantic	South Atlantic	E-N Central	E-S Central	W-N Central	W-S Central	Moun-tain	Pacific
BASE SALARY:	Highest 25%	–	$40,000	$38,978	$37,825	$37,000	$35,000	$39,130	$34,450	$36,000
	Average	–	$30,785	$31,791	$30,579	$30,337	$29,029	$31,918	$27,298	$29,229
	Lowest 25%	–	$21,000	$24,829	$22,550	$23,319	$20,900	$26,200	$20,235	$21,294
HOUSING:	Highest 25%	–	$14,000	$24,000	$20,400	$19,200	$17,501	$19,000	$21,148	$24,000
	Average	–	$7,316	$13,927	$12,862	$9,292	$10,535	$11,875	$13,135	$15,311
	Lowest 25%	–	–	–	–	–	–	–	–	–
PARSONAGE:	Highest 25%	–	–	–	–	–	–	–	–	–
	Average	–	$1,434	$417	$1,522	$2,302	$426	$607	$661	$1,745
	Lowest 25%	–	–	–	–	–	–	–	–	–
TOTAL COMPENSATION	Highest 25%	–	$46,800	$55,823	$53,664	$49,939	$48,000	$51,950	$48,000	$55,000
	Average	–	$39,535	$46,136	$44,963	$41,931	$39,991	$44,400	$41,093	$46,284
	Lowest 25%	–	$32,000	$35,262	$35,360	$32,216	$33,000	$33,000	$30,632	$34,008

– Not enough responses to provide meaningful data

TABLE 9-8: ANNUAL COMPENSATION OF YOUTH PASTOR BY REGION

BENEFITS		New England	Middle Atlantic	South Atlantic	E-N Central	E-S Central	W-N Central	W-S Central	Moun-tain	Pacific
RETIREMENT:	Highest 25%	–	$2,630	$3,216	$2,400	$2,300	$3,140	$3,000	$1,200	$2,464
	Average	–	$1,648	$2,100	$1,318	$1,338	$1,679	$1,645	$846	$1,254
	Lowest 25%	–	–	–	–	–	–	–	–	–
LIFE INSURANCE:	Highest 25%	–	–	–	$160	$275	–	–	–	–
	Average	–	–	–	$101	$172	$125	–	$214	–
	Lowest 25%	–	–	–	–	–	–	–	–	–
HEALTH INSURANCE:	Highest 25%	–	$10,000	$8,758	$11,151	$7,435	$9,951	$9,000	$6,461	$8,402
	Average	–	$6,915	$5,525	$6,502	$3,288	$5,389	$5,074	$4,204	$5,549
	Lowest 25%	–	$1,933	–	–	–	–	–	–	$2,400
CONTINUING EDUCATION	Highest 25%	–	$1,001	$1,001	$748	$600	$752	$1,002	$600	$623
	Average	–	$712	$664	$506	$459	$503	$525	$368	$442
	Lowest 25%	–	–	–	–	–	–	–	–	–
TOTAL BENEFITS	Highest 25%	–	$13,000	$13,075	$13,450	$8,136	$12,072	$10,800	$10,070	$10,956
	Average	–	$9,340	$8,376	$8,426	$5,256	$7,696	$7,283	$5,631	$7,323
	Lowest 25%	–	$5,000	$2,766	$3,200	–	$3,752	$3,371	$1,512	$3,270
TOTAL COMPENSATION AND BENEFIT		New England	Middle Atlantic	South Atlantic	E-N Central	E-S Central	W-N Central	W-S Central	Moun-tain	Pacific
	Highest 25%	–	$58,960	$69,046	$63,368	$60,372	$62,054	$61,718	$55,540	$60,884
	Average	–	$48,875	$54,751	$53,390	$47,187	$47,687	$51,683	$46,725	$53,608
	Lowest 25%	–	$40,155	$43,354	$43,857	$36,641	$38,460	$40,101	$36,893	$40,177
NUMBER OF RESPONDENTS		6	38	92	95	34	53	55	38	79

– Not enough responses to provide meaningful data

179

TABLE 9-9: ANNUAL COMPENSATION OF YOUTH PASTOR BY GENDER

CHARACTERISTICS	GENDER	
	Male	Female
AVERAGE SUNDAY AM WORSHIP ATTENDANCE	807	609
AVERAGE CHURCH INCOME	$1,558,848	$1,107,265
AVERAGE # of YEARS EMPLOYED	4	4
AVERAGE # of WEEKS OF PAID VACATION	3	3
% COLLEGE GRADUATE OR HIGHER	89%	93%
% WHO RECEIVE AUTO REIMBURSEMENT	70%	72%
% ORDAINED	71%	31%
AVERAGE % SALARY INCREASE THIS YEAR	4%	5%

COMPENSATION		Male	Female
BASE SALARY:	Highest 25%	$38,000	$35,024
	Average	$30,554	$28,089
	Lowest 25%	$21,886	$25,376
HOUSING:	Highest 25%	$20,515	–
	Average	$13,055	$4,504
	Lowest 25%	–	–
PARSONAGE:	Highest 25%	–	–
	Average	$1,066	$2,424
	Lowest 25%	–	–
TOTAL COMPENSATION	Highest 25%	$52,257	$40,200
	Average	$44,675	$35,017
	Lowest 25%	$35,000	$27,126

– Not enough responses to provide meaningful data

TABLE 9-9: ANNUAL COMPENSATION OF YOUTH PASTOR BY GENDER

BENEFITS		GENDER	
		Male	Female
RETIREMENT:	Highest 25%	$2,640	$2,426
	Average	$1,541	$1,427
	Lowest 25%	–	–
LIFE INSURANCE:	Highest 25%	–	–
	Average	–	$101
	Lowest 25%	–	–
HEALTH INSURANCE:	Highest 25%	$9,500	$7,473
	Average	$5,720	$3,739
	Lowest 25%	–	–
CONTINUING EDUCATION	Highest 25%	$804	$950
	Average	$525	$535
	Lowest 25%	–	–
TOTAL BENEFITS	Highest 25%	$12,000	$10,063
	Average	$7,878	$5,802
	Lowest 25%	$2,800	$934
TOTAL COMPENSATION AND BENEFIT		Male	Female
	Highest 25%	$63,033	$49,200
	Average	$52,601	$40,818
	Lowest 25%	$41,225	$29,997
NUMBER OF RESPONDENTS		454	36

– Not enough responses to provide meaningful data

TABLE 9-10: ANNUAL COMPENSATION OF YOUTH PASTOR BY EDUCATION

CHARACTERISTICS	EDUCATION			
	< than Bachelor	Bachelor	Master	Doctorate
AVERAGE SUNDAY AM WORSHIP ATTENDANCE	650	782	825	–
AVERAGE CHURCH INCOME	$1,346,301	$1,416,038	$1,634,639	–
AVERAGE # of YEARS EMPLOYED	4	4	5	–
AVERAGE # of WEEKS OF PAID VACATION	3	3	3	–
% COLLEGE GRADUATE OR HIGHER	–	100%	100%	–
% WHO RECEIVE AUTO REIMBURSEMENT	61%	69%	77%	–
% ORDAINED	67%	62%	82%	–
AVERAGE % SALARY INCREASE THIS YEAR	5%	4%	4%	–

COMPENSATION		< than Bachelor	Bachelor	Master	Doctorate
BASE SALARY:	Highest 25%	$38,536	$36,400	$39,350	–
	Average	$29,216	$29,680	$32,501	–
	Lowest 25%	$18,678	$21,760	$25,000	–
HOUSING:	Highest 25%	$20,457	$19,740	$24,000	–
	Average	$11,155	$11,327	$15,495	–
	Lowest 25%	–	–	$5,999	–
PARSONAGE:	Highest 25%	–	–	–	–
	Average	$1,638	$1,194	$1,334	–
	Lowest 25%	–	–	–	–
TOTAL COMPENSATION	Highest 25%	$51,494	$49,384	$56,576	–
	Average	$42,009	$42,200	$49,329	–
	Lowest 25%	$33,000	$32,500	$40,200	–

– Not enough responses to provide meaningful data

TABLE 9-10: ANNUAL COMPENSATION OF YOUTH PASTOR BY EDUCATION

BENEFITS		EDUCATION			
		< than Bachelor	Bachelor	Master	Doctorate
RETIREMENT:	Highest 25%	$1,012	$2,200	$4,928	–
	Average	$827	$1,258	$2,642	–
	Lowest 25%	–	–	–	–
LIFE INSURANCE:	Highest 25%	–	–	–	–
	Average	–	–	$150	–
	Lowest 25%	–	–	–	–
HEALTH INSURANCE:	Highest 25%	$10,000	$9,000	$10,128	–
	Average	$5,300	$5,458	$6,361	–
	Lowest 25%	–	–	$1,130	–
CONTINUING EDUCATION	Highest 25%	$400	$901	$999	–
	Average	$320	$501	$639	–
	Lowest 25%	–	–	–	–
TOTAL BENEFITS	Highest 25%	$11,850	$11,197	$14,539	–
	Average	$6,494	$7,300	$9,792	–
	Lowest 25%	$1,436	$2,640	$5,262	–
TOTAL COMPENSATION AND BENEFIT		< than Bachelor	Bachelor	Master	Doctorate
	Highest 25%	$60,360	$59,014	$69,472	–
	Average	$48,503	$49,538	$59,223	–
	Lowest 25%	$34,947	$38,802	$50,300	–
NUMBER OF RESPONDENTS		48	291	109	3

– Not enough responses to provide meaningful data

TABLE 9-11: ANNUAL COMPENSATION OF YOUTH PASTOR BY YEARS EMPLOYED

CHARACTERISTICS		YEARS EMPLOYED			
		< 6 years	6-10 years	11-15 years	Over 15 years
AVERAGE SUNDAY AM WORSHIP ATTENDANCE		709	1,117	825	–
AVERAGE CHURCH INCOME		$1,379,486	$2,026,486	$1,725,119	–
AVERAGE # of YEARS EMPLOYED		2	8	13	–
AVERAGE # of WEEKS OF PAID VACATION		3	3	4	–
% COLLEGE GRADUATE OR HIGHER		89%	91%	95%	–
% WHO RECEIVE AUTO REIMBURSEMENT		70%	70%	65%	–
% ORDAINED		65%	75%	76%	–
AVERAGE % SALARY INCREASE THIS YEAR		4%	4%	4%	–

COMPENSATION		< 6 years	6-10 years	11-15 years	Over 15 years
BASE SALARY:	Highest 25%	$37,000	$36,424	$40,500	–
	Average	$30,140	$29,940	$32,760	–
	Lowest 25%	$22,600	$20,500	$24,863	–
HOUSING:	Highest 25%	$19,999	$23,451	$25,001	–
	Average	$11,048	$16,538	$17,396	–
	Lowest 25%	–	$9,665	–	–
PARSONAGE:	Highest 25%	–	–	–	–
	Average	$1,169	$835	$3,029	–
	Lowest 25%	–	–	–	–
TOTAL COMPENSATION	Highest 25%	$49,939	$54,424	$57,230	–
	Average	$42,358	$47,313	$53,184	–
	Lowest 25%	$32,000	$36,356	$42,000	–

– Not enough responses to provide meaningful data

TABLE 9-11: ANNUAL COMPENSATION OF YOUTH PASTOR BY YEARS EMPLOYED

BENEFITS		YEARS EMPLOYED			
		< 6 years	6-10 years	11-15 years	Over 15 years
RETIREMENT:	Highest 25%	$2,400	$2,680	$3,999	–
	Average	$1,414	$1,455	$2,817	–
	Lowest 25%	–	–	$1,671	–
LIFE INSURANCE:	Highest 25%	–	–	$146	–
	Average	–	$179	–	–
	Lowest 25%	–	–	–	–
HEALTH INSURANCE:	Highest 25%	$8,815	$10,128	$11,088	–
	Average	$5,312	$6,128	$6,995	–
	Lowest 25%	–	$946	$2,296	–
CONTINUING EDUCATION	Highest 25%	$850	$999	$499	–
	Average	$514	$637	$271	–
	Lowest 25%	–	–	–	–
TOTAL BENEFITS	Highest 25%	$11,350	$12,240	$15,429	–
	Average	$7,305	$8,398	$10,141	–
	Lowest 25%	$2,360	$3,979	$5,992	–
TOTAL COMPENSATION AND BENEFIT		< 6 years	6-10 years	11-15 years	Over 15 years
	Highest 25%	$59,100	$65,907	$68,709	–
	Average	$49,693	$55,711	$63,326	–
	Lowest 25%	$39,479	$44,050	$53,403	–
NUMBER OF RESPONDENTS		358	97	21	7

– Not enough responses to provide meaningful data

185

TABLE 9-12: ANNUAL COMPENSATION OF YOUTH PASTOR BY DENOMINATION

CHARACTERISTICS	DENOMINATION					
	Assemblies of God	Baptist	Independent/ Nondenom	Lutheran	Methodist	Presbyterian
AVERAGE SUNDAY AM WORSHIP ATTENDANCE	598	803	966	447	715	580
AVERAGE CHURCH INCOME	$1,143,288	$1,820,540	$1,560,949	$1,042,089	$1,296,942	$1,349,111
AVERAGE # of YEARS EMPLOYED	3	5	4	4	4	3
AVERAGE # of WEEKS OF PAID VACATION	2	3	3	3	3	3
% COLLEGE GRADUATE OR HIGHER	77%	93%	86%	100%	87%	93%
% WHO RECEIVE AUTO REIMBURSEMENT	59%	73%	60%	71%	63%	79%
% ORDAINED	94%	82%	74%	33%	26%	26%
AVERAGE % SALARY INCREASE THIS YEAR	5%	4%	5%	4%	4%	4%

COMPENSATION		Assemblies of God	Baptist	Independent/ Nondenom	Lutheran	Methodist	Presbyterian
BASE SALARY:	Highest 25%	$34,452	$38,902	$38,000	$36,000	$39,175	$41,193
	Average	$25,983	$31,109	$30,661	$32,426	$31,158	$33,664
	Lowest 25%	$17,268	$21,419	$21,630	$26,286	$26,000	$28,893
HOUSING:	Highest 25%	$21,680	$22,008	$20,513	$16,800	$4,250	–
	Average	$15,797	$15,069	$13,129	$7,240	$3,332	$3,957
	Lowest 25%	$10,000	$2,400	–	–	–	–
PARSONAGE:	Highest 25%	–	–	–	–	–	–
	Average	$375	$1,114	$320	–	$761	$1,946
	Lowest 25%	–	–	–	–	–	–
TOTAL COMPENSATION	Highest 25%	$49,550	$54,500	$52,000	$47,057	$41,800	$48,000
	Average	$42,155	$47,292	$44,110	$39,666	$35,250	$39,566
	Lowest 25%	$31,000	$37,479	$34,320	$30,632	$31,060	$30,000

– Not enough responses to provide meaningful data

TABLE 9-12: ANNUAL COMPENSATION OF YOUTH PASTOR BY DENOMINATION

BENEFITS		DENOMINATION					
		Assemblies of God	Baptist	Independent/ Nondenom	Lutheran	Methodist	Presbyterian
RETIREMENT:	Highest 25%	$735	$3,736	$1,660	$2,772	$2,426	$2,505
	Average	$510	$2,262	$1,090	$2,303	$1,535	$1,475
	Lowest 25%	–	–	–	–	–	–
LIFE INSURANCE:	Highest 25%	–	–	–	–	–	$173
	Average	–	$171	$108	–	–	$114
	Lowest 25%	–	–	–	–	–	–
HEALTH INSURANCE:	Highest 25%	$7,951	$9,749	$10,956	$8,180	$3,950	$6,960
	Average	$4,415	$6,174	$7,091	$5,523	$2,612	$4,096
	Lowest 25%	–	$2,592	$3,000	$2,000	–	–
CONTINUING EDUCATION	Highest 25%	–	$798	$999	$1,798	$550	$1,075
	Average	$113	$493	$593	$1,114	$546	$861
	Lowest 25%	–	–	–	$303	–	–
TOTAL BENEFITS	Highest 25%	$9,300	$13,311	$13,000	$10,070	$8,390	$9,436
	Average	$5,083	$9,100	$8,882	$8,949	$4,702	$6,545
	Lowest 25%	$565	$5,260	$4,846	$4,285	$1,173	$2,217
TOTAL COMPENSATION AND BENEFIT		Assemblies of God	Baptist	Independent/ Nondenom	Lutheran	Methodist	Presbyterian
	Highest 25%	$56,350	$66,350	$61,450	$54,468	$48,796	$58,455
	Average	$47,237	$56,392	$52,992	$48,616	$39,952	$46,112
	Lowest 25%	$35,416	$44,508	$43,201	$40,455	$32,791	$33,550
NUMBER OF RESPONDENTS		32	134	119	15	28	44

– Not enough responses to provide meaningful data

187

TABLE 9-13: AVERAGE COMPENSATION PACKAGE FOR YOUTH PASTORS*

	Overall	Base Salary Only	No Base Salary	Base Salary and Parsonage	Base Salary and Housing	Base Salary and Parsonage and Housing
PASTORS WHO RECIEVE ...						
BASE SALARY	$30,382	$36,620		$31,179	$28,232	$28,790
PARSONAGE**	$1,159		$11,710	$15,513		$14,517
HOUSING ALLOWANCE	$12,351		$18,325		$19,044	$10,265
TOTAL COMPENSATION PACKAGE	$43,892	$36,620	$30,035	$46,692	$47,276	$53,572
NUMBER OF RESPONDENTS	493	150	9	16	303	15

*All $ values are annual averages
**Parsonage = Rental value of parsonage plus allowance
– Not enough responses to provide meaningful data

For an explanation of the Average Compensation Table, please refer to Chapter 1.

TABLE 9-14: COMPENSATION OF PART-TIME YOUTH PASTOR BY WORSHIP ATTENDANCE

CHARACTERISTICS	WORSHIP ATTENDANCE					
	100 or less	101 - 300	301 - 500	501 - 750	751 - 1,000	Over 1,000
AVERAGE SUNDAY AM WORSHIP ATTENDANCE	84	183	400	–	–	–
AVERAGE CHURCH INCOME	$136,059	$315,007	$787,933	–	–	–
AVERAGE # of YEARS EMPLOYED	2	3	3	–	–	–
AVERAGE # of WEEKS OF PAID VACATION	2	2	3	–	–	–
% COLLEGE GRADUATE OR HIGHER	59%	69%	77%	–	–	–
% WHO RECEIVE AUTO REIMBURSEMENT	52%	48%	69%	–	–	–
% ORDAINED	19%	20%	26%	–	–	–
AVERAGE % SALARY INCREASE THIS YEAR	–	6%	4%	–	–	–
HOURLY RATES						
AVERAGE BASE RATE	$7.77	$8.74	$9.84			
ANNUAL COMPENSATION						
AVERAGE BASE SALARY:	$8,903	$10,969	$14,528	–	–	–
AVERAGE HOUSING:	$526	$893	$1,609	–	–	–
AVERAGE PARSONAGE:	–	–	–	–	–	–
AVERAGE TOTAL COMPENSATION	$9,641	$11,963	$16,136	–	–	–
ANNUAL BENEFITS						
AVERAGE RETIREMENT	–	–	$266	–	–	–
AVERAGE LIFE INSURANCE	–	–	–	–	–	–
AVERAGE HEALTH INSURANCE	$133	$284	$601	–	–	–
AVERAGE CONTINUING EDUCATION	$39	$160	$140	–	–	–
AVERAGE TOTAL BENEFITS	$224	$478	$1,031	–	–	–
ANNUAL COMPENSATION & BENEFIT						
AVERAGE	$9,865	$12,441	$17,167	–	–	–
NUMBER OF RESPONDENTS	31	89	36	7	1	3

– Not enough responses to provide meaningful data

TABLE 9-15: COMPENSATION OF PART-TIME YOUTH PASTOR BY CHURCH INCOME

CHARACTERISTICS	CHURCH INCOME				
	$250 K & Under	$251 - $500K	$501 - $750K	$751K - $1M	Over $1 Million
AVERAGE SUNDAY AM WORSHIP ATTENDANCE	117	252	376	398	612
AVERAGE CHURCH INCOME	$166,874	$376,971	$633,856	$881,515	$1,743,434
AVERAGE # of YEARS EMPLOYED	3	3	4	4	3
AVERAGE # of WEEKS OF PAID VACATION	2	2	3	3	2
% COLLEGE GRADUATE OR HIGHER	64%	65%	78%	80%	83%
% WHO RECEIVE AUTO REIMBURSEMENT	47%	50%	–	75%	70%
% ORDAINED	16%	20%	36%	29%	23%
AVERAGE % SALARY INCREASE THIS YEAR	9%	4%	–	–	–
HOURLY RATES					
AVERAGE BASE RATE	$8.65	$8.49	$9.85	$11.49	$7.56
ANNUAL COMPENSATION	$250 K & Under	$251 - $500K	$501 - $750K	$751K - $1M	Over $1 Million
AVERAGE BASE SALARY:	$9,421	$11,461	$16,160	$12,944	$11,372
AVERAGE HOUSING:	–	–	–	$2,467	$4,301
AVERAGE PARSONAGE:	–	–	–	–	$5,000
AVERAGE TOTAL COMPENSATION	$10,089	$12,426	$16,160	$15,690	$20,673
ANNUAL BENEFITS					
AVERAGE RETIREMENT	–	–	$165	$384	$407
AVERAGE LIFE INSURANCE	–	–	–	–	–
AVERAGE HEALTH INSURANCE	$121	$578	$423	$546	$1,179
AVERAGE CONTINUING EDUCATION	$115	$150	–	–	$112
AVERAGE TOTAL BENEFITS	$271	$807	$670	$1,069	$1,709
ANNUAL COMPENSATION & BENEFIT					
AVERAGE	$10,360	$13,233	$16,830	$17,956	$24,246
NUMBER OF RESPONDENTS	67	52	11	15	13

– Not enough responses to provide meaningful data

10

MUSIC/
CHOIR
DIRECTORS

Employment Profile

Of the reported Music/Choir Directors position, about half are part-time and half are full-time. While men occupy most of the full-time positions, part-time positions are divided almost equally between males and females. Music/Choir Directors provided the following employment profile:

	FULL-TIME	PART-TIME
Ordained	63%	10%
Average years employed	8	7
Male	87%	46%
Female	13%	54%
Self-employed (receives 1099)	3%	7%
Church employee (receives W-2)	97%	93%
High school diploma	7%	12%
Associate's degree	2%	2%
Bachelor's degree	50%	58%
Master's degree	37%	22%
Doctorate	4%	6%
Number of respondents	*297*	*331*

Total Compensation plus Benefits Package Analysis

The analysis below is based upon the tables found later in this chapter. The tables present compensation data according to worship attendance, church income, combinations of size and setting, region, gender, education, years employed, and denomination for Music/Choir Directors who serve full-time. The final tables provide data for part-time Music/Choir Directors by worship attendance and church income. In this way, the compensation of Music/Choir Directors can be viewed from a variety of useful perspectives. The total compensation plus benefits amount found in the box at the bottom of each page includes the base salary, housing and/or parsonage amount, life and health insurance payments, retirement contribution, and educational funds.

Full-time staff members. Most benefits are comparable to those of adult ministry directors. Few receive a parsonage allowance, although 57% receive a housing allowance.

Part-time staff members. Part-time workers receive similar benefits to those of the other staff positions, except senior/solo pastor and associate pastor positions.

COMPENSATION PLUS BENEFITS	FULL TIME	PART TIME
Base salary	99%	97%
Housing	57%	5%
Parsonage	3%	0%
Retirement	61%	3%
Life insurance	35%	1%
Health insurance	74%	4%
Paid vacation	93%	44%
Auto reimbursement	54%	16%
Continuing education	34%	10%

KEY POINTS

➲ **Compensation and benefits of Music/Choir Directors higher for bigger church sizes.** The greatest gain occurs between 101 to 300 and 301 to 500 (about $14,000) in attendance, and then increases steadily after that. Nearly half of the reported Music/Choir Directors serve in churches over 750 people. *See Table 10-1.*

➲ **Church income impacts the compensation and benefits package in a pattern similar to church attendance.** Compensation and benefits start off much lower than the national average of $64,075, but increase steadily . The vast majority of Music/Choir Directors work in churches with an annual income over $1,000,000. These individuals receive, on average, $29,000 a year more compensation than choir directors in churches with an annual income of $500,000 or less. *See Table 10-2.*

➲ **Compensation and benefits of Music/Choir Directors fluctuate by geographical setting.** Music and choir directors in suburban churches, accounting for 44% of the reported positions, consistently earn more across attendance levels than those in small town or rural areas. The same is true compared to those in metropolitan churches, except in the highest attendance bracket (over 1,000) where directors in this region out-earn those in the suburbs. *See Tables 10-3, 10-4, 10-5, 10-6, and 10.7.*

⮑ **The region in which a church is located affects the compensation and benefits of the music or choir director.** With the exception of two regions (Middle Atlantic and the North West of Central U.S.), compensation and benefits packages were all close to or above the national average. These two regions also had two of the lowest three church incomes, which could account for some of the difference. . Music and choir directors in the Pacific region earn the highest compensation yet serve in relatively smaller churches. *See Table10-8.*

⮑ **Male directors earn considerably more than female directors.** On average, females earn approximately $19,600 less compensation and benefits than their male counterparts. While their salaries were comparable, women received about half as much as men in benefits. However, the women were found in churches with slightly over half the attendance and church income as the males, which affects compensation and benefits. *See Table 10-9.*

⮑ **Compensation increases across education levels.** Music and choir directors possessing a bachelor's degree receive substantially higher (over $10,000) compensation than those who do not have a college degree. Having a college degree increases the compensation above the national average. Those with a doctorate degree receive substantially higher compensation than those with a college degree. This year's findings indicate only a slight increase for those with a Master's degree from those with a Bachelor's (less than $500 on average), but a significant increase for those with a doctoral degree. *See Table 10-10.*

⮑ **Length of employment has some impact upon compensation levels.** Those with ten years or less of service receive a compensation below the national average. This represented 74% of all Music/Choir Directors. Compensation rose slowly, but somewhat inconsistently, with years of service. Slight differences emerge between less than 6 years and 6 to 10 years and then between 11 to 15 years and over 15 years. The greatest increase of about $15,000 is between 6 to 11 years and 11 to 15 years. *See Table 10-11.*

⮑ **A church's denominational affiliation has an effect on the compensation and benefits package of the choir or music director.** The compensation and benefits packages of all but two denominations were $6,000 or more below the national average. 71% of music directors worked for Baptist and Independent/Nondenominational churches, both of whose directors made above the national average. *See Table 10-12*

⮑ **Consistent with compensation and benefit packages for full-time Music/Choir Directors, church attendance and church income for part-time music directors impacts compensation.** In general, part-time music directors serving in larger churches earn more than those serving in smaller churches. Most part-time music directors serve in congregations with an attendance under 500 and $750,000 or less in church income. Similar with other positions, those serving part-time receive fewer fringe benefits than those serving full-time. *See Tables 10-14 and 10-15.*

Ten Year Compensation & Benefits Trend: National Average for Music/Choir Director

FULL TIME

1997	$43,598
1998	$45,603
1999	$49,383
2000	$50,911
2001	$53,200
2002	$55,046
2003	$56,875
2004	$57,279
2005	$60,316
2006	$64,075

TABLE 10-1: ANNUAL COMPENSATION OF MUSIC DIRECTOR BY WORSHIP ATTENDANCE

CHARACTERISTICS		WORSHIP ATTENDANCE					
		100 or less	101-300	301-500	501-750	751-1000	Over 1000
AVERAGE SUNDAY AM WORSHIP ATTENDANCE		–	225	429	606	889	2,023
AVERAGE CHURCH INCOME		–	$531,908	$994,598	$1,314,108	$1,927,944	$3,659,377
AVERAGE # of YEARS EMPLOYED		–	6	6	9	8	8
AVERAGE # of WEEKS OF PAID VACATION		–	3	3	3	3	3
% COLLEGE GRADUATE OR HIGHER		–	85%	92%	94%	89%	93%
% WHO RECEIVE AUTO REIMBURSEMENT		–	43%	59%	63%	66%	65%
% ORDAINED		–	39%	56%	68%	70%	70%
AVERAGE % SALARY INCREASE THIS YEAR		–	4%	4%	4%	4%	4%
COMPENSATION		100 or less	101-300	301-500	501-750	751-1000	Over 1000
BASE SALARY:	Highest 25%	–	$37,500	$44,085	$51,114	$56,327	$60,000
	Average	–	$30,121	$37,190	$39,733	$43,020	$46,381
	Lowest 25%	–	$25,100	$27,382	$30,655	$29,500	$30,835
HOUSING:	Highest 25%	–	$11,618	$22,499	$23,350	$25,502	$31,861
	Average	–	$6,394	$11,145	$12,193	$14,793	$20,124
	Lowest 25%	–	–	–	–	–	–
PARSONAGE:	Highest 25%	–	–	–	–	–	–
	Average	–	$1,167	$1,556	–	$1,008	–
	Lowest 25%	–	–	–	–	–	–
TOTAL COMPENSATION	Highest 25%	–	$41,427	$62,642	$57,633	$64,090	$75,000
	Average	–	$37,682	$49,891	$51,926	$58,820	$66,581
	Lowest 25%	–	$29,305	$40,000	$45,876	$50,348	$51,000

– Not enough responses to provide meaningful data

TABLE 10-1: ANNUAL COMPENSATION OF MUSIC DIRECTOR BY WORSHIP ATTENDANCE

BENEFITS		WORSHIP ATTENDANCE					
		100 or less	101-300	301-500	501-750	751-1000	Over 1000
RETIREMENT:	Highest 25%	–	$2,309	$4,150	$4,383	$3,900	$4,274
	Average	–	$1,308	$2,440	$2,592	$2,227	$2,735
	Lowest 25%	–	–	–	–	–	–
LIFE INSURANCE:	Highest 25%	–	–	–	–	–	–
	Average	–	–	–	$228	–	$171
	Lowest 25%	–	–	–	–	–	–
HEALTH INSURANCE:	Highest 25%	–	$8,845	$8,751	$10,423	$8,750	$10,560
	Average	–	$3,844	$4,623	$6,471	$5,527	$7,344
	Lowest 25%	–	–	–	$1,181	$2,200	$3,624
CONTINUING EDUCATION	Highest 25%	–	–	$999	$500	$1,001	–
	Average	–	$277	$558	$501	$553	$404
	Lowest 25%	–	–	–	–	–	–
TOTAL BENEFITS	Highest 25%	–	$10,629	$13,000	$14,558	$12,700	$14,338
	Average	–	$5,517	$7,714	$9,793	$8,386	$10,654
	Lowest 25%	–	–	$1,000	$5,256	$3,200	$6,792
TOTAL COMPENSATION AND BENEFIT		100 or less	101-300	301-500	501-750	751-1000	Over 1000
	Highest 25%	–	$51,250	$71,199	$69,860	$74,001	$90,301
	Average	–	$43,198	$57,606	$61,719	$67,206	$77,364
	Lowest 25%	–	$34,100	$41,201	$51,335	$57,099	$59,659
NUMBER OF RESPONDENTS		1	36	55	56	45	93

– Not enough responses to provide meaningful data

TABLE 10-2: ANNUAL COMPENSATION OF MUSIC DIRECTOR BY CHURCH INCOME

CHARACTERISTICS	CHURCH INCOME				
	$250K & under	$251K-$500K	$501K-$750K	$751K-$1M	Over $1 Million
AVERAGE SUNDAY AM WORSHIP ATTENDANCE	–	210	390	477	1,321
AVERAGE CHURCH INCOME	–	$389,233	$636,221	$887,710	$2,579,956
AVERAGE # of YEARS EMPLOYED	–	6	6	5	8
AVERAGE # of WEEKS OF PAID VACATION	–	3	3	3	3
% COLLEGE GRADUATE OR HIGHER	–	86%	92%	94%	91%
% WHO RECEIVE AUTO REIMBURSEMENT	–	28%	52%	71%	63%
% ORDAINED	–	43%	41%	61%	68%
AVERAGE % SALARY INCREASE THIS YEAR	–	4%	4%	5%	4%

COMPENSATION		$250K & under	$251K-$500K	$501K-$750K	$751K-$1M	Over 1 Million
BASE SALARY:	Highest 25%	–	$38,400	$38,642	$48,800	$55,400
	Average	–	$29,539	$31,919	$39,318	$43,613
	Lowest 25%	–	$18,011	$27,250	$30,294	$30,000
HOUSING:	Highest 25%	–	$19,440	$11,999	$16,700	$28,973
	Average	–	$6,766	$7,768	$8,218	$17,311
	Lowest 25%	–	–	–	–	–
PARSONAGE:	Highest 25%	–	–	–	–	–
	Average	–	$1,043	$1,111	$353	–
	Lowest 25%	–	–	–	–	–
TOTAL COMPENSATION	Highest 25%	–	$45,000	$46,800	$56,000	$68,000
	Average	–	$37,348	$40,798	$47,889	$61,023
	Lowest 25%	–	$28,000	$31,540	$40,000	$49,384

– Not enough responses to provide meaningful data

TABLE 10-2: ANNUAL COMPENSATION OF MUSIC DIRECTOR BY CHURCH INCOME

BENEFITS		CHURCH INCOME				
		$250K & under	$251K-$500K	$501K-$750K	$751K-$1M	Over $1 Million
RETIREMENT:	Highest 25%	–	$2,518	$3,610	$3,233	$4,787
	Average	–	$1,259	$2,104	$1,841	$2,673
	Lowest 25%	–	–	–	–	–
LIFE INSURANCE:	Highest 25%	–	–	–	–	–
	Average	–	–	–	$124	$158
	Lowest 25%	–	–	–	–	–
HEALTH INSURANCE:	Highest 25%	–	$5,571	$7,907	$7,620	$10,225
	Average	–	$3,150	$3,330	$4,220	$6,924
	Lowest 25%	–	–	–	–	$3,000
CONTINUING EDUCATION	Highest 25%	–	$503	$996	$750	$805
	Average	–	$329	$422	$418	$498
	Lowest 25%	–	–	–	–	–
TOTAL BENEFITS	Highest 25%	–	$8,871	$11,146	$10,174	$14,270
	Average	–	$4,852	$5,885	$6,603	$10,253
	Lowest 25%	–	–	–	$1,660	$5,600
TOTAL COMPENSATION AND BENEFIT		$250K & under	$251K-$500K	$501K-$750K	$751K-$1M	Over 1 Million
	Highest 25%	–	$49,999	$57,945	$66,294	$81,941
	Average	–	$42,200	$46,683	$54,492	$71,338
	Lowest 25%	–	$34,001	$36,001	$43,900	$59,219
NUMBER OF RESPONDENTS		3	23	27	34	193

– Not enough responses to provide meaningful data

TABLE 10-3: ANNUAL COMPENSATION OF MUSIC DIRECTOR BY CHURCH SETTING & SIZE

ATTENDANCE 250 & UNDER	CHURCH SETTING			
	Metropoli-tan city	Suburb of large city	Small town or rural city	Farming area
AVERAGE SUNDAY AM WORSHIP ATTENDANCE	–	–	195	–
AVERAGE CHURCH INCOME	–	–	$368,069	–
AVERAGE # of YEARS EMPLOYED	–	–	4	–
AVERAGE # of WEEKS OF PAID VACATION	–	–	3	–
% COLLEGE GRADUATE OR HIGHER	–	–	73%	–
% WHO RECEIVE AUTO REIMBURSEMENT	–	–	27%	–
% ORDAINED	–	–	33%	–
AVERAGE % SALARY INCREASE THIS YEAR	–	–	–	–

COMPENSATION		Metropoli-tan city	Suburb of large city	Small town or rural city	Farming area
BASE SALARY:	Highest 25%	–	–	$35,541	–
	Average	–	–	$25,211	–
	Lowest 25%	–	–	$13,210	–
HOUSING:	Highest 25%	–	–	$7,429	–
	Average	–	–	$4,688	–
	Lowest 25%	–	–	–	–
PARSONAGE:	Highest 25%	–	–	–	–
	Average	–	–	–	–
	Lowest 25%	–	–	–	–
TOTAL COMPENSATION	Highest 25%	–	–	$39,374	–
	Average	–	–	$29,899	–
	Lowest 25%	–	–	$26,249	–

– Not enough responses to provide meaningful data

TABLE 10-3: ANNUAL COMPENSATION OF MUSIC DIRECTOR BY CHURCH SETTING & SIZE

BENEFITS		CHURCH SETTING			
		Metropoli-tan city	Suburb of large city	Small town or rural city	Farming area
RETIREMENT:	Highest 25%	–	–	–	–
	Average	–	–	$440	–
	Lowest 25%	–	–	–	–
LIFE INSURANCE:	Highest 25%	–	–	$231	–
	Average	–	–	$206	–
	Lowest 25%	–	–	–	–
HEALTH INSURANCE:	Highest 25%	–	–	$9,152	–
	Average	–	–	$4,376	–
	Lowest 25%	–	–	–	–
CONTINUING EDUCATION	Highest 25%	–	–	$350	–
	Average	–	–	$183	–
	Lowest 25%	–	–	–	–
TOTAL BENEFITS	Highest 25%	–	–	$9,877	–
	Average	–	–	$5,205	–
	Lowest 25%	–	–	$195	–
TOTAL COMPENSATION AND BENEFIT		Metropoli-tan city	Suburb of large city	Small town or rural city	Farming area
	Highest 25%	–	–	$44,618	–
	Average	–	–	$35,104	–
	Lowest 25%	–	–	$30,951	–
NUMBER OF RESPONDENTS		5	7	12	0

– Not enough responses to provide meaningful data

TABLE 10-4: ANNUAL COMPENSATION OF MUSIC DIRECTOR BY CHURCH SETTING & SIZE

ATTENDANCE 251 - 500	CHURCH SETTING			
	Metropoli-tan city	Suburb of large city	Small town or rural city	Farming area
AVERAGE SUNDAY AM WORSHIP ATTENDANCE	409	418	378	–
AVERAGE CHURCH INCOME	$1,111,393	$1,003,170	$815,720	–
AVERAGE # of YEARS EMPLOYED	8	5	6	–
AVERAGE # of WEEKS OF PAID VACATION	3	3	3	–
% COLLEGE GRADUATE OR HIGHER	100%	83%	96%	–
% WHO RECEIVE AUTO REIMBURSEMENT	50%	55%	75%	–
% ORDAINED	50%	46%	55%	–
AVERAGE % SALARY INCREASE THIS YEAR	–	4%	4%	–

COMPENSATION		Metropoli-tan city	Suburb of large city	Small town or rural city	Farming area
BASE SALARY:	Highest 25%	$59,870	$44,085	$38,000	–
	Average	$44,824	$39,232	$30,535	–
	Lowest 25%	$35,582	$30,400	$22,000	–
HOUSING:	Highest 25%	–	$25,350	$19,470	–
	Average	$3,230	$11,654	$9,941	–
	Lowest 25%	–	–	–	–
PARSONAGE:	Highest 25%	–	–	$993	–
	Average	$2,160	$2,462	$600	–
	Lowest 25%	–	–	–	–
TOTAL COMPENSATION	Highest 25%	$65,000	$62,642	$47,939	–
	Average	$50,214	$53,347	$41,076	–
	Lowest 25%	$36,050	$40,040	$30,894	–

– Not enough responses to provide meaningful data

TABLE 10-4: ANNUAL COMPENSATION OF MUSIC DIRECTOR BY CHURCH SETTING & SIZE

		CHURCH SETTING			
BENEFITS		Metropoli-tan city	Suburb of large city	Small town or rural city	Farming area
RETIREMENT:	Highest 25%	$4,150	$3,720	$4,190	–
	Average	$1,970	$1,958	$2,883	–
	Lowest 25%	–	–	$1,023	–
LIFE INSURANCE:	Highest 25%	–	–	–	–
	Average	–	–	–	–
	Lowest 25%	–	–	–	–
HEALTH INSURANCE:	Highest 25%	$6,228	$6,600	$8,966	–
	Average	$3,390	$3,831	$5,647	–
	Lowest 25%	–	–	–	–
CONTINUING EDUCATION	Highest 25%	$1,006	$995	$994	–
	Average	$720	$467	$504	–
	Lowest 25%	–	–	–	–
TOTAL BENEFITS	Highest 25%	$6,588	$11,550	$14,600	–
	Average	$6,116	$6,338	$9,122	–
	Lowest 25%	$1,000	$952	$3,753	–
TOTAL COMPENSATION AND BENEFIT		Metropoli-tan city	Suburb of large city	Small town or rural city	Farming area
	Highest 25%	$73,650	$71,200	$62,250	–
	Average	$56,329	$59,686	$50,198	–
	Lowest 25%	$41,000	$42,000	$36,000	–
NUMBER OF RESPONDENTS		10	26	30	0

– Not enough responses to provide meaningful data

TABLE 10-5: ANNUAL COMPENSATION OF MUSIC DIRECTOR BY CHURCH SETTING & SIZE

ATTENDANCE 501 - 750	CHURCH SETTING			
	Metropoli-tan city	Suburb of large city	Small town or rural city	Farming area
AVERAGE SUNDAY AM WORSHIP ATTENDANCE	574	628	588	–
AVERAGE CHURCH INCOME	$1,313,106	$1,345,844	$1,306,017	–
AVERAGE # of YEARS EMPLOYED	6	8	11	–
AVERAGE # of WEEKS OF PAID VACATION	3	3	3	–
% COLLEGE GRADUATE OR HIGHER	89%	95%	93%	–
% WHO RECEIVE AUTO REIMBURSEMENT	60%	56%	69%	–
% ORDAINED	50%	68%	78%	–
AVERAGE % SALARY INCREASE THIS YEAR	4%	5%	4%	–

COMPENSATION		Metropoli-tan city	Suburb of large city	Small town or rural city	Farming area
BASE SALARY:	Highest 25%	$47,942	$48,602	$53,568	–
	Average	$38,497	$39,333	$40,834	–
	Lowest 25%	$23,660	$30,295	$33,000	–
HOUSING:	Highest 25%	$23,000	$29,015	$21,600	–
	Average	$9,286	$13,791	$12,543	–
	Lowest 25%	–	–	$24	–
PARSONAGE:	Highest 25%	–	–	–	–
	Average	–	–	–	–
	Lowest 25%	–	–	–	–
TOTAL COMPENSATION	Highest 25%	$48,800	$60,003	$56,355	–
	Average	$47,783	$53,125	$53,377	–
	Lowest 25%	$40,000	$47,197	$47,600	–

– Not enough responses to provide meaningful data

TABLE 10-5: ANNUAL COMPENSATION OF MUSIC DIRECTOR BY CHURCH SETTING & SIZE

BENEFITS		CHURCH SETTING			
		Metropoli-tan city	Suburb of large city	Small town or rural city	Farming area
RETIREMENT:	Highest 25%	$5,238	$3,601	$3,982	–
	Average	$3,436	$2,629	$2,124	–
	Lowest 25%	–	$1,230	–	–
LIFE INSURANCE:	Highest 25%	–	–	–	–
	Average	$132	$256	$270	–
	Lowest 25%	–	–	–	–
HEALTH INSURANCE:	Highest 25%	$7,155	$11,901	$10,225	–
	Average	$5,220	$7,582	$6,074	–
	Lowest 25%	$663	$4,564	–	–
CONTINUING EDUCATION	Highest 25%	$250	–	–	–
	Average	$200	$715	$372	–
	Lowest 25%	–	–	–	–
TOTAL BENEFITS	Highest 25%	$13,504	$16,034	$13,902	–
	Average	$8,988	$11,183	$8,840	–
	Lowest 25%	$5,000	$6,775	$4,920	–
TOTAL COMPENSATION AND BENEFIT		Metropoli-tan city	Suburb of large city	Small town or rural city	Farming area
	Highest 25%	$66,980	$73,152	$69,653	–
	Average	$56,772	$64,307	$62,217	–
	Lowest 25%	$50,944	$51,669	$54,172	–
NUMBER OF RESPONDENTS		10	25	18	2

– *Not enough responses to provide meaningful data*

205

TABLE 10-6: ANNUAL COMPENSATION OF MUSIC DIRECTOR BY CHURCH SETTING & SIZE

ATTENDANCE 751 - 1,000	CHURCH SETTING			
	Metropoli-tan city	Suburb of large city	Small town or rural city	Farming area
AVERAGE SUNDAY AM WORSHIP ATTENDANCE	916	842	895	–
AVERAGE CHURCH INCOME	$2,075,566	$1,773,780	$1,939,179	–
AVERAGE # of YEARS EMPLOYED	10	6	7	–
AVERAGE # of WEEKS OF PAID VACATION	4	3	3	–
% COLLEGE GRADUATE OR HIGHER	93%	83%	90%	–
% WHO RECEIVE AUTO REIMBURSEMENT	56%	69%	73%	–
% ORDAINED	65%	64%	82%	–
AVERAGE % SALARY INCREASE THIS YEAR	4%	5%	5%	–

COMPENSATION		Metropoli-tan city	Suburb of large city	Small town or rural city	Farming area
BASE SALARY:	Highest 25%	$62,445	$57,271	$41,403	–
	Average	$49,592	$47,047	$34,008	–
	Lowest 25%	$30,774	$32,058	$24,762	–
HOUSING:	Highest 25%	$23,013	$29,000	$24,250	–
	Average	$12,905	$13,926	$15,525	–
	Lowest 25%	–	–	$6,900	–
PARSONAGE:	Highest 25%	–	–	–	–
	Average	–	$857	–	–
	Lowest 25%	–	–	–	–
TOTAL COMPENSATION	Highest 25%	$65,796	$65,000	$55,364	–
	Average	$62,503	$61,830	$49,533	–
	Lowest 25%	$52,991	$54,703	$47,738	–

– Not enough responses to provide meaningful data

TABLE 10-6: ANNUAL COMPENSATION OF MUSIC DIRECTOR BY CHURCH SETTING & SIZE

BENEFITS		CHURCH SETTING			
		Metropoli-tan city	Suburb of large city	Small town or rural city	Farming area
RETIREMENT:	Highest 25%	$4,800	$5,022	$2,185	–
	Average	$2,376	$2,560	$1,581	–
	Lowest 25%	–	–	–	–
LIFE INSURANCE:	Highest 25%	–	$240	–	–
	Average	–	$122	–	–
	Lowest 25%	–	–	–	–
HEALTH INSURANCE:	Highest 25%	$5,996	$10,872	$9,675	–
	Average	$4,140	$7,209	$5,712	–
	Lowest 25%	$2,686	$2,200	$1,250	–
CONTINUING EDUCATION	Highest 25%	$1,019	$1,000	$1,000	–
	Average	$626	$602	$408	–
	Lowest 25%	–	–	–	–
TOTAL BENEFITS	Highest 25%	$9,904	$14,225	$11,275	–
	Average	$7,186	$10,493	$7,702	–
	Lowest 25%	$2,694	$5,322	$4,550	–
TOTAL COMPENSATION AND BENEFIT		Metropoli-tan city	Suburb of large city	Small town or rural city	Farming area
	Highest 25%	$82,580	$74,900	$64,696	–
	Average	$69,689	$72,323	$57,235	–
	Lowest 25%	$55,535	$62,872	$50,152	–
NUMBER OF RESPONDENTS		17	14	12	0

Not enough responses to provide meaningful data

TABLE 10-7: ANNUAL COMPENSATION OF MUSIC DIRECTOR BY CHURCH SETTING & SIZE

ATTENDANCE OVER 1,000		Metropolitan city	Suburb of large city	Small town or rural city	Farming area
AVERAGE SUNDAY AM WORSHIP ATTENDANCE		2,382	2,059	1,761	–
AVERAGE CHURCH INCOME		$4,672,418	$3,702,912	$3,020,796	–
AVERAGE # of YEARS EMPLOYED		10	8	7	–
AVERAGE # of WEEKS OF PAID VACATION		3	3	3	–
% COLLEGE GRADUATE OR HIGHER		93%	93%	91%	–
% WHO RECEIVE AUTO REIMBURSEMENT		67%	64%	64%	–
% ORDAINED		53%	70%	77%	–
AVERAGE % SALARY INCREASE THIS YEAR		4%	4%	4%	–

COMPENSATION		Metropolitan city	Suburb of large city	Small town or rural city	Farming area
BASE SALARY:	Highest 25%	$72,531	$60,001	$44,438	–
	Average	$52,469	$49,156	$36,657	–
	Lowest 25%	$38,150	$31,999	$23,563	–
HOUSING:	Highest 25%	$31,858	$35,328	$31,600	–
	Average	$20,642	$19,300	$21,386	–
	Lowest 25%	–	–	$1,600	–
PARSONAGE:	Highest 25%	$2,115	–	–	–
	Average	$465	–	–	–
	Lowest 25%	–	–	–	–
TOTAL COMPENSATION	Highest 25%	$109,999	$75,972	$67,090	–
	Average	$73,576	$68,456	$58,043	–
	Lowest 25%	$50,976	$51,701	$47,000	–

– Not enough responses to provide meaningful data

TABLE 10-7: ANNUAL COMPENSATION OF MUSIC DIRECTOR BY CHURCH SETTING & SIZE

BENEFITS		CHURCH SETTING			
		Metropoli-tan city	Suburb of large city	Small town or rural city	Farming area
RETIREMENT:	Highest 25%	$3,372	$4,099	$4,800	–
	Average	$1,666	$2,876	$2,841	–
	Lowest 25%	–	–	–	–
LIFE INSURANCE:	Highest 25%	$204	–	$121	–
	Average	$163	$213	–	–
	Lowest 25%	–	–	–	–
HEALTH INSURANCE:	Highest 25%	$12,053	$11,579	$9,936	–
	Average	$8,781	$7,174	$6,934	–
	Lowest 25%	$6,794	$3,002	$4,092	–
CONTINUING EDUCATION	Highest 25%	$488	–	$1,100	–
	Average	$353	$410	$438	–
	Lowest 25%	–	–	–	–
TOTAL BENEFITS	Highest 25%	$13,849	$14,678	$14,338	–
	Average	$10,963	$10,673	$10,300	–
	Lowest 25%	$7,201	$5,401	$5,180	–
TOTAL COMPENSATION AND BENEFIT		Metropoli-tan city	Suburb of large city	Small town or rural city	Farming area
	Highest 25%	$117,799	$91,778	$84,980	–
	Average	$84,540	$79,364	$68,343	–
	Lowest 25%	$61,001	$60,722	$57,843	–
NUMBER OF RESPONDENTS		15	51	26	0

– Not enough responses to provide meaningful data

TABLE 10-8: ANNUAL COMPENSATION OF MUSIC DIRECTOR BY REGION

CHARACTERISTICS	New England	Middle Atlantic	South Atlantic	E-N Central	E-S Central	W-N Central	W-S Central	Mountain	Pacific
AVERAGE SUNDAY AM WORSHIP ATTENDANCE	–	734	796	1,342	1,077	877	1,099	1,228	973
AVERAGE CHURCH INCOME	–	$1,384,637	$1,645,976	$2,174,321	$2,590,148	$1,796,850	$2,423,101	$2,013,592	$1,891,963
AVERAGE # of YEARS EMPLOYED	–	5	7	6	9	8	11	7	6
AVERAGE # of WEEKS OF PAID VACATION	–	4	3	3	3	3	3	3	3
% COLLEGE GRADUATE OR HIGHER	–	92%	92%	88%	94%	96%	95%	79%	91%
% WHO RECEIVE AUTO REIMBURSEMENT	–	55%	63%	81%	44%	65%	48%	68%	48%
% ORDAINED	–	29%	62%	61%	60%	59%	71%	70%	72%
AVERAGE % SALARY INCREASE THIS YEAR	–	5%	4%	4%	4%	4%	4%	4%	4%

COMPENSATION		New England	Middle Atlantic	South Atlantic	E-N Central	E-S Central	W-N Central	W-S Central	Mountain	Pacific
BASE SALARY:	Highest 25%	–	$48,118	$49,826	$48,600	$67,304	$49,420	$55,000	$41,000	$53,363
	Average	–	$35,551	$39,944	$40,800	$46,487	$36,648	$45,534	$35,244	$40,513
	Lowest 25%	–	$28,167	$30,000	$30,068	$26,852	$28,000	$34,093	$22,000	$23,723
HOUSING:	Highest 25%	–	$18,778	$22,500	$23,519	$24,000	$17,999	$23,701	$34,001	$38,500
	Average	–	$7,655	$11,367	$13,209	$11,901	$9,796	$14,594	$19,683	$22,343
	Lowest 25%	–	–	–	–	–	–	–	–	–
PARSONAGE:	Highest 25%	–	–	–	–	–	–	–	–	–
	Average	–	–	$309	$588	$1,663	–	–	–	$1,600
	Lowest 25%	–	–	–	–	–	–	–	–	–
TOTAL COMPENSATION	Highest 25%	–	$51,173	$64,090	$62,429	$74,713	$55,400	$75,000	$62,000	$70,750
	Average	–	$43,206	$51,620	$54,597	$60,051	$46,444	$60,280	$54,931	$64,456
	Lowest 25%	–	$31,540	$40,000	$43,495	$39,170	$31,500	$44,085	$47,939	$50,500

– Not enough responses to provide meaningful data

TABLE 10-8: ANNUAL COMPENSATION OF MUSIC DIRECTOR BY REGION

BENEFITS		REGION								
		New England	Middle Atlantic	South Atlantic	E-N Central	E-S Central	W-N Central	W-S Central	Moun-tain	Pacific
RETIREMENT:	Highest 25%	–	$4,331	$4,794	$2,041	$4,801	$3,720	$4,044	$1,500	$4,475
	Average	–	$2,062	$2,744	$1,510	$3,260	$2,456	$2,607	$1,337	$2,538
	Lowest 25%	–	–	–	–	–	–	–	–	–
LIFE INSURANCE:	Highest 25%	–	$250	–	$159	$553	–	–	–	–
	Average	–	$133	–	$141	$453	–	$124	$196	–
	Lowest 25%	–	–	–	–	–	–	–	–	–
HEALTH INSURANCE:	Highest 25%	–	$8,966	$9,266	$12,665	$8,014	$9,052	$9,936	$9,028	$9,681
	Average	–	$5,857	$5,269	$7,287	$4,280	$5,742	$6,150	$5,572	$5,928
	Lowest 25%	–	–	–	–	–	$1,698	$663	$1,000	–
CONTINUING EDUCATION	Highest 25%	–	$750	$875	–	$950	$995	$500	$705	$995
	Average	–	$311	$538	$246	$520	$531	$368	$312	$636
	Lowest 25%	–	–	–	–	–	–	–	–	–
TOTAL BENEFITS	Highest 25%	–	$10,911	$13,771	$14,437	$13,102	$13,637	$12,654	$12,507	$14,058
	Average	–	$8,343	$8,645	$9,185	$8,513	$8,814	$9,249	$7,417	$9,195
	Lowest 25%	–	$5,347	$2,601	$1,980	$2,842	$5,180	$4,138	$3,393	$2,480
TOTAL COMPENSATION AND BENEFIT		New England	Middle Atlantic	South Atlantic	E-N Central	E-S Central	W-N Central	W-S Central	Moun-tain	Pacific
	Highest 25%	–	$60,721	$71,654	$74,899	$86,267	$69,894	$88,170	$67,621	$83,753
	Average	–	$51,548	$60,265	$63,782	$68,564	$55,259	$69,529	$62,348	$73,950
	Lowest 25%	–	$38,133	$45,616	$50,601	$49,842	$36,001	$47,360	$55,539	$61,844
NUMBER OF RESPONDENTS		3	14	70	51	20	27	46	25	40

– Not enough responses to provide meaningful data

TABLE 10-9: ANNUAL COMPENSATION OF MUSIC DIRECTOR BY GENDER

CHARACTERISTICS	GENDER	
	Male	Female
AVERAGE SUNDAY AM WORSHIP ATTENDANCE	1,087	609
AVERAGE CHURCH INCOME	$2,089,457	$1,282,376
AVERAGE # of YEARS EMPLOYED	8	8
AVERAGE # of WEEKS OF PAID VACATION	3	3
% COLLEGE GRADUATE OR HIGHER	91%	91%
% WHO RECEIVE AUTO REIMBURSEMENT	64%	33%
% ORDAINED	69%	14%
AVERAGE % SALARY INCREASE THIS YEAR	4%	5%

COMPENSATION		Male	Female
BASE SALARY:	Highest 25%	$53,000	$47,942
	Average	$40,824	$37,865
	Lowest 25%	$28,882	$28,400
HOUSING:	Highest 25%	$25,974	–
	Average	$15,830	$3,125
	Lowest 25%	–	–
PARSONAGE:	Highest 25%	–	–
	Average	$525	$1,232
	Lowest 25%	–	–
TOTAL COMPENSATION	Highest 25%	$65,000	$52,227
	Average	$57,179	$42,223
	Lowest 25%	$44,691	$30,220

– Not enough responses to provide meaningful data

TABLE 10-9: ANNUAL COMPENSATION OF MUSIC DIRECTOR BY GENDER

		GENDER	
BENEFITS		Male	Female
RETIREMENT:	Highest 25%	$4,190	$2,518
	Average	$2,553	$1,227
	Lowest 25%	–	
LIFE INSURANCE:	Highest 25%	–	–
	Average	$153	–
	Lowest 25%	–	–
HEALTH INSURANCE:	Highest 25%	$9,918	$5,100
	Average	$6,271	$2,974
	Lowest 25%	$1,116	–
CONTINUING EDUCATION	Highest 25%	$750	$805
	Average	$441	$530
	Lowest 25%	–	–
TOTAL BENEFITS	Highest 25%	$13,901	$8,525
	Average	$9,418	$4,778
	Lowest 25%	$4,815	$500
TOTAL COMPENSATION AND BENEFIT		Male	Female
	Highest 25%	$76,244	$62,873
	Average	$66,644	$47,000
	Lowest 25%	$51,010	$32,726
NUMBER OF RESPONDENTS		256	37

– Not enough responses to provide meaningful data

213

TABLE 10-10: ANNUAL COMPENSATION OF MUSIC DIRECTOR BY EDUCATION

CHARACTERISTICS	EDUCATION			
	< than Bachelor	Bachelor	Master	Doctorate
AVERAGE SUNDAY AM WORSHIP ATTENDANCE	1,281	1,039	888	1,245
AVERAGE CHURCH INCOME	$1,915,061	$1,859,621	$1,860,454	$2,975,698
AVERAGE # of YEARS EMPLOYED	6	6	10	9
AVERAGE # of WEEKS OF PAID VACATION	3	3	3	4
% COLLEGE GRADUATE OR HIGHER	–	100%	100%	100%
% WHO RECEIVE AUTO REIMBURSEMENT	43%	63%	63%	64%
% ORDAINED	55%	65%	70%	27%
AVERAGE % SALARY INCREASE THIS YEAR	6%	4%	4%	–

COMPENSATIÓN		< than Bachelor	Bachelor	Master	Doctorate
BASE SALARY:	Highest 25%	$51,468	$46,165	$53,000	$68,443
	Average	$39,896	$39,191	$41,236	$54,139
	Lowest 25%	$29,811	$28,000	$30,220	$30,600
HOUSING:	Highest 25%	$14,999	$25,351	$25,000	$19,999
	Average	$8,052	$15,241	$14,318	$8,182
	Lowest 25%	–	–	–	–
PARSONAGE:	Highest 25%	–	–	–	–
	Average	–	$957	$470	$633
	Lowest 25%	–	–	–	–
TOTAL COMPENSATION	Highest 25%	$59,867	$64,165	$65,000	$80,900
	Average	$47,952	$55,389	$56,024	$62,954
	Lowest 25%	$38,224	$40,040	$45,619	$53,000

– Not enough responses to provide meaningful data

TABLE 10-10: ANNUAL COMPENSATION OF MUSIC DIRECTOR BY EDUCATION

BENEFITS		EDUCATION			
		< than Bachelor	Bachelor	Master	Doctorate
RETIREMENT:	Highest 25%	$1,231	$3,610	$4,381	$4,800
	Average	$909	$2,296	$2,869	$2,870
	Lowest 25%	–	–	–	–
LIFE INSURANCE:	Highest 25%	–	–	–	$180
	Average	–	$155	$165	–
	Lowest 25%	–	–	–	–
HEALTH INSURANCE:	Highest 25%	$8,871	$10,200	$9,685	$8,940
	Average	$4,840	$6,446	$5,705	$5,807
	Lowest 25%	$272	–	–	$4,090
CONTINUING EDUCATION	Highest 25%	–	$748	$805	$1,495
	Average	$226	$417	$470	$1,027
	Lowest 25%	–	–	–	–
TOTAL BENEFITS	Highest 25%	$9,641	$13,390	$14,516	$13,312
	Average	$6,048	$9,314	$9,210	$9,809
	Lowest 25%	$2,200	$4,270	$3,250	$7,079

TOTAL COMPENSATION AND BENEFIT		< than Bachelor	Bachelor	Master	Doctorate
	Highest 25%	$65,399	$75,483	$78,377	$91,778
	Average	$54,001	$64,793	$65,233	$72,763
	Lowest 25%	$41,201	$49,820	$50,927	$63,695
NUMBER OF RESPONDENTS		23	133	97	11

– Not enough responses to provide meaningful data

215

TABLE 10-11: ANNUAL COMPENSATION OF MUSIC DIRECTOR BY YEARS EMPLOYED

CHARACTERISTICS		< 6 years	6-10 years	11-15 years	Over 15 years
AVERAGE SUNDAY AM WORSHIP ATTENDANCE		1,000	1,000	1,232	1,004
AVERAGE CHURCH INCOME		$1,747,130	$1,869,676	$2,796,840	$2,296,980
AVERAGE # of YEARS EMPLOYED		3	7	13	22
AVERAGE # of WEEKS OF PAID VACATION		3	4	4	4
% COLLEGE GRADUATE OR HIGHER		92%	87%	90%	97%
% WHO RECEIVE AUTO REIMBURSEMENT		59%	64%	57%	62%
% ORDAINED		60%	70%	63%	68%
AVERAGE % SALARY INCREASE THIS YEAR		4%	4%	5%	4%

COMPENSATION		< 6 years	6-10 years	11-15 years	Over 15 years
BASE SALARY:	Highest 25%	$48,000	$47,935	$63,000	$59,870
	Average	$37,731	$36,756	$50,386	$47,367
	Lowest 25%	$27,250	$28,000	$30,790	$34,093
HOUSING:	Highest 25%	$23,704	$24,960	$28,973	$29,856
	Average	$13,084	$13,933	$15,380	$17,218
	Lowest 25%	–	–	–	–
PARSONAGE:	Highest 25%	–	–	–	–
	Average	$623	$1,037	–	$527
	Lowest 25%	–	–	–	–
TOTAL COMPENSATION	Highest 25%	$62,000	$57,271	$80,000	$74,327
	Average	$51,438	$51,727	$65,767	$65,111
	Lowest 25%	$40,000	$47,200	$45,750	$52,227

– Not enough responses to provide meaningful data

TABLE 10-11: ANNUAL COMPENSATION OF MUSIC DIRECTOR BY YEARS EMPLOYED

BENEFITS		YEARS EMPLOYED			
		< 6 years	6-10 years	11-15 years	Over 15 years
RETIREMENT:	Highest 25%	$3,500	$4,274	$5,452	$5,241
	Average	$1,828	$2,616	$3,691	$3,043
	Lowest 25%	–	–	$900	–
LIFE INSURANCE:	Highest 25%	–	$155	–	–
	Average	$155	$130	$100	$125
	Lowest 25%	–	–	–	–
HEALTH INSURANCE:	Highest 25%	$10,000	$9,052	$8,856	$9,600
	Average	$5,849	$6,098	$5,436	$5,991
	Lowest 25%	–	$2,200	–	–
CONTINUING EDUCATION	Highest 25%	$695	$1,000	–	$705
	Average	$370	$573	$508	$511
	Lowest 25%	–	–	–	–
TOTAL BENEFITS	Highest 25%	$12,754	$14,250	$13,899	$14,270
	Average	$8,202	$9,416	$9,735	$9,670
	Lowest 25%	$2,518	$3,983	$4,820	$4,800
TOTAL COMPENSATION AND BENEFIT		< 6 years	6-10 years	11-15 years	Over 15 years
	Highest 25%	$70,250	$69,037	$88,416	$86,501
	Average	$59,640	$61,143	$75,865	$74,782
	Lowest 25%	$43,901	$55,132	$55,450	$55,787
NUMBER OF RESPONDENTS		151	62	33	41

– Not enough responses to provide meaningful data

217

TABLE 10-12: ANNUAL COMPENSATION OF MUSIC DIRECTOR BY DENOMINATION

CHARACTERISTICS		Assemblies of God	Baptist	Independent/ Nondenom	Lutheran	Methodist	Presbyterian
AVERAGE SUNDAY AM WORSHIP ATTENDANCE		1,056	891	1,405	513	790	687
AVERAGE CHURCH INCOME		$1,900,014	$1,895,573	$2,296,069	$1,457,243	$1,446,155	$1,766,398
AVERAGE # of YEARS EMPLOYED		4	9	6	12	9	7
AVERAGE # of WEEKS OF PAID VACATION		3	3	3	4	3	3
% COLLEGE GRADUATE OR HIGHER		89%	98%	78%	100%	88%	96%
% WHO RECEIVE AUTO REIMBURSEMENT		67%	68%	53%	44%	30%	55%
% ORDAINED		82%	82%	78%	30%	23%	8%
AVERAGE % SALARY INCREASE THIS YEAR		–	4%	4%	–	5%	4%
COMPENSATION		Assemblies of God	Baptist	Independent/ Nondenom	Lutheran	Methodist	Presbyterian
BASE SALARY:	Highest 25%	$42,000	$52,614	$48,276	$47,942	$54,500	$60,864
	Average	$34,865	$39,769	$37,930	$41,061	$43,962	$47,742
	Lowest 25%	$29,340	$25,671	$25,480	$34,192	$32,000	$38,000
HOUSING:	Highest 25%	$24,959	$26,850	$30,001	$23,700	–	–
	Average	$14,848	$17,591	$18,350	$9,115	$2,169	$2,771
	Lowest 25%	$7,671	–	–	–	–	–
PARSONAGE:	Highest 25%	–	–	–	–	–	–
	Average	–	$572	–	–	$1,565	–
	Lowest 25%	–	–	–	–	–	–
TOTAL COMPENSATION	Highest 25%	$60,369	$66,744	$61,700	$67,192	$55,408	$62,429
	Average	$49,713	$57,932	$56,572	$50,176	$47,697	$50,513
	Lowest 25%	$41,000	$46,688	$45,840	$36,050	$38,000	$38,463

– Not enough responses to provide meaningful data

TABLE 10-12: ANNUAL COMPENSATION OF MUSIC DIRECTOR BY DENOMINATION

BENEFITS		DENOMINATION					
		Assemblies of God	Baptist	Independent/ Nondenom	Lutheran	Methodist	Presbyte-rian
RETIREMENT:	Highest 25%	–	$5,240	$2,000	$4,794	$3,258	$3,720
	Average	$794	$3,323	$1,294	$2,242	$1,604	$2,118
	Lowest 25%	–	–	–	–	–	–
LIFE INSURANCE:	Highest 25%	$166	–	–	–	–	–
	Average	–	$260	–	–	–	–
	Lowest 25%	–	–	–	–	–	–
HEALTH INSURANCE:	Highest 25%	$7,600	$9,762	$11,238	$9,000	$5,436	$8,488
	Average	$5,370	$6,192	$7,196	$4,575	$3,002	$4,475
	Lowest 25%	$2,364	$332	$1,698	–	–	–
CONTINUING EDUCATION	Highest 25%	–	$563	$994	$995	$501	$1,250
	Average	$455	$426	$451	$595	$337	$770
	Lowest 25%	–	–	–	–	–	–
TOTAL BENEFITS	Highest 25%	$8,741	$15,286	$12,945	$13,771	$7,780	$13,312
	Average	$6,681	$10,200	$9,018	$7,420	$4,950	$7,445
	Lowest 25%	$3,250	$5,218	$3,610	$1,000	$952	$2,100
TOTAL COMPENSATION AND BENEFIT		Assemblies of God	Baptist	Independent/ Nondenom	Lutheran	Methodist	Presbyte-rian
	Highest 25%	$64,799	$81,191	$74,304	$81,940	$62,041	$70,251
	Average	$56,395	$68,133	$65,590	$57,595	$52,646	$57,958
	Lowest 25%	$47,765	$52,202	$54,975	$37,255	$38,001	$44,153
NUMBER OF RESPONDENTS		11	108	62	10	23	26

– Not enough responses to provide meaningful data

THE 2007 COMPENSATION HANDBOOK FOR CHURCH STAFF

TABLE 10-13: AVERAGE COMPENSATION PACKAGE FOR MUSIC / CHOIR DIRECTOR*

	Overall	MUSIC / CHOIR DIRECTORS WHO RECIEVE...				
		Base Salary Only	No Base Salary	Base Salary and Parsonage	Base Salary and Housing	Base Salary and Parsonage and Housing
BASE SALARY	$40,516	$48,002		–	$35,941	–
PARSONAGE**	$606		–	–		–
HOUSING ALLOWANCE	$14,112		–		$24,888	–
TOTAL COMPENSATION PACKAGE	$55,234	$48,002	–	–	$60,829	–
NUMBER OF RESPONDENTS	297	125	3	3	160	6

*All $ values are annual averages
**Parsonage = Rental value of parsonage plus allowance
– Not enough responses to provide meaningful data

**For an explanation of the Average Compensation Table,
please refer to Chapter 1.**

TABLE 10-14: COMPENSATION OF PART-TIME MUSIC DIRECTOR BY WORSHIP ATTENDANCE

CHARACTERISTICS	WORSHIP ATTENDANCE					
	100 or less	101 - 300	301 - 500	501 - 750	751 - 1,000	Over 1,000
AVERAGE SUNDAY AM WORSHIP ATTENDANCE	74	187	400	632	–	1,481
AVERAGE CHURCH INCOME	$143,984	$375,831	$747,338	$1,129,382	–	$2,200,920
AVERAGE # of YEARS EMPLOYED	7	7	7	6	–	6
AVERAGE # of WEEKS OF PAID VACATION	3	3	3	2	–	–
% COLLEGE GRADUATE OR HIGHER	88%	84%	88%	90%	–	90%
% WHO RECEIVE AUTO REIMBURSEMENT	11%	18%	31%	55%	–	50%
% ORDAINED	12%	9%	16%	4%	–	15%
AVERAGE % SALARY INCREASE THIS YEAR	5%	6%	4%	7%	–	4%
HOURLY RATES						
AVERAGE BASE RATE	$14.20	$10.66	$12.81	$12.22	–	$13.67
ANNUAL COMPENSATION						
AVERAGE BASE SALARY:	$6,074	$10,983	$14,519	$15,080	–	$23,177
AVERAGE HOUSING:	–	–	–	–	–	–
AVERAGE PARSONAGE:	–	–	–	–	–	–
AVERAGE TOTAL COMPENSATION	$6,530	$11,698	$15,359	$15,939	–	$23,177
ANNUAL BENEFITS						
AVERAGE RETIREMENT	–	–	–	–	–	–
AVERAGE LIFE INSURANCE	–	–	–	–	–	–
AVERAGE HEALTH INSURANCE	–	$125	$149	–	–	$1,358
AVERAGE CONTINUING EDUCATION	–	–	–	–	–	$107
AVERAGE TOTAL BENEFITS	$170	$267	$215	$104	–	$1,489
ANNUAL COMPENSATION & BENEFIT						
AVERAGE	$6,700	$12,039	$15,575	$16,659	–	$24,667
NUMBER OF RESPONDENTS	35	165	74	27	7	14

– Not enough responses to provide meaningful data

TABLE 10-15: COMPENSATION OF PART-TIME MUSIC DIRECTOR BY CHURCH INCOME

	CHURCH INCOME				
CHARACTERISTICS	$250 K & Under	$251 - $500K	$501 - $750K	$751K - $1M	Over $1 Million
AVERAGE SUNDAY AM WORSHIP ATTENDANCE	138	230	374	420	829
AVERAGE CHURCH INCOME	$173,941	$369,284	$613,067	$879,666	$1,678,145
AVERAGE # of YEARS EMPLOYED	8	6	6	6	6
AVERAGE # of WEEKS OF PAID VACATION	3	2	2	2	2
% COLLEGE GRADUATE OR HIGHER	84%	85%	76%	96%	93%
% WHO RECEIVE AUTO REIMBURSEMENT	18%	16%	23%	45%	55%
% ORDAINED	10%	10%	16%	13%	9%
AVERAGE % SALARY INCREASE THIS YEAR	9%	5%	4%	3%	3%
HOURLY RATES					
AVERAGE BASE RATE	$11.80	$11.37	$9.96	$11.36	$13.07
ANNUAL COMPENSATION	$250 K & Under	$251 - $500K	$501 - $750K	$751K - $1M	Over $1 Million
AVERAGE BASE SALARY:	$7,555	$10,973	$14,295	$14,487	$17,350
AVERAGE HOUSING:	–	–	$1,041	–	$1,012
AVERAGE PARSONAGE:	–	–	–	–	–
AVERAGE TOTAL COMPENSATION	$8,028	$11,592	$15,336	$14,855	$18,616
ANNUAL BENEFITS					
AVERAGE RETIREMENT	–	–	–	–	–
AVERAGE LIFE INSURANCE	–	–	–	–	–
AVERAGE HEALTH INSURANCE	–	$122	$176	$285	$515
AVERAGE CONTINUING EDUCATION	–	–	–	–	–
AVERAGE TOTAL BENEFITS	$125	$279	$244	$350	$629
ANNUAL COMPENSATION & BENEFIT					
AVERAGE	$8,153	$11,984	$15,580	$15,627	$19,245
NUMBER OF RESPONDENTS	82	106	40	37	47

– Not enough responses to provide meaningful data

11

CHILDREN'S/ PRESCHOOL DIRECTORS

Employment Profile

Of the reported Children's/Preschool Directors, just over half are full-time (58%). The typical Children's/Preschool Director is a full-time female college graduate. Women also hold over 90% of the part-time positions. Children's/Preschool Directors provided the following employment profile:

	FULL-TIME	PART-TIME
Ordained	36%	5%
Average years employed	5	5
Male	27%	8%
Female	73%	92%
Self-employed (receives 1099)	2%	1%
Church employee (receives W-2)	98%	99%
High school diploma	14%	29%
Associate's degree	7%	5%
Bachelor's degree	59%	55%
Master's degree	19%	11%
Doctorate	2%	1%
Number of respondents	*276*	*204*

Total Compensation plus Benefits Package Analysis

The analysis below is based upon the tables found later in this chapter. The tables present compensation data according to worship attendance, church income, combinations of size and setting, region, gender, education, years employed, and denomination for Children's/Preschool Directors who serve full-time. The final tables provide data for part-time Children's/Preschool Directors by worship attendance and church income. In this way, the compensation of Children's/Preschool Directors can be viewed from a variety of useful perspectives. The total compensation plus benefits amount found in the box at the bottom of each page includes the base salary, housing and/or parsonage amount, life and health insurance payments, retirement contribution, and educational funds.

Full-time staff members. Most benefits are comparable to those of Music/Choir Directors. Few receive a parsonage allowance, though 31% receive a housing allowance.

Part-time staff members. Part-time workers receive similar benefits to those of the other part-time staff positions, except senior/solo pastor and associate pastor positions.

COMPENSATION PLUS BENEFITS	FULL TIME	PART TIME
Base salary	99%	99%
Housing	31%	2%
Parsonage	2%	0%
Retirement	47%	7%
Life insurance	28%	2%
Health insurance	56%	6%
Paid vacation	92%	48%
Auto reimbursement	53%	26%
Continuing education	32%	23%

KEY POINTS

◐ **Compensation and benefits of Children's/Preschool Directors are higher for bigger church sizes.** The greatest gain (about $6,790) occurs between churches with 751-1,000 and over 1,000 in attendance. Nearly half of the reported Children's/Preschool Directors serve in churches over 750 people. *See Table 11-1.*

◐ **Church income impacts the compensation and benefits package.** Compensation and benefits start off far below the national average of $46,361, and stay below it until the church incomes surpasses $1 million. The vast majority (about 67%) of Children's/Preschool Directors work in churches with an annual income over $1,000,000. These individuals receive, on average, about $15,700 a year more compensation than directors in churches with an annual income of $500,000 or less. *See Table 11-2.*

◐ **Compensation and benefits of Children's/Preschool Directors fluctuate by geographical setting.** Directors in metropolitan areas consistently earn more than those who are in other settings. However, the majority of Children's/Preschool Directors are found in suburban churches, and usually earn more across attendance levels than those in small town or rural areas. *See Tables 11-3, 11-4, 11-5, 11-6, and 11-7.*

◐ **The region in which a church is located affects the compensation and benefits of the Children's/Preschool Director.** Directors in the Pacific region earn the highest compensation yet serve in relatively smaller churches. With the exception of two regions (Middle Atlantic and Mountain), compensation and benefits packages were all close to or above the national average. *See Table 11-8.*

◑ **Male directors earn considerably more than female directors.** On average, females earn approximately $11,677 less compensation and benefits than do their male counterparts. While their salaries are comparable, women receive less in benefits. The church incomes of the churches women serve in are, on average, higher than the males'. The difference in packages can be attributed to gender more than church income. *See Table 11-9.*

◑ **Compensation increases across education levels.** Children's/Preschool Directors possessing a bachelor's degree receive substantially higher (about $12,000) compensation than those who do not have a college degree. Having a college degree increases the compensation above the national average. *See Table 11-10.*

◑ **Length of employment has some impact upon compensation levels. In general, as years of employment increases, compensation for directors increases.** Those with six or more years of service receive compensation above the national average. However the average number of years worked by 67% of Children's/Preschool Directors is 3 years. *See Table 11-11.*

◑ **Consistent with compensation and benefit packages for full-time Children's/ Preschool Directors, church attendance and church income for part-time directors impacts compensation.** However, there is a drop-off in compensation among directors in larger congregations (attendance over 1,000 and church income over $1,000,000.) Most part-time Children's/Preschool Directors serve in congregations with an attendance of 500 or less (73%), and $750,000 or less in church income (58%). Similar with other positions, those serving part-time receive fewer fringe benefits than those serving full-time. *See Tables 11-14 and 11-15.*

Compensation & Benefits: National Average for Children's/ Preschool Directors**

FULL TIME

2006	$46,361

** *No historical data available*

TABLE 11-1: ANNUAL COMPENSATION OF CHILDREN'S DIRECTOR BY WORSHIP ATTENDANCE

CHARACTERISTICS		WORSHIP ATTENDANCE					
		100 or less	101-300	301-500	501-750	751-1000	Over 1000
AVERAGE SUNDAY AM WORSHIP ATTENDANCE		–	215	430	627	890	2,001
AVERAGE CHURCH INCOME		–	$496,069	$925,620	$1,447,857	$1,689,378	$3,646,734
AVERAGE # of YEARS EMPLOYED		–	3	5	7	6	5
AVERAGE # of WEEKS OF PAID VACATION		–	3	3	3	3	3
% COLLEGE GRADUATE OR HIGHER		–	74%	75%	82%	76%	87%
% WHO RECEIVE AUTO REIMBURSEMENT		–	44%	61%	64%	61%	60%
% ORDAINED		–	16%	36%	33%	31%	48%
AVERAGE % SALARY INCREASE THIS YEAR		–	5%	4%	4%	5%	5%
COMPENSATION		100 or less	101-300	301-500	501-750	751-1000	Over 1000
BASE SALARY:	Highest 25%	–	$34,600	$39,000	$41,456	$43,500	$45,369
	Average	–	$29,330	$31,193	$34,443	$34,197	$37,287
	Lowest 25%	–	$23,715	$23,700	$27,000	$27,954	$28,000
HOUSING:	Highest 25%	–	–	$7,389	$11,400	$16,600	$21,710
	Average	–	$4,159	$4,757	$5,414	$6,691	$9,270
	Lowest 25%	–	–	–	–	–	–
PARSONAGE:	Highest 25%	–	$438	–	–	–	$412
	Average	–	$375	$1,042	–	$990	$26
	Lowest 25%	–	–	–	–	–	–
TOTAL COMPENSATION	Highest 25%	–	$41,882	$44,880	$45,120	$46,168	$55,000
	Average	–	$33,864	$36,991	$39,857	$41,878	$46,582
	Lowest 25%	–	$25,001	$28,214	$33,031	$36,238	$36,000

– Not enough responses to provide meaningful data

TABLE 11-1: ANNUAL COMPENSATION OF CHILDREN'S DIRECTOR BY WORSHIP ATTENDANCE

BENEFITS		WORSHIP ATTENDANCE					
		100 or less	101-300	301-500	501-750	751-1000	Over 1000
RETIREMENT:	Highest 25%	–	–	$2,244	$3,346	$2,010	$2,911
	Average	–	$589	$1,250	$1,801	$1,012	$1,628
	Lowest 25%	–	–	–	–	–	–
LIFE INSURANCE:	Highest 25%	–	–	–	–	–	$147
	Average	–	$106	–	–	–	$140
	Lowest 25%	–	–	–	–	–	–
HEALTH INSURANCE:	Highest 25%	–	$4,418	$5,160	$7,718	$6,298	$8,922
	Average	–	$2,334	$2,325	$4,170	$3,564	$4,734
	Lowest 25%	–	–	–	–	–	–
CONTINUING EDUCATION	Highest 25%	–	$450	$775	$510	$300	–
	Average	–	$255	$396	$429	$258	$310
	Lowest 25%	–	–	–	–	–	–
TOTAL BENEFITS	Highest 25%	–	$6,160	$6,150	$10,404	$7,492	$10.411
	Average	–	$3,283	$4,008	$6,496	$4,869	$6,812
	Lowest 25%	–	–	$450	$1,770	–	$2,000
TOTAL COMPENSATION AND BENEFIT		100 or less	101-300	301-500	501-750	751-1000	Over 1000
	Highest 25%	–	$44,925	$48,920	$50,516	$56,738	$62,911
	Average	–	$37,147	$40,999	$46,353	$46,747	$53,540
	Lowest 25%	–	$26,200	$29,075	$37,435	$36,950	$40,599
NUMBER OF RESPONDENTS		4	32	48	54	40	93

– Not enough responses to provide meaningful data

TABLE 11-2: ANNUAL COMPENSATION OF CHILDREN'S DIRECTOR BY CHURCH INCOME

CHARACTERISTICS	CHURCH INCOME				
	$250K & under	$251K-$500K	$501K-$750K	$751K-$1M	Over $1 Million
AVERAGE SUNDAY AM WORSHIP ATTENDANCE	376	236	430	504	1,381
AVERAGE CHURCH INCOME	$172,188	$399,123	$638,977	$875,040	$2,694,184
AVERAGE # of YEARS EMPLOYED	3	4	5	4	6
AVERAGE # of WEEKS OF PAID VACATION	2	3	3	2	3
% COLLEGE GRADUATE OR HIGHER	78%	74%	58%	91%	82%
% WHO RECEIVE AUTO REIMBURSEMENT	–	47%	44%	64%	63%
% ORDAINED	–	22%	22%	38%	39%
AVERAGE % SALARY INCREASE THIS YEAR	–	6%	4%	4%	5%

COMPENSATION		$250K & under	$251K-$500K	$501K-$750K	$751K-$1M	Over 1 Million
BASE SALARY:	Highest 25%	$34,200	$32,375	$39,140	$38,640	$45,000
	Average	$30,856	$28,109	$32,197	$28,566	$36,741
	Lowest 25%	$25,000	$23,715	$25,000	$20,746	$28,635
HOUSING:	Highest 25%	–	–	–	$11,995	$15,250
	Average	$2,000	$3,418	$2,109	$6,294	$7,629
	Lowest 25%	–	–	–	–	–
PARSONAGE:	Highest 25%	–	–	–	$436	$406
	Average	–	$500	–	$364	–
	Lowest 25%	–	–	–	–	–
TOTAL COMPENSATION	Highest 25%	$34,201	$38,000	$42,140	$40,001	$51,692
	Average	$32,856	$32,026	$34,306	$35,224	$44,383
	Lowest 25%	$25,000	$25,000	$26,000	$30,000	$34,999

– Not enough responses to provide meaningful data

TABLE 11-2: ANNUAL COMPENSATION OF CHILDREN'S DIRECTOR BY CHURCH INCOME

BENEFITS		CHURCH INCOME				
		$250K & under	$251K-$500K	$501K-$750K	$751K-$1M	Over $1 Million
RETIREMENT:	Highest 25%	–	–	–	$1,519	$3,000
	Average	$256	$653	$665	$904	$1,660
	Lowest 25%			–	–	–
LIFE INSURANCE:	Highest 25%	–	–	–	–	–
	Average	$337	–	–	–	$104
	Lowest 25%	–	–	–	–	–
HEALTH INSURANCE:	Highest 25%	$4,501	$5,250	–	$5,120	$7,996
	Average	$2,328	$2,435	$1,158	$2,602	$4,478
	Lowest 25%	–	–	–	–	–
CONTINUING EDUCATION	Highest 25%	$706	$450	$250	$994	$500
	Average	$272	$210	$213	$495	$367
	Lowest 25%	–	–	–	–	–
TOTAL BENEFITS	Highest 25%	$5,400	$6.410	$3,182	$6,099	$10,404
	Average	$3,193	$3,305	$2,045	$4,061	$6,609
	Lowest 25%	$700	–	–	$750	$1,757
TOTAL COMPENSATION AND BENEFIT		$250K & under	$251K-$500K	$501K-$750K	$751K-$1M	Over 1 Million
	Highest 25%	$37,537	$43,385	$45,250	$46,649	$59,897
	Average	$36,048	$35,331	$36,351	$39,285	$51,070
	Lowest 25%	$27,499	$25,950	$26,000	$32,999	$39,935
NUMBER OF RESPONDENTS		9	24	20	33	174

– Not enough responses to provide meaningful data

TABLE 11-3: ANNUAL COMPENSATION OF CHILDREN'S DIRECTOR BY CHURCH SETTING & SIZE

ATTENDANCE 250 & UNDER		CHURCH SETTING			
		Metropoli-tan city	Suburb of large city	Small town or rural city	Farming area
AVERAGE SUNDAY AM WORSHIP ATTENDANCE		–	210	158	–
AVERAGE CHURCH INCOME		–	$629,096	$320,051	–
AVERAGE # of YEARS EMPLOYED		–	5	3	–
AVERAGE # of WEEKS OF PAID VACATION		–	4	2	–
% COLLEGE GRADUATE OR HIGHER		–	88%	50%	–
% WHO RECEIVE AUTO REIMBURSEMENT		–	–	17%	–
% ORDAINED		–	13%	8%	–
AVERAGE % SALARY INCREASE THIS YEAR		–	–	3%	–

COMPENSATION		Metropoli-tan city	Suburb of large city	Small town or rural city	Farming area
BASE SALARY:	Highest 25%	–	$46,632	$34,250	–
	Average	–	$32,346	$28,136	–
	Lowest 25%	–	$22,500	$22,950	–
HOUSING:	Highest 25%	–	$4,300	–	–
	Average	–	$2,575	$2,467	–
	Lowest 25%	–	–	–	–
PARSONAGE:	Highest 25%	–	–	$3,750	–
	Average	–	–	$923	–
	Lowest 25%	–	–	–	–
TOTAL COMPENSATION	Highest 25%	–	$46,632	$37,113	–
	Average	–	$34,921	$31,527	–
	Lowest 25%	–	$25,500	$22,950	–

— Not enough responses to provide meaningful data

TABLE 11-3: ANNUAL COMPENSATION OF CHILDREN'S DIRECTOR BY CHURCH SETTING & SIZE

		CHURCH SETTING			
BENEFITS		Metropoli-tan city	Suburb of large city	Small town or rural city	Farming area
RETIREMENT:	Highest 25%	–	–	–	–
	Average	–	$288	$404	–
	Lowest 25%	–	–	–	–
LIFE INSURANCE:	Highest 25%	–	–	–	–
	Average	–	–	$241	–
	Lowest 25%	–	–	–	–
HEALTH INSURANCE:	Highest 25%	–	$6,000	$3,313	–
	Average	–	$4,036	$1,970	–
	Lowest 25%	–	–	–	–
CONTINUING EDUCATION	Highest 25%	–	–	$550	–
	Average	–	$250	$281	–
	Lowest 25%	–	–	–	–
TOTAL BENEFITS	Highest 25%	–	$7,000	$5,386	–
	Average	–	$4,586	$2,895	–
	Lowest 25%	–	–	$495	–
TOTAL COMPENSATION AND BENEFIT		Metropoli-tan city	Suburb of large city	Small town or rural city	Farming area
	Highest 25%	–	$51,800	$43,820	–
	Average	–	$39,506	$34,422	–
	Lowest 25%	–	$26,200	$26,150	–
NUMBER OF RESPONDENTS		4	8	13	0

– Not enough responses to provide meaningful data

TABLE 11-4: ANNUAL COMPENSATION OF CHILDREN'S DIRECTOR BY CHURCH SETTING & SIZE

ATTENDANCE 251 - 500	CHURCH SETTING			
	Metropoli-tan city	Suburb of large city	Small town or rural city	Farming area
AVERAGE SUNDAY AM WORSHIP ATTENDANCE	418	416	367	–
AVERAGE CHURCH INCOME	$948,080	$916,283	$630,950	–
AVERAGE # of YEARS EMPLOYED	7	4	3	–
AVERAGE # of WEEKS OF PAID VACATION	3	3	2	–
% COLLEGE GRADUATE OR HIGHER	83%	77%	73%	–
% WHO RECEIVE AUTO REIMBURSEMENT	100%	48%	67%	–
% ORDAINED	17%	48%	29%	–
AVERAGE % SALARY INCREASE THIS YEAR	4%	5%	6%	–

COMPENSATION		Metropoli-tan city	Suburb of large city	Small town or rural city	Farming area
BASE SALARY:	Highest 25%	$40,013	$38,628	$29,213	–
	Average	$39,065	$28,123	$26,262	–
	Lowest 25%	$29,398	$20,013	$21,828	–
HOUSING:	Highest 25%	–	$13,699	–	–
	Average	$3,860	$7,783	$2,849	–
	Lowest 25%	–	–	–	–
PARSONAGE:	Highest 25%	–	$3,720	–	–
	Average	–	$1,852	–	–
	Lowest 25%	–	–	–	–
TOTAL COMPENSATION	Highest 25%	$49,619	$44,981	$30,513	–
	Average	$42,925	$37,758	$29,110	–
	Lowest 25%	$34,088	$30,013	$24,288	–

– Not enough responses to provide meaningful data

TABLE 11-4: ANNUAL COMPENSATION OF CHILDREN'S DIRECTOR BY CHURCH SETTING & SIZE

BENEFITS		CHURCH SETTING			
		Metropoli-tan city	Suburb of large city	Small town or rural city	Farming area
RETIREMENT:	Highest 25%	$2,503	$1,997	–	–
	Average	$1,835	$1,209	$574	–
	Lowest 25%	–	–	–	–
LIFE INSURANCE:	Highest 25%	–	–	–	–
	Average	–	–	–	–
	Lowest 25%	–	–	–	–
HEALTH INSURANCE:	Highest 25%	$5,213	$5,106	$1,818	–
	Average	$2,277	$2,574	$1,531	–
	Lowest 25%	–	–	–	–
CONTINUING EDUCATION	Highest 25%	$1,013	$756	$713	–
	Average	$650	$293	$344	–
	Lowest 25%	–	–	–	–
TOTAL BENEFITS	Highest 25%	$5,986	$7,534	$6,101	–
	Average	$4,792	$4,114	$2,481	–
	Lowest 25%	$1,703	–	–	–
TOTAL COMPENSATION AND BENEFIT		Metropoli-tan city	Suburb of large city	Small town or rural city	Farming area
	Highest 25%	$51,762	$48,987	$35,149	–
	Average	$47,716	$41,871	$31,591	–
	Lowest 25%	$37,264	$35,493	$24,292	–
NUMBER OF RESPONDENTS		13	27	17	1

– Not enough responses to provide meaningful data

TABLE 11-5: ANNUAL COMPENSATION OF CHILDREN'S DIRECTOR BY CHURCH SETTING & SIZE

ATTENDANCE 501 - 750	CHURCH SETTING			
	Metropolitan city	Suburb of large city	Small town or rural city	Farming area
AVERAGE SUNDAY AM WORSHIP ATTENDANCE	633	647	595	–
AVERAGE CHURCH INCOME	$1,601,598	$1,317,161	$1,579,831	–
AVERAGE # of YEARS EMPLOYED	6	7	6	–
AVERAGE # of WEEKS OF PAID VACATION	4	3	3	–
% COLLEGE GRADUATE OR HIGHER	–	79%	82%	–
% WHO RECEIVE AUTO REIMBURSEMENT	63%	58%	69%	–
% ORDAINED	13%	30%	39%	–
AVERAGE % SALARY INCREASE THIS YEAR	–	4%	4%	–

COMPENSATION		Metropolitan city	Suburb of large city	Small town or rural city	Farming area
BASE SALARY:	Highest 25%	$40,311	$40,440	$44,097	–
	Average	$31,387	$35,267	$34,229	–
	Lowest 25%	$22,114	$26,470	$27,003	–
HOUSING:	Highest 25%	$10,000	–	$14,953	–
	Average	$5,875	$4,267	$6,455	–
	Lowest 25%	–	–	–	–
PARSONAGE:	Highest 25%	–	–	–	–
	Average	–	–	–	–
	Lowest 25%	–	–	–	–
TOTAL COMPENSATION	Highest 25%	$40,311	$42,008	$48,906	–
	Average	$37,262	$39,504	$40,683	–
	Lowest 25%	$33,254	$34,992	$30,008	–

– Not enough responses to provide meaningful data

TABLE 11-5: ANNUAL COMPENSATION OF CHILDREN'S DIRECTOR BY CHURCH SETTING & SIZE

		CHURCH SETTING			
BENEFITS		Metropoli- tan city	Suburb of large city	Small town or rural city	Farming area
RETIREMENT:	Highest 25%	$5,544	$3,005	$3,342	–
	Average	$2,764	$1,647	$1,460	–
	Lowest 25%	–	–	–	–
LIFE INSURANCE:	Highest 25%	$240	–	–	–
	Average	$111	–	–	–
	Lowest 25%	–	–	–	–
HEALTH INSURANCE:	Highest 25%	$13,227	$5,408	$7,228	–
	Average	$7,693	$3,539	$3,352	–
	Lowest 25%	$2,500	–	–	–
CONTINUING EDUCATION	Highest 25%	$500	$589	–	–
	Average	$313	$522	$321	–
	Lowest 25%	–	–	–	–
TOTAL BENEFITS	Highest 25%	$16,609	$7,907	$9,586	–
	Average	$10,879	$5,764	$5,216	–
	Lowest 25%	$6,500	$1,768	–	–
TOTAL COMPENSATION AND BENEFIT		Metropoli- tan city	Suburb of large city	Small town or rural city	Farming area
	Highest 25%	$52,244	$48,634	$49,627	–
	Average	$48,141	$45,268	$45,899	–
	Lowest 25%	$44,400	$38,998	$34,435	–
NUMBER OF RESPONDENTS		8	25	19	1

— Not enough responses to provide meaningful data

237

TABLE 11-6: ANNUAL COMPENSATION OF CHILDREN'S DIRECTOR BY CHURCH SETTING & SIZE

ATTENDANCE 751 - 1,000	CHURCH SETTING			
	Metropoli-tan city	Suburb of large city	Small town or rural city	Farming area
AVERAGE SUNDAY AM WORSHIP ATTENDANCE	925	855	900	–
AVERAGE CHURCH INCOME	$1,738,851	$1,746,408	$1,619,106	–
AVERAGE # of YEARS EMPLOYED	5	7	6	–
AVERAGE # of WEEKS OF PAID VACATION	3	3	3	–
% COLLEGE GRADUATE OR HIGHER	82%	87%	55%	–
% WHO RECEIVE AUTO REIMBURSEMENT	50%	53%	73%	–
% ORDAINED	50%	29%	18%	–
AVERAGE % SALARY INCREASE THIS YEAR	6%	5%	6%	–

COMPENSATION		Metropoli-tan city	Suburb of large city	Small town or rural city	Farming area
BASE SALARY:	Highest 25%	$41,500	$45,998	$40,831	–
	Average	$34,814	$37,201	$32,161	–
	Lowest 25%	$32,950	$25,010	$24,002	–
HOUSING:	Highest 25%	$21,050	$19,700	$10,151	–
	Average	$11,175	$6,000	$3,959	–
	Lowest 25%	–	–	–	–
PARSONAGE:	Highest 25%	–	–	–	–
	Average	–	–	–	–
	Lowest 25%	–	–	–	–
TOTAL COMPENSATION	Highest 25%	$52,500	$48,189	$41,692	–
	Average	$45,989	$43,201	$36,120	–
	Lowest 25%	$35,950	$40,708	$32,261	–

– Not enough responses to provide meaningful data

TABLE 11-6: ANNUAL COMPENSATION OF CHILDREN'S DIRECTOR BY CHURCH SETTING & SIZE

BENEFITS		CHURCH SETTING			
		Metropoli-tan city	Suburb of large city	Small town or rural city	Farming area
RETIREMENT:	Highest 25%	$1,750	$1,693	$2,308	–
	Average	$715	$1,008	$1,165	–
	Lowest 25%	–	–	–	–
LIFE INSURANCE:	Highest 25%	–	–	–	–
	Average	–	–	–	–
	Lowest 25%	–	–	–	–
HEALTH INSURANCE:	Highest 25%	$6,250	$8,123	$4,781	–
	Average	$3,782	$4,279	$1,953	–
	Lowest 25%	–	–	–	–
CONTINUING EDUCATION	Highest 25%	$300	$619	–	–
	Average	$300	$242	$200	–
	Lowest 25%	–	–	–	–
TOTAL BENEFITS	Highest 25%	$7,310	$8,995	$6,963	–
	Average	$4,812	$5,576	$3,317	–
	Lowest 25%	–	–	$1,231	–
TOTAL COMPENSATION AND BENEFIT		Metropoli-tan city	Suburb of large city	Small town or rural city	Farming area
	Highest 25%	$59,750	$58,115	$46,112	–
	Average	$50,801	$48,778	$39,437	–
	Lowest 25%	$36,950	$41,520	$34,915	–
NUMBER OF RESPONDENTS		12	15	11	1

– Not enough responses to provide meaningful data

239

TABLE 11-7: ANNUAL COMPENSATION OF CHILDREN'S DIRECTOR BY CHURCH SETTING & SIZE

ATTENDANCE OVER 1,000	CHURCH SETTING			
	Metropoli-tan city	Suburb of large city	Small town or rural city	Farming area
AVERAGE SUNDAY AM WORSHIP ATTENDANCE	2,411	1,984	1,791	–
AVERAGE CHURCH INCOME	$5,014,580	$3,590,073	$2,929,273	–
AVERAGE # of YEARS EMPLOYED	5	6	5	–
AVERAGE # of WEEKS OF PAID VACATION	3	3	3	–
% COLLEGE GRADUATE OR HIGHER	100%	84%	86%	–
% WHO RECEIVE AUTO REIMBURSEMENT	53%	63%	57%	–
% ORDAINED	31%	47%	64%	–
AVERAGE % SALARY INCREASE THIS YEAR	5%	4%	5%	–

COMPENSATION		Metropoli-tan city	Suburb of large city	Small town or rural city	Farming area
BASE SALARY:	Highest 25%	$46,678	$46,168	$35,507	–
	Average	$40,142	$39,631	$30,410	–
	Lowest 25%	$32,482	$30,843	$22,943	–
HOUSING:	Highest 25%	$12,738	$19,990	$26,010	–
	Average	$6,017	$8,226	$13,852	–
	Lowest 25%	–	–	–	–
PARSONAGE:	Highest 25%	$720	–	–	–
	Average	$150	–	–	–
	Lowest 25%	–	–	–	–
TOTAL COMPENSATION	Highest 25%	$51,216	$57,994	$52,999	–
	Average	$46,309	$47,857	$44,261	–
	Lowest 25%	$36,925	$35,998	$34,896	–

– Not enough responses to provide meaningful data

TABLE 11-7: ANNUAL COMPENSATION OF CHILDREN'S DIRECTOR BY CHURCH SETTING & SIZE

BENEFITS		CHURCH SETTING			
		Metropoli-tan city	Suburb of large city	Small town or rural city	Farming area
RETIREMENT:	Highest 25%	$3,666	$2,511	$3,061	–
	Average	$1,706	$1,442	$1,848	–
	Lowest 25%	–	–	–	–
LIFE INSURANCE:	Highest 25%	$196	–	$119	–
	Average	$176	$154	–	–
	Lowest 25%	–	–	–	–
HEALTH INSURANCE:	Highest 25%	$8,908	$7,997	$9,207	–
	Average	$5,020	$4,670	$4,509	–
	Lowest 25%	–	–	–	–
CONTINUING EDUCATION	Highest 25%	–	–	$1,106	–
	Average	$308	$233	$480	–
	Lowest 25%	–	–	–	–
TOTAL BENEFITS	Highest 25%	$10,799	$10,410	$9,618	–
	Average	$7,210	$6,500	$6,914	–
	Lowest 25%	$3,350	$1,282	$3,059	–
TOTAL COMPENSATION AND BENEFIT		Metropoli-tan city	Suburb of large city	Small town or rural city	Farming area
	Highest 25%	$63,357	$64,320	$62,336	–
	Average	$54,370	$54,356	$51,175	–
	Lowest 25%	$40,922	$39,939	$40,011	–
NUMBER OF RESPONDENTS		16	51	25	0

– Not enough responses to provide meaningful data

TABLE 11-8: ANNUAL COMPENSATION OF CHILDREN'S DIRECTOR BY REGION

CHARACTERISTICS	REGION								
	New England	Middle Atlantic	South Atlantic	E-N Central	E-S Central	W-N Central	W-S Central	Mountain	Pacific
AVERAGE SUNDAY AM WORSHIP ATTENDANCE	–	744	915	1,331	1,049	878	1,101	1,284	821
AVERAGE CHURCH INCOME	–	$1,276,470	$1,964,075	$1,995,419	$2,640,713	$1,893,266	$2,582,706	$1,841,190	$1,377,202
AVERAGE # of YEARS EMPLOYED	–	4	5	5	7	4	6	5	6
AVERAGE # of WEEKS OF PAID VACATION	–	3	3	3	3	3	3	3	3
% COLLEGE GRADUATE OR HIGHER	–	73%	85%	83%	88%	80%	76%	78%	78%
% WHO RECEIVE AUTO REIMBURSEMENT	–	56%	62%	78%	53%	75%	50%	61%	38%
% ORDAINED	–	9%	31%	47%	37%	38%	34%	24%	42%
AVERAGE % SALARY INCREASE THIS YEAR	–	5%	4%	5%	4%	4%	4%	4%	6%

COMPENSATION		New England	Middle Atlantic	South Atlantic	E-N Central	E-S Central	W-N Central	W-S Central	Mountain	Pacific
BASE SALARY:	Highest 25%	–	$36,000	$44,000	$42,080	$45,120	$39,481	$40,621	$40,000	$43,264
	Average	–	$32,555	$34,332	$33,906	$33,231	$32,572	$34,273	$32,621	$35,229
	Lowest 25%	–	$28,000	$25,000	$23,800	$23,600	$27,000	$26,000	$26,000	$27,750
HOUSING:	Highest 25%	–	–	$10,683	$16,990	$11,390	$10,361	–	–	$20,010
	Average	–	$4,439	$5,150	$8,769	$4,576	$6,225	$5,523	$4,447	$8,926
	Lowest 25%	–	–	–	–	–	–	–	–	–
PARSONAGE:	Highest 25%	–	–	–	$423	–	–	$429	–	–
	Average	–	–	–	$235	$2,084	–	–	–	$1,020
	Lowest 25%	–	–	–	–	–	–	–	–	–
TOTAL COMPENSATION	Highest 25%	–	$45,648	$46,335	$53,039	$48,000	$47,850	$49,607	$42,000	$52,996
	Average	–	$36,994	$39,482	$42,910	$39,891	$38,797	$39,855	$37,067	$45,175
	Lowest 25%	–	$28,001	$32,000	$30,001	$33,729	$31,500	$28,000	$32,001	$33,120

– Not enough responses to provide meaningful data

TABLE 11-8: ANNUAL COMPENSATION OF CHILDREN'S DIRECTOR BY REGION

BENEFITS		REGION								
		New England	Middle Atlantic	South Atlantic	E-N Central	E-S Central	W-N Central	W-S Central	Mountain	Pacific
RETIREMENT:	Highest 25%	–	$3,346	$3,060	$2,040	$2,580	$2,933	$3,001	$1,600	$2,001
	Average	–	$1,293	$1,659	$1,189	$1,466	$1,778	$1,487	$661	$1,170
	Lowest 25%	–	–	–	–	–	–	–	–	–
LIFE INSURANCE:	Highest 25%	–	–	–	–	$285	–	–	–	–
	Average	–	–	–	–	$266	$134	$134	–	–
	Lowest 25%	–	–	–	–	–	–	–	–	–
HEALTH INSURANCE:	Highest 25%	–	$7,000	$6,900	$8,400	$8,000	$8,352	$7,237	$3,600	$5,801
	Average	–	$2,755	$3,890	$3,847	$4,795	$3,965	$4,532	$1,951	$3,191
	Lowest 25%	–	–	–	–	$574	–	–	–	–
CONTINUING EDUCATION	Highest 25%	–	–	$990	$703	$503	$747	–	$394	$406
	Average	–	$200	$401	$337	$368	$458	$312	$235	$328
	Lowest 25%	–	–	–	–	–	–	–	–	–
TOTAL BENEFITS	Highest 25%	–	$8,000	$10,600	$8,733	$10,786	$11,214	$10,108	$4,641	$8,100
	Average	–	$4,287	$6,040	$5,413	$6,896	$6,335	$6,465	$2,879	$4,744
	Lowest 25%	–	–	$960	$500	$1,260	$1,705	$1,260	–	$750
TOTAL COMPENSATION AND BENEFIT		New England	Middle Atlantic	South Atlantic	E-N Central	E-S Central	W-N Central	W-S Central	Mountain	Pacific
	Highest 25%	–	$50,370	$55,440	$60,537	$56,474	$58,000	$57,714	$47,199	$55,045
	Average	–	$41,281	$45,522	$48,589	$46,786	$45,133	$46,320	$39,946	$49,919
	Lowest 25%	–	$28,901	$36,725	$32,444	$37,436	$35,804	$31,939	$34,201	$35,483
NUMBER OF RESPONDENTS		1	11	54	51	19	25	41	23	49

– Not enough responses to provide meaningful data

TABLE 11-9: ANNUAL COMPENSATION OF CHILDREN'S DIRECTOR BY GENDER

CHARACTERISTICS	GENDER	
	Male	Female
AVERAGE SUNDAY AM WORSHIP ATTENDANCE	1,054	1,046
AVERAGE CHURCH INCOME	$1,970,365	$2,042,835
AVERAGE # of YEARS EMPLOYED	4	6
AVERAGE # of WEEKS OF PAID VACATION	3	3
% COLLEGE GRADUATE OR HIGHER	79%	80%
% WHO RECEIVE AUTO REIMBURSEMENT	53%	62%
% ORDAINED	77%	21%
AVERAGE % SALARY INCREASE THIS YEAR	5%	5%

COMPENSATION		Male	Female
BASE SALARY:	Highest 25%	$43,260	$41,700
	Average	$32,921	$34,332
	Lowest 25%	$23,600	$27,000
HOUSING:	Highest 25%	$24,190	–
	Average	$13,472	$4,067
	Lowest 25%	–	–
PARSONAGE:	Highest 25%	–	$411
	Average	$718	$259
	Lowest 25%	–	–
TOTAL COMPENSATION	Highest 25%	$52,996	$45,369
	Average	$47,112	$38,659
	Lowest 25%	$37,063	$30,001

– Not enough responses to provide meaningful data

TABLE 11-9: ANNUAL COMPENSATION OF CHILDREN'S DIRECTOR BY GENDER

BENEFITS		GENDER	
		Male	Female
RETIREMENT:	Highest 25%	$3,212	$2,112
	Average	$1,777	$1,198
	Lowest 25%	–	–
LIFE INSURANCE:	Highest 25%	–	–
	Average	–	–
	Lowest 25%	–	–
HEALTH INSURANCE:	Highest 25%	$9,085	$5,904
	Average	$5,459	$3,087
	Lowest 25%	–	–
CONTINUING EDUCATION	Highest 25%	$806	$498
	Average	$417	$312
	Lowest 25%	–	–
TOTAL BENEFITS	Highest 25%	$11,980	$7,900
	Average	$7,731	$4,693
	Lowest 25%	$2,000	–
TOTAL COMPENSATION AND BENEFIT		Male	Female
	Highest 25%	$64,712	$51,036
	Average	$55,029	$43,352
	Lowest 25%	$43,363	$33,000
NUMBER OF RESPONDENTS		73	199

– Not enough responses to provide meaningful data

TABLE 11-10: ANNUAL COMPENSATION OF CHILDREN'S DIRECTOR BY EDUCATION

CHARACTERISTICS	EDUCATION			
	< than Bachelor	Bachelor	Master	Doctorate
AVERAGE SUNDAY AM WORSHIP ATTENDANCE	905	1,025	1,241	–
AVERAGE CHURCH INCOME	$1,527,158	$1,960,202	$2,333,748	–
AVERAGE # of YEARS EMPLOYED	6	5	7	–
AVERAGE # of WEEKS OF PAID VACATION	2	3	3	–
% COLLEGE GRADUATE OR HIGHER	–	100%	100%	–
% WHO RECEIVE AUTO REIMBURSEMENT	49%	59%	67%	–
% ORDAINED	20%	35%	47%	–
AVERAGE % SALARY INCREASE THIS YEAR	5%	4%	5%	–

COMPENSATION		< than Bachelor	Bachelor	Master	Doctorate
BASE SALARY:	Highest 25%	$37,200	$43,184	$45,000	–
	Average	$30,120	$35,037	$34,927	–
	Lowest 25%	$23,466	$26,717	$26,230	–
HOUSING:	Highest 25%	–	$11,993	$22,110	–
	Average	$2,674	$6,449	$10,754	–
	Lowest 25%	–	–	–	–
PARSONAGE:	Highest 25%	–	–	–	–
	Average	–	$447	–	–
	Lowest 25%	–	–	–	–
TOTAL COMPENSATION	Highest 25%	$40,000	$48,100	$52,441	–
	Average	$32,794	$41,932	$45,681	–
	Lowest 25%	$24,500	$31,715	$35,140	–

– Not enough responses to provide meaningful data

TABLE 11-10: ANNUAL COMPENSATION OF CHILDREN'S DIRECTOR BY EDUCATION

BENEFITS		EDUCATION			
		< than Bachelor	Bachelor	Master	Doctorate
RETIREMENT:	Highest 25%	$1,260	$2,309	$2,910	–
	Average	$729	$1,439	$1,717	–
	Lowest 25%	–	–	–	–
LIFE INSURANCE:	Highest 25%	–	–	–	–
	Average	–	–	$168	–
	Lowest 25%	–	–	–	–
HEALTH INSURANCE:	Highest 25%	$2,641	$7,106	$7,054	–
	Average	$2,083	$4,045	$4,215	–
	Lowest 25%	–	–	–	–
CONTINUING EDUCATION	Highest 25%	–	$570	$992	–
	Average	$238	$383	$385	–
	Lowest 25%	–	–	–	–
TOTAL BENEFITS	Highest 25%	$4,195	$9,465	$10,600	–
	Average	$3,065	$5,958	$6,485	–
	Lowest 25%	–	$1,113	$1,624	–
TOTAL COMPENSATION AND BENEFIT		< than Bachelor	Bachelor	Master	Doctorate
	Highest 25%	$44,001	$57,885	$61,141	–
	Average	$35,859	$47,985	$52,167	–
	Lowest 25%	$26,676	$37,050	$39,500	–
NUMBER OF RESPONDENTS		49	144	46	4

– Not enough responses to provide meaningful data

TABLE 11-11: ANNUAL COMPENSATION OF CHILDREN'S DIRECTOR BY YEARS EMPLOYED

CHARACTERISTICS		YEARS EMPLOYED			
		< 6 years	6-10 years	11-15 years	Over 15 years
AVERAGE SUNDAY AM WORSHIP ATTENDANCE		983	1,152	1,255	1,276
AVERAGE CHURCH INCOME		$1,799,415	$2,442,645	$2,410,243	$2,379,874
AVERAGE # of YEARS EMPLOYED		3	8	13	22
AVERAGE # of WEEKS OF PAID VACATION		2	3	4	3
% COLLEGE GRADUATE OR HIGHER		82%	75%	71%	89%
% WHO RECEIVE AUTO REIMBURSEMENT		57%	68%	44%	67%
% ORDAINED		36%	33%	33%	36%
AVERAGE % SALARY INCREASE THIS YEAR		4%	5%	5%	–

COMPENSATION		< 6 years	6-10 years	11-15 years	Over 15 years
BASE SALARY:	Highest 25%	$41,240	$43,260	$45,369	$43,108
	Average	$33,110	$34,939	$36,619	$37,229
	Lowest 25%	$25,000	$27,750	$23,466	$28,027
HOUSING:	Highest 25%	$10,673	$15,000	–	$19,190
	Average	$5,982	$8,025	$6,614	$9,003
	Lowest 25%	–	–	–	–
PARSONAGE:	Highest 25%	–	$420	–	–
	Average	$568	–	–	–
	Lowest 25%	–	–	–	–
TOTAL COMPENSATION	Highest 25%	$46,335	$51,916	$48,355	$53,570
	Average	$39,660	$43,005	$43,232	$46,231
	Lowest 25%	$30,000	$33,228	$28,594	$35,001

– Not enough responses to provide meaningful data

TABLE 11-11: ANNUAL COMPENSATION OF CHILDREN'S DIRECTOR BY YEARS EMPLOYED

BENEFITS		YEARS EMPLOYED			
		< 6 years	6-10 years	11-15 years	Over 15 years
RETIREMENT:	Highest 25%	$1,999	$2,501	$2,910	$4,192
	Average	$1,162	$1,505	$1,656	$3,172
	Lowest 25%	–	–	–	$801
LIFE INSURANCE:	Highest 25%	–	$120	–	$121
	Average	–	–	$191	–
	Lowest 25%	–	–	–	–
HEALTH INSURANCE:	Highest 25%	$6,756	$6,576	$5,256	$7,996
	Average	$3,531	$4,021	$3,016	$5,125
	Lowest 25%	–	–	–	–
CONTINUING EDUCATION	Highest 25%	$492	$991	$500	$844
	Average	$295	$441	$406	$323
	Lowest 25%	–	–	–	–
TOTAL BENEFITS	Highest 25%	$8,600	$10,384	$9,952	$12,188
	Average	$5,070	$6,059	$5,269	$8,705
	Lowest 25%	$400	$1,624	–	$3,900
TOTAL COMPENSATION AND BENEFIT		< 6 years	6-10 years	11-15 years	Over 15 years
	Highest 25%	$54,935	$57,695	$62,500	$64,593
	Average	$44,806	$49,064	$48,502	$54,936
	Lowest 25%	$33,002	$39,131	$33,031	$39,001
NUMBER OF RESPONDENTS		179	58	18	11

– Not enough responses to provide meaningful data

TABLE 11-12: ANNUAL COMPENSATION OF CHILDREN'S DIRECTOR BY DENOMINATION

CHARACTERISTICS		Assemblies of God	Baptist	Independent/ Nondenom	Lutheran	Methodist	Presbyterian
AVERAGE SUNDAY AM WORSHIP ATTENDANCE		634	1,066	1,407	400	792	652
AVERAGE CHURCH INCOME		$1,271,035	$2,344,610	$2,160,814	$1,008,603	$1,428,049	$1,643,497
AVERAGE # of YEARS EMPLOYED		4	6	5	7	7	5
AVERAGE # of WEEKS OF PAID VACATION		3	3	3	3	3	3
% COLLEGE GRADUATE OR HIGHER		60%	80%	75%	94%	100%	88%
% WHO RECEIVE AUTO REIMBURSEMENT		45%	67%	51%	33%	50%	62%
% ORDAINED		64%	32%	47%	6%	21%	4%
AVERAGE % SALARY INCREASE THIS YEAR		7%	4%	5%	3%	4%	4%

COMPENSATION		Assemblies of God	Baptist	Independent/ Nondenom	Lutheran	Methodist	Presbyterian
BASE SALARY:	Highest 25%	$37,063	$45,000	$43,108	$41,456	$40,000	$43,358
	Average	$27,604	$36,032	$33,890	$34,307	$34,796	$36,376
	Lowest 25%	$22,050	$28,000	$24,000	$27,000	$33,660	$27,500
HOUSING:	Highest 25%	$22,090	–	$15,240	–	–	–
	Average	$10,105	$4,806	$7,794	$1,765	$1,197	$2,145
	Lowest 25%	–	–	–	–	–	–
PARSONAGE:	Highest 25%	–	–	–	–	–	–
	Average	$522	$560	–	–	–	–
	Lowest 25%	–	–	–	–	–	–
TOTAL COMPENSATION	Highest 25%	$43,775	$48,000	$50,000	$41,457	$42,080	$45,000
	Average	$38,231	$41,398	$41,684	$36,072	$35,993	$38,521
	Lowest 25%	$25,001	$32,444	$32,001	$27,245	$35,000	$27,500

– Not enough responses to provide meaningful data

TABLE 11-12: ANNUAL COMPENSATION OF CHILDREN'S DIRECTOR BY DENOMINATION

BENEFITS		DENOMINATION					
		Assemblies of God	Baptist	Independent/ Nondenom	Lutheran	Methodist	Presbyterian
RETIREMENT:	Highest 25%	–	$3,900	$1,200	$1,789	$2,580	$3,500
	Average	$295	$2,050	$796	$783	$1,600	$1,888
	Lowest 25%	–	–	–	–	–	–
LIFE INSURANCE:	Highest 25%	–	–	–	–	–	–
	Average	–	$156	–	$192	–	–
	Lowest 25%	–	–	–	–	–	–
HEALTH INSURANCE:	Highest 25%	$8,500	$7,500	$9,164	$6,000	$5,119	$6,497
	Average	$3,826	$3,977	$4,458	$2,763	$2,007	$3,186
	Lowest 25%	–	–	–	–	–	–
CONTINUING EDUCATION	Highest 25%	–	$490	$573	$497	$508	$992
	Average	$141	$333	$343	$347	$307	$433
	Lowest 25%	–	–	–	–	–	–
TOTAL BENEFITS	Highest 25%	$8,500	$10,583	$9,566	$6,000	$6,180	$8,770
	Average	$4,294	$6,517	$5,639	$4,085	$3,949	$5,562
	Lowest 25%	–	$1,260	$1,000	$1,625	$1,500	$500
TOTAL COMPENSATION AND BENEFIT		Assemblies of God	Baptist	Independent/ Nondenom	Lutheran	Methodist	Presbyterian
	Highest 25%	$49,628	$57,694	$59,549	$45,985	$49,180	$56,801
	Average	$42,525	$47,915	$47,539	$40,157	$39,942	$44,084
	Lowest 25%	$27,547	$37,221	$34,601	$28,999	$36,900	$27,500
NUMBER OF RESPONDENTS		23	75	63	17	14	26

– Not enough responses to provide meaningful data

TABLE 11-13: AVERAGE COMPENSATION PACKAGE FOR CHILDREN'S / PRESCHOOL DIRECTOR*

		CHILDREN'S / PRESCHOOL DIRECTORS WHO RECIEVE...				
	Overall	Base Salary Only	No Base Salary	Base Salary and Parsonage	Base Salary and Housing	Base Salary and Parsonage and Housing
BASE SALARY	$33,969	$36,725		–	$29,196	–
PARSONAGE**	$377		–	–		–
HOUSING ALLOWANCE	$6,496		–		$21,022	–
TOTAL COMPENSATION PACKAGE	$40,842	$36,725	–	–	$50,218	–
NUMBER OF RESPONDENTS	276	187	3	2	82	2

*All $ values are annual averages

**Parsonage = Rental value of parsonage plus allowance

– Not enough responses to provide meaningful data

For an explanation of the Average Compensation Table, please refer to Chapter 1.

TABLE 11-14: COMPENSATION OF PART-TIME CHILDREN'S DIRECTOR BY WORSHIP ATTENDANCE

CHARACTERISTICS	WORSHIP ATTENDANCE					
	100 or less	101 - 300	301 - 500	501 - 750	751 - 1,000	Over 1,000
AVERAGE SUNDAY AM WORSHIP ATTENDANCE	72	208	405	603	902	1,284
AVERAGE CHURCH INCOME	$185,185	$432,655	$807,602	$1,150,375	$2,014,109	$2,005,099
AVERAGE # of YEARS EMPLOYED	3	4	4	7	5	5
AVERAGE # of WEEKS OF PAID VACATION	–	2	2	3	–	3
% COLLEGE GRADUATE OR HIGHER		57%	67%	73%	73%	70%
% WHO RECEIVE AUTO REIMBURSEMENT	–	42%	28%	50%	50%	50%
% ORDAINED	–	6%	–	7%	9%	8%
AVERAGE % SALARY INCREASE THIS YEAR	–	6%	5%	5%	–	17%
HOURLY RATES						
AVERAGE BASE RATE	$9.04	$8.29	$10.19	$12.32	$15.78	$10.91
ANNUAL COMPENSATION						
AVERAGE BASE SALARY:	$8,479	$10,077	$14,155	$18,843	$23,526	$19,694
AVERAGE HOUSING:	–	–	–	–	–	–
AVERAGE PARSONAGE:	–	–	–	–	–	–
AVERAGE TOTAL COMPENSATION	$8,479	$10,854	$14,155	$19,218	$23,526	$19,694
ANNUAL BENEFITS						
AVERAGE RETIREMENT	–	–	–	–	$287	$433
AVERAGE LIFE INSURANCE	–	–	–	–	–	–
AVERAGE HEALTH INSURANCE	–	$274	$384	$475	$322	$0
AVERAGE CONTINUING EDUCATION	–	$119	$184	$119	$258	$135
AVERAGE TOTAL BENEFITS	–	$441	$651	$662	$867	$569
ANNUAL COMPENSATION & BENEFIT						
AVERAGE	$8,568	$11,295	$15,031	$19,880	$24,394	$20,262
NUMBER OF RESPONDENTS	9	68	87	29	12	12

– Not enough responses to provide meaningful data

TABLE 11-15: COMPENSATION OF PART-TIME CHILDREN'S DIRECTOR BY CHURCH INCOME

CHARACTERISTICS	CHURCH INCOME				
	$250 K & Under	$251 - $500K	$501 - $750K	$751K - $1M	Over $1 Million
AVERAGE SUNDAY AM WORSHIP ATTENDANCE	132	245	379	470	755
AVERAGE CHURCH INCOME	$164,259	$379,052	$626,245	$895,309	$1,682,718
AVERAGE # of YEARS EMPLOYED	4	4	4	5	6
AVERAGE # of WEEKS OF PAID VACATION	2	2	2	3	2
% COLLEGE GRADUATE OR HIGHER	67%	64%	69%	70%	67%
% WHO RECEIVE AUTO REIMBURSEMENT	22%	38%	35%	47%	43%
% ORDAINED	13%	6%	–	4%	6%
AVERAGE % SALARY INCREASE THIS YEAR	11%	6%	4%	6%	8%
HOURLY RATES					
AVERAGE BASE RATE	$9.75	$8.37	$9.81	$13.30	$10.92
ANNUAL COMPENSATION	$250 K & Under	$251 - $500K	$501 - $750K	$751K - $1M	Over $1 Million
AVERAGE BASE SALARY:	$10,233	$9,671	$12,822	$19,276	$18,624
AVERAGE HOUSING:	–	–	–	–	–
AVERAGE PARSONAGE:	–	–	–	–	–
AVERAGE TOTAL COMPENSATION	$10,852	$10,026	$13,433	$19,693	$18,802
ANNUAL BENEFITS					
AVERAGE RETIREMENT	–	–	–	$179	$204
AVERAGE LIFE INSURANCE	–	–	–	–	–
AVERAGE HEALTH INSURANCE	$125	$153	$404	$585	$379
AVERAGE CONTINUING EDUCATION	–	$143	$165	$183	$136
AVERAGE TOTAL BENEFITS	$200	$314	$575	$982	$721
ANNUAL COMPENSATION & BENEFIT					
AVERAGE	$11,052	$10,340	$14,408	$20,676	$19,524
NUMBER OF RESPONDENTS	16	59	36	26	56

– Not enough responses to provide meaningful data

12

ADMINSTRATORS

Employment Profile

The majority of administrators serve in a full-time capacity. In this study, 23% of those working full-time are ordained ministers, although this percentage declines significantly for those serving part-time. Gender is evenly split among those working full-time while women are in a majority for those working part-time. This group of administrators provided the following employment profile:

	FULL-TIME	PART-TIME
Ordained	23%	5%
Average years employed	7	6
Male	49%	25%
Female	51%	75%
Self-employed (receives 1099)	2%	7%
Church employee (receives W-2)	98%	93%
High school diploma	16%	31%
Associate's degree	8%	16%
Bachelor's degree	49%	41%
Master's degree	24%	11%
Doctorate	2%	1%
Number of respondents	*330*	*106*

Total Compensation plus Benefits Package Analysis

The analysis below is based upon the tables found later in this chapter. The tables present compensation data according to worship attendance, church income, combinations of size and setting, region, gender, education, years employed, and denomination for administrators who serve full-time. The final two tables provide data for part-time administrators by worship attendance and church income. In this way, the administrator's compensation can be viewed from a variety of useful perspectives. The total compensation plus benefits amount found in a box at the bottom of each chart includes the base salary, housing and/or parsonage amount, life and health insurance payments, retirement contribution, and educational funds.

Full-time staff members. In general, average compensation and benefit packages among administrators are lower than the pastoral and director positions reported. Few church administrators receive housing or parsonage allowances.

Part-time staff members. Twenty-four percent of the administrators positions reported work part-time. Females comprise 75% of this group. Slightly over half of the part-time administrator positions reported have a college degree.

COMPENSATION PLUS BENEFITS	FULL TIME	PART TIME
Base salary	100%	99%
Housing	21%	2%
Parsonage	1%	0%
Retirement	49%	10%
Life insurance	32%	0%
Health insurance	64%	14%
Paid vacation	91%	56%
Auto reimbursement	51%	24%
Continuing education	28%	3%

KEY POINTS

⮑ **Compensation and benefits increase with church size.** Base salary and total compensation plus benefits steadily increases with church size. The largest gains of approximately $10,000 occur in the larger churches from 501 to 750 and 751 to 1,000 and then from 751 to 1,000 and over 1,000. Nearly 60% work in churches with an attendance over 500. 30% worked in churches over 1,000. The national average compensation plus benefits corresponded to a church attendance of over 750. *See Table 12-1.*

⮑ **Church income impacts compensation and benefits in the churches with the largest incomes.** Generally, compensation and benefits increase as church income increases at each level. For administrators, this increase did not emerge until $751,000 and higher income levels. 74% of the administrators participating in this study work in churches within these higher levels. *See Table 12-2.*

⮑ **Geographic setting across attendance levels impacts compensation and benefit packages. Administrators serving in** metropolitan churches receive the highest compensation and benefit packages for churches with attendance above 250 compared to suburban and small town or rural churches. However, those serving in metropolitan churches with attendance 250 and under receive the lowest compensation. About 77% of administrators in this group work in metropolitan and suburban churches. Few farming area churches employ administrators. *See Tables 12-3, 12-4, 12-5, 12-6, and 12-7.*

⮑ **The region in which a church is located has some effect on the compensation and benefits of the administrator.** Consistent with other positions, Administrators located in the Pacific region earn more than those in the other areas. With the exception of two regions (Middle Atlantic and South Atlantic), compensation and benefits packages were all close to or above the national average for administrators. *See Table 12-8.*

⮑ **On average, male administrators receive 55% more in compensation and benefits than did females.** This represent the largest earning gap of any church staff position with a sufficient sample size of women and men. Women earn well below the national average. In terms of salary alone, women administrators earn about $10,000 per year less. Similar with other positions, women generally serve in significantly smaller churches than men, which impacts compensation and benefit packages. *See Table 12-9.*

⮑ **College graduates receive substantially higher compensation and benefits than do high school graduates; having a graduate degree increases the package amount significantly as well.** College graduates with a bachelor's degree earn over $13,500 more than those with a high school education. A similar difference emerges among those with a bachelor's degree compared to those with a doctorate degree. Significant increases occurred over the national average once the administrator earned a graduate degree. *See Table 12-10.*

⮑ **A church's denominational affiliation has some effect on the compensation and benefits package of the administrator. However, it is directly related to church income and attendance. In general, the administrators serving in denominations of larger churches earn more than those in denominations of smaller churches.** The compensation and benefits packages of all but two denominations are below the national average. The churches whose packages average above the national average are Assemblies of God and Baptist denominations. Over one-third of administrators work for these denominations. *See Table 12-12.*

⮑ **Average church income and attendance impact compensation and benefit packages similarly for part-time administrators as full-time administrators.** As both church income and attendance increase, part-time compensation increases. Hourly rate does not have a similar relationship with income and attendance as total compensation. *See Tables 12-13 and 12-14.*

Ten Year Compensation & Benefits Trend: National Average for Administrators

FULL TIME

1997	$37,413
1998	$40,207
1999	$42,277
2000	$44,768
2001	$48,064
2002	$47,305
2003	$50,615
2004	$49,907
2005	$53,153
2006	$52,036

TABLE 12-1: ANNUAL COMPENSATION OF ADMINISTRATOR BY WORSHIP ATTENDANCE

CHARACTERISTICS		100 or less	101–300	301–500	501–750	751–1000	Over 1000
AVERAGE SUNDAY AM WORSHIP ATTENDANCE		–	220	409	626	884	2,119
AVERAGE CHURCH INCOME		–	$478,809	$909,609	$1,460,073	$2,012,485	$3,741,924
AVERAGE # of YEARS EMPLOYED		–	7	8	6	7	8
AVERAGE # of WEEKS OF PAID VACATION		–	3	3	3	3	3
% COLLEGE GRADUATE OR HIGHER		–	66%	74%	71%	76%	88%
% WHO RECEIVE AUTO REIMBURSEMENT		–	46%	66%	52%	53%	60%
% ORDAINED		–	10%	18%	22%	18%	35%
AVERAGE % SALARY INCREASE THIS YEAR		–	5%	6%	5%	6%	5%
COMPENSATION		100 or less	101–300	301–500	501–750	751–1000	Over 1000
BASE SALARY:	Highest 25%	–	$36,500	$41,381	$45,000	$55,319	$65,288
	Average	–	$30,577	$34,310	$38,152	$44,286	$52,331
	Lowest 25%	–	$23,600	$25,000	$29,370	$32,082	$36,250
HOUSING:	Highest 25%	–	–	–	–	–	$15,810
	Average	–	$1,866	$4,131	$3,272	$5,139	$7,749
	Lowest 25%	–	–	–	–	–	–
PARSONAGE:	Highest 25%	–	–	–	–	–	–
	Average	–	–	–	–	$1,672	–
	Lowest 25%	–	–	–	–	–	–
TOTAL COMPENSATION	Highest 25%	–	$38,000	$46,000	$50,544	$60,443	$75,500
	Average	–	$32,443	$38,440	$41,424	$51,098	$60,080
	Lowest 25%	–	$24,000	$27,380	$30,000	$36,850	$43,250

– Not enough responses to provide meaningful data

TABLE 12-1: ANNUAL COMPENSATION OF ADMINISTRATOR BY WORSHIP ATTENDANCE

BENEFITS		WORSHIP ATTENDANCE					
		100 or less	101-300	301-500	501-750	751-1000	Over 1000
RETIREMENT:	Highest 25%	–	$2,541	$2,842	$2,800	$4,050	$3,128
	Average	–	$1,290	$1,529	$1,733	$2,425	$2,028
	Lowest 25%	–	–	–	–	–	–
LIFE INSURANCE:	Highest 25%	–	–	–	–	–	–
	Average	–	$151	–	$158	–	$206
	Lowest 25%	–	–	–	–	–	–
HEALTH INSURANCE:	Highest 25%	–	$6,000	$5,762	$7,708	$7,852	$8,514
	Average	–	$3,248	$3,661	$3,992	$4,282	$5,432
	Lowest 25%	–	–	–	–	–	$693
CONTINUING EDUCATION	Highest 25%	–	–	$493	–	$503	–
	Average	–	$297	$304	$307	$294	$296
	Lowest 25%	–	–	–	–	–	–
TOTAL BENEFITS	Highest 25%	–	$8,911	$8,951	$9,600	$12,934	$11,906
	Average	–	$4,986	$5,563	$6,190	$7,068	$7,963
	Lowest 25%	–	–	–	$1,732	$967	$2,643
TOTAL COMPENSATION AND BENEFIT		100 or less	101-300	301-500	501-750	751-1000	Over 1000
	Highest 25%	–	$45,778	$53,072	$57,120	$73,835	$86,064
	Average	–	$37,429	$44,144	$47,615	$58,166	$68,042
	Lowest 25%	–	$28,300	$31,700	$36,861	$39,600	$48,150
NUMBER OF RESPONDENTS		4	54	71	57	36	96

– Not enough responses to provide meaningful data

TABLE 12-2: ANNUAL COMPENSATION OF ADMINISTRATOR BY CHURCH INCOME

CHARACTERISTICS		CHURCH INCOME				
		$250K & under	$251K-$500K	$501K-$750K	$751K-$1M	Over $1 Million
AVERAGE SUNDAY AM WORSHIP ATTENDANCE		332	268	349	470	1,400
AVERAGE CHURCH INCOME		$198,490	$412,902	$613,602	$890,666	$2,744,515
AVERAGE # of YEARS EMPLOYED		5	9	6	7	8
AVERAGE # of WEEKS OF PAID VACATION		–	3	3	3	3
% COLLEGE GRADUATE OR HIGHER		75%	43%	77%	69%	84%
% WHO RECEIVE AUTO REIMBURSEMENT		75%	51%	40%	67%	58%
% ORDAINED		20%	10%	4%	13%	31%
AVERAGE % SALARY INCREASE THIS YEAR		–	5%	6%	6%	5%

COMPENSATION		$250K & under	$251K-$500K	$501K-$750K	$751K-$1M	Over 1 Million
BASE SALARY:	Highest 25%	$31,000	$35,784	$37,400	$39,667	$57,745
	Average	$29,346	$29,253	$30,557	$35,154	$46,696
	Lowest 25%	$19,230	$23,000	$23,600	$27,808	$33,395
HOUSING:	Highest 25%	$14,400	–	–	–	$9,600
	Average	$7,023	$2,339	$780	$2,980	$6,746
	Lowest 25%	–	–	–	–	–
PARSONAGE:	Highest 25%	–	–	–	–	–
	Average	–	–	–	–	–
	Lowest 25%	–	–	–	–	–
TOTAL COMPENSATION	Highest 25%	$47,969	$36,720	$39,000	$41,409	$66,708
	Average	$36,369	$31,592	$31,337	$38,134	$53,554
	Lowest 25%	$21,000	$25,000	$23,600	$30,285	$39,074

– Not enough responses to provide meaningful data

TABLE 12-2: ANNUAL COMPENSATION OF ADMINISTRATOR BY CHURCH INCOME

		CHURCH INCOME				
BENEFITS		$250K & under	$251K-$500K	$501K-$750K	$751K-$1M	Over $1 Million
RETIREMENT:	Highest 25%	–	$2,750	$1,560	$1,624	$3,406
	Average	–	$1,372	$776	$1,284	$2,167
	Lowest 25%	–	–	–	–	–
LIFE INSURANCE:	Highest 25%	–	–	–	–	–
	Average	$200	$147	$144	$107	$163
	Lowest 25%	–	–	–	–	–
HEALTH INSURANCE:	Highest 25%	–	$7,830	$4,000	$5,650	$8,068
	Average	$1,920	$3,756	$2,035	$3,678	$4,830
	Lowest 25%	–	–	–	–	–
CONTINUING EDUCATION	Highest 25%	–	$245	–	$625	–
	Average	$300	$214	$81	$355	$349
	Lowest 25%	–	–	–	–	–
TOTAL BENEFITS	Highest 25%	$3,000	$9,940	$6,330	$9,183	$11,181
	Average	$2,450	$5,489	$3,036	$5,424	$7,509
	Lowest 25%	–	–	–	$1,132	$2,400
TOTAL COMPENSATION AND BENEFIT		$250K & under	$251K-$500K	$501K-$750K	$751K-$1M	Over 1 Million
	Highest 25%	$47,969	$43,600	$43,020	$50,356	$77,107
	Average	$38,819	$37,391	$34,373	$43,808	$61,063
	Lowest 25%	$21,000	$28,000	$26,537	$36,316	$43,706
NUMBER OF RESPONDENTS		10	42	29	40	188

– Not enough responses to provide meaningful data

TABLE 12-3: ANNUAL COMPENSATION OF ADMINISTRATOR BY CHURCH SETTING & SIZE

ATTENDANCE 250 & UNDER	CHURCH SETTING			
	Metropolitan city	Suburb of large city	Small town or rural city	Farming area
AVERAGE SUNDAY AM WORSHIP ATTENDANCE	187	203	188	–
AVERAGE CHURCH INCOME	$389,075	$547,896	$370,128	–
AVERAGE # of YEARS EMPLOYED	7	8	9	–
AVERAGE # of WEEKS OF PAID VACATION	3	3	3	–
% COLLEGE GRADUATE OR HIGHER	80%	71%	53%	–
% WHO RECEIVE AUTO REIMBURSEMENT	44%	60%	32%	–
% ORDAINED	9%	15%	15%	–
AVERAGE % SALARY INCREASE THIS YEAR	4%	4%	7%	–

COMPENSATION		Metropolitan city	Suburb of large city	Small town or rural city	Farming area
BASE SALARY:	Highest 25%	$35,650	$38,000	$30,224	–
	Average	$29,458	$31,291	$27,521	–
	Lowest 25%	$22,100	$23,992	$22,985	–
HOUSING:	Highest 25%	–	–	–	–
	Average	$1,200	$3,000	$2,938	–
	Lowest 25%	–	–	–	–
PARSONAGE:	Highest 25%	–	–	–	–
	Average	–	–	–	–
	Lowest 25%	–	–	–	–
TOTAL COMPENSATION	Highest 25%	$35,650	$39,281	$36,142	–
	Average	$30,658	$34,291	$30,458	–
	Lowest 25%	$22,500	$23,992	$25,615	–

– Not enough responses to provide meaningful data

TABLE 12-3: ANNUAL COMPENSATION OF ADMINISTRATOR BY CHURCH SETTING & SIZE

BENEFITS		CHURCH SETTING			
		Metropoli-tan city	Suburb of large city	Small town or rural city	Farming area
RETIREMENT:	Highest 25%	–	$3,535	$2,540	–
	Average	$1,297	$1,199	$1,149	–
	Lowest 25%	–	–	–	–
LIFE INSURANCE:	Highest 25%	–	$240	–	–
	Average	–	$111	$527	–
	Lowest 25%	–	–	–	–
HEALTH INSURANCE:	Highest 25%	–	$5,124	$7,680	–
	Average	$1,206	$2,863	$3,878	–
	Lowest 25%	–	–	–	–
CONTINUING EDUCATION	Highest 25%	–	$1,000	$125	
	Average	–	$736	$288	–
	Lowest 25%	–	–	–	–
TOTAL BENEFITS	Highest 25%	$5,510	$10,115	$9,666	–
	Average	$2,599	$4,910	$5,841	–
	Lowest 25%	$0	$2	$2,358	–
TOTAL COMPENSATION AND BENEFIT		Metropoli-tan city	Suburb of large city	Small town or rural city	Farming area
	Highest 25%	$43,342	$49,396	$45,102	–
	Average	$33,257	$39,201	$36,299	–
	Lowest 25%	$22,500	$24,480	$29,240	–
NUMBER OF RESPONDENTS		12	14	20	0

– Not enough responses to provide meaningful data

TABLE 12-4: ANNUAL COMPENSATION OF ADMINISTRATOR BY CHURCH SETTING & SIZE

ATTENDANCE 251 - 500	CHURCH SETTING			
	Metropolitan city	Suburb of large city	Small town or rural city	Farming area
AVERAGE SUNDAY AM WORSHIP ATTENDANCE	391	399	384	–
AVERAGE CHURCH INCOME	$994,269	$940,498	$753,076	–
AVERAGE # of YEARS EMPLOYED	9	6	9	–
AVERAGE # of WEEKS OF PAID VACATION	3	3	3	–
% COLLEGE GRADUATE OR HIGHER	93%	68%	69%	–
% WHO RECEIVE AUTO REIMBURSEMENT	93%	48%	66%	–
% ORDAINED	13%	17%	16%	–
AVERAGE % SALARY INCREASE THIS YEAR	4%	9%	5%	–

COMPENSATION		Metropolitan city	Suburb of large city	Small town or rural city	Farming area
BASE SALARY:	Highest 25%	$43,650	$41,001	$37,051	–
	Average	$40,197	$34,424	$30,567	–
	Lowest 25%	$34,360	$25,001	$23,001	–
HOUSING:	Highest 25%	–	–	–	–
	Average	$3,063	$4,200	$3,457	–
	Lowest 25%	–	–	–	–
PARSONAGE:	Highest 25%	–	–	–	–
	Average	–	–	–	–
	Lowest 25%	–	–	–	–
TOTAL COMPENSATION	Highest 25%	$46,150	$50,149	$37,509	–
	Average	$43,259	$38,624	$34,024	–
	Lowest 25%	$34,360	$30,571	$24,999	–

– Not enough responses to provide meaningful data

TABLE 12-4: ANNUAL COMPENSATION OF ADMINISTRATOR BY CHURCH SETTING & SIZE

BENEFITS		CHURCH SETTING			
		Metropoli-tan city	Suburb of large city	Small town or rural city	Farming area
RETIREMENT:	Highest 25%	$2,369	$2,030	$2,846	–
	Average	$1,670	$1,070	$1,818	–
	Lowest 25%	–	–	–	–
LIFE INSURANCE:	Highest 25%	–	–	–	–
	Average	–	$106	–	–
	Lowest 25%	–	–	–	–
HEALTH INSURANCE:	Highest 25%	$4,272	$5,853	$6,695	–
	Average	$2,529	$3,474	$4,601	–
	Lowest 25%	–	–	–	–
CONTINUING EDUCATION	Highest 25%	$900	–	$505	–
	Average	$469	$196	$299	–
	Lowest 25%	–	–	–	–
TOTAL BENEFITS	Highest 25%	$7,335	$8,724	$9,944	–
	Average	$4,683	$4,845	$6,761	–
	Lowest 25%	$2,333	–	–	–
TOTAL COMPENSATION AND BENEFIT		Metropoli-tan city	Suburb of large city	Small town or rural city	Farming area
	Highest 25%	$50,626	$53,900	$45,779	–
	Average	$47,942	$43,469	$41,088	–
	Lowest 25%	$39,810	$31,701	$28,300	–
NUMBER OF RESPONDENTS		16	31	33	2

– Not enough responses to provide meaningful data

TABLE 12-5: ANNUAL COMPENSATION OF ADMINISTRATOR BY CHURCH SETTING & SIZE

ATTENDANCE 501 - 750	CHURCH SETTING			
	Metropoli-tan city	Suburb of large city	Small town or rural city	Farming area
AVERAGE SUNDAY AM WORSHIP ATTENDANCE	617	650	597	–
AVERAGE CHURCH INCOME	$1,485,469	$1,474,884	$1,443,783	–
AVERAGE # of YEARS EMPLOYED	7	6	6	–
AVERAGE # of WEEKS OF PAID VACATION	4	3	3	–
% COLLEGE GRADUATE OR HIGHER	80%	74%	67%	–
% WHO RECEIVE AUTO REIMBURSEMENT	67%	44%	53%	–
% ORDAINED	20%	15%	33%	–
AVERAGE % SALARY INCREASE THIS YEAR	3%	7%	3%	–

COMPENSATION		Metropoli-tan city	Suburb of large city	Small town or rural city	Farming area
BASE SALARY:	Highest 25%	$44,850	$50,989	$44,247	–
	Average	$41,266	$38,374	$36,146	–
	Lowest 25%	$30,000	$29,011	$28,210	–
HOUSING:	Highest 25%	–	–	$9,905	–
	Average	$4,371	$719	$6,494	–
	Lowest 25%	–	–	–	–
PARSONAGE:	Highest 25%	–	–	–	–
	Average	–	–	–	–
	Lowest 25%	–	–	–	–
TOTAL COMPENSATION	Highest 25%	$50,922	$51,292	$48,992	–
	Average	$45,637	$39,094	$42,640	–
	Lowest 25%	$34,100	$29,009	$29,379	–

– Not enough responses to provide meaningful data

TABLE 12-5: ANNUAL COMPENSATION OF ADMINISTRATOR BY CHURCH SETTING & SIZE

BENEFITS		CHURCH SETTING			
		Metropoli-tan city	Suburb of large city	Small town or rural city	Farming area
RETIREMENT:	Highest 25%	$5,420	$2,798	$2,518	–
	Average	$3,255	$1,469	$1,400	–
	Lowest 25%	–	–	–	–
LIFE INSURANCE:	Highest 25%	–	–	$406	–
	Average	–	$100	$290	–
	Lowest 25%	–	–	–	–
HEALTH INSURANCE:	Highest 25%	$4,320	$7,196	$8,661	–
	Average	$3,764	$3,350	$5,235	–
	Lowest 25%	$2,382	–	–	–
CONTINUING EDUCATION	Highest 25%	$513	–	–	–
	Average	$380	$267	$342	–
	Lowest 25%	–	–	–	–
TOTAL BENEFITS	Highest 25%	$9,740	$9,055	$11,495	–
	Average	$7,477	$5,185	$7,267	–
	Lowest 25%	$3,900	–	$2,324	–
TOTAL COMPENSATION AND BENEFIT		Metropoli-tan city	Suburb of large city	Small town or rural city	Farming area
	Highest 25%	$59,443	$57,116	$62,343	–
	Average	$53,114	$44,278	$49,907	–
	Lowest 25%	$42,000	$32,118	$36,865	–
NUMBER OF RESPONDENTS		10	27	19	1

– Not enough responses to provide meaningful data

TABLE 12-6: ANNUAL COMPENSATION OF ADMINISTRATOR BY CHURCH SETTING & SIZE

ATTENDANCE 751 - 1,000		Metropolitan city	Suburb of large city	Small town or rural city	Farming area
AVERAGE SUNDAY AM WORSHIP ATTENDANCE		930	844	–	–
AVERAGE CHURCH INCOME		$2,202,622	$1,969,194	–	–
AVERAGE # of YEARS EMPLOYED		7	5	–	–
AVERAGE # of WEEKS OF PAID VACATION		3	4	–	–
% COLLEGE GRADUATE OR HIGHER		79%	67%	–	–
% WHO RECEIVE AUTO REIMBURSEMENT		38%	62%	–	–
% ORDAINED		14%	8%	–	–
AVERAGE % SALARY INCREASE THIS YEAR		7%	5%	–	–

COMPENSATION		Metropolitan city	Suburb of large city	Small town or rural city	Farming area
BASE SALARY:	Highest 25%	$60,883	$54,064	–	–
	Average	$47,764	$45,478	–	–
	Lowest 25%	$34,936	$36,436	–	–
HOUSING:	Highest 25%	–	–	–	–
	Average	$6,067	$2,615	–	–
	Lowest 25%	–	–	–	–
PARSONAGE:	Highest 25%	$5,525	–	–	–
	Average	$1,400	–	–	–
	Lowest 25%	–	–	–	–
TOTAL COMPENSATION	Highest 25%	$77,605	$56,033	–	–
	Average	$55,230	$48,093	–	–
	Lowest 25%	$35,054	$39,168	–	–

– Not enough responses to provide meaningful data

TABLE 12-6: ANNUAL COMPENSATION OF ADMINISTRATOR BY CHURCH SETTING & SIZE

BENEFITS		CHURCH SETTING			
		Metropoli-tan city	Suburb of large city	Small town or rural city	Farming area
RETIREMENT:	Highest 25%	$4,097	$4,004	–	–
	Average	$2,606	$1,926	–	–
	Lowest 25%	–	–	–	–
LIFE INSURANCE:	Highest 25%	–	$242	–	–
	Average	–	$121	–	–
	Lowest 25%	–	–	–	–
HEALTH INSURANCE:	Highest 25%	$5,994	$9,606	–	–
	Average	$3,280	$5,549	–	–
	Lowest 25%	–	–	–	–
CONTINUING EDUCATION	Highest 25%	$458	$975	–	–
	Average	$177	$411	–	–
	Lowest 25%	–	–	–	–
TOTAL BENEFITS	Highest 25%	$10,212	$14,702	–	–
	Average	$6,087	$8,007	–	–
	Lowest 25%	–	$1,097	–	
TOTAL COMPENSATION AND BENEFIT		Metropoli-tan city	Suburb of large city	Small town or rural city	Farming area
	Highest 25%	$81,688	$71,020	–	–
	Average	$61,317	$56,100	–	–
	Lowest 25%	$40,049	$39,151	–	–
NUMBER OF RESPONDENTS		15	13	6	1

– Not enough responses to provide meaningful data

TABLE 12-7: ANNUAL COMPENSATION OF ADMINISTRATOR BY CHURCH SETTING & SIZE

ATTENDANCE OVER 1,000		CHURCH SETTING			
		Metropoli-tan city	Suburb of large city	Small town or rural city	Farming area
AVERAGE SUNDAY AM WORSHIP ATTENDANCE		2,465	2,154	1,815	–
AVERAGE CHURCH INCOME		$5,038,127	$3,729,990	$2,956,496	–
AVERAGE # of YEARS EMPLOYED		10	7	9	–
AVERAGE # of WEEKS OF PAID VACATION		3	3	3	–
% COLLEGE GRADUATE OR HIGHER		100%	82%	90%	–
% WHO RECEIVE AUTO REIMBURSEMENT		56%	58%	65%	–
% ORDAINED		38%	28%	52%	–
AVERAGE % SALARY INCREASE THIS YEAR		5%	6%	5%	–

COMPENSATION		Metropoli-tan city	Suburb of large city	Small town or rural city	Farming area
BASE SALARY:	Highest 25%	$73,786	$71,001	$55,029	–
	Average	$57,108	$55,560	$41,368	–
	Lowest 25%	$39,452	$39,900	$28,533	–
HOUSING:	Highest 25%	$15,500	–	$24,983	–
	Average	$7,933	$5,473	$13,499	–
	Lowest 25%	–	–	–	–
PARSONAGE:	Highest 25%	–	–	–	–
	Average	–	–	–	–
	Lowest 25%	–	–	–	–
TOTAL COMPENSATION	Highest 25%	$81,874	$76,620	$69,829	–
	Average	$65,041	$61,033	$54,867	–
	Lowest 25%	$41,500	$44,000	$43,503	–

– Not enough responses to provide meaningful data

TABLE 12-7: ANNUAL COMPENSATION OF ADMINISTRATOR BY CHURCH SETTING & SIZE

BENEFITS		CHURCH SETTING			
		Metropoli-tan city	Suburb of large city	Small town or rural city	Farming area
RETIREMENT:	Highest 25%	$2,642	$3,393	$3,068	–
	Average	$1,456	$2,097	$2,142	–
	Lowest 25%	–	–	–	–
LIFE INSURANCE:	Highest 25%	$218	–	$155	–
	Average	$216	$226	$146	–
	Lowest 25%	–	–	–	–
HEALTH INSURANCE:	Highest 25%	$10,327	$8,497	$8,337	–
	Average	$6,839	$5,318	$4,664	–
	Lowest 25%	$2,897	$400	$273	–
CONTINUING EDUCATION	Highest 25%	$650	–	–	–
	Average	$394	$268	$309	–
	Lowest 25%	–	–	–	–
TOTAL BENEFITS	Highest 25%	$13,523	$11,181	$11,811	–
	Average	$8,904	$7,908	$7,261	–
	Lowest 25%	$4,099	$2,643	$894	–
TOTAL COMPENSATION AND BENEFIT		Metropoli-tan city	Suburb of large city	Small town or rural city	Farming area
	Highest 25%	$99,307	$87,014	$75,992	–
	Average	$73,945	$68,941	$62,128	–
	Lowest 25%	$44,108	$49,400	$46,250	–
NUMBER OF RESPONDENTS		16	56	23	0

– Not enough responses to provide meaningful data

273

TABLE 12-8: ANNUAL COMPENSATION OF ADMINISTRATOR BY REGION

CHARACTERISTICS	REGION								
	New England	Middle Atlantic	South Atlantic	E-N Central	E-S Central	W-N Central	W-S Central	Moun-tain	Pacific
AVERAGE SUNDAY AM WORSHIP ATTENDANCE	–	638	771	1,454	1,017	735	927	1,124	1,038
AVERAGE CHURCH INCOME	–	$1,207,150	$1,648,054	$2,267,145	$2,431,762	$1,506,489	$2,158,056	$1,867,222	$1,978,150
AVERAGE # of YEARS EMPLOYED	–	7	7	7	6	9	9	8	7
AVERAGE # of WEEKS OF PAID VACATION	–	3	3	3	3	3	3	3	3
% COLLEGE GRADUATE OR HIGHER	–	68%	77%	74%	85%	63%	80%	79%	73%
% WHO RECEIVE AUTO REIMBURSEMENT	–	67%	60%	75%	54%	65%	40%	55%	49%
% ORDAINED	–	10%	15%	25%	22%	24%	25%	32%	34%
AVERAGE % SALARY INCREASE THIS YEAR	–	5%	7%	4%	6%	4%	5%	6%	6%

COMPENSATION		New England	Middle Atlantic	South Atlantic	E-N Central	E-S Central	W-N Central	W-S Central	Moun-tain	Pacific
BASE SALARY:	Highest 25%	–	$40,320	$47,872	$60,000	$54,534	$51,051	$45,170	$44,258	$51,300
	Average	–	$34,312	$38,161	$43,828	$43,551	$39,221	$39,506	$41,167	$42,916
	Lowest 25%	–	$29,120	$27,190	$26,500	$29,685	$23,600	$27,375	$34,000	$30,500
HOUSING:	Highest 25%	–	–	–	–	–	$10,000	–	$9,578	$22,643
	Average	–	–	$3,517	$4,336	$4,699	$5,323	$5,565	$5,714	$9,182
	Lowest 25%	–	–	–	–	–	–	–	–	–
PARSONAGE:	Highest 25%	–	–	–	–	–	–	–	–	–
	Average	–	–	–	–	$1,400	–	–	–	–
	Lowest 25%	–	–	–	–	–	–	–	–	–
TOTAL COMPENSATION	Highest 25%	–	$40,320	$52,525	$65,000	$65,774	$57,050	$53,770	$56,630	$66,950
	Average	–	$34,683	$41,954	$48,164	$49,651	$44,543	$45,071	$46,880	$52,112
	Lowest 25%	–	$29,120	$29,882	$30,000	$31,000	$30,815	$30,000	$36,500	$36,720

— Not enough responses to provide meaningful data

TABLE 12-8: ANNUAL COMPENSATION OF ADMINISTRATOR BY REGION

BENEFITS		REGION								
		New England	Middle Atlantic	South Atlantic	E-N Central	E-S Central	W-N Central	W-S Central	Mountain	Pacific
RETIREMENT:	Highest 25%	–	$1,325	$3,211	$2,200	$4,170	$4,230	$2,945	$2,541	$2,835
	Average	–	$957	$1,935	$1,511	$2,549	$2,058	$1,893	$1,402	$1,684
	Lowest 25%	–	–	–	–	–	–	–	–	–
LIFE INSURANCE:	Highest 25%	–	–	–	–	–	$222	–	–	–
	Average	–	$239	$129	$159	$129	$163	$201	$207	–
	Lowest 25%	–	–	–	–	–	–	–	–	–
HEALTH INSURANCE:	Highest 25%	–	$7,812	$5,574	$8,425	$7,032	$8,258	$7,559	$8,000	$7,320
	Average	–	$4,533	$3,113	$4,311	$3,822	$5,369	$4,979	$4,710	$4,323
	Lowest 25%	–	–	–	–	–	–	–	–	–
CONTINUING EDUCATION	Highest 25%	–	–	–	–	$700	–	$302	$998	–
	Average	–	$310	$315	$297	$479	$273	$275	$399	$297
	Lowest 25%	–	–	–	–	–	–	–	–	–
TOTAL BENEFITS	Highest 25%	–	$10,115	$9,005	$10,397	$12,519	$12,913	$10,388	$9,867	$10,200
	Average	–	$6,039	$5,492	$6,279	$6,978	$7,863	$7,347	$6,718	$6,376
	Lowest 25%	–	–	–	$974	$1,600	$2,319	$2,000	$1,816	$894
TOTAL COMPENSATION AND BENEFIT		New England	Middle Atlantic	South Atlantic	E-N Central	E-S Central	W-N Central	W-S Central	Mountain	Pacific
	Highest 25%	–	$49,000	$58,276	$73,230	$69,977	$71,960	$64,740	$56,685	$75,300
	Average	–	$40,722	$47,577	$54,442	$57,093	$52,407	$52,418	$53,598	$58,488
	Lowest 25%	–	$34,057	$34,820	$31,135	$35,920	$36,551	$37,570	$42,900	$40,362
NUMBER OF RESPONDENTS		2	21	76	51	28	26	53	26	45

– Not enough responses to provide meaningful data

TABLE 12-9: ANNUAL COMPENSATION OF ADMINISTRATOR BY GENDER

CHARACTERISTICS	GENDER	
	Male	Female
AVERAGE SUNDAY AM WORSHIP ATTENDANCE	1,144	826
AVERAGE CHURCH INCOME	$2,288,111	$1,531,478
AVERAGE # of YEARS EMPLOYED	7	8
AVERAGE # of WEEKS OF PAID VACATION	3	3
% COLLEGE GRADUATE OR HIGHER	90%	61%
% WHO RECEIVE AUTO REIMBURSEMENT	63%	52%
% ORDAINED	45%	2%
AVERAGE % SALARY INCREASE THIS YEAR	5%	6%

COMPENSATION		Male	Female
BASE SALARY:	Highest 25%	$58,100	$40,000
	Average	$45,339	$35,571
	Lowest 25%	$30,886	$27,000
HOUSING:	Highest 25%	$20,897	–
	Average	$9,719	–
	Lowest 25%	–	–
PARSONAGE:	Highest 25%	–	–
	Average	–	–
	Lowest 25%	–	–
TOTAL COMPENSATION	Highest 25%	$67,770	$40,320
	Average	$55,191	$36,096
	Lowest 25%	$40,618	$27,375

– Not enough responses to provide meaningful data

TABLE 12-9: ANNUAL COMPENSATION OF ADMINISTRATOR BY GENDER

		GENDER	
BENEFITS		Male	Female
RETIREMENT:	Highest 25%	$3,500	$2,200
	Average	$2,197	$1,352
	Lowest 25%	–	–
LIFE INSURANCE:	Highest 25%	–	–
	Average	$206	$100
	Lowest 25%	–	–
HEALTH INSURANCE:	Highest 25%	$8,460	$6,000
	Average	$5,198	$3,293
	Lowest 25%	–	–
CONTINUING EDUCATION	Highest 25%	–	$491
	Average	$313	$321
	Lowest 25%	–	–
TOTAL BENEFITS	Highest 25%	$11,811	$8,727
	Average	$7,914	$5,066
	Lowest 25%	$2,882	–
TOTAL COMPENSATION AND BENEFIT		Male	Female
	Highest 25%	$79,348	$48,791
	Average	$63,105	$41,299
	Lowest 25%	$46,400	$30,107
NUMBER OF RESPONDENTS		162	167

– *Not enough responses to provide meaningful data*

TABLE 12-10: ANNUAL COMPENSATION OF ADMINISTRATOR BY EDUCATION

CHARACTERISTICS	EDUCATION			
	< than Bachelor	Bachelor	Master	Doctorate
AVERAGE SUNDAY AM WORSHIP ATTENDANCE	733	1,005	1,221	–
AVERAGE CHURCH INCOME	$1,246,986	$1,921,220	$2,552,615	–
AVERAGE # of YEARS EMPLOYED	8	7	7	–
AVERAGE # of WEEKS OF PAID VACATION	3	3	3	–
% COLLEGE GRADUATE OR HIGHER	–	100%	100%	–
% WHO RECEIVE AUTO REIMBURSEMENT	48%	56%	68%	–
% ORDAINED	7%	27%	35%	–
AVERAGE % SALARY INCREASE THIS YEAR	6%	5%	5%	–

COMPENSATION		< than Bachelor	Bachelor	Master	Doctorate
BASE SALARY:	Highest 25%	$39,000	$48,100	$65,575	–
	Average	$33,775	$40,273	$47,104	–
	Lowest 25%	$24,000	$30,000	$30,886	–
HOUSING:	Highest 25%	–	–	$16,023	–
	Average	$1,674	$5,893	$8,160	–
	Lowest 25%	–	–	–	–
PARSONAGE:	Highest 25%	–	–	–	–
	Average	–	–	$545	–
	Lowest 25%	–	–	–	–
TOTAL COMPENSATION	Highest 25%	$40,000	$54,500	$68,600	–
	Average	$34,939	$46,309	$55,809	–
	Lowest 25%	$25,384	$32,302	$42,000	–

– Not enough responses to provide meaningful data

TABLE 12-10: ANNUAL COMPENSATION OF ADMINISTRATOR BY EDUCATION

		EDUCATION			
BENEFITS		< than Bachelor	Bachelor	Master	Doctorate
RETIREMENT:	Highest 25%	$900	$2,983	$5,377	–
	Average	$703	$1,811	$2,915	–
	Lowest 25%	–	–	–	–
LIFE INSURANCE:	Highest 25%	–	–	–	–
	Average	$139	$136	$243	–
	Lowest 25%	–	–	–	–
HEALTH INSURANCE:	Highest 25%	$4,898	$7,108	$9,905	–
	Average	$2,939	$4,001	$6,409	–
	Lowest 25%	–	–	$460	–
CONTINUING EDUCATION	Highest 25%	–	–	$999	–
	Average	$158	$298	$514	–
	Lowest 25%	–	–	–	–
TOTAL BENEFITS	Highest 25%	$7,320	$9,734	$14,698	–
	Average	$3,939	$6,246	$10,081	–
	Lowest 25%	–	$1,916	$4,937	–
TOTAL COMPENSATION AND BENEFIT		< than Bachelor	Bachelor	Master	Doctorate
	Highest 25%	$45,816	$62,033	$82,323	–
	Average	$39,056	$52,622	$65,891	–
	Lowest 25%	$27,380	$37,946	$50,320	–
NUMBER OF RESPONDENTS		73	148	73	7

– Not enough responses to provide meaningful data

TABLE 12-11: ANNUAL COMPENSATION OF ADMINISTRATOR BY YEARS EMPLOYED

CHARACTERISTICS	YEARS EMPLOYED			
	< 6 years	6-10 years	11-15 years	Over 15 years
AVERAGE SUNDAY AM WORSHIP ATTENDANCE	970	875	1,066	1,114
AVERAGE CHURCH INCOME	$1,833,151	$1,670,291	$2,145,389	$2,364,499
AVERAGE # of YEARS EMPLOYED	3	8	13	20
AVERAGE # of WEEKS OF PAID VACATION	3	3	4	4
% COLLEGE GRADUATE OR HIGHER	78%	76%	71%	68%
% WHO RECEIVE AUTO REIMBURSEMENT	51%	59%	63%	69%
% ORDAINED	17%	25%	31%	33%
AVERAGE % SALARY INCREASE THIS YEAR	6%	5%	5%	6%

COMPENSATION		< 6 years	6-10 years	11-15 years	Over 15 years
BASE SALARY:	Highest 25%	$51,051	$42,052	$56,161	$42,000
	Average	$40,115	$38,746	$44,112	$39,730
	Lowest 25%	$28,199	$27,717	$30,570	$26,500
HOUSING:	Highest 25%	–	–	$14,423	$9,634
	Average	$3,849	$5,584	$6,667	$6,410
	Lowest 25%	–	–	–	–
PARSONAGE:	Highest 25%	–	–	–	–
	Average	–	–	–	$956
	Lowest 25%	–	–	–	–
TOTAL COMPENSATION	Highest 25%	$55,000	$51,300	$63,800	$63,413
	Average	$44,097	$44,330	$50,779	$47,095
	Lowest 25%	$30,000	$33,280	$33,886	$28,941

– Not enough responses to provide meaningful data

TABLE 12-11: ANNUAL COMPENSATION OF ADMINISTRATOR BY YEARS EMPLOYED

BENEFITS		YEARS EMPLOYED			
		< 6 years	6-10 years	11-15 years	Over 15 years
RETIREMENT:	Highest 25%	$2,520	$3,055	$2,808	$3,920
	Average	$1,368	$2,268	$1,794	$2,272
	Lowest 25%	–	–	–	–
LIFE INSURANCE:	Highest 25%	–	–	–	$315
	Average	–	$219	$282	$289
	Lowest 25%	–	–	–	–
HEALTH INSURANCE:	Highest 25%	$7,200	$7,930	$7,200	$8,160
	Average	$3,658	$4,289	$4,860	$5,853
	Lowest 25%	–	–	$475	–
CONTINUING EDUCATION	Highest 25%	–	$505	–	$405
	Average	$287	$382	$319	$345
	Lowest 25%	–	–	–	–
TOTAL BENEFITS	Highest 25%	$8,976	$10,707	$9,431	$12,642
	Average	$5,370	$7,159	$7,255	$8,759
	Lowest 25%	–	$1,648	$3,300	$2,400
TOTAL COMPENSATION AND BENEFIT		< 6 years	6-10 years	11-15 years	Over 15 years
	Highest 25%	$62,564	$57,650	$75,300	$87,052
	Average	$49,467	$51,622	$58,034	$56,172
	Lowest 25%	$33,437	$38,000	$43,317	$35,660
NUMBER OF RESPONDENTS		162	75	45	41

– Not enough responses to provide meaningful data

TABLE 12-12: ANNUAL COMPENSATION OF ADMINISTRATOR BY DENOMINATION

CHARACTERISTICS	DENOMINATION					
	Assemblies of God	Baptist	Independent/ Nondenom	Lutheran	Methodist	Presbyterian
AVERAGE SUNDAY AM WORSHIP ATTENDANCE	1,016	1,016	1,249	479	667	632
AVERAGE CHURCH INCOME	1,899,463	$2,258,169	$2,011,229	$1,090,391	$1,213,749	$1,748,820
AVERAGE # of YEARS EMPLOYED	7	9	6	6	6	7
AVERAGE # of WEEKS OF PAID VACATION	3	3	3	3	3	3
% COLLEGE GRADUATE OR HIGHER	71%	82%	76%	68%	63%	82%
% WHO RECEIVE AUTO REIMBURSEMENT	38%	56%	52%	60%	43%	68%
% ORDAINED	46%	37%	31%	–	–	–
AVERAGE % SALARY INCREASE THIS YEAR	7%	5%	6%	5%	6%	46

COMPENSATION		Assemblies of God	Baptist	Independent/ Nondenom	Lutheran	Methodist	Presbyterian
BASE SALARY:	Highest 25%	$52,000	$53,813	$45,450	$38,617	$42,650	$51,650
	Average	$40,491	$41,184	$38,527	$34,343	$37,931	$43,906
	Lowest 25%	$26,500	$27,000	$27,000	$27,000	$31,813	$33,619
HOUSING:	Highest 25%	$25,380	$16,620	$10,202	–	–	–
	Average	$13,220	$7,768	$6,242	–	–	–
	Lowest 25%	–	–	–	–	–	–
PARSONAGE:	Highest 25%	–	–	–	–	–	–
	Average	–	$734	–	–	–	–
	Lowest 25%	–	–	–	–	–	–
TOTAL COMPENSATION	Highest 25%	$57,389	$65,000	$55,500	$38,617	$42,650	$51,650
	Average	$53,711	$49,686	$44,770	$34,367	$37,931	$43,906
	Lowest 25%	$46,530	$32,715	$30,000	$27,000	$31,813	$33,619

– Not enough responses to provide meaningful data

TABLE 12-12: ANNUAL COMPENSATION OF ADMINISTRATOR BY DENOMINATION

BENEFITS		DENOMINATION					
		Assemblies of God	Baptist	Independent/ Nondenom	Lutheran	Methodist	Presbyte-rian
RETIREMENT:	Highest 25%	$3,000	$4,730	$1,568	$2,500	$2,088	$3,360
	Average	$1,250	$2,792	$1,098	$1,098	$928	$1,975
	Lowest 25%	–	–	–	–	–	–
LIFE INSURANCE:	Highest 25%	–	$420	–	–	–	–
	Average	–	$362	–	–	–	–
	Lowest 25%	–	–	–	–	–	–
HEALTH INSURANCE:	Highest 25%	$6,393	$7,357	$8,425	$5,467	$4,518	$7,760
	Average	$3,035	$4,908	$4,642	$3,053	$2,478	$3,664
	Lowest 25%	–	–	–	–	–	–
CONTINUING EDUCATION	Highest 25%	–	–	–	–	$494	$1,075
	Average	$143	$312	$301	$340	$183	$558
	Lowest 25%	–	–	–	–	–	–
TOTAL BENEFITS	Highest 25%	$9,523	$12,533	$9,812	$8,727	$6,660	$10,164
	Average	$4,499	$8,374	$6,106	$4,586	$3,592	$6,256
	Lowest 25%	–	$2,945	$1,050	–	–	$1,782
TOTAL COMPENSATION AND BENEFIT		Assemblies of God	Baptist	Independent/ Nondenom	Lutheran	Methodist	Presbyte-rian
	Highest 25%	$61,320	$78,520	$67,094	$45,816	$49,653	$54,288
	Average	$58,210	$58,219	$50,876	$39,353	$41,523	$50,162
	Lowest 25%	$47,969	$38,000	$35,750	$28,351	$32,695	$38,136
NUMBER OF RESPONDENTS		14	82	80	25	24	40

– Not enough responses to provide meaningful data

TABLE 12-13: COMPENSATION OF PART-TIME ADMINISTRATOR BY WORSHIP ATTENDANCE

CHARACTERISTICS	WORSHIP ATTENDANCE					
	100 or less	101 - 300	301 - 500	501 - 750	751 - 1,000	Over 1,000
AVERAGE SUNDAY AM WORSHIP ATTENDANCE	75	192	411	593	–	–
AVERAGE CHURCH INCOME	$142,305	$389,116	$778,412	$1,019,585	–	–
AVERAGE # of YEARS EMPLOYED	6	6	6	6	–	–
AVERAGE # of WEEKS OF PAID VACATION	2	2	3	–	–	–
% COLLEGE GRADUATE OR HIGHER	38%	45%	79%	50%	–	–
% WHO RECEIVE AUTO REIMBURSEMENT	33%	27%	18%	–	–	–
% ORDAINED	–	2%	5%	10%	–	–
AVERAGE % SALARY INCREASE THIS YEAR	–	5%	4%	–	–	–
HOURLY RATES						
AVERAGE BASE RATE	$6.36	$9.35	$13.20	$11.07	–	–
ANNUAL COMPENSATION						
AVERAGE BASE SALARY:	$8,681	$16,292	$18,766	$24,927	–	–
AVERAGE HOUSING:	–	–	–	–	–	–
AVERAGE PARSONAGE:	–	–	–	–	–	–
AVERAGE TOTAL COMPENSATION	$8,681	$16,292	$18,766	$24,927	–	–
ANNUAL BENEFITS						
AVERAGE RETIREMENT	–	–	–	$694	–	–
AVERAGE LIFE INSURANCE	–	–	–	–	–	–
AVERAGE HEALTH INSURANCE	–	$783	$128	$727	–	–
AVERAGE CONTINUING EDUCATION	–	–	–	–	–	–
AVERAGE TOTAL BENEFITS	–	$825	$128	$1,447	–	–
ANNUAL COMPENSATION & BENEFIT						
AVERAGE	$8,772	$17,481	$18,893	$26,373	–	–
NUMBER OF RESPONDENTS	14	48	21	10	5	4

– Not enough responses to provide meaningful data

TABLE 12-14: COMPENSATION OF PART-TIME ADMINISTRATOR BY CHURCH INCOME

	CHURCH INCOME				
CHARACTERISTICS	$250 K & Under	$251 - $500K	$501 - $750K	$751K - $1M	Over $1 Million
AVERAGE SUNDAY AM WORSHIP ATTENDANCE	122	218	409	436	758
AVERAGE CHURCH INCOME	$163,360	$366,386	$644,439	$872,103	$1,512,456
AVERAGE # of YEARS EMPLOYED	7	5	6	5	7
AVERAGE # of WEEKS OF PAID VACATION	2	2	–	3	3
% COLLEGE GRADUATE OR HIGHER	36%	48%	67%	75%	65%
% WHO RECEIVE AUTO REIMBURSEMENT	26%	20%	–	56%	53%
% ORDAINED	–	3%	8%	7%	12%
AVERAGE % SALARY INCREASE THIS YEAR	6%	4%	–	4%	6%
HOURLY RATES					
AVERAGE BASE RATE	$8.33	$9.03	$11.06	$14.59	$10.71
ANNUAL COMPENSATION	$250 K & Under	$251 - $500K	$501 - $750K	$751K - $1M	Over $1 Million
AVERAGE BASE SALARY:	$9,679	$16,959	$18,381	$20,952	$24,848
AVERAGE HOUSING:	–	–	–	–	$2,647
AVERAGE PARSONAGE:	–	–	–	–	–
AVERAGE TOTAL COMPENSATION	$9,679	$16,959	$18,381	$20,952	$27,495
ANNUAL BENEFITS					
AVERAGE RETIREMENT	–	–	–	$207	$519
AVERAGE LIFE INSURANCE	–	–	–	–	–
AVERAGE HEALTH INSURANCE	–	$819	$253	$419	$893
AVERAGE CONTINUING EDUCATION	–	–	–	–	–
AVERAGE TOTAL BENEFITS	–	$843	$296	$626	$1,426
ANNUAL COMPENSATION & BENEFIT					
AVERAGE	$10,135	$17,802	$18,677	$21,578	$28,921
NUMBER OF RESPONDENTS	25	32	12	14	17

– Not enough responses to provide meaningful data

TABLE 12-15: AVERAGE COMPENSATION PACKAGE FOR ADMINISTRATOR*

	Overall	ADMINISTRATORS WHO RECIEVE...				
		Base Salary Only	No Base Salary	Base Salary and Parsonage	Base Salary and Housing	Base Salary and Parsonage and Housing
BASE SALARY	$40,416	$41,173		–	$38,076	–
PARSONAGE**	$184		–	–		–
HOUSING ALLOWANCE	$4,918		–		$23,866	–
TOTAL COMPENSATION PACKAGE	$45,518	$41,173	–	–	$61,942	–
NUMBER OF RESPONDENTS	330	259	1	2	68	0

*All $ values are annual averages
**Parsonage = Rental value of parsonage plus allowance
– Not enough responses to provide meaningful data

For an explanation of the Average Compensation Table,
please refer to Chapter 1.

13

BOOKKEEPERS

Employment Profile

From an employment standpoint, bookkeepers are aligned with secretaries and custodians. Very few are ordained ministers. The majority are female, whether full-time or part-time. The bookkeeper positions reported in this study provide the following employment profile:

	FULL-TIME	PART-TIME
Ordained	1%	1%
Average years employed	9	6
Male	9%	11%
Female	91%	89%
Self-employed (receives 1099)	1%	5%
Church employee (receives W-2)	99%	95%
High school diploma	43%	32%
Associate's degree	12%	13%
Bachelor's degree	41%	44%
Master's degree	5%	10%
Doctorate	0%	2%
Number of respondents	*178*	*237*

Total Compensation plus Benefits Package Analysis

The analysis below is based upon the tables found later in this chapter. The tables present compensation and benefits data according to worship attendance, church income, combinations of size and setting, region, gender, education, years employed, and denomination for bookkeepers who serve full-time. The final two tables provide data for part-time bookkeepers by worship attendance and church income. In this way, the bookkeeper's compensation can be viewed from a variety of useful perspectives. The total compensation and benefits amount found in a separate box at the bottom of each page includes the base salary, housing and/or parsonage amount, life and health insurance payments, retirement contribution, and educational funds.

Full-time staff members. Bookkeepers receive less benefits in the areas of housing, auto allowance, and continuing education than do administrators or ministerial staff. 1% receives a housing allowance. Slightly more bookkeepers, however, receive insurance and retirement benefits than secretaries and custodians.

Part-time staff members. Over half (57%) of the reported bookkeeper positions work part-time for their churches. Eighty-nine percent of part-time bookkeepers are women. As with other part-time positions, few receive fringe benefits other than a paid vacation or an auto allowance.

COMPENSATION PLUS BENEFITS	FULL TIME	PART TIME
Base salary	99%	97%
Housing	1%	1%
Parsonage	0%	0%
Retirement	46%	5%
Life insurance	33%	3%
Health insurance	65%	5%
Paid vacation	94%	38%
Auto reimbursement	38%	19%
Continuing education	15%	5%

KEY POINTS

⊃ **The compensation and benefits of bookkeepers increases significantly with church size.** Total compensation and benefits increases with attendance, with the fastest growth occurring once church attendance exceeds 1,000. About 40% of all reported church bookkeepers work in churches of that size or larger. *See Table 13-1.*

⊃ **Compensation increases steadily as church income increases.** About 75% of reported bookkeepers work in congregations with an annual income in excess of $1,000,000. The national average compensation was not achieved until the church's income, on average, was over $1,000,000. *See Table 13-2.*

⊃ **Suburban and metropolitan churches provide the highest compensation for bookkeepers.** On average, among churches of all sizes, the suburban and metropolitan churches provide the highest packages to bookkeepers. Generally, compensation does not reach the national average until church attendance reach over 1,000. Very few reported bookkeepers are from farming areas. *See Table 13-3, 13-4, 13-5, 13-6, and 13-7.*

⊃ **Female bookkeepers earn less than males.** Historically, females have earned less than their male counterparts, although four years ago they earned slightly more. Men represent only a small percentage of all reported bookkeepers (9%). This year, females earn about $8,460 less in total compensation. Both men and women tend to work in larger congregations. However, men work in significantly larger churches than women, which directly impacts compensation. *See Table 13-9.*

⊃ **Educational achievement has a minor impact on total compensation and benefits.** Bookkeepers with college degrees earn slightly higher than the national average, while those without a college education tend to earn slightly less. The difference in compensation between those with a college education and those without one is about $4,200. *See Table 13-10.*

⊃ **In general, part-time bookkeepers receive compensation in line with part-time secretaries.** Part-time bookkeepers earn less than most other part-time professional staff, but more than part-time custodians and organists. *See Tables 13-14 and 13-15.*

Ten Year Compensation & Benefits Trend: National Average for Bookkeepers

FULL TIME

1997	$23,839
1998	$24,623
1999	$26,229
2000	$27,992
2001	$29,220
2002	$29,398
2003	$30,457
2004	$32,765
2005	$33,336
2006	$36,122

TABLE 13-1: ANNUAL COMPENSATION OF BOOKKEEPER BY WORSHIP ATTENDANCE

CHARACTERISTICS	WORSHIP ATTENDANCE					
	100 or less	101-300	301-500	501-750	751-1000	Over 1000
AVERAGE SUNDAY AM WORSHIP ATTENDANCE	–	210	428	631	882	2,122
AVERAGE CHURCH INCOME	–	$475,382	$1,138,523	$1,556,462	$1,943,599	$3,985,129
AVERAGE # of YEARS EMPLOYED	–	9	10	10	8	8
AVERAGE # of WEEKS OF PAID VACATION	–	2	3	3	3	3
% COLLEGE GRADUATE OR HIGHER	–	33%	44%	37%	29%	63%
% WHO RECEIVE AUTO REIMBURSEMENT	–	30%	35%	46%	40%	55%
% ORDAINED	–	–	4%	4%	–	–
AVERAGE % SALARY INCREASE THIS YEAR	–	4%	4%	4%	4%	5%

COMPENSATION		100 or less	101-300	301-500	501-750	751-1000	Over 1000
BASE SALARY:	Highest 25%	–	$27,777	$31,100	$32,791	$35,362	$42,014
	Average	–	$24,560	$27,775	$30,122	$29,220	$35,844
	Lowest 25%	–	$20,402	$25,559	$28,202	$22,306	$28,598
HOUSING:	Highest 25%	–	–	$3,972	–	–	–
	Average	–	–	–	–	–	–
	Lowest 25%	–	–	–	–	–	–
PARSONAGE:	Highest 25%	–	–	–	–	–	–
	Average	–	–	–	–	–	–
	Lowest 25%	–	–	–	–	–	–
TOTAL COMPENSATION	Highest 25%	–	$27,777	$31,100	$32,791	$35,362	$42,014
	Average	–	$24,560	$28,255	$30,122	$29,220	$35,844
	Lowest 25%	–	$20,402	$25,559	$28,202	$22,306	$28,598

– Not enough responses to provide meaningful data

TABLE 13-1: ANNUAL COMPENSATION OF BOOKKEEPER BY WORSHIP ATTENDANCE

BENEFITS		WORSHIP ATTENDANCE					
		100 or less	101-300	301-500	501-750	751-1000	Over 1000
RETIREMENT:	Highest 25%	–	–	$1,446	$1,639	$1,687	$2,065
	Average	–	$422	$673	$967	$984	$1,065
	Lowest 25%	–	–	–	–	–	–
LIFE INSURANCE:	Highest 25%	–	–	–	$125	–	–
	Average	–	–	–	$100	$154	$168
	Lowest 25%	–	–	–	–	–	–
HEALTH INSURANCE:	Highest 25%	–	$4,441	$5,211	$4,816	$5,425	$6,757
	Average	–	$2,581	$3,234	$3,182	$3,660	$3,904
	Lowest 25%	–	–	–	–	–	–
CONTINUING EDUCATION	Highest 25%	–	–	–	–	–	–
	Average	–	–	$100	–	–	$131
	Lowest 25%	–	–	–	–	–	–
TOTAL BENEFITS	Highest 25%	–	$5,110	$7,150	$5,446	$7,401	$7,588
	Average	–	$3,105	$4,024	$4,333	$4,860	$5,269
	Lowest 25%	–	–	–	$1,030	$1,260	$2,300
TOTAL COMPENSATION AND BENEFIT		100 or less	101-300	301-500	501-750	751-1000	Over 1000
	Highest 25%	–	$31,541	$36,997	$38,921	$43,001	$47,479
	Average	–	$27,665	$32,613	$34,456	$34,081	$41,403
	Lowest 25%	–	$22,000	$29,428	$31,165	$28,358	$32,400
NUMBER OF RESPONDENTS		1	17	30	27	29	69

– Not enough responses to provide meaningful data

293

TABLE 13-2: ANNUAL COMPENSATION OF BOOKKEEPER BY CHURCH INCOME

CHARACTERISTICS		$250K & under	$251K-$500K	$501K-$750K	$751K-$1M	Over $1 Million
AVERAGE SUNDAY AM WORSHIP ATTENDANCE		–	410	390	549	1,461
AVERAGE CHURCH INCOME		–	$386,032	$635,339	$894,596	$3,002,122
AVERAGE # of YEARS EMPLOYED		–	8	7	9	9
AVERAGE # of WEEKS OF PAID VACATION		–	2	2	3	3
% COLLEGE GRADUATE OR HIGHER		–	44%	38%	47%	50%
% WHO RECEIVE AUTO REIMBURSEMENT		–	10%	13%	36%	52%
% ORDAINED		–	–	8%	–	1%
AVERAGE % SALARY INCREASE THIS YEAR		–	–	–	4%	4%

COMPENSATION		$250K & under	$251K-$500K	$501K-$750K	$751K-$1M	Over 1 Million
BASE SALARY:	Highest 25%	–	$28,000	$28,202	$34,859	$37,900
	Average	–	$24,378	$24,305	$30,060	$33,234
	Lowest 25%	–	$23,660	$23,694	$24,998	$26,847
HOUSING:	Highest 25%	–	–	$4,500	–	–
	Average	–	–	$1,108	–	–
	Lowest 25%	–	–	–	–	–
PARSONAGE:	Highest 25%	–	–	–	–	–
	Average	–	–	–	–	–
	Lowest 25%	–	–	–	–	–
TOTAL COMPENSATION	Highest 25%	–	$28,000	$28,202	$34,859	$37,900
	Average	–	$24,378	$25,413	$30,060	$33,234
	Lowest 25%	–	$23,660	$23,694	$24,998	$26,847

– Not enough responses to provide meaningful data

TABLE 13-2: ANNUAL COMPENSATION OF BOOKKEEPER BY CHURCH INCOME

		CHURCH INCOME				
		$250K & under	$251K-$500K	$501K-$750K	$751K-$1M	Over $1 Million
BENEFITS						
RETIREMENT:	Highest 25%	–	–	–	$541	$2,092
	Average	–	–	$243	$345	$1,147
	Lowest 25%	–	–	–	–	–
LIFE INSURANCE:	Highest 25%	–	–	–	–	–
	Average	–	–	–	$123	$108
	Lowest 25%	–	–	–	–	–
HEALTH INSURANCE:	Highest 25%	–	$3,700	$5,110	$3,601	$6,460
	Average	–	$2,843	$4,328	$1,931	$3,806
	Lowest 25%	–	–	–	–	–
CONTINUING EDUCATION	Highest 25%	–	–	–	–	–
	Average	–	–	–	$136	$103
	Lowest 25%	–	–	–	–	–
TOTAL BENEFITS	Highest 25%	–	$3,900	$5,110	$5,001	$8,000
	Average	–	$2,960	$4,609	$2,535	$5,164
	Lowest 25%	–	–	$2,999	–	$1,358
TOTAL COMPENSATION AND BENEFIT		$250K & under	$251K-$500K	$501K-$750K	$751K-$1M	Over 1 Million
	Highest 25%	–	$29,755	$33,000	$36,719	$44,902
	Average	–	$27,338	$30,022	$33,184	$38,559
	Lowest 25%	–	$23,660	$29,428	$25,559	$31,467
NUMBER OF RESPONDENTS		3	10	13	17	124

– *Not enough responses to provide meaningful data*

TABLE 13-3: ANNUAL COMPENSATION OF BOOKKEEPER BY CHURCH SETTING & SIZE

ATTENDANCE 251 - 500	CHURCH SETTING			
	Metropolitan city	Suburb of large city	Small town or rural city	Farming area
AVERAGE SUNDAY AM WORSHIP ATTENDANCE	385	422	422	–
AVERAGE CHURCH INCOME	–	$1,283,617	$985,166	–
AVERAGE # of YEARS EMPLOYED	13	5	10	–
AVERAGE # of WEEKS OF PAID VACATION	–	2	3	–
% COLLEGE GRADUATE OR HIGHER	–	64%	33%	–
% WHO RECEIVE AUTO REIMBURSEMENT	–	50%	20%	–
% ORDAINED	–	–	8%	–
AVERAGE % SALARY INCREASE THIS YEAR	–	–	4%	–

COMPENSATION		Metropolitan city	Suburb of large city	Small town or rural city	Farming area
BASE SALARY:	Highest 25%	$28,529	$34,846	$28,945	–
	Average	$27,211	$31,154	$23,813	–
	Lowest 25%	$24,348	$26,012	$23,493	–
HOUSING:	Highest 25%	–	–	$4,500	–
	Average	–	–	$1,108	–
	Lowest 25%	–	–	–	–
PARSONAGE:	Highest 25%	–	–	–	–
	Average	–	–	–	–
	Lowest 25%	–	–	–	–
TOTAL COMPENSATION	Highest 25%	$28,529	$34,846	$28,945	–
	Average	$27,211	$31,154	$24,921	–
	Lowest 25%	$24,348	$26,012	$23,493	–

– Not enough responses to provide meaningful data

TABLE 13-3: ANNUAL COMPENSATION OF BOOKKEEPER BY CHURCH SETTING & SIZE

BENEFITS		CHURCH SETTING			
		Metropoli-tan city	Suburb of large city	Small town or rural city	Farming area
RETIREMENT:	Highest 25%	$1,497	$1,624	$776	–
	Average	$879	$690	$538	–
	Lowest 25%	–	–	–	–
LIFE INSURANCE:	Highest 25%	–	–	–	–
	Average	–	–	–	–
	Lowest 25%	–	–	–	–
HEALTH INSURANCE:	Highest 25%	$6,021	$5,104	$5,226	–
	Average	$4,414	$2,841	$3,118	–
	Lowest 25%	–	–	–	–
CONTINUING EDUCATION	Highest 25%	$175	–	–	–
	Average	$169	$127	–	–
	Lowest 25%	–	–	–	–
TOTAL BENEFITS	Highest 25%	$8,505	$6,377	$7,165	–
	Average	$5,486	$3,681	$3,681	–
	Lowest 25%	$1,349	$762	–	–
TOTAL COMPENSATION AND BENEFIT		Metropoli-tan city	Suburb of large city	Small town or rural city	Farming area
	Highest 25%	$41,032	$39,328	$35,140	–
	Average	$32,697	$34,836	$29,371	–
	Lowest 25%	$27,734	$29,430	$26,587	–
NUMBER OF RESPONDENTS		8	11	13	0

– Not enough responses to provide meaningful data

297

TABLE 13-4: ANNUAL COMPENSATION OF BOOKKEEPER BY CHURCH SETTING & SIZE

ATTENDANCE 501 - 750		CHURCH SETTING			
		Metropoli-tan city	Suburb of large city	Small town or rural city	Farming area
AVERAGE SUNDAY AM WORSHIP ATTENDANCE		–	631	631	–
AVERAGE CHURCH INCOME		–	$1,498,260	$1,742,201	–
AVERAGE # of YEARS EMPLOYED		–	10	10	–
AVERAGE # of WEEKS OF PAID VACATION		–	3	3	–
% COLLEGE GRADUATE OR HIGHER		–	38%	–	–
% WHO RECEIVE AUTO REIMBURSEMENT		–	45%	–	–
% ORDAINED		–	9%	–	–
AVERAGE % SALARY INCREASE THIS YEAR		–	–	–	–

COMPENSATION		Metropoli-tan city	Suburb of large city	Small town or rural city	Farming area
BASE SALARY:	Highest 25%	–	$36,138	$30,950	–
	Average	–	$32,543	$28,417	–
	Lowest 25%	–	$29,775	$26,617	–
HOUSING:	Highest 25%	–	–	–	–
	Average	–	–	–	–
	Lowest 25%	–	–	–	–
PARSONAGE:	Highest 25%	–	–	–	–
	Average	–	–	–	–
	Lowest 25%	–	–	–	–
TOTAL COMPENSATION	Highest 25%	–	$36,138	$30,950	–
	Average	–	$32,543	$28,417	–
	Lowest 25%	–	$29,775	$26,617	–

– Not enough responses to provide meaningful data

TABLE 13-4: ANNUAL COMPENSATION OF BOOKKEEPER BY CHURCH SETTING & SIZE

BENEFITS		CHURCH SETTING			
		Metropoli-tan city	Suburb of large city	Small town or rural city	Farming area
RETIREMENT:	Highest 25%	–	$2,794	$636	–
	Average	–	$1,279	$538	–
	Lowest 25%	–	–	–	–
LIFE INSURANCE:	Highest 25%	–	$154	–	–
	Average	–	–	$136	–
	Lowest 25%	–	–	–	–
HEALTH INSURANCE:	Highest 25%	–	$3,488	$8,223	–
	Average	–	$2,246	$5,469	–
	Lowest 25%	–	–	$2,396	–
CONTINUING EDUCATION	Highest 25%	–	–	–	–
	Average	–	–	$156	–
	Lowest 25%	–	–	–	–
TOTAL BENEFITS	Highest 25%	–	$5,388	$10,479	–
	Average	–	$3,670	$6,300	–
	Lowest 25%	–	$578	$2,393	–
TOTAL COMPENSATION AND BENEFIT		Metropoli-tan city	Suburb of large city	Small town or rural city	Farming area
	Highest 25%	–	$39,640	$39,684	–
	Average	–	$36,213	$34,716	–
	Lowest 25%	–	$31,116	$31,304	–
NUMBER OF RESPONDENTS		7	11	9	0

– Not enough responses to provide meaningful data

TABLE 13-5: ANNUAL COMPENSATION OF BOOKKEEPER BY CHURCH SETTING & SIZE

ATTENDANCE 751 - 1,000		CHURCH SETTING			
		Metropoli-tan city	Suburb of large city	Small town or rural city	Farming area
AVERAGE SUNDAY AM WORSHIP ATTENDANCE		920	856	875	–
AVERAGE CHURCH INCOME		$2,355,563	$1,724,699	$1,765,495	–
AVERAGE # of YEARS EMPLOYED		12	4	7	–
AVERAGE # of WEEKS OF PAID VACATION		3	2	3	–
% COLLEGE GRADUATE OR HIGHER		38%	38%	–	–
% WHO RECEIVE AUTO REIMBURSEMENT		33%	67%	–	–
% ORDAINED		–	–	–	–
AVERAGE % SALARY INCREASE THIS YEAR		4%	–	–	–

COMPENSATION		Metropoli-tan city	Suburb of large city	Small town or rural city	Farming area
BASE SALARY:	Highest 25%	$35,360	$31,925	$37,835	–
	Average	$32,126	$30,132	$26,448	–
	Lowest 25%	$31,000	$25,965	$20,765	–
HOUSING:	Highest 25%	–	–	–	–
	Average	–	–	–	–
	Lowest 25%	–	–	–	–
PARSONAGE:	Highest 25%	–	–	–	–
	Average	–	–	–	–
	Lowest 25%	–	–	–	–
TOTAL COMPENSATION	Highest 25%	$35,360	$31,925	$37,835	–
	Average	$32,126	$30,132	$26,448	–
	Lowest 25%	$31,000	$25,965	$20,765	–

– Not enough responses to provide meaningful data

TABLE 13-5: ANNUAL COMPENSATION OF BOOKKEEPER BY CHURCH SETTING & SIZE

BENEFITS		CHURCH SETTING			
		Metropoli-tan city	Suburb of large city	Small town or rural city	Farming area
RETIREMENT:	Highest 25%	$2,500	$1,264	$1,690	–
	Average	$1,447	$649	$914	–
	Lowest 25%	–	–	–	–
LIFE INSURANCE:	Highest 25%	–	–	–	–
	Average	–	–	$411	–
	Lowest 25%	–	–	–	–
HEALTH INSURANCE:	Highest 25%	$8,000	$6,010	$3,535	–
	Average	$5,363	$3,787	$2,047	–
	Lowest 25%	$4,000	–	–	–
CONTINUING EDUCATION	Highest 25%	–	–	–	–
	Average	–	–	$167	–
	Lowest 25%	–	–	–	–
TOTAL BENEFITS	Highest 25%	$8,040	$7,801	$5,927	–
	Average	$6,897	$4,459	$3,539	–
	Lowest 25%	$5,453	$1,260	$1,053	–
TOTAL COMPENSATION AND BENEFIT		Metropoli-tan city	Suburb of large city	Small town or rural city	Farming area
	Highest 25%	$43,400	$37,806	$43,431	–
	Average	$39,024	$34,590	$29,988	–
	Lowest 25%	$36,720	$30,570	$24,042	–
NUMBER OF RESPONDENTS		10	9	9	1

– Not enough responses to provide meaningful data

TABLE 13-6: ANNUAL COMPENSATION OF BOOKKEEPER BY CHURCH SETTING & SIZE

ATTENDANCE OVER 1,000		Metropoli-tan city	Suburb of large city	Small town or rural city	Farming area
AVERAGE SUNDAY AM WORSHIP ATTENDANCE		2,224	2,049	2,211	–
AVERAGE CHURCH INCOME		$4,317,094	$3,984,500	$3,696,074	–
AVERAGE # of YEARS EMPLOYED		10	7	8	–
AVERAGE # of WEEKS OF PAID VACATION		3	3	3	–
% COLLEGE GRADUATE OR HIGHER		85%	63%	43%	–
% WHO RECEIVE AUTO REIMBURSEMENT		50%	54%	62%	–
% ORDAINED		–	–	–	–
AVERAGE % SALARY INCREASE THIS YEAR		6%	4%	5%	–

COMPENSATION		Metropoli-tan city	Suburb of large city	Small town or rural city	Farming area
BASE SALARY:	Highest 25%	$40,009	$46,991	$35,718	–
	Average	$36,501	$37,413	$31,446	–
	Lowest 25%	$30,004	$28,009	$25,935	–
HOUSING:	Highest 25%	–	–	–	–
	Average	–	–	–	–
	Lowest 25%	–	–	–	–
PARSONAGE:	Highest 25%	–	–	–	–
	Average	–	–	–	–
	Lowest 25%	–	–	–	–
TOTAL COMPENSATION	Highest 25%	$40,009	$46,991	$35,718	–
	Average	$36,501	$37,413	$31,446	–
	Lowest 25%	$30,004	$28,009	$25,935	–

– Not enough responses to provide meaningful data

TABLE 13-6: ANNUAL COMPENSATION OF BOOKKEEPER BY CHURCH SETTING & SIZE

		CHURCH SETTING			
BENEFITS		Metropoli-tan city	Suburb of large city	Small town or rural city	Farming area
RETIREMENT:	Highest 25%	$2,228	$2,345	$1,744	–
	Average	$1,255	$1,074	$878	–
	Lowest 25%	–	–	–	–
LIFE INSURANCE:	Highest 25%	–	–	–	–
	Average	$265	$123	$194	–
	Lowest 25%	–	–	–	–
HEALTH INSURANCE:	Highest 25%	$6,792	$5,435	$8,201	–
	Average	$3,977	$3,490	$4,852	–
	Lowest 25%	–	–	$429	–
CONTINUING EDUCATION	Highest 25%	–	–	–	–
	Average	$168	$156	–	–
	Lowest 25%	–	–	–	–
TOTAL BENEFITS	Highest 25%	$9,250	$7,323	$9,177	–
	Average	$5,665	$4,843	$5,961	–
	Lowest 25%	$2,400	–	$2,793	–
TOTAL COMPENSATION AND BENEFIT		Metropoli-tan city	Suburb of large city	Small town or rural city	Farming area
	Highest 25%	$46,249	$51,611	$41,858	–
	Average	$42,166	$42,257	$38,657	–
	Lowest 25%	$39,250	$31,190	$31,927	–
NUMBER OF RESPONDENTS		14	39	16	0

– *Not enough responses to provide meaningful data*

TABLE 13-7: ANNUAL COMPENSATION OF BOOKKEEPER BY REGION

CHARACTERISTICS	REGION								
	New England	Middle Atlantic	South Atlantic	E-N Central	E-S Central	W-N Central	W-S Central	Mountain	Pacific
AVERAGE SUNDAY AM WORSHIP ATTENDANCE	–	666	935	1,494	1,112	1,083	1,297	1,771	1,272
AVERAGE CHURCH INCOME	–	$1,282,651	$2,101,307	$2,344,302	$2,932,576	$2,792,283	$2,996,463	$2,650,121	$2,281,508
AVERAGE # of YEARS EMPLOYED	–	10	7	8	10	7	11	5	10
AVERAGE # of WEEKS OF PAID VACATION	–	3	3	3	3	3	3	3	3
% COLLEGE GRADUATE OR HIGHER	–	50%	48%	33%	36%	44%	56%	64%	33%
% WHO RECEIVE AUTO REIMBURSEMENT	–	–	51%	72%	31%	45%	28%	73%	21%
% ORDAINED	–	–	–	–	–	–	4%	–	4%
AVERAGE % SALARY INCREASE THIS YEAR	–	–	4%	4%	4%	4%	5%	7%	5%

COMPENSATION		New England	Middle Atlantic	South Atlantic	E-N Central	E-S Central	W-N Central	W-S Central	Mountain	Pacific
BASE SALARY:	Highest 25%	–	$26,412	$36,146	$36,748	$35,000	$33,598	$40,001	$39,998	$37,991
	Average	–	$23,259	$30,280	$32,572	$31,252	$29,660	$34,364	$33,852	$30,907
	Lowest 25%	–	$20,799	$25,777	$26,629	$26,589	$22,310	$26,870	$26,825	$24,821
HOUSING:	Highest 25%	–	–	–	–	–	–	–	–	$4,070
	Average	–	–	–	–	–	–	–	–	$600
	Lowest 25%	–	–	–	–	–	–	–	–	–
PARSONAGE:	Highest 25%	–	–	–	–	–	–	–	–	–
	Average	–	–	–	–	–	–	–	–	–
	Lowest 25%	–	–	–	–	–	–	–	–	–
TOTAL COMPENSATION	Highest 25%	–	$26,412	$36,146	$36,748	$35,000	$33,598	$40,001	$39,998	$37,991
	Average	–	$23,259	$30,280	$32,572	$31,252	$29,660	$34,364	$33,852	$31,507
	Lowest 25%	–	$20,799	$25,777	$26,629	$26,589	$22,310	$26,870	$26,825	$24,821

– Not enough responses to provide meaningful data

TABLE 13-7: ANNUAL COMPENSATION OF BOOKKEEPER BY REGION

BENEFITS		REGION								
		New England	Middle Atlantic	South Atlantic	E-N Central	E-S Central	W-N Central	W-S Central	Moun-tain	Pacific
RETIREMENT:	Highest 25%	–	–	$2,227	$1,685	$2,084	$2,230	$2,044	$1,630	–
	Average	–	$298	$1,190	$763	$971	$1,198	$1,163	$709	$407
	Lowest 25%	–	–	–	–	–	–	–	–	–
LIFE INSURANCE:	Highest 25%	–	–	–	–	$270	–	–	$120	–
	Average	–	$138	–	–	$241	$372	$154	–	–
	Lowest 25%	–	–	–	–	–	–	–	–	–
HEALTH INSURANCE:	Highest 25%	–	$4,440	$5,762	$8,760	$6,883	$6,792	$5,000	$5,211	$5,924
	Average	–	$2,405	$3,417	$4,800	$3,642	$3,126	$3,409	$3,271	$3,235
	Lowest 25%	–	–	–	–	–	–	–	–	–
CONTINUING EDUCATION	Highest 25%	–	–	–	–	–	–	–	–	–
	Average	–	–	$101	$152	$113	$227	$109	–	–
	Lowest 25%	–	–	–	–	–	–	–	–	–
TOTAL BENEFITS	Highest 25%	–	$5,017	$6,814	$10,122	$8,000	$8,830	$7,326	$7,016	$7,054
	Average	–	$2,887	$4,784	$5,762	$4,966	$4,923	$4,835	$4,100	$3,661
	Lowest 25%	–	–	$601	$1,604	$1,200	$1,457	$2,058	$1,750	$270
TOTAL COMPENSATION AND BENEFIT		New England	Middle Atlantic	South Atlantic	E-N Central	E-S Central	W-N Central	W-S Central	Moun-tain	Pacific
	Highest 25%	–	$31,660	$41,572	$43,425	$42,900	$39,745	$48,828	$43,000	$43,934
	Average	–	$26,146	$35,277	$39,203	$36,218	$34,583	$39,200	$37,952	$35,169
	Lowest 25%	–	$21,831	$30,386	$32,577	$29,755	$28,359	$30,740	$30,654	$30,088
NUMBER OF RESPONDENTS		2	11	47	23	18	11	27	14	24

– Not enough responses to provide meaningful data

TABLE 13-8: ANNUAL COMPENSATION OF BOOKKEEPER BY GENDER

CHARACTERISTICS	GENDER	
	Male	Female
AVERAGE SUNDAY AM WORSHIP ATTENDANCE	1,738	1,132
AVERAGE CHURCH INCOME	$3,081,781	$2,323,874
AVERAGE # of YEARS EMPLOYED	5	9
AVERAGE # of WEEKS OF PAID VACATION	3	3
% COLLEGE GRADUATE OR HIGHER	64%	43%
% WHO RECEIVE AUTO REIMBURSEMENT	62%	43%
% ORDAINED	–	1%
AVERAGE % SALARY INCREASE THIS YEAR	5%	4%

COMPENSATION		Male	Female
BASE SALARY:	Highest 25%	$51,625	$35,360
	Average	$39,720	$30,401
	Lowest 25%	$29,560	$25,559
HOUSING:	Highest 25%	–	$3,667
	Average	–	–
	Lowest 25%	–	–
PARSONAGE:	Highest 25%	–	–
	Average	–	–
	Lowest 25%	–	–
TOTAL COMPENSATION	Highest 25%	$51,625	$35,360
	Average	$39,720	$30,490
	Lowest 25%	$29,560	$25,559

– Not enough responses to provide meaningful data

TABLE 13-8: ANNUAL COMPENSATION OF BOOKKEEPER BY GENDER

BENEFITS		GENDER	
		Male	Female
RETIREMENT:	Highest 25%	$1,715	$1,648
	Average	$1,013	$884
	Lowest 25%	–	–
LIFE INSURANCE:	Highest 25%	$121	–
	Average	–	$116
	Lowest 25%	–	–
HEALTH INSURANCE:	Highest 25%	$4,850	$5,619
	Average	$2,783	$3,601
	Lowest 25%	–	–
CONTINUING EDUCATION	Highest 25%	–	–
	Average	$238	–
	Lowest 25%	–	–
TOTAL BENEFITS	Highest 25%	$7,343	$7,326
	Average	$4,102	$4,687
	Lowest 25%	$1,154	$747
TOTAL COMPENSATION AND BENEFIT		Male	Female
	Highest 25%	$52,885	$41,411
	Average	$43,822	$35,362
	Lowest 25%	$32,657	$29,620
NUMBER OF RESPONDENTS		16	162

– Not enough responses to provide meaningful data

TABLE 13-9: ANNUAL COMPENSATION OF BOOKKEEPER BY EDUCATION

CHARACTERISTICS	EDUCATION			
	< than Bachelor	Bachelor	Master	Doctorate
AVERAGE SUNDAY AM WORSHIP ATTENDANCE	1,017	1,347	–	–
AVERAGE CHURCH INCOME	$1,980,891	$2,567,699	–	–
AVERAGE # of YEARS EMPLOYED	9	7	–	–
AVERAGE # of WEEKS OF PAID VACATION	3	3	–	–
% COLLEGE GRADUATE OR HIGHER	–	100%	–	–
% WHO RECEIVE AUTO REIMBURSEMENT	39%	48%	–	–
% ORDAINED	3%	–	–	–
AVERAGE % SALARY INCREASE THIS YEAR	4%	4%	–	–

COMPENSATION		< than Bachelor	Bachelor	Master	Doctorate
BASE SALARY:	Highest 25%	$35,000	$40,002	–	–
	Average	$29,349	$33,684	–	–
	Lowest 25%	$24,000	$26,553	–	–
HOUSING:	Highest 25%	$3,733	–	–	–
	Average	–	–	–	–
	Lowest 25%	–	–	–	–
PARSONAGE:	Highest 25%	–	–	–	–
	Average	–	–	–	–
	Lowest 25%	–	–	–	–
TOTAL COMPENSATION	Highest 25%	$35,000	$40,002	–	–
	Average	$29,524	$33,684	–	–
	Lowest 25%	$24,000	$26,553	–	–

– Not enough responses to provide meaningful data

TABLE 13-9: ANNUAL COMPENSATION OF BOOKKEEPER BY EDUCATION

BENEFITS		EDUCATION			
		< than Bachelor	Bachelor	Master	Doctorate
RETIREMENT:	Highest 25%	$1,456	$2,046	–	–
	Average	$770	$1,044	–	–
	Lowest 25%	–	–	–	–
LIFE INSURANCE:	Highest 25%	–	–	–	–
	Average	–	$131	–	–
	Lowest 25%	–	–	–	–
HEALTH INSURANCE:	Highest 25%	$5,762	$5,437	–	–
	Average	$3,671	$3,462	–	–
	Lowest 25%	–	–	–	–
CONTINUING EDUCATION	Highest 25%	–	–	–	–
	Average	–	$148	–	–
	Lowest 25%	–	–	–	–
TOTAL BENEFITS	Highest 25%	$7,150	$7,327	–	–
	Average	$4,605	$4,785	–	–
	Lowest 25%	$1,456	$747	–	–
TOTAL COMPENSATION AND BENEFIT		< than Bachelor	Bachelor	Master	Doctorate
	Highest 25%	$40,022	$46,347	–	–
	Average	$34,251	$38,469	–	–
	Lowest 25%	$28,975	$31,299	–	–
NUMBER OF RESPONDENTS		82	61	7	0

– Not enough responses to provide meaningful data

TABLE 13-10: ANNUAL COMPENSATION OF BOOKKEEPER BY YEARS EMPLOYED

CHARACTERISTICS	YEARS EMPLOYED			
	< 6 years	6-10 years	11-15 years	Over 15 years
AVERAGE SUNDAY AM WORSHIP ATTENDANCE	1,237	1,311	1,112	1,009
AVERAGE CHURCH INCOME	$2,330,979	$2,306,177	$2,878,395	$2,523,833
AVERAGE # of YEARS EMPLOYED	3	7	13	23
AVERAGE # of WEEKS OF PAID VACATION	2	3	4	4
% COLLEGE GRADUATE OR HIGHER	52%	30%	60%	35%
% WHO RECEIVE AUTO REIMBURSEMENT	43%	43%	60%	43%
% ORDAINED	–	–	6%	3%
AVERAGE % SALARY INCREASE THIS YEAR	4%	5%	4%	4%

COMPENSATION		< 6 years	6-10 years	11-15 years	Over 15 years
BASE SALARY:	Highest 25%	$35,722	$36,280	$37,800	$36,874
	Average	$30,934	$30,914	$33,802	$31,494
	Lowest 25%	$24,639	$25,628	$29,120	$26,002
HOUSING:	Highest 25%	–	–	$4,235	–
	Average	–	–	$800	–
	Lowest 25%	–	–	–	–
PARSONAGE:	Highest 25%	–	–	–	–
	Average	–	–	–	–
	Lowest 25%	–	–	–	–
TOTAL COMPENSATION	Highest 25%	$35,722	$36,280	$37,800	$36,874
	Average	$30,934	$30,914	$34,602	$31,494
	Lowest 25%	$24,639	$25,628	$29,120	$26,002

– Not enough responses to provide meaningful data

TABLE 13-10: ANNUAL COMPENSATION OF BOOKKEEPER BY YEARS EMPLOYED

BENEFITS		YEARS EMPLOYED			
		< 6 years	6-10 years	11-15 years	Over 15 years
RETIREMENT:	Highest 25%	$1,274	$1,637	$2,100	$2,580
	Average	$683	$942	$1,121	$1,297
	Lowest 25%	–	–	–	–
LIFE INSURANCE:	Highest 25%	–	–	–	$116
	Average	–	$174	–	$194
	Lowest 25%	–	–	–	–
HEALTH INSURANCE:	Highest 25%	$5,001	$6,067	$6,720	$6,939
	Average	$3,436	$3,221	$4,470	$3,647
	Lowest 25%	–	–	–	–
CONTINUING EDUCATION	Highest 25%	–	–	–	–
	Average	$134	–	$100	–
	Lowest 25%	–	–	–	–
TOTAL BENEFITS	Highest 25%	$6,393	$7,107	$7,587	$9,373
	Average	$4,325	$4,421	$5,731	$5,169
	Lowest 25%	$1,029	–	$3,234	$541
TOTAL COMPENSATION AND BENEFIT		< 6 years	6-10 years	11-15 years	Over 15 years
	Highest 25%	$42,242	$42,236	$43,425	$43,842
	Average	$35,495	$35,585	$40,333	$36,662
	Lowest 25%	$29,428	$29,722	$31,299	$29,621
NUMBER OF RESPONDENTS		85	40	18	31

– Not enough responses to provide meaningful data

TABLE 13-11: ANNUAL COMPENSATION OF BOOKKEEPER BY DENOMINATION

CHARACTERISTICS		DENOMINATION					
		Assemblies of God	Baptist	Independent/ Nondenom	Lutheran	Methodist	Presbyterian
AVERAGE SUNDAY AM WORSHIP ATTENDANCE		759	1,093	1,676	–	936	865
AVERAGE CHURCH INCOME		$1,328,273	$2,686,939	$2,647,325	–	$1,529,665	$2,484,015
AVERAGE # of YEARS EMPLOYED		12	8	8	–	9	11
AVERAGE # of WEEKS OF PAID VACATION		3	3	3	–	3	3
% COLLEGE GRADUATE OR HIGHER		36%	43%	42%	–	67%	38%
% WHO RECEIVE AUTO REIMBURSEMENT		56%	46%	39%	–	40%	47%
% ORDAINED		–	–	2%	–	–	–
AVERAGE % SALARY INCREASE THIS YEAR		5%	4%	5%	–	–	4%

COMPENSATION		Assemblies of God	Baptist	Independent/ Nondenom	Lutheran	Methodist	Presbyterian
BASE SALARY:	Highest 25%	$40,471	$33,389	$39,956	–	$34,878	$36,227
	Average	$31,371	$30,821	$31,373	–	$30,702	$30,857
	Lowest 25%	$20,402	$25,775	$24,002	–	$26,961	$25,557
HOUSING:	Highest 25%	–	–	$3,857	–	–	–
	Average	–	–	–	–	–	–
	Lowest 25%	–	–	–	–	–	–
PARSONAGE:	Highest 25%	–	–	–	–	–	–
	Average	–	–	–	–	–	–
	Lowest 25%	–	–	–	–	–	–
TOTAL COMPENSATION	Highest 25%	$40,471	$33,389	$39,956	–	$34,878	$36,227
	Average	$31,371	$30,821	$31,708	–	$30,702	$30,857
	Lowest 25%	$20,402	$25,775	$24,002	–	$26,961	$25,557

– Not enough responses to provide meaningful data

TABLE 13-11: ANNUAL COMPENSATION OF BOOKKEEPER BY DENOMINATION

BENEFITS		DENOMINATION					
		Assemblies of God	Baptist	Independent/ Nondenom	Lutheran	Methodist	Presbyte-rian
RETIREMENT:	Highest 25%	–	$2,231	$999	–	$1,611	$2,851
	Average	$534	$1,188	$580	–	$706	$1,386
	Lowest 25%	–	–	–	–	–	–
LIFE INSURANCE:	Highest 25%	–	–	–	–	–	–
	Average	–	$189	$130	–	$122	–
	Lowest 25%	–	–	–	–	–	–
HEALTH INSURANCE:	Highest 25%	$5,110	$6,372	$6,935	–	$5,718	$6,884
	Average	$3,081	$3,988	$4,112	–	$3,600	$3,409
	Lowest 25%	–	–	–	–	$755	–
CONTINUING EDUCATION	Highest 25%	–	–	–	–	–	–
	Average	–	$109	$150	–	–	–
	Lowest 25%	–	–	–	–	–	–
TOTAL BENEFITS	Highest 25%	$5,110	$7,991	$8,000	–	$7,563	$9,166
	Average	$3,667	$5,474	$4,972	–	$4,460	$4,880
	Lowest 25%	$500	$2,300	$895	–	$790	$600
TOTAL COMPENSATION AND BENEFIT		Assemblies of God	Baptist	Independent/ Nondenom	Lutheran	Methodist	Presbyte-rian
	Highest 25%	$43,704	$41,411	$43,425	–	$39,483	$40,023
	Average	$35,039	$36,294	$36,680	–	$35,162	$35,736
	Lowest 25%	$29,344	$30,385	$27,001	–	$31,270	$25,559
NUMBER OF RESPONDENTS		13	58	43	6	12	17

– Not enough responses to provide meaningful data

313

TABLE 13-12: COMPENSATION OF PART-TIME BOOKKEEPER BY WORSHIP ATTENDANCE

CHARACTERISTICS	WORSHIP ATTENDANCE					
	100 or less	101 - 300	301 - 500	501 - 750	751 - 1,000	Over 1,000
AVERAGE SUNDAY AM WORSHIP ATTENDANCE	75	203	403	623	895	1,740
AVERAGE CHURCH INCOME	$163,478	$416,708	$737,686	$1,138,190	$1,368,888	$2,589,427
AVERAGE # of YEARS EMPLOYED	4	6	6	4	7	6
AVERAGE # of WEEKS OF PAID VACATION	–	2	2	2	–	3
% COLLEGE GRADUATE OR HIGHER	47%	53%	64%	43%	60%	70%
% WHO RECEIVE AUTO REIMBURSEMENT	11%	17%	37%	33%	63%	71%
% ORDAINED	5%	–	–	–	–	–
AVERAGE % SALARY INCREASE THIS YEAR	6%	4%	4%	10%	5%	4%
HOURLY RATES						
AVERAGE BASE RATE	–	$7.67	$10.83	$11.63	$8.72	$14.11
ANNUAL COMPENSATION						
AVERAGE BASE SALARY:	$3,268	$8,241	$12,356	$16,141	$14,379	$22,876
AVERAGE HOUSING:	–	–	–	–	–	–
AVERAGE PARSONAGE:	–	–	–	–	–	–
AVERAGE TOTAL COMPENSATION	$3,533	$8,241	$12,356	$16,141	$14,379	$22,876
ANNUAL BENEFITS						
AVERAGE RETIREMENT	–	–	–	$145	–	$248
AVERAGE LIFE INSURANCE	–	–	–	–	–	–
AVERAGE HEALTH INSURANCE	$273	–	$104	$278	–	$1,421
AVERAGE CONTINUING EDUCATION	–	–	–	$100	–	–
AVERAGE TOTAL BENEFITS	$273	–	$253	$528	–	$1,709
ANNUAL COMPENSATION & BENEFIT						
AVERAGE	$3,997	$8,483	$12,847	$16,669	$14,401	$25,755
NUMBER OF RESPONDENTS	21	89	54	31	11	22

– Not enough responses to provide meaningful data

TABLE 13-13: COMPENSATION OF PART-TIME BOOKKEEPER BY CHURCH INCOME

CHARACTERISTICS	CHURCH INCOME				
	$250 K & Under	$251 - $500K	$501 - $750K	$751K - $1M	Over $1 Million
AVERAGE SUNDAY AM WORSHIP ATTENDANCE	125	240	397	447	1,030
AVERAGE CHURCH INCOME	$176,428	$370,522	$625,687	$897,872	$1,820,689
AVERAGE # of YEARS EMPLOYED	7	5	5	10	5
AVERAGE # of WEEKS OF PAID VACATION	–	2	2	2	2
% COLLEGE GRADUATE OR HIGHER	38%	58%	65%	56%	54%
% WHO RECEIVE AUTO REIMBURSEMENT	9%	11%	29%	47%	55%
% ORDAINED	3%	–	–	–	–
AVERAGE % SALARY INCREASE THIS YEAR	5%	5%	7%	4%	5%
HOURLY RATES					
AVERAGE BASE RATE	$5.78	$8.07	$9.49	$13.07	$11.44
ANNUAL COMPENSATION	$250 K & Under	$251 - $500K	$501 - $750K	$751K - $1M	Over $1 Million
AVERAGE BASE SALARY:	$4,883	$8,270	$10,704	$14,340	$18,791
AVERAGE HOUSING:	–	–	–	–	–
AVERAGE PARSONAGE:	–	–	–	–	–
AVERAGE TOTAL COMPENSATION	$5,043	$8,270	$10,704	$14,340	$18,791
ANNUAL BENEFITS					
AVERAGE RETIREMENT	–	–	–	–	$190
AVERAGE LIFE INSURANCE	–	–	–	–	–
AVERAGE HEALTH INSURANCE	$164	–	–	–	$692
AVERAGE CONTINUING EDUCATION	–	–	–	$110	–
AVERAGE TOTAL BENEFITS	$164	$102	–	$152	$957
ANNUAL COMPENSATION & BENEFIT					
AVERAGE	$5,360	$8,503	$11,064	$15,096	$20,072
NUMBER OF RESPONDENTS	35	65	38	25	62

– Not enough responses to provide meaningful data

14

SECRETARIES

Employment Profile

The title of Secretary can encompass a number of clerical and administrative roles within the church office. Secretaries are the most common paid position on the church staff (full-time or part-time). Almost all are church employees (receiving W-2s for their tax form) with 97% being female. 1% are ordained ministers. The reported secretary positions provide the following employment profile:

	FULL-TIME	PART-TIME
Ordained	1%	1%
Average years employed	8	6
Male	3%	1%
Female	97%	99%
Self-employed (receives 1099)	1%	2%
Church employee (receives W-2)	99%	98%
High school diploma	59%	58%
Associate's degree	10%	10%
Bachelor's degree	30%	30%
Master's degree	1%	2%
Doctorate	<1%	<1%
Number of respondents	460	469

Total Compensation plus Benefits Package Analysis

The analysis below is based upon the tables found later in this chapter. The tables present compensation and benefits data according to worship attendance, church income, combinations of size and setting, region, gender, education, years employed, and denomination for church secretaries who serve full-time. The final two tables provide data for part-time church secretaries by worship attendance and church income. In this way, the secretary's compensation can be viewed from a variety of useful perspectives. The total compensation amount found in a separate box at the bottom of each page includes the base salary, housing and/or parsonage amount, life and health insurance payments, retirement contribution, and educational funds.

Full-time staff members. Secretaries receive fewer benefits for full-time work than ministerial and professional staff. The majority do not receive, housing allowances, retirement, life insurance, auto allowances, or continuing education funds. 50% receive health insurance, less than any other position surveyed in this study.

Part-time staff members. Fifty percent of secretaries work part-time. Ninety-eight percent of secretaries working part-time are employees of the church and 2% are self-employed. Few benefits are provided for part-time secretaries apart from a paid vacation.

COMPENSATION PLUS BENEFITS	FULL TIME	PART TIME
Base salary	99%	96%
Housing	0%	0%
Parsonage	0%	0%
Retirement	37%	7%
Life insurance	25%	2%
Health insurance	50%	5%
Paid vacation	90%	46%
Auto reimbursement	35%	13%
Continuing education	12%	5%

KEY POINTS

⮑ **Secretarial compensation and benefits are affected by church size.** Compensation and benefits for secretaries increase gradually with size. Secretaries in churches with attendance of 501-750 receive compensation right around the national average level. Compensation and benefits for secretaries serving church size of over 750 people exceed the national average exceeds the national average. *See Table 14-1.*

⮑ **Church income has an impact on compensation and benefits.** Similar to attendance, total compensation increases with church income. The national average compensation is obtained as a church approaches $1,000,000 in income. Slightly more than half of the reported secretaries are in churches with income over $1,000,000. The biggest increases occur from under $250,000 and $251-$500,000 and then once church income exceeds $1,000,000. *See Table 14-2.*

⮑ **Suburban churches provide the best compensation for smaller churches.** Suburban churches consistently pay the highest compensation and benefits for smaller churches (sizes of 500 or less). Suburban churches with attendance between 251 and 500 achieve the national average while metropolitan churches do not exceed the national average until they are between 501 and 750 people. *See Table 14-3, 14-4, 14-5, 14-6, and 14-7.*

⊃ **The region in which a church is located has some effect on the compensation and benefits of a secretary.** In general, secretaries in the Pacific or South Atlantic earn more than those in the other areas, although they serve in mid-size churches. East and West South Central have the largest churches yet compensation for secretaries in these areas are about average. The compensation and benefits packages of all regions are comparable to the national average, though the Mountain region is below. *See Table 14-8.*

⊃ **Educational attainment slightly increases compensation.** Those with a college degree made about $1,500 more than those with a less than a bachelor's degree. *See Table 14-10.*

⊃ **Years employed had some impact on compensation.** As years of employment increase, compensation and benefits totals also increase. However, the greater the years of service, the greater the church income, which may explain the increases in the package amounts. Close to 50% of these secretaries have worked on average only three years. About 13% have worked more than fifteen years. *See Table 14-11.*

⊃ **Part-time secretaries earn compensation and benefit packages similar to part-time bookkeepers.** The typical part-time secretary works about three days per week. Some part-time secretaries do not receive a salary, but rather receive their compensation as fringe benefits. Part-time secretaries earn less than most other part-time professional staff, but more than part-time custodians and organists. *See Tables 14-13 and 14-14.*

Ten Year Compensation & Benefits Trend: National Average for Secretaries

FULL TIME

1997	$20,232
1998	$20,353
1999	$21,354
2000	$21,965
2001	$23,316
2002	$24,132
2003	$24,875
2004	$25,007
2005	$26,624
2006	$29,551

THE 2007 COMPENSATION HANDBOOK FOR CHURCH STAFF

TABLE 14-1: ANNUAL COMPENSATION OF SECRETARY BY WORSHIP ATTENDANCE

CHARACTERISTICS		WORSHIP ATTENDANCE					
		100 or less	101-300	301-500	501-750	751-1000	Over 1000
AVERAGE SUNDAY AM WORSHIP ATTENDANCE		–	219	416	619	886	1,957
AVERAGE CHURCH INCOME		–	$477,404	$872,759	$1,372,439	$1,736,429	$3,580,349
AVERAGE # of YEARS EMPLOYED		–	8	7	7	8	9
AVERAGE # of WEEKS OF PAID VACATION		–	2	3	3	3	3
% COLLEGE GRADUATE OR HIGHER		–	30%	22%	32%	33%	39%
% WHO RECEIVE AUTO REIMBURSEMENT		–	27%	46%	53%	47%	48%
% ORDAINED		–	–	2%	–	–	–
AVERAGE % SALARY INCREASE THIS YEAR		–	5%	4%	4%	4%	5%
COMPENSATION		100 or less	101-300	301-500	501-750	751-1000	Over 1000
BASE SALARY:	Highest 25%	–	$27,500	$29,666	$30,000	$32,510	$32,550
	Average	–	$22,600	$25,942	$25,522	$27,080	$29,493
	Lowest 25%	–	$18,000	$22,180	$21,320	$22,650	$25,000
HOUSING:	Highest 25%	–	$309	–	–	–	–
	Average	–	–	–	–	–	–
	Lowest 25%	–	–	–	–	–	–
PARSONAGE:	Highest 25%	–	–	–	–	$5,605	–
	Average	–	–	–	–	$407	–
	Lowest 25%	–	–	–	–	–	–
TOTAL COMPENSATION	Highest 25%	–	$27,500	$29,666	$30,000	$32,510	$32,550
	Average	–	$22,614	$25,942	$25,522	$27,487	$29,493
	Lowest 25%	–	$18,000	$22,180	$21,320	$22,650	$25,000

– Not enough responses to provide meaningful data

TABLE 14-1: ANNUAL COMPENSATION OF SECRETARY BY WORSHIP ATTENDANCE

BENEFITS		WORSHIP ATTENDANCE					
		100 or less	101-300	301-500	501-750	751-1000	Over 1000
RETIREMENT:	Highest 25%	–	–	$1,260	$935	$1,182	$1,530
	Average	–	$184	$689	$609	$743	$849
	Lowest 25%	–	–	–	–	–	–
LIFE INSURANCE:	Highest 25%	–	–	–	$116	–	$125
	Average	–	–	–	$122	–	$115
	Lowest 25%	–	–	–	–	–	–
HEALTH INSURANCE:	Highest 25%	–	$2,700	$3,600	$4,668	$5,952	$5,919
	Average	–	$1,441	$2,095	$2,560	$3,229	$3,708
	Lowest 25%	–	–	–	–	–	–
CONTINUING EDUCATION	Highest 25%	–	–	–	–	–	–
	Average	–	–	–	–	–	–
	Lowest 25%	–	–	–	–	–	–
TOTAL BENEFITS	Highest 25%	–	$3,000	$4,032	$5,142	$7,377	$7,212
	Average	–	$1,691	$2,949	$3,385	$4,034	$4,711
	Lowest 25%	–	–	–	–	–	$186
TOTAL COMPENSATION AND BENEFIT		100 or less	101-300	301-500	501-750	751-1000	Over 1000
	Highest 25%	–	$29,250	$32,559	$33,990	$37,749	$41,029
	Average	–	$24,305	$28,986	$29,243	$31,521	$35,281
	Lowest 25%	–	$18,000	$25,200	$24,075	$24,270	$28,846
NUMBER OF RESPONDENTS		6	85	106	87	52	105

– Not enough responses to provide meaningful data

TABLE 14-2: ANNUAL COMPENSATION OF SECRETARY BY CHURCH INCOME

CHARACTERISTICS	CHURCH INCOME				
	$250K & under	$251K-$500K	$501K-$750K	$751K-$1M	Over $1 Million
AVERAGE SUNDAY AM WORSHIP ATTENDANCE	206	267	436	460	1,206
AVERAGE CHURCH INCOME	$211,163	$385,702	$622,982	$879,563	$2,417,474
AVERAGE # of YEARS EMPLOYED	9	7	8	6	8
AVERAGE # of WEEKS OF PAID VACATION	3	2	3	2	3
% COLLEGE GRADUATE OR HIGHER	36%	26%	39%	24%	31%
% WHO RECEIVE AUTO REIMBURSEMENT	33%	28%	48%	39%	50%
% ORDAINED	–	2%	–	–	0%
AVERAGE % SALARY INCREASE THIS YEAR	4%	4%	4%	4%	4%

COMPENSATION		$250K & under	$251K-$500K	$501K-$750K	$751K-$1M	Over 1 Million
BASE SALARY:	Highest 25%	$21,840	$28,000	$29,666	$28,686	$32,219
	Average	$18,981	$23,417	$24,920	$24,518	$27,966
	Lowest 25%	$15,000	$20,000	$21,000	$20,300	$23,300
HOUSING:	Highest 25%	–	$312	–	–	–
	Average	–	–	–	–	–
	Lowest 25%	–	–	–	–	–
PARSONAGE:	Highest 25%	–	–	–	–	–
	Average	–	–	–	–	–
	Lowest 25%	–	–	–	–	–
TOTAL COMPENSATION	Highest 25%	$21,840	$28,000	$29,666	$28,686	$32,219
	Average	$18,981	$23,435	$24,920	$24,518	$27,966
	Lowest 25%	$15,000	$20,000	$21,000	$20,300	$23,300

– Not enough responses to provide meaningful data

TABLE 14-2: ANNUAL COMPENSATION OF SECRETARY BY CHURCH INCOME

BENEFITS		CHURCH INCOME				
		$250K & under	$251K-$500K	$501K-$750K	$751K-$1M	Over $1 Million
RETIREMENT:	Highest 25%	–	–	$624	$1,000	$1,392
	Average	$214	$264	$468	$524	$795
	Lowest 25%	–	–	–	–	–
LIFE INSURANCE:	Highest 25%	–	–	–	–	–
	Average	–	–	–	$204	–
	Lowest 25%	–	–	–	–	–
HEALTH INSURANCE:	Highest 25%	$1,594	$3,900	$2,340	$2,688	$5,436
	Average	$852	$2,050	$1,321	$1,450	$3,344
	Lowest 25%	–	–	–	–	–
CONTINUING EDUCATION	Highest 25%	–	–	–	–	–
	Average	–	–	–	–	–
	Lowest 25%	–	–	–	–	–
TOTAL BENEFITS	Highest 25%	$2,100	$4,000	$3,000	$3,875	$7,061
	Average	$1,152	$2,376	$1,829	$2,271	$4,286
	Lowest 25%	–	–	–	–	–
TOTAL COMPENSATION AND BENEFIT		$250K & under	$251K-$500K	$501K-$750K	$751K-$1M	Over 1 Million
	Highest 25%	$23,080	$31,000	$31,122	$32,100	$37,913
	Average	$20,132	$25,811	$26,748	$26,961	$32,718
	Lowest 25%	$15,851	$21,000	$21,340	$21,603	$26,295
NUMBER OF RESPONDENTS		14	66	53	58	237

– Not enough responses to provide meaningful data

TABLE 14-3: ANNUAL COMPENSATION OF SECRETARY BY CHURCH SETTING & SIZE

ATTENDANCE 250 & UNDER	CHURCH SETTING			
	Metropoli- tan city	Suburb of large city	Small town or rural city	Farming area
AVERAGE SUNDAY AM WORSHIP ATTENDANCE	155	189	193	–
AVERAGE CHURCH INCOME	$436,342	$514,506	$349,906	–
AVERAGE # of YEARS EMPLOYED	8	5	9	–
AVERAGE # of WEEKS OF PAID VACATION	2	2	3	–
% COLLEGE GRADUATE OR HIGHER	–	43%	25%	–
% WHO RECEIVE AUTO REIMBURSEMENT	–	39%	12%	–
% ORDAINED	–	–	–	–
AVERAGE % SALARY INCREASE THIS YEAR	–	4%	5%	–

COMPENSATION		Metropoli- tan city	Suburb of large city	Small town or rural city	Farming area
BASE SALARY:	Highest 25%	$21,003	$27,998	$23,650	–
	Average	$20,325	$23,672	$20,874	–
	Lowest 25%	$13,498	$20,002	$16,498	–
HOUSING:	Highest 25%	–	$333	–	–
	Average	–	–	–	–
	Lowest 25%	–	–	–	–
PARSONAGE:	Highest 25%	–	–	–	–
	Average	–	–	–	–
	Lowest 25%	–	–	–	–
TOTAL COMPENSATION	Highest 25%	$21,003	$27,998	$23,650	–
	Average	$20,325	$23,716	$20,874	–
	Lowest 25%	$13,498	$20,002	$16,498	–

– Not enough responses to provide meaningful data

TABLE 14-3: ANNUAL COMPENSATION OF SECRETARY BY CHURCH SETTING & SIZE

BENEFITS		CHURCH SETTING			
		Metropoli-tan city	Suburb of large city	Small town or rural city	Farming area
RETIREMENT:	Highest 25%	–	–	–	–
	Average	$556	–	$276	–
	Lowest 25%	–	–	–	–
LIFE INSURANCE:	Highest 25%	–	–	–	–
	Average	–	–		–
	Lowest 25%	–	–	–	–
HEALTH INSURANCE:	Highest 25%	$3,302	$3,358	$2,700	–
	Average	$1,226	$1,410	$1,366	–
	Lowest 25%	–	–	–	–
CONTINUING EDUCATION	Highest 25%	–	–	–	–
	Average	–	–	–	–
	Lowest 25%	–	–	–	–
TOTAL BENEFITS	Highest 25%	$3,301	$3,484	$3,881	–
	Average	$1,781	$1,485	$1,706	–
	Lowest 25%	–	–	–	–
TOTAL COMPENSATION AND BENEFIT		Metropoli-tan city	Suburb of large city	Small town or rural city	Farming area
	Highest 25%	$23,533	$29,999	$26,500	–
	Average	$22,107	$25,202	$22,580	–
	Lowest 25%	$13,499	$20,501	$16,501	–
NUMBER OF RESPONDENTS		9	27	30	2

– Not enough responses to provide meaningful data

TABLE 14-4: ANNUAL COMPENSATION OF SECRETARY BY CHURCH SETTING & SIZE

ATTENDANCE 251 - 500	CHURCH SETTING			
	Metropoli-tan city	Suburb of large city	Small town or rural city	Farming area
AVERAGE SUNDAY AM WORSHIP ATTENDANCE	393	403	384	–
AVERAGE CHURCH INCOME	$874,881	$926,128	$721,803	–
AVERAGE # of YEARS EMPLOYED	5	6	9	–
AVERAGE # of WEEKS OF PAID VACATION	2	3	3	–
% COLLEGE GRADUATE OR HIGHER	25%	21%	23%	–
% WHO RECEIVE AUTO REIMBURSEMENT	43%	49%	43%	–
% ORDAINED	–	3%	2%	–
AVERAGE % SALARY INCREASE THIS YEAR	4%	4%	3%	–

COMPENSATION		Metropoli-tan city	Suburb of large city	Small town or rural city	Farming area
BASE SALARY:	Highest 25%	$28,900	$31,200	$26,700	–
	Average	$26,309	$27,760	$23,512	–
	Lowest 25%	$24,999	$23,505	$20,600	–
HOUSING:	Highest 25%	–	–	–	–
	Average	–	–	–	–
	Lowest 25%	–	–	–	–
PARSONAGE:	Highest 25%	–	–	–	–
	Average	–	–	–	–
	Lowest 25%	–	–	–	–
TOTAL COMPENSATION	Highest 25%	$28,900	$31,200	$26,700	–
	Average	$26,309	$27,760	$23,512	–
	Lowest 25%	$24,999	$23,505	$20,600	–

– Not enough responses to provide meaningful data

TABLE 14-4: ANNUAL COMPENSATION OF SECRETARY BY CHURCH SETTING & SIZE

BENEFITS		CHURCH SETTING			
		Metropoli-tan city	Suburb of large city	Small town or rural city	Farming area
RETIREMENT:	Highest 25%	$1,606	$859	$560	–
	Average	$825	$552	$478	–
	Lowest 25%	–	–	–	–
LIFE INSURANCE:	Highest 25%	–	–	–	–
	Average	$285	–	–	–
	Lowest 25%	–	–	–	–
HEALTH INSURANCE:	Highest 25%	$4,080	$4,000	$3,105	–
	Average	$2,242	$2,260	$1,881	–
	Lowest 25%	–	–	–	–
CONTINUING EDUCATION	Highest 25%	–	–	–	–
	Average	$132	–	–	–
	Lowest 25%	–	–	–	–
TOTAL BENEFITS	Highest 25%	$6,342	$4,000	$3,500	–
	Average	$3,484	$2,910	$2,422	–
	Lowest 25%	–	–	–	–
TOTAL COMPENSATION AND BENEFIT		Metropoli-tan city	Suburb of large city	Small town or rural city	Farming area
	Highest 25%	$34,007	$34,999	$31,033	–
	Average	$29,792	$30,670	$26,106	–
	Lowest 25%	$26,145	$26,357	$21,600	–
NUMBER OF RESPONDENTS		28	39	58	2

– Not enough responses to provide meaningful data

327

TABLE 14-5: ANNUAL COMPENSATION OF SECRETARY BY CHURCH SETTING & SIZE

ATTENDANCE 501 - 750	CHURCH SETTING			
	Metropoli- tan city	Suburb of large city	Small town or rural city	Farming area
AVERAGE SUNDAY AM WORSHIP ATTENDANCE	632	634	596	–
AVERAGE CHURCH INCOME	$1,552,182	$1,408,468	$1,343,499	–
AVERAGE # of YEARS EMPLOYED	6	5	8	–
AVERAGE # of WEEKS OF PAID VACATION	2	2	3	–
% COLLEGE GRADUATE OR HIGHER	18%	39%	38%	–
% WHO RECEIVE AUTO REIMBURSEMENT	73%	45%	45%	–
% ORDAINED	–	–	–	–
AVERAGE % SALARY INCREASE THIS YEAR	5%	4%	4%	–

COMPENSATION		Metropoli- tan city	Suburb of large city	Small town or rural city	Farming area
BASE SALARY:	Highest 25%	$31,075	$32,100	$27,552	–
	Average	$27,467	$26,466	$23,502	–
	Lowest 25%	$22,860	$21,320	$19,997	–
HOUSING:	Highest 25%	–	–	–	–
	Average	–	–	–	–
	Lowest 25%	–	–	–	–
PARSONAGE:	Highest 25%	–	–	–	–
	Average	–	–	–	–
	Lowest 25%	–	–	–	–
TOTAL COMPENSATION	Highest 25%	$31,075	$32,100	$27,552	–
	Average	$27,467	$26,466	$23,502	–
	Lowest 25%	$22,860	$21,320	$19,997	–

– Not enough responses to provide meaningful data

TABLE 14-5: ANNUAL COMPENSATION OF SECRETARY BY CHURCH SETTING & SIZE

BENEFITS		CHURCH SETTING			
		Metropolitan city	Suburb of large city	Small town or rural city	Farming area
RETIREMENT:	Highest 25%	$880	$993	–	–
	Average	$829	$610	$490	–
	Lowest 25%	–	–	–	–
LIFE INSURANCE:	Highest 25%	$180	$121	–	–
	Average	$122	$106	$150	–
	Lowest 25%	–	–	–	–
HEALTH INSURANCE:	Highest 25%	$3,455	$4,500	$4,829	–
	Average	$1,775	$2,822	$2,562	–
	Lowest 25%	–	–	–	–
CONTINUING EDUCATION	Highest 25%	–	–	–	–
	Average	$171	–	–	–
	Lowest 25%	–	–	–	–
TOTAL BENEFITS	Highest 25%	$4,395	$6,300	$5,142	–
	Average	$2,896	$3,579	$3,295	–
	Lowest 25%	$741	$800	–	–
TOTAL COMPENSATION AND BENEFIT		Metropolitan city	Suburb of large city	Small town or rural city	Farming area
	Highest 25%	$32,825	$36,000	$31,901	–
	Average	$30,363	$30,046	$27,541	–
	Lowest 25%	$25,949	$24,440	$21,481	–
NUMBER OF RESPONDENTS		12	34	37	4

– Not enough responses to provide meaningful data

329

TABLE 14-6: ANNUAL COMPENSATION OF SECRETARY BY CHURCH SETTING & SIZE

ATTENDANCE 751 - 1,000		CHURCH SETTING			
		Metropolitan city	Suburb of large city	Small town or rural city	Farming area
AVERAGE SUNDAY AM WORSHIP ATTENDANCE		922	854	884	–
AVERAGE CHURCH INCOME		$2,017,280	$1,506,767	$1,765,697	–
AVERAGE # of YEARS EMPLOYED		7	8	11	–
AVERAGE # of WEEKS OF PAID VACATION		3	3	3	–
% COLLEGE GRADUATE OR HIGHER		33%	33%	33%	–
% WHO RECEIVE AUTO REIMBURSEMENT		50%	43%	45%	–
% ORDAINED		–	–	–	–
AVERAGE % SALARY INCREASE THIS YEAR		4%	4%	4%	–

COMPENSATION		Metropolitan city	Suburb of large city	Small town or rural city	Farming area
BASE SALARY:	Highest 25%	$32,711	$33,121	$29,100	–
	Average	$26,386	$29,982	$25,452	–
	Lowest 25%	$22,650	$25,000	$20,427	–
HOUSING:	Highest 25%	–	–	–	–
	Average	–	–	–	–
	Lowest 25%	–	–	–	–
PARSONAGE:	Highest 25%	–	–	–	–
	Average	–	–	–	–
	Lowest 25%	–	–	–	–
TOTAL COMPENSATION	Highest 25%	$32,711	$33,121	$29,100	–
	Average	$26,386	$29,982	$25,452	–
	Lowest 25%	$22,650	$25,000	$20,427	–

– Not enough responses to provide meaningful data

TABLE 14-6: ANNUAL COMPENSATION OF SECRETARY BY CHURCH SETTING & SIZE

BENEFITS		CHURCH SETTING			
		Metropoli- tan city	Suburb of large city	Small town or rural city	Farming area
RETIREMENT:	Highest 25%	$2,042	$994	$1,164	–
	Average	$1,055	$534	$676	–
	Lowest 25%	–	–	–	–
LIFE INSURANCE:	Highest 25%	–	–	–	–
	Average	–	–	–	–
	Lowest 25%	–	–	–	–
HEALTH INSURANCE:	Highest 25%	$5,712	$5,908	$8,750	–
	Average	$3,336	$2,934	$3,781	–
	Lowest 25%	–	–	–	–
CONTINUING EDUCATION	Highest 25%	–	–	–	–
	Average	–	–	–	–
	Lowest 25%	–	–	–	–
TOTAL BENEFITS	Highest 25%	$7,260	$7,330	$8,750	–
	Average	$4,469	$3,529	$4,507	–
	Lowest 25%	$686	–	–	–
TOTAL COMPENSATION AND BENEFIT		Metropoli- tan city	Suburb of large city	Small town or rural city	Farming area
	Highest 25%	$37,356	$37,704	$38,025	–
	Average	$30,855	$33,511	$29,959	–
	Lowest 25%	$23,220	$24,993	$22,100	–
NUMBER OF RESPONDENTS		16	21	14	0

– Not enough responses to provide meaningful data

331

TABLE 14-7: ANNUAL COMPENSATION OF SECRETARY BY CHURCH SETTING & SIZE

ATTENDANCE OVER 1,000		Metropoli-tan city	Suburb of large city	Small town or rural city	Farming area
AVERAGE SUNDAY AM WORSHIP ATTENDANCE		2,266	2,002	1,670	–
AVERAGE CHURCH INCOME		$4,017,294	$3,673,606	$3,115,763	–
AVERAGE # of YEARS EMPLOYED		9	8	10	–
AVERAGE # of WEEKS OF PAID VACATION		3	3	3	–
% COLLEGE GRADUATE OR HIGHER		63%	36%	29%	–
% WHO RECEIVE AUTO REIMBURSEMENT		42%	49%	48%	–
% ORDAINED		–	–	–	–
AVERAGE % SALARY INCREASE THIS YEAR		4%	5%	4%	–

COMPENSATION		Metropoli-tan city	Suburb of large city	Small town or rural city	Farming area
BASE SALARY:	Highest 25%	$35,069	$33,218	$29,754	–
	Average	$30,181	$30,677	$26,721	–
	Lowest 25%	$25,663	$27,004	$22,247	–
HOUSING:	Highest 25%	–	–	–	–
	Average	–	–	–	–
	Lowest 25%	–	–	–	–
PARSONAGE:	Highest 25%	–	–	–	–
	Average	–	–	–	–
	Lowest 25%	–	–	–	–
TOTAL COMPENSATION	Highest 25%	$35,069	$33,218	$29,754	–
	Average	$30,181	$30,677	$26,721	–
	Lowest 25%	$25,663	$27,004	$22,247	–

– Not enough responses to provide meaningful data

TABLE 14-7: ANNUAL COMPENSATION OF SECRETARY BY CHURCH SETTING & SIZE

		CHURCH SETTING			
BENEFITS		Metropoli-tan city	Suburb of large city	Small town or rural city	Farming area
RETIREMENT:	Highest 25%	$1,805	$1,529	$1,025	–
	Average	$834	$916	$654	–
	Lowest 25%	–	–	–	–
LIFE INSURANCE:	Highest 25%	$138	$177	$108	–
	Average	$118	$136	$65	–
	Lowest 25%	–	–	–	–
HEALTH INSURANCE:	Highest 25%	$5,256	$6,119	$4,743	–
	Average	$3,511	$3,807	$3,440	–
	Lowest 25%	–	–	–	–
CONTINUING EDUCATION	Highest 25%	–	–	–	–
	Average	–	–	–	–
	Lowest 25%	–	–	–	–
TOTAL BENEFITS	Highest 25%	$7,278	$7,490	$6,466	–
	Average	$4,481	$4,916	$4,180	–
	Lowest 25%	–	–	$1,038	–
TOTAL COMPENSATION AND BENEFIT		Metropoli-tan city	Suburb of large city	Small town or rural city	Farming area
	Highest 25%	$42,355	$40,999	$36,478	–
	Average	$36,486	$35,592	$33,583	–
	Lowest 25%	$30,101	$30,001	$26,746	–
NUMBER OF RESPONDENTS		20	55	29	0

– Not enough responses to provide meaningful data

333

TABLE 14-8: ANNUAL COMPENSATION OF SECRETARY BY REGION

CHARACTERISTICS	REGION								
	New England	Middle Atlantic	South Atlantic	E-N Central	E-S Central	W-N Central	W-S Central	Mountain	Pacific
AVERAGE SUNDAY AM WORSHIP ATTENDANCE	–	598	761	1,160	836	685	893	861	911
AVERAGE CHURCH INCOME	–	$1,026,960	$1,599,727	$1,861,447	$2,064,440	$1,282,009	$1,968,174	$1,427,391	$1,608,916
AVERAGE # of YEARS EMPLOYED	–	7	8	8	8	8	8	8	7
AVERAGE # of WEEKS OF PAID VACATION	–	3	3	3	3	3	3	3	3
% COLLEGE GRADUATE OR HIGHER	–	38%	29%	28%	46%	29%	19%	28%	35%
% WHO RECEIVE AUTO REIMBURSEMENT	–	47%	53%	60%	45%	50%	22%	46%	30%
% ORDAINED	–	–	1%	–	–	–	–	3%	–
AVERAGE % SALARY INCREASE THIS YEAR	–	4%	4%	4%	4%	4%	5%	4%	5%

COMPENSATION		New England	Middle Atlantic	South Atlantic	E-N Central	E-S Central	W-N Central	W-S Central	Mountain	Pacific
BASE SALARY:	Highest 25%	–	$30,000	$31,000	$30,000	$31,000	$32,120	$30,000	$25,858	$33,920
	Average	–	$24,846	$27,315	$24,981	$24,779	$25,669	$25,516	$22,446	$28,831
	Lowest 25%	–	$21,000	$22,566	$20,474	$21,000	$20,214	$20,000	$19,200	$23,504
HOUSING:	Highest 25%	–	–	$307	–	–	–	–	–	–
	Average	–	–	–	–	–	–	–	–	–
	Lowest 25%	–	–	–	–	–	–	–	–	–
PARSONAGE:	Highest 25%	–	–	–	–	–	–	–	–	–
	Average	–	–	–	–	–	–	–	–	–
	Lowest 25%	–	–	–	–	–	–	–	–	–
TOTAL COMPENSATION	Highest 25%	–	$30,000	$31,000	$30,000	$31,000	$31,120	$30,000	$25,858	$33,920
	Average	–	$24,846	$27,326	$24,981	$25,421	$25,669	$25,516	$22,446	$28,831
	Lowest 25%	–	$21,000	$22,566	$20,474	$21,174	$20,214	$20,000	$19,200	$23,504

– Not enough responses to provide meaningful data

TABLE 14-8: ANNUAL COMPENSATION OF SECRETARY BY REGION

BENEFITS		New England	Middle Atlantic	South Atlantic	E-N Central	E-S Central	W-N Central	W-S Central	Mountain	Pacific
RETIREMENT:	Highest 25%	–	–	$1,601	$750	–	$1,097	$1,047	–	$900
	Average	–	$330	$911	$537	$430	$645	$562	$371	$630
	Lowest 25%	–	–	–	–	–	–	–	–	–
LIFE INSURANCE:	Highest 25%	–	–	–	–	–	–	–	–	–
	Average	–	–	$141	–	$107	–	–	$120	–
	Lowest 25%	–	–	–	–	–	–	–	–	–
HEALTH INSURANCE:	Highest 25%	–	$4,636	$4,624	$4,682	$4,900	$4,575	$4,542	$3,105	$3,991
	Average	–	$2,588	$2,510	$2,457	$2,909	$2,981	$2,293	$2,211	$2,507
	Lowest 25%	–	–	–	–	–	–	–	–	–
CONTINUING EDUCATION	Highest 25%	–	–	–	–	–	–	–	–	–
	Average	–	–	–	–	$107	–	–	–	–
	Lowest 25%	–	–	–	–	–	–	–	–	–
TOTAL BENEFITS	Highest 25%	–	$4,668	$5,836	$4,920	$7,200	$5,243	$5,346	$6,000	$4,437
	Average	–	$3,048	$3,625	$3,083	$3,553	$3,695	$2,960	$2,782	$3,236
	Lowest 25%	–	–	–	–	–	–	–	–	–
TOTAL COMPENSATION AND BENEFIT		New England	Middle Atlantic	South Atlantic	E-N Central	E-S Central	W-N Central	W-S Central	Mountain	Pacific
	Highest 25%	–	$34,585	$35,345	$33,559	$36,078	$35,899	$33,236	$30,708	$37,490
	Average	–	$27,895	$31,043	$28,865	$28,974	$29,364	$28,476	$25,929	$33,081
	Lowest 25%	–	$22,000	$24,120	$21,669	$22,234	$23,040	$21,840	$20,100	$26,804
NUMBER OF RESPONDENTS		6	43	108	61	33	48	63	37	57

– Not enough responses to provide meaningful data

335

TABLE 14-9: ANNUAL COMPENSATION OF SECRETARY BY GENDER

CHARACTERISTICS	GENDER	
	Male	Female
AVERAGE SUNDAY AM WORSHIP ATTENDANCE	536	849
AVERAGE CHURCH INCOME	$1,093,289	$1,627,198
AVERAGE # of YEARS EMPLOYED	10	8
AVERAGE # of WEEKS OF PAID VACATION	3	3
% COLLEGE GRADUATE OR HIGHER	31%	30%
% WHO RECEIVE AUTO REIMBURSEMENT	33%	44%
% ORDAINED	–	0%
AVERAGE % SALARY INCREASE THIS YEAR	–	4%

COMPENSATION		Male	Female
BASE SALARY:	Highest 25%	$31,304	$30,544
	Average	$24,850	$25,950
	Lowest 25%	$18,920	$21,268
HOUSING:	Highest 25%	–	$300
	Average	–	–
	Lowest 25%	–	–
PARSONAGE:	Highest 25%	–	–
	Average	–	–
	Lowest 25%	–	–
TOTAL COMPENSATION	Highest 25%	$31,304	$30,544
	Average	$24,850	$26,000
	Lowest 25%	$18,920	$21,268

– Not enough responses to provide meaningful data

SECRETARIES—TABLE 14-9

TABLE 14-9: ANNUAL COMPENSATION OF SECRETARY BY GENDER

BENEFITS		GENDER	
		Male	Female
RETIREMENT:	Highest 25%	$1,000	$1,000
	Average	$712	$612
	Lowest 25%	–	–
LIFE INSURANCE:	Highest 25%	–	–
	Average	$142	–
	Lowest 25%	–	–
HEALTH INSURANCE:	Highest 25%	$6,423	$4,404
	Average	$3,346	$2,525
	Lowest 25%	–	–
CONTINUING EDUCATION	Highest 25%	–	–
	Average	–	–
	Lowest 25%	–	–
TOTAL BENEFITS	Highest 25%	$6,468	$5,373
	Average	$4,271	$3,274
	Lowest 25%	$450	–
TOTAL COMPENSATION AND BENEFIT		Male	Female
	Highest 25%	$38,746	$35,425
	Average	$29,121	$29,608
	Lowest 25%	$23,700	$23,000
NUMBER OF RESPONDENTS		14	440

– Not enough responses to provide meaningful data

337

TABLE 14-10: ANNUAL COMPENSATION OF SECRETARY BY EDUCATION

CHARACTERISTICS	EDUCATION			
	< than Bachelor	Bachelor	Master	Doctorate
AVERAGE SUNDAY AM WORSHIP ATTENDANCE	816	861	–	–
AVERAGE CHURCH INCOME	$1,794,054	$1,609,373	–	–
AVERAGE # of YEARS EMPLOYED	8	7	–	–
AVERAGE # of WEEKS OF PAID VACATION	3	3	–	–
% COLLEGE GRADUATE OR HIGHER	–	100%	–	–
% WHO RECEIVE AUTO REIMBURSEMENT	47%	40%	–	–
% ORDAINED	0%	1%	–	–
AVERAGE % SALARY INCREASE THIS YEAR	4%	4%	–	–

COMPENSATION		< than Bachelor	Bachelor	Master	Doctorate
BASE SALARY:	Highest 25%	$29,400	$31,356	–	–
	Average	$25,488	$26,798	–	–
	Lowest 25%	$21,000	$22,000	–	–
HOUSING:	Highest 25%	–	$307	–	–
	Average	–	–	–	–
	Lowest 25%	–	–	–	–
PARSONAGE:	Highest 25%	–	–	–	–
	Average	–	–	–	–
	Lowest 25%	–	–	–	–
TOTAL COMPENSATION	Highest 25%	$29,400	$31,356	–	–
	Average	$25,488	$26,809	–	–
	Lowest 25%	$21,000	$22,000	–	–

– Not enough responses to provide meaningful data

TABLE 14-10: ANNUAL COMPENSATION OF SECRETARY BY EDUCATION

BENEFITS		EDUCATION			
		< than Bachelor	Bachelor	Master	Doctorate
RETIREMENT:	Highest 25%	$1,000	$1,382	–	–
	Average	$633	$697	–	–
	Lowest 25%	–	–	–	–
LIFE INSURANCE:	Highest 25%	–	–	–	–
	Average	–	–	–	–
	Lowest 25%	–	–	–	–
HEALTH INSURANCE:	Highest 25%	$4,760	$4,521	–	–
	Average	$2,620	$2,933	–	–
	Lowest 25%	–	–	–	–
CONTINUING EDUCATION	Highest 25%	–		–	–
	Average	–	–	–	–
	Lowest 25%	–	–	–	–
TOTAL BENEFITS	Highest 25%	$5,862	$6,186	–	–
	Average	$3,385	$3,766	–	–
	Lowest 25%	–	–	–	–
TOTAL COMPENSATION AND BENEFIT		< than Bachelor	Bachelor	Master	Doctorate
	Highest 25%	$34,250	$36,392	–	–
	Average	$28,995	$30,575	–	–
	Lowest 25%	$23,000	$24,538	–	–
NUMBER OF RESPONDENTS		247	104	3	1

– Not enough responses to provide meaningful data

TABLE 14-11: ANNUAL COMPENSATION OF SECRETARY BY YEARS EMPLOYED

CHARACTERISTICS		YEARS EMPLOYED			
		< 6 years	6-10 years	11-15 years	Over 15 years
AVERAGE SUNDAY AM WORSHIP ATTENDANCE		775	852	972	916
AVERAGE CHURCH INCOME		$1,469,922	$1,548,353	$1,723,603	$2,075,420
AVERAGE # of YEARS EMPLOYED		3	8	13	23
AVERAGE # of WEEKS OF PAID VACATION		2	3	3	4
% COLLEGE GRADUATE OR HIGHER		37%	27%	22%	23%
% WHO RECEIVE AUTO REIMBURSEMENT		46%	40%	38%	48%
% ORDAINED		–	2%	–	–
AVERAGE % SALARY INCREASE THIS YEAR		5%	4%	4%	4%

COMPENSATION		< 6 years	6-10 years	11-15 years	Over 15 years
BASE SALARY:	Highest 25%	$29,000	$31,304	$31,000	$32,500
	Average	$24,368	$26,445	$28,012	$28,291
	Lowest 25%	$20,800	$21,271	$24,564	$23,099
HOUSING:	Highest 25%	–	–	$321	–
	Average	–	–	–	–
	Lowest 25%	–	–	–	–
PARSONAGE:	Highest 25%	–	–	–	–
	Average	–	–	–	–
	Lowest 25%	–	–	–	–
TOTAL COMPENSATION	Highest 25%	$29,000	$31,304	$31,000	$32,500
	Average	$24,469	$26,445	$28,041	$28,291
	Lowest 25%	$20,930	$21,271	$24,564	$23,099

– Not enough responses to provide meaningful data

TABLE 14-11: ANNUAL COMPENSATION OF SECRETARY BY YEARS EMPLOYED

BENEFITS		YEARS EMPLOYED			
		< 6 years	6-10 years	11-15 years	Over 15 years
RETIREMENT:	Highest 25%	$496	$1,086	$624	$2,100
	Average	$432	$693	$527	$1,112
	Lowest 25%	–	–	–	–
LIFE INSURANCE:	Highest 25%	–	–	–	–
	Average	–	–	$162	$104
	Lowest 25%	–	–	–	–
HEALTH INSURANCE:	Highest 25%	$3,550	$4,900	$4,488	$5,919
	Average	$2,041	$2,685	$2,669	$3,808
	Lowest 25%	–	–	–	–
CONTINUING EDUCATION	Highest 25%	–	–	–	–
	Average	–	–	–	–
	Lowest 25%	–	–	–	–
TOTAL BENEFITS	Highest 25%	$4,500	$6,423	$4,741	$8,300
	Average	$2,618	$3,483	$3,405	$5,079
	Lowest 25%	–	–	–	$2,340
TOTAL COMPENSATION AND BENEFIT		< 6 years	6-10 years	11-15 years	Over 15 years
	Highest 25%	$32,900	$36,477	$35,877	$40,520
	Average	$27,588	$30,002	$31,446	$33,369
	Lowest 25%	$21,600	$23,000	$25,825	$26,238
NUMBER OF RESPONDENTS		210	134	41	58

– Not enough responses to provide meaningful data

341

TABLE 14-12: ANNUAL COMPENSATION OF SECRETARY BY DENOMINATION

CHARACTERISTICS	DENOMINATION					
	Assemblies of God	Baptist	Independent/ Nondenom	Lutheran	Methodist	Presbyterian
AVERAGE SUNDAY AM WORSHIP ATTENDANCE	642	772	1,142	431	768	609
AVERAGE CHURCH INCOME	1,264,536	$1,683,632	$1,864,578	$954,980	$1,277,347	$1,502,265
AVERAGE # of YEARS EMPLOYED	7	9	7	9	8	9
AVERAGE # of WEEKS OF PAID VACATION	2	3	3	3	3	3
% COLLEGE GRADUATE OR HIGHER	17%	34%	31%	20%	29%	26%
% WHO RECEIVE AUTO REIMBURSEMENT	40%	38%	41%	58%	30%	53%
% ORDAINED	–	1%	–	4%	–	–
AVERAGE % SALARY INCREASE THIS YEAR	4%	4%	4%	4%	4%	4%

COMPENSATION		Assemblies of God	Baptist	Independent/ Nondenom	Lutheran	Methodist	Presbyterian
BASE SALARY:	Highest 25%	$25,000	$29,800	$31,000	$28,000	$29,800	$33,112
	Average	$23,056	$25,231	$26,068	$24,511	$26,152	$29,170
	Lowest 25%	$21,000	$20,904	$21,538	$21,000	$21,650	$24,829
HOUSING:	Highest 25%	–	–	–	–	–	–
	Average	–	–	–	–	–	–
	Lowest 25%	–	–	–	–	–	–
PARSONAGE:	Highest 25%	–	–	–	–	–	–
	Average	–	–	–	–	–	–
	Lowest 25%	–	–	–	–	–	–
TOTAL COMPENSATION	Highest 25%	$25,000	$29,800	$31,000	$28,000	$29,800	$33,112
	Average	$23,056	$25,366	$26,068	$24,511	$26,152	$29,170
	Lowest 25%	$21,000	$21,000	$21,538	$21,000	$21,650	$24,829

– Not enough responses to provide meaningful data

TABLE 14-12: ANNUAL COMPENSATION OF SECRETARY BY DENOMINATION

BENEFITS		DENOMINATION					
		Assemblies of God	Baptist	Independent/ Nondenom	Lutheran	Methodist	Presbyterian
RETIREMENT:	Highest 25%	–	$1,392	$565	$1,000	$1,360	$2,100
	Average	$175	$774	$340	$618	$583	$1,145
	Lowest 25%	–	–	–	–	–	–
LIFE INSURANCE:	Highest 25%	–	–	–	–	–	$100
	Average	–	$102	–	–	–	–
	Lowest 25%	–	–	–	–	–	–
HEALTH INSURANCE:	Highest 25%	$2,911	$4,010	$5,424	$4,542	$3,441	$5,543
	Average	$1,600	$2,349	$3,197	$2,182	$1,635	$3,305
	Lowest 25%	–	–	–	–	–	–
CONTINUING EDUCATION	Highest 25%	–	–	–	–	–	–
	Average	–	–	–	–	–	–
	Lowest 25%	–	–	–	–	–	–
TOTAL BENEFITS	Highest 25%	$2,995	$5,648	$6,000	$4,920	$3,441	$7,413
	Average	$1,832	$3,270	$3,649	$2,864	$2,284	$4,623
	Lowest 25%	–	–	–	–	–	$748
TOTAL COMPENSATION AND BENEFIT		Assemblies of God	Baptist	Independent/ Nondenom	Lutheran	Methodist	Presbyterian
	Highest 25%	$27,730	$34,929	$36,800	$32,100	$33,487	$39,745
	Average	$24,888	$28,637	$30,734	$27,760	$28,436	$33,793
	Lowest 25%	$21,603	$22,061	$23,485	$22,200	$22,825	$29,495
NUMBER OF RESPONDENTS		30	156	87	26	32	40

– Not enough responses to provide meaningful data

343

TABLE 14-13: COMPENSATION OF PART-TIME SECRETARY BY WORSHIP ATTENDANCE

CHARACTERISTICS	WORSHIP ATTENDANCE					
	100 or less	101 - 300	301 - 500	501 - 750	751 - 1,000	Over 1,000
AVERAGE SUNDAY AM WORSHIP ATTENDANCE	78	185	406	606	862	1,379
AVERAGE CHURCH INCOME	$157,115	$325,731	$694,138	$1,095,314	$1,450,497	$1,939,265
AVERAGE # of YEARS EMPLOYED	5	6	6	6	4	4
AVERAGE # of WEEKS OF PAID VACATION	2	2	2	2	–	3
% COLLEGE GRADUATE OR HIGHER	33%	30%	41%	33%	38%	26%
% WHO RECEIVE AUTO REIMBURSEMENT	18%	15%	14%	55%	–	30%
% ORDAINED	1%	–	2%	–	–	–
AVERAGE % SALARY INCREASE THIS YEAR	5%	4%	4%	4%	7%	3%
HOURLY RATES						
AVERAGE BASE RATE	$6.69	$7.39	$8.89	$9.65	$9.40	$10.30
ANNUAL COMPENSATION						
AVERAGE BASE SALARY:	$7,006	$11,191	$13,456	$15,259	$13,671	$13,775
AVERAGE HOUSING:	–	–	–	–	–	–
AVERAGE PARSONAGE:	–	–	–	–	–	–
AVERAGE TOTAL COMPENSATION	$7,065	$11,236	$13,603	$15,259	$13,671	$13,775
ANNUAL BENEFITS						
AVERAGE RETIREMENT	–	–	$165	$158	$233	$100
AVERAGE LIFE INSURANCE	–	–	–	–	–	–
AVERAGE HEALTH INSURANCE	$131	$124	$154	$685	–	$519
AVERAGE CONTINUING EDUCATION	–	–	–	–	–	–
AVERAGE TOTAL BENEFITS	$169	$192	$339	$850	$330	$654
ANNUAL COMPENSATION & BENEFIT						
AVERAGE	$7,319	$11,634	$14,352	$17,629	$16,546	$14,429
NUMBER OF RESPONDENTS	85	226	70	42	13	22

– Not enough responses to provide meaningful data

TABLE 14-14: COMPENSATION OF PART-TIME SECRETARY BY CHURCH INCOME

	CHURCH INCOME				
CHARACTERISTICS	$250 K & Under	$251 - $500K	$501 - $750K	$751K - $1M	Over $1 Million
AVERAGE SUNDAY AM WORSHIP ATTENDANCE	125	223	376	476	886
AVERAGE CHURCH INCOME	$161,933	$359,602	$625,570	$884,311	$1,595,901
AVERAGE # of YEARS EMPLOYED	6	6	6	6	5
AVERAGE # of WEEKS OF PAID VACATION	2	2	3	2	2
% COLLEGE GRADUATE OR HIGHER	31%	31%	41%	35%	33%
% WHO RECEIVE AUTO REIMBURSEMENT	16%	13%	6%	39%	42%
% ORDAINED	1%	–	2%	–	
AVERAGE % SALARY INCREASE THIS YEAR	5%	4%	4%	4%	4%
HOURLY RATES					
AVERAGE BASE RATE	$6.98	$7.47	$8.31	$9.61	$9.13
ANNUAL COMPENSATION	$250 K & Under	$251 - $500K	$501 - $750K	$751K - $1M	Over $1 Million
AVERAGE BASE SALARY:	$8,257	$12,480	$12,912	$13,901	$15,030
AVERAGE HOUSING:	–	–	–	–	–
AVERAGE PARSONAGE:	–	–	–	–	–
AVERAGE TOTAL COMPENSATION	$8,285	$12,480	$10,704	$14,340	$18,791
ANNUAL BENEFITS					
AVERAGE RETIREMENT	–	$107	–	–	$206
AVERAGE LIFE INSURANCE	–	–	–	–	–
AVERAGE HEALTH INSURANCE	$120	–	–	$443	$690
AVERAGE CONTINUING EDUCATION	–	–	–	–	–
AVERAGE TOTAL BENEFITS	$152	$200	$70	$544	$931
ANNUAL COMPENSATION & BENEFIT					
AVERAGE	$8,535	$12,781	$14,215	$15,650	$16,806
NUMBER OF RESPONDENTS	174	127	43	39	65

– Not enough responses to provide meaningful data

15
CUSTODIANS

Employment Profile

Slightly more than half of the reported custodians serve part-time. Most are men, although women represent 44% of those working part-time. Some custodians are ordained ministers. The reported custodian positions provided the following employment profile:

	FULL-TIME	PART-TIME
Ordained	2%	2%
Average years employed	7	5
Male	81%	56%
Female	19%	44%
Self-employed (receives 1099)	3%	11%
Church employee (receives W-2)	97%	89%
High school diploma	80%	81%
Associate's degree	6%	2%
Bachelor's degree	13%	16%
Master's degree	1%	‹1%
Doctorate	‹1%	0%
Number of respondents	342	447

Total Compensation plus Benefits Package Analysis

The analysis below is based upon the tables found later in this chapter. The tables present compensation and benefits data according to worship attendance, church income, combinations of size and setting, region, gender, education, years employed, and denomination for church custodians who serve full-time. The final two tables provide data for part-time church custodians by worship attendance and church income. In this way, the custodian's compensation and benefits can be viewed from a variety of useful perspectives. The total compensation plus benefits package amount found in a separate box at the bottom of each page includes the base salary, housing and/or parsonage amount, life and health insurance payments, retirement contribution, and educational funds.

Full-time staff members. Custodians receive fewer and smaller benefits than full-time ministerial or professional staff. 60% receive health insurance, but only 38% have a retirement program from the church. Benefits are about the same as bookkeepers and secretaries.

Part-time staff members. More than 50% of custodians work part-time rather than full-time. Of this group, 44% were women. Eleven percent of the part-time custodians are self-employed. Churches provide part-time custodial workers very few benefits as compared to full-time employees.

COMPENSATION PLUS BENEFITS	FULL TIME	PART TIME
Base salary	99%	98%
Housing	1%	0%
Parsonage	1%	1%
Retirement	38%	2%
Life insurance	29%	0%
Health insurance	60%	2%
Paid vacation	88%	25%
Auto reimbursement	34%	9%
Continuing education	4%	0%

KEY POINTS

⮑ **Compensation increases gradually with church size.** As church size increases, the total compensation and benefits package does as well, although the increase plateaus over 750 people. The national average compensation corresponded to a church size of over 500 people. *See Table 15-1.*

⮑ **Churches with larger incomes offer larger total packages to custodians.** Compensation increases steadily with church income. The largest rate of increase (about 30% higher) is between $251 to $500,000 and $501 to $750,000. Rate of increases drops from there to about a 5% increase in larger churches. *See Table 15-2.*

⮑ **Suburban churches provide the best income and benefits for churches with an average attendance of 500 or less.** Custodians in metropolitan areas earn higher compensation and benefit packages for churches with an average attendance over 500. Almost all congregations with an attendance above 500 provided compensation levels above the national average (with the exception of those in the rural city with an attendance between 751-1,000). *See Table 15-3, 15-4, 15-5, 15-6, and 15-7.*

⮑ **The region in which a church is located has some effect on the compensation and benefits of the custodian.** In general, custodians in the Pacific region earn more than those in the other areas, although they serve in mid-size churches. East and West South Central have the largest churches yet compensation for custodians are below average. Despite the region, most of the total packages offered to custodians are comparable to the national average. The only regions where the amounts fall greatly below (about $4,000) the national average are in the West South Central U.S. and Mountain regions. This does not appear to be related to church size or attendance. *See Table 15-8.*

⮕ **A difference exists in compensation and benefits levels between men and women.**
On average, female custodians earn 80% of their male counterparts' total package. In general, men earn about $6,800 per year more than women do. Males work in slightly larger congregations with slightly larger incomes. The differences are not enough to account for the disparity in compensation. *See Table 15-9.*

⮕ **Education has some impact on compensation and benefit packages of custodians.**
Most custodians have less than a Bachelor's degree. About 14% are college graduates. In general, compensation increases for those with higher education. *See Table 15-10.*

⮕ **A church's denominational affiliation has some effect on the compensation and benefits package of custodian. Custodians who work for the Lutheran denomination churches earn the highest compensation, yet serve in some of the smallest churches.**
All denominations have packages comparable with the national average. About 40% of custodians work in the Baptist denomination. *See Table 15-12.*

⮕ **In general, part-time custodians earn among the lowest compensation and benefit packages of all positions, except organist.** Nearly three-quarters of the custodians serve in smaller churches (less than 300 in attendance and less than $500,000 in church income). *See Tables 15-13 and 15-14.*

Ten Year Compensation & Benefits Trend: National Average for Custodian

FULL TIME

1997	$22,493
1998	$23,271
1999	$24,401
2000	$26,161
2001	$26,725
2002	$27,913
2003	$29,047
2004	$30,052
2005	$31,026
2006	$32,884

TABLE 15-1: ANNUAL COMPENSATION OF CUSTODIAN BY WORSHIP ATTENDANCE

CHARACTERISTICS		WORSHIP ATTENDANCE					
		100 or less	101-300	301-500	501-750	751-1000	Over 1000
AVERAGE SUNDAY AM WORSHIP ATTENDANCE		–	222	400	612	890	2,001
AVERAGE CHURCH INCOME		–	$545,224	$920,618	$1,403,731	$1,978,557	$3,717,931
AVERAGE # of YEARS EMPLOYED		–	8	9	7	8	6
AVERAGE # of WEEKS OF PAID VACATION		–	3	3	3	3	3
% COLLEGE GRADUATE OR HIGHER		–	15%	17%	12%	13%	13%
% WHO RECEIVE AUTO REIMBURSEMENT		–	20%	46%	50%	46%	48%
% ORDAINED		–	–	3%	–	–	4%
AVERAGE % SALARY INCREASE THIS YEAR		–	4%	3%	3%	4%	4%
COMPENSATION		100 or less	101-300	301-500	501-750	751-1000	Over 1000
BASE SALARY:	Highest 25%	–	$28,000	$29,620	$31,951	$37,199	$33,280
	Average	–	$23,147	$26,982	$28,636	$30,485	$29,424
	Lowest 25%	–	$18,700	$22,568	$24,000	$23,523	$23,000
HOUSING:	Highest 25%	–	–	–	–	–	$257
	Average	–	–	–	–	$768	–
	Lowest 25%	–	–	–	–	–	–
PARSONAGE:	Highest 25%	–	–	–	–	–	$408
	Average	–	–	–	–	$637	$170
	Lowest 25%	–	–	–	–	–	–
TOTAL COMPENSATION	Highest 25%	–	$28,000	$29,620	$31,951	$37,867	$34,145
	Average	–	$23,147	$26,982	$28,636	$31,890	$29,690
	Lowest 25%	–	$18,700	$22,568	$24,000	$24,565	$23,000

– Not enough responses to provide meaningful data

TABLE 15-1: ANNUAL COMPENSATION OF CUSTODIAN BY WORSHIP ATTENDANCE

BENEFITS		WORSHIP ATTENDANCE					
		100 or less	101-300	301-500	501-750	751-1000	Over 1000
RETIREMENT:	Highest 25%	–	–	$950	$1,048	$1,611	$1,405
	Average	–	$431	$602	$753	$1,041	$934
	Lowest 25%	–	–	–	–	–	–
LIFE INSURANCE:	Highest 25%	–	–	–	–	–	–
	Average	–	–	–	$128	–	$113
	Lowest 25%	–	–	–	–	–	–
HEALTH INSURANCE:	Highest 25%	–	$6,200	$4,650	$5,748	$5,424	$7,200
	Average	–	$3,123	$2,449	$3,391	$3,297	$4,864
	Lowest 25%	–	–	–	–	–	$792
CONTINUING EDUCATION	Highest 25%	–	–	–	–	–	–
	Average	–	–	–	–	–	–
	Lowest 25%	–	–	–	–	–	–
TOTAL BENEFITS	Highest 25%	–	$7,137	$5,152	$7,500	$7,621	$8,712
	Average	–	$3,595	$3,090	$4,287	$4,382	$5,949
	Lowest 25%	–	–	–	–	–	$2,476

TOTAL COMPENSATION AND BENEFIT		100 or less	101-300	301-500	501-750	751-1000	Over 1000
	Highest 25%	–	$32,880	$35,748	$38,000	$40,600	$42,062
	Average	–	$26,742	$30,346	$32,924	$36,272	$35,829
	Lowest 25%	–	$20,000	$24,294	$27,231	$27,643	$27.000
NUMBER OF RESPONDENTS		3	35	73	67	48	105

– Not enough responses to provide meaningful data

351

TABLE 15-2: ANNUAL COMPENSATION OF CUSTODIAN BY CHURCH INCOME

	CHURCH INCOME				
CHARACTERISTICS	$250K & under	$251K-$500K	$501K-$750K	$751K-$1M	Over $1 Million
AVERAGE SUNDAY AM WORSHIP ATTENDANCE	–	268	523	433	1,294
AVERAGE CHURCH INCOME	–	$406,729	$624,159	$884,244	$2,660,370
AVERAGE # of YEARS EMPLOYED	–	9	7	9	7
AVERAGE # of WEEKS OF PAID VACATION	–	2	3	3	3
% COLLEGE GRADUATE OR HIGHER	–	16%	18%	15%	11%
% WHO RECEIVE AUTO REIMBURSEMENT	–	11%	38%	42%	49%
% ORDAINED	–	–	3%	–	2%
AVERAGE % SALARY INCREASE THIS YEAR	–	4%	4%	3%	4%

COMPENSATION		$250K & under	$251K-$500K	$501K-$750K	$751K-$1M	Over 1 Million
BASE SALARY:	Highest 25%	–	$26,000	$32,000	$30,139	$33,779
	Average	–	$22,046	$27,567	$28,296	$29,207
	Lowest 25%	–	$17,680	$23,977	$23,566	$22,880
HOUSING:	Highest 25%	–	–	–	–	$261
	Average	–	–	–	–	$216
	Lowest 25%	–	–	–	–	–
PARSONAGE:	Highest 25%	–	–	–	–	$391
	Average	–	–	–	–	–
	Lowest 25%	–	–	–	–	–
TOTAL COMPENSATION	Highest 25%	–	$26,000	$32,000	$30,139	$34,608
	Average	–	$22,046	$27,567	$28,296	$29,505
	Lowest 25%	–	$17,680	$23,977	$23,566	$23,000

– Not enough responses to provide meaningful data

TABLE 15-2: ANNUAL COMPENSATION OF CUSTODIAN BY CHURCH INCOME

BENEFITS		CHURCH INCOME				
		$250K & under	$251K-$500K	$501K-$750K	$751K-$1M	Over $1 Million
RETIREMENT:	Highest 25%	–	–	$1,397	$1,500	$1,414
	Average	–	$121	$757	$742	$884
	Lowest 25%	–	–	–	–	–
LIFE INSURANCE:	Highest 25%	–	–	–	–	–
	Average	–	–	–	–	–
	Lowest 25%	–	–	–	–	–
HEALTH INSURANCE:	Highest 25%	–	$3,600	$4,865	$5,152	$6,006
	Average	–	$2,002	$3,237	$3,117	$4,009
	Lowest 25%	–	–	–	–	–
CONTINUING EDUCATION	Highest 25%	–	–	–	–	–
	Average	–	–	–	–	–
	Lowest 25%	–	–	–	–	–
TOTAL BENEFITS	Highest 25%	–	$3,868	$5,825	$6,357	$7,778
	Average	–	$2,168	$4,007	$3,955	$5,013
	Lowest 25%	–	–	–	–	–
TOTAL COMPENSATION AND BENEFIT		$250K & under	$251K-$500K	$501K-$750K	$751K-$1M	Over 1 Million
	Highest 25%	–	$29,000	$36,200	$35,917	$40,000
	Average	–	$24,213	$31,574	$32,777	$34,610
	Lowest 25%	–	$18,000	$24,294	$26,900	$26,661
NUMBER OF RESPONDENTS		3	29	37	38	217

– Not enough responses to provide meaningful data

TABLE 15-3: ANNUAL COMPENSATION OF CUSTODIAN BY CHURCH SETTING & SIZE

ATTENDANCE 250 & UNDER	CHURCH SETTING			
	Metropoli-tan city	Suburb of large city	Small town or rural city	Farming area
AVERAGE SUNDAY AM WORSHIP ATTENDANCE	–	199	194	–
AVERAGE CHURCH INCOME	–	$670,175	$376,658	–
AVERAGE # of YEARS EMPLOYED	–	12	6	–
AVERAGE # of WEEKS OF PAID VACATION	–	3	3	–
% COLLEGE GRADUATE OR HIGHER	–	–	13%	–
% WHO RECEIVE AUTO REIMBURSEMENT	–	22%	10%	–
% ORDAINED	–	–	–	–
AVERAGE % SALARY INCREASE THIS YEAR	–	–	–	–

COMPENSATION		Metropoli-tan city	Suburb of large city	Small town or rural city	Farming area
BASE SALARY:	Highest 25%	–	$26,163	$24,794	–
	Average	–	$21,513	$20,662	–
	Lowest 25%	–	$16,500	$17,306	–
HOUSING:	Highest 25%	–	–	–	–
	Average	–	–	–	–
	Lowest 25%	–	–	–	–
PARSONAGE:	Highest 25%	–	–	–	–
	Average	–	–	–	–
	Lowest 25%	–	–	–	–
TOTAL COMPENSATION	Highest 25%	–	$26,163	$24,794	–
	Average	–	$21,513	$20,662	–
	Lowest 25%	–	$16,500	$17,306	–

– Not enough responses to provide meaningful data

TABLE 15-3: ANNUAL COMPENSATION OF CUSTODIAN BY CHURCH SETTING & SIZE

BENEFITS		CHURCH SETTING			
		Metropoli-tan city	Suburb of large city	Small town or rural city	Farming area
RETIREMENT:	Highest 25%	–	–	–	–
	Average	–	–	$377	–
	Lowest 25%	–	–	–	–
LIFE INSURANCE:	Highest 25%	–	–	–	–
	Average	–	–		–
	Lowest 25%	–	–	–	–
HEALTH INSURANCE:	Highest 25%	–	$4,850	$3,584	–
	Average	–	$2,170	$1,809	–
	Lowest 25%	–	–	–	–
CONTINUING EDUCATION	Highest 25%	–	–	–	–
	Average	–	–	–	–
	Lowest 25%	–	–	–	–
TOTAL BENEFITS	Highest 25%	–	$5,432	$4,689	–
	Average	–	$2,267	$2,193	–
	Lowest 25%	–	–		–
TOTAL COMPENSATION AND BENEFIT		Metropoli-tan city	Suburb of large city	Small town or rural city	Farming area
	Highest 25%	–	$31,260	$26,978	–
	Average	–	$23,779	$22,855	–
	Lowest 25%	–	$16,500	$18,745	–
NUMBER OF RESPONDENTS		7	12	11	0

– Not enough responses to provide meaningful data

TABLE 15-4: ANNUAL COMPENSATION OF CUSTODIAN BY CHURCH SETTING & SIZE

ATTENDANCE 251 - 500	CHURCH SETTING			
	Metropoli-tan city	Suburb of large city	Small town or rural city	Farming area
AVERAGE SUNDAY AM WORSHIP ATTENDANCE	375	411	378	–
AVERAGE CHURCH INCOME	$909,139	$1,021,166	$772,376	–
AVERAGE # of YEARS EMPLOYED	8	7	9	–
AVERAGE # of WEEKS OF PAID VACATION	2	3	3	–
% COLLEGE GRADUATE OR HIGHER	14%	13%	21%	–
% WHO RECEIVE AUTO REIMBURSEMENT	38%	59%	39%	–
% ORDAINED	–	–	7%	–
AVERAGE % SALARY INCREASE THIS YEAR	3%	3%	4%	–

COMPENSATION		Metropoli-tan city	Suburb of large city	Small town or rural city	Farming area
BASE SALARY:	Highest 25%	$29,382	$30,139	$29,000	–
	Average	$24,767	$29,299	$25,283	–
	Lowest 25%	$19,000	$25,750	$19,964	–
HOUSING:	Highest 25%	–	–	–	–
	Average	–	–	–	–
	Lowest 25%	–	–	–	–
PARSONAGE:	Highest 25%	–	–	–	–
	Average	–	–	–	–
	Lowest 25%	–	–	–	–
TOTAL COMPENSATION	Highest 25%	$29,382	$30,139	$29,000	–
	Average	$24,767	$29,299	$25,283	–
	Lowest 25%	$19,000	$25,750	$19,964	–

– Not enough responses to provide meaningful data

TABLE 15-4: ANNUAL COMPENSATION OF CUSTODIAN BY CHURCH SETTING & SIZE

BENEFITS		CHURCH SETTING			
		Metropoli-tan city	Suburb of large city	Small town or rural city	Farming area
RETIREMENT:	Highest 25%	$1,400	$589	$700	–
	Average	$841	$400	$581	–
	Lowest 25%	–	–	–	–
LIFE INSURANCE:	Highest 25%	–	–	–	–
	Average	–	–	–	–
	Lowest 25%	–	–	–	–
HEALTH INSURANCE:	Highest 25%	$5,400	$4,398	$4,966	–
	Average	$3,061	$2,060	$2,382	–
	Lowest 25%	–	–	–	–
CONTINUING EDUCATION	Highest 25%	–	–	–	–
	Average	–	–	–	–
	Lowest 25%	–	–	–	–
TOTAL BENEFITS	Highest 25%	$6,423	$4,511	$5,825	–
	Average	$3,915	$2,500	$3,013	–
	Lowest 25%	$1,285	$0	$0	–
TOTAL COMPENSATION AND BENEFIT		Metropoli-tan city	Suburb of large city	Small town or rural city	Farming area
	Highest 25%	$36,550	$35,748	$31,400	–
	Average	$28,682	$31,799	$28,884	–
	Lowest 25%	$20,400	$26,242	$21,500	–
NUMBER OF RESPONDENTS		18	26	34	2

– Not enough responses to provide meaningful data

TABLE 15-5: ANNUAL COMPENSATION OF CUSTODIAN BY CHURCH SETTING & SIZE

ATTENDANCE 501 - 750		CHURCH SETTING			
		Metropolitan city	Suburb of large city	Small town or rural city	Farming area
AVERAGE SUNDAY AM WORSHIP ATTENDANCE		590	628	603	–
AVERAGE CHURCH INCOME		$1,574,340	$1,425,491	$1,405,984	–
AVERAGE # of YEARS EMPLOYED		9	7	7	–
AVERAGE # of WEEKS OF PAID VACATION		3	3	3	–
% COLLEGE GRADUATE OR HIGHER		–	12%	18%	–
% WHO RECEIVE AUTO REIMBURSEMENT		38%	57%	35%	–
% ORDAINED		–	–	–	–
AVERAGE % SALARY INCREASE THIS YEAR		3%	3%	4%	–

COMPENSATION		Metropolitan city	Suburb of large city	Small town or rural city	Farming area
BASE SALARY:	Highest 25%	$33,982	$31,677	$31,079	–
	Average	$30,423	$29,092	$26,668	–
	Lowest 25%	$25,000	$26,457	$21,736	–
HOUSING:	Highest 25%	–	–	–	–
	Average	–	–	–	–
	Lowest 25%	–	–	–	–
PARSONAGE:	Highest 25%	–	–	–	–
	Average	–	–	–	–
	Lowest 25%	–	–	–	–
TOTAL COMPENSATION	Highest 25%	$33,982	$31,677	$31,079	–
	Average	$30,423	$29,092	$26,668	–
	Lowest 25%	$25,000	$26,457	$21,736	–

– Not enough responses to provide meaningful data

TABLE 15-5: ANNUAL COMPENSATION OF CUSTODIAN BY CHURCH SETTING & SIZE

		CHURCH SETTING			
BENEFITS		Metropoli-tan city	Suburb of large city	Small town or rural city	Farming area
RETIREMENT:	Highest 25%	$1,020	$1,411	$585	–
	Average	$868	$872	$581	–
	Lowest 25%	–	–	–	–
LIFE INSURANCE:	Highest 25%	–	–	–	–
	Average	–	$114	$218	–
	Lowest 25%	–	–	–	–
HEALTH INSURANCE:	Highest 25%	$4,104	$5,400	$7,996	–
	Average	$2,371	$3,059	$4,143	–
	Lowest 25%	–	–	–	–
CONTINUING EDUCATION	Highest 25%	$308	–	–	–
	Average	–	–	–	–
	Lowest 25%	–	–	–	–
TOTAL BENEFITS	Highest 25%	$6,400	$6,565	$8,895	–
	Average	$3,339	$4,045	$4,943	–
	Lowest 25%	–	$1,439	–	–
TOTAL COMPENSATION AND BENEFIT		Metropoli-tan city	Suburb of large city	Small town or rural city	Farming area
	Highest 25%	$37,866	$35,631	$37,039	–
	Average	$33,762	$33,137	$31,611	–
	Lowest 25%	$27,285	$29,644	$24,809	–
NUMBER OF RESPONDENTS		14	22	26	5

– Not enough responses to provide meaningful data

TABLE 15-6: ANNUAL COMPENSATION OF CUSTODIAN BY CHURCH SETTING & SIZE

ATTENDANCE 751 - 1,000		CHURCH SETTING			
		Metropoli-tan city	Suburb of large city	Small town or rural city	Farming area
AVERAGE SUNDAY AM WORSHIP ATTENDANCE		923	840	883	–
AVERAGE CHURCH INCOME		$2,318,684	$1,750,346	$1,746,212	–
AVERAGE # of YEARS EMPLOYED		9	7	10	–
AVERAGE # of WEEKS OF PAID VACATION		3	3	3	–
% COLLEGE GRADUATE OR HIGHER		15%	11%	11%	–
% WHO RECEIVE AUTO REIMBURSEMENT		43%	33%	55%	–
% ORDAINED		–	–	–	–
AVERAGE % SALARY INCREASE THIS YEAR		3%	4%	5%	–

COMPENSATION		Metropoli-tan city	Suburb of large city	Small town or rural city	Farming area
BASE SALARY:	Highest 25%	$39,199	$43,000	$32,718	–
	Average	$30,017	$34,576	$29,778	–
	Lowest 25%	$21,851	$27,225	$24,998	–
HOUSING:	Highest 25%	$3,000	–	–	–
	Average	$1,844	–	–	–
	Lowest 25%	–	–	–	–
PARSONAGE:	Highest 25%	–	–	–	–
	Average	–	–	–	–
	Lowest 25%	–	–	–	–
TOTAL COMPENSATION	Highest 25%	$39,199	$43,000	$32,718	–
	Average	$31,860	$34,576	$29,778	–
	Lowest 25%	$22,451	$27,225	$24,998	–

– Not enough responses to provide meaningful data

TABLE 15-6: ANNUAL COMPENSATION OF CUSTODIAN BY CHURCH SETTING & SIZE

BENEFITS		CHURCH SETTING			
		Metropoli-tan city	Suburb of large city	Small town or rural city	Farming area
RETIREMENT:	Highest 25%	$2,389	$547	$1,801	–
	Average	$1,368	$524	$1,137	–
	Lowest 25%	–	–	–	–
LIFE INSURANCE:	Highest 25%	–	$150	–	–
	Average	–	–	–	–
	Lowest 25%	–	–	–	–
HEALTH INSURANCE:	Highest 25%	$5,712	$7,506	$4,784	–
	Average	$3,469	$4,071	$3,078	–
	Lowest 25%	–	–	–	–
CONTINUING EDUCATION	Highest 25%	–	–	–	–
	Average	–	–	–	–
	Lowest 25%	–	–	–	–
TOTAL BENEFITS	Highest 25%	$8,108	$7,728	$6,998	–
	Average	$4,894	$4,677	$4,217	–
	Lowest 25%	–	–	–	–
TOTAL COMPENSATION AND BENEFIT		Metropoli-tan city	Suburb of large city	Small town or rural city	Farming area
	Highest 25%	$42,856	$49,449	$38,478	–
	Average	$36,754	$39,252	$33,994	–
	Lowest 25%	$27,643	$29,801	$26,761	–
NUMBER OF RESPONDENTS		20	12	13	1

– Not enough responses to provide meaningful data

TABLE 15-7: ANNUAL COMPENSATION OF CUSTODIAN BY CHURCH SETTING & SIZE

		CHURCH SETTING			
ATTENDANCE OVER 1,000		Metropoli-tan city	Suburb of large city	Small town or rural city	Farming area
AVERAGE SUNDAY AM WORSHIP ATTENDANCE		2,258	2,019	1,738	–
AVERAGE CHURCH INCOME		$4,263,558	$3,799,252	$2,977,350	–
AVERAGE # of YEARS EMPLOYED		6	6	6	–
AVERAGE # of WEEKS OF PAID VACATION		3	3	3	–
% COLLEGE GRADUATE OR HIGHER		13%	16%	9%	–
% WHO RECEIVE AUTO REIMBURSEMENT		38%	50%	57%	–
% ORDAINED		5%	4%	4%	–
AVERAGE % SALARY INCREASE THIS YEAR		5%	4%	4%	–
COMPENSATION		Metropoli-tan city	Suburb of large city	Small town or rural city	Farming area
BASE SALARY:	Highest 25%	$34,000	$31,599	$33,279	–
	Average	$29,792	$28,814	$29,085	–
	Lowest 25%	$23,566	$23,002	$22,618	–
HOUSING:	Highest 25%	–	$2,639	–	–
	Average	–	–	–	–
	Lowest 25%	–	–	–	–
PARSONAGE:	Highest 25%	–	$440	–	–
	Average	–	$325	–	–
	Lowest 25%	–	–	–	–
TOTAL COMPENSATION	Highest 25%	$34,000	$35,044	$33,279	–
	Average	$29,792	$29,322	$29,085	–
	Lowest 25%	$23,566	$23,002	$22,618	–

– Not enough responses to provide meaningful data

TABLE 15-7: ANNUAL COMPENSATION OF CUSTODIAN BY CHURCH SETTING & SIZE

BENEFITS		CHURCH SETTING			
		Metropoli-tan city	Suburb of large city	Small town or rural city	Farming area
RETIREMENT:	Highest 25%	$1,940	$1,200	$2,157	–
	Average	$1,077	$745	$1,236	–
	Lowest 25%	–	–	–	–
LIFE INSURANCE:	Highest 25%	$192	–	–	–
	Average	$184	$106	–	–
	Lowest 25%	–	–	–	–
HEALTH INSURANCE:	Highest 25%	$7,357	$6,261	$8,623	–
	Average	$5,841	$4,554	$4,878	–
	Lowest 25%	$3,000	$793	–	–
CONTINUING EDUCATION	Highest 25%	–	–	–	–
	Average	–	–	–	–
	Lowest 25%	–	–	–	–
TOTAL BENEFITS	Highest 25%	$9,250	$8,712	$9,708	–
	Average	$7,114	$5,457	$6,220	–
	Lowest 25%	$4,895	$1,603	$2,793	–
TOTAL COMPENSATION AND BENEFIT		Metropoli-tan city	Suburb of large city	Small town or rural city	Farming area
	Highest 25%	$44,446	$40,312	$41,588	–
	Average	$36,906	$34,779	$36,046	–
	Lowest 25%	$29,193	$26,547	$27,643	–
NUMBER OF RESPONDENTS		22	55	27	0

– Not enough responses to provide meaningful data

TABLE 15-8: ANNUAL COMPENSATION OF CUSTODIAN BY REGION

CHARACTERISTICS	REGION								
	New England	Middle Atlantic	South Atlantic	E-N Central	E-S Central	W-N Central	W-S Central	Moun-tain	Pacific
AVERAGE SUNDAY AM WORSHIP ATTENDANCE	–	848	849	1,438	1,061	791	990	1,041	1,080
AVERAGE CHURCH INCOME	–	$1,310,548	$1,849,364	$2,312,761	$2,854,232	$1,572,016	$2,314,062	$1,832,442	$2,060,433
AVERAGE # of YEARS EMPLOYED	–	6	7	7	9	9	7	7	8
AVERAGE # of WEEKS OF PAID VACATION	–	3	3	3	3	3	3	3	3
% COLLEGE GRADUATE OR HIGHER	–	27%	14%	10%	12%	8%	13%	9%	12%
% WHO RECEIVE AUTO REIMBURSEMENT	–	47%	56%	61%	22%	46%	21%	59%	40%
% ORDAINED	–	4%	3%	–	4%	–	2%	4%	–
AVERAGE % SALARY INCREASE THIS YEAR	–	4%	4%	4%	4%	4%	3%	4%	4%

COMPENSATION		New England	Middle Atlantic	South Atlantic	E-N Central	E-S Central	W-N Central	W-S Central	Moun-tain	Pacific
BASE SALARY:	Highest 25%	–	$34,000	$32,000	$33,573	$29,000	$29,810	$30,750	$29,975	$35,000
	Average	–	$28,698	$28,722	$29,955	$26,412	$26,708	$25,417	$24,705	$32,341
	Lowest 25%	–	$24,000	$23,000	$23,309	$20,000	$24,147	$20,000	$20,000	$26,242
HOUSING:	Highest 25%	–	–	$260	–	–	–	–	–	$269
	Average	–	–	$115	–	–	–	–	$961	$244
	Lowest 25%	–	–	–	–	–	–	–	–	–
PARSONAGE:	Highest 25%	–	–	–	$401	–	–	–	–	–
	Average	–	$566	–	–	$1,132	–	–	–	–
	Lowest 25%	–	–	–	–	–	–	–	–	–
TOTAL COMPENSATION	Highest 25%	–	$34,090	$32,250	$33,573	$30,000	$29,810	$30,750	$30,000	$35,388
	Average	–	$29,263	$28,838	$29,989	$27,545	$26,708	$25,417	$25,666	$32,585
	Lowest 25%	–	$24,000	$23,000	$23,309	$20,000	$24,147	$20,000	$20,317	$26,242

– Not enough responses to provide meaningful data

TABLE 15-8: ANNUAL COMPENSATION OF CUSTODIAN BY REGION

BENEFITS		New England	Middle Atlantic	South Atlantic	E-N Central	E-S Central	W-N Central	W-S Central	Mountain	Pacific
						REGION				
RETIREMENT:	Highest 25%	–	–	$2,200	$1,138	$1,248	$1,715	$1,048	$1,020	$1,000
	Average	–	$531	$1,077	$845	$641	$913	$477	$590	$815
	Lowest 25%	–	–	–	–	–	–	–	–	–
LIFE INSURANCE:	Highest 25%	–	–	–	–	–	–	–	–	–
	Average	–	–	–	–	–	–	–	$175	–
	Lowest 25%	–	–	–	–	–	–	–	–	–
HEALTH INSURANCE:	Highest 25%	–	$5,743	$5,762	$6,978	$4,900	$5,300	$5,000	$5,400	$6,216
	Average	–	$4,210	$3,573	$4,331	$2,857	$3,367	$3,071	$2,912	$4,415
	Lowest 25%	–	–	–	–	–	–	–	–	–
CONTINUING EDUCATION	Highest 25%	–	–	–	–	–	–	–	–	–
	Average	–	–	–	–	–	–	–	–	–
	Lowest 25%	–	–	–	–	–	–	–	–	–
TOTAL BENEFITS	Highest 25%	–	$8,282	$7,617	$7,618	$6,400	$6,913	$6,055	$7,320	$8,217
	Average	–	$4,826	$4,740	$5,258	$3,671	$4,351	$3,610	$3,683	$5,313
	Lowest 25%	–	–	–	$690	–	–	–	–	–
TOTAL COMPENSATION AND BENEFIT		New England	Middle Atlantic	South Atlantic	E-N Central	E-S Central	W-N Central	W-S Central	Mountain	Pacific
	Highest 25%	–	$41,200	$39,678	$44,460	$34,504	$38,358	$35,500	$36,200	$42,000
	Average	–	$34,090	$33,834	$35,702	$31,216	$31,058	$29,027	$29,349	$37,899
	Lowest 25%	–	$26,045	$26,348	$28,097	$23,876	$25,500	$21,067	$22,568	$30,279
NUMBER OF RESPONDENTS		6	29	78	44	27	32	55	29	41

– Not enough responses to provide meaningful data

365

TABLE 15-9: ANNUAL COMPENSATION OF CUSTODIAN BY GENDER

CHARACTERISTICS	GENDER	
	Male	Female
AVERAGE SUNDAY AM WORSHIP ATTENDANCE	1,017	937
AVERAGE CHURCH INCOME	$2,002,334	$1,918,225
AVERAGE # of YEARS EMPLOYED	8	7
AVERAGE # of WEEKS OF PAID VACATION	3	3
% COLLEGE GRADUATE OR HIGHER	15%	9%
% WHO RECEIVE AUTO REIMBURSEMENT	45%	36%
% ORDAINED	2%	3%
AVERAGE % SALARY INCREASE THIS YEAR	4%	3%

COMPENSATION		Male	Female
BASE SALARY:	Highest 25%	$32,340	$26,460
	Average	$29,138	$23,502
	Lowest 25%	$23,296	$19,240
HOUSING:	Highest 25%	$256	$262
	Average	$140	$145
	Lowest 25%	–	–
PARSONAGE:	Highest 25%	$392	–
	Average	$179	–
	Lowest 25%	–	–
TOTAL COMPENSATION	Highest 25%	$32,448	$26,771
	Average	$29,457	$23,648
	Lowest 25%	$23,566	$19,240

– Not enough responses to provide meaningful data

TABLE 15-9: ANNUAL COMPENSATION OF CUSTODIAN BY GENDER

BENEFITS		GENDER	
		Male	Female
RETIREMENT:	Highest 25%	$1,500	$663
	Average	$854	$476
	Lowest 25%	–	–
LIFE INSURANCE:	Highest 25%	–	–
	Average	–	–
	Lowest 25%	–	–
HEALTH INSURANCE:	Highest 25%	$6,006	$4,398
	Average	$3,796	$2,772
	Lowest 25%	–	–
CONTINUING EDUCATION	Highest 25%	–	–
	Average	–	–
	Lowest 25%	–	–
TOTAL BENEFITS	Highest 25%	$7,712	$5,152
	Average	$4,753	$3,295
	Lowest 25%	–	–
TOTAL COMPENSATION AND BENEFIT		Male	Female
	Highest 25%	$39,491	$31,817
	Average	$34,247	$27,427
	Lowest 25%	$27,000	$21,590
NUMBER OF RESPONDENTS		271	62

– Not enough responses to provide meaningful data

TABLE 15-10: ANNUAL COMPENSATION OF CUSTODIAN BY EDUCATION

CHARACTERISTICS	EDUCATION			
	< than Bachelor	Bachelor	Master	Doctorate
AVERAGE SUNDAY AM WORSHIP ATTENDANCE	951	991	–	–
AVERAGE CHURCH INCOME	$1,822,738	$1,603,083	–	–
AVERAGE # of YEARS EMPLOYED	7	7	–	–
AVERAGE # of WEEKS OF PAID VACATION	3	3	–	–
% COLLEGE GRADUATE OR HIGHER	–	100%	–	–
% WHO RECEIVE AUTO REIMBURSEMENT	44%	52%	–	–
% ORDAINED	1%	10%	–	–
AVERAGE % SALARY INCREASE THIS YEAR	4%	4%	–	–

COMPENSATION		< than Bachelor	Bachelor	Master	Doctorate
BASE SALARY:	Highest 25%	$31,900	$32,000	–	–
	Average	$27,634	$29,247	–	–
	Lowest 25%	$21,840	$22,000	–	–
HOUSING:	Highest 25%	$254	–	–	–
	Average	–	$300	–	–
	Lowest 25%	–	–	–	–
PARSONAGE:	Highest 25%	–	$414	–	–
	Average	–	$200	–	–
	Lowest 25%	–	–	–	–
TOTAL COMPENSATION	Highest 25%	$31,900	$35,000	–	–
	Average	$27,682	$29,747	–	–
	Lowest 25%	$21,840	$22,000	–	–

— Not enough responses to provide meaningful data

TABLE 15-10: ANNUAL COMPENSATION OF CUSTODIAN BY EDUCATION

BENEFITS		EDUCATION			
		< than Bachelor	Bachelor	Master	Doctorate
RETIREMENT:	Highest 25%	$1,405	$900	–	–
	Average	$814	$782	–	–
	Lowest 25%	–	–	–	–
LIFE INSURANCE:	Highest 25%	–	–	–	–
	Average	–	$203	–	–
	Lowest 25%	–	–	–	–
HEALTH INSURANCE:	Highest 25%	$5,968	$5,748	–	–
	Average	$3,880	$3,511	–	–
	Lowest 25%	–	–		–
CONTINUING EDUCATION	Highest 25%	–	–	–	–
	Average	–	–	–	–
	Lowest 25%	–	–	–	–
TOTAL BENEFITS	Highest 25%	$7,571	$7,320	–	–
	Average	$4,773	$4,496	–	–
	Lowest 25%	–	–	–	–
TOTAL COMPENSATION AND BENEFIT		< than Bachelor	Bachelor	Master	Doctorate
	Highest 25%	$37,866	$41,266	–	–
	Average	$32,503	$34,576	–	–
	Lowest 25%	$26,000	$26,547	–	–
NUMBER OF RESPONDENTS		207	30	2	1

– Not enough responses to provide meaningful data

TABLE 15-11: ANNUAL COMPENSATION OF CUSTODIAN BY YEARS EMPLOYED

CHARACTERISTICS	YEARS EMPLOYED			
	< 6 years	6-10 years	11-15 years	Over 15 years
AVERAGE SUNDAY AM WORSHIP ATTENDANCE	1,070	986	718	904
AVERAGE CHURCH INCOME	$1,989,128	$1,896,961	$1,683,039	$2,198,581
AVERAGE # of YEARS EMPLOYED	3	8	13	22
AVERAGE # of WEEKS OF PAID VACATION	2	3	3	4
% COLLEGE GRADUATE OR HIGHER	15%	8%	13%	18%
% WHO RECEIVE AUTO REIMBURSEMENT	43%	45%	32%	55%
% ORDAINED	3%	–	–	3%
AVERAGE % SALARY INCREASE THIS YEAR	4%	4%	3%	4%

COMPENSATION		< 6 years	6-10 years	11-15 years	Over 15 years
BASE SALARY:	Highest 25%	$31,200	$32,000	$32,340	$32,200
	Average	$27,270	$28,751	$28,216	$30,021
	Lowest 25%	$21,230	$23,500	$22,568	$24,783
HOUSING:	Highest 25%	$259	–	–	$270
	Average	$217	–	–	$256
	Lowest 25%	–	–	–	–
PARSONAGE:	Highest 25%	$382	$388	–	–
	Average	–	–	–	$784
	Lowest 25%	–	–	–	–
TOTAL COMPENSATION	Highest 25%	$31,677	$32,000	$32,340	$39,400
	Average	$27,495	$28,870	$28,216	$31,061
	Lowest 25%	$21,500	$23,500	$22,568	$25,000

– Not enough responses to provide meaningful data

TABLE 15-11: ANNUAL COMPENSATION OF CUSTODIAN BY YEARS EMPLOYED

BENEFITS		YEARS EMPLOYED			
		< 6 years	6-10 years	11-15 years	Over 15 years
RETIREMENT:	Highest 25%	$950	$1,158	$1,940	$2,253
	Average	$624	$782	$1,032	$1,045
	Lowest 25%	–	–	–	–
LIFE INSURANCE:	Highest 25%	–	–	$113	$180
	Average	–	–	$150	$105
	Lowest 25%	–	–	–	–
HEALTH INSURANCE:	Highest 25%	$5,000	$6,557	$4,824	$7,704
	Average	$3,308	$4,072	$2,755	$4,792
	Lowest 25%	–	–	–	–
CONTINUING EDUCATION	Highest 25%	–	–	–	–
	Average	–	–	–	–
	Lowest 25%	–	–	–	–
TOTAL BENEFITS	Highest 25%	$6,262	$8,275	$6,624	$9,141
	Average	$4,005	$4,946	$3,937	$5,969
	Lowest 25%	–	–	–	–
TOTAL COMPENSATION AND BENEFIT		< 6 years	6-10 years	11-15 years	Over 15 years
	Highest 25%	$37,560	$39,036	$35,748	$44,446
	Average	$31,677	$33,816	$32,153	$37,287
	Lowest 25%	$24,000	$26,300	$26,985	$31,318
NUMBER OF RESPONDENTS		170	87	39	39

– Not enough responses to provide meaningful data

TABLE 15-12: ANNUAL COMPENSATION OF CUSTODIAN BY DENOMINATION

CHARACTERISTICS	Assemblies of God	Baptist	Independent/ Nondenom	Lutheran	Methodist	Presbyte-rian
AVERAGE SUNDAY AM WORSHIP ATTENDANCE	880	963	1,293	596	766	661
AVERAGE CHURCH INCOME	1,781,254	$2,238,679	$2,209,923	$1,547,830	$1,286,157	$1,686,876
AVERAGE # of YEARS EMPLOYED	7	8	6	11	6	10
AVERAGE # of WEEKS OF PAID VACATION	3	3	3	3	3	3
% COLLEGE GRADUATE OR HIGHER	17%	18%	12%	8%	5%	10%
% WHO RECEIVE AUTO REIMBURSEMENT	50%	40%	44%	57%	36%	55%
% ORDAINED	7%	1%	5%	–	–	–
AVERAGE % SALARY INCREASE THIS YEAR	5%	3%	4%	3%	4%	3%

COMPENSATION		Assemblies of God	Baptist	Independent/ Nondenom	Lutheran	Methodist	Presbyte-rian
BASE SALARY:	Highest 25%	$28,776	$32,125	$32,000	$32,000	$29,640	$34,573
	Average	$26,122	$28,487	$27,635	$29,290	$26,164	$30,567
	Lowest 25%	$21,695	$22,055	$23,250	$24,000	$21,000	$25,000
HOUSING:	Highest 25%	–	$257	–	–	–	–
	Average	$625	–	–	–	–	–
	Lowest 25%	–	–	–	–	–	–
PARSONAGE:	Highest 25%	$450	$395	$392	–	–	–
	Average	–	$366	–	–	–	–
	Lowest 25%	–	–	–	–	–	–
TOTAL COMPENSATION	Highest 25%	$33,275	$32,360	$32,000	$32,000	$29,640	$34,573
	Average	$26,841	$28,933	$27,726	$29,290	$26,164	$30,567
	Lowest 25%	$21,790	$22,339	$23,250	$24,000	$21,000	$25,000

– Not enough responses to provide meaningful data

TABLE 15-12: ANNUAL COMPENSATION OF CUSTODIAN BY DENOMINATION

BENEFITS		DENOMINATION					
		Assemblies of God	Baptist	Independent/ Nondenom	Lutheran	Methodist	Presbyterian
RETIREMENT:	Highest 25%	$402	$1,737	$750	$1,861	$1,285	$2,519
	Average	$258	$913	$591	$974	$656	$1,286
	Lowest 25%	–	–		–	–	–
LIFE INSURANCE:	Highest 25%	–	–	–	–	–	–
	Average	–	$129	–	–	–	–
	Lowest 25%	–	–	–	–	–	–
HEALTH INSURANCE:	Highest 25%	$4,575	$6,371	$6,074	$5,376	$4,636	$5,856
	Average	$3,037	$3,780	$4,024	$4,220	$2,377	$3,587
	Lowest 25%	–	–	–	$2,700	–	–
CONTINUING EDUCATION	Highest 25%	–	–	–	–	–	–
	Average	–	–	–	–	–	–
	Lowest 25%	–	–	–	–	–	–
TOTAL BENEFITS	Highest 25%	$5,190	$7,559	$7,680	$7,173	$5,597	$8,250
	Average	$3,310	$4,844	$4,676	$5,216	$3,088	$4,992
	Lowest 25%	–	–	–	$2,700	–	–
TOTAL COMPENSATION AND BENEFIT		Assemblies of God	Baptist	Independent/ Nondenom	Lutheran	Methodist	Presbyterian
	Highest 25%	$39,127	$39,339	$36,200	$38,208	$32,835	$39,572
	Average	$30,151	$33,777	$32,402	$35,840	$29,252	$35,559
	Lowest 25%	$22,136	$26,398	$25,000	$29,380	$21,745	$28,012
NUMBER OF RESPONDENTS		16	112	66	15	34	40

– Not enough responses to provide meaningful data

TABLE 15-13: COMPENSATION OF PART-TIME CUSTODIAN BY WORSHIP ATTENDANCE

CHARACTERISTICS	100 or less	101 - 300	301 - 500	501 - 750	751 - 1,000	Over 1,000
AVERAGE SUNDAY AM WORSHIP ATTENDANCE	76	192	408	610	861	1,667
AVERAGE CHURCH INCOME	$122,205	$342,583	$694,396	$970,661	$1,317,405	$1,897,837
AVERAGE # of YEARS EMPLOYED	5	6	6	5	2	6
AVERAGE # of WEEKS OF PAID VACATION	2	2	2	2	–	–
% COLLEGE GRADUATE OR HIGHER	9%	19%	26%	13%	–	–
% WHO RECEIVE AUTO REIMBURSEMENT	3%	13%	29%	37%	38%	21%
% ORDAINED	1%	1%	2%	3%	–	7%
AVERAGE % SALARY INCREASE THIS YEAR	4%	5%	4%	4%	–	3%
HOURLY RATES						
AVERAGE BASE RATE	$7.61	$8.76	$9.31	$7.70	$7.51	$5.83
ANNUAL COMPENSATION						
AVERAGE BASE SALARY:	$4,240	$8,614	$11,354	$11,439	$11,276	$11,706
AVERAGE HOUSING:	–	–	–	–	–	–
AVERAGE PARSONAGE:	–	–	–	–	–	–
AVERAGE TOTAL COMPENSATION	$4,240	$8,706	$11,604	$11,439	$11,276	$11,706
ANNUAL BENEFITS						
AVERAGE RETIREMENT	–	–	–	–	$100	–
AVERAGE LIFE INSURANCE	–	–	–	–	–	–
AVERAGE HEALTH INSURANCE	–	–	–	$536	$683	–
AVERAGE CONTINUING EDUCATION	–	–	–	–	–	–
AVERAGE TOTAL BENEFITS	–	–	–	$570	$783	–
ANNUAL COMPENSATION & BENEFIT						
AVERAGE	$4,285	$8,815	$11,664	$12,809	$14,471	$11,746
NUMBER OF RESPONDENTS	95	221	60	32	12	15

– Not enough responses to provide meaningful data

TABLE 15-14: COMPENSATION OF PART-TIME CUSTODIAN BY CHURCH INCOME

CHARACTERISTICS	CHURCH INCOME				
	$250 K & Under	$251 - $500K	$501 - $750K	$751K - $1M	Over $1 Million
AVERAGE SUNDAY AM WORSHIP ATTENDANCE	120	229	482	447	844
AVERAGE CHURCH INCOME	$153,408	$365,849	$602,743	$894,035	$1,480,126
AVERAGE # of YEARS EMPLOYED	5	5	6	5	6
AVERAGE # of WEEKS OF PAID VACATION	2	2	2	2	2
% COLLEGE GRADUATE OR HIGHER	17%	13%	22%	28%	7%
% WHO RECEIVE AUTO REIMBURSEMENT	6%	13%	42%	35%	36%
% ORDAINED	1%	1%	3%	–	5%
AVERAGE % SALARY INCREASE THIS YEAR	4%	5%	3%	4%	4%
HOURLY RATES					
AVERAGE BASE RATE	$8.09	$8.26	$9.84	$10.01	$7.80
ANNUAL COMPENSATION	$250 K & Under	$251 - $500K	$501 - $750K	$751K - $1M	Over $1 Million
AVERAGE BASE SALARY:	$5,368	$9,096	$10,967	$13,175	$11,777
AVERAGE HOUSING:	–	–	–	–	–
AVERAGE PARSONAGE:	–	–	–	–	–
AVERAGE TOTAL COMPENSATION	$5,526	$9,194	$10,967	$13,175	$12,162
ANNUAL BENEFITS					
AVERAGE RETIREMENT	–	–	–	–	–
AVERAGE LIFE INSURANCE	–	–	–	–	–
AVERAGE HEALTH INSURANCE	–	–	–	$107	$684
AVERAGE CONTINUING EDUCATION	–	–	–	–	–
AVERAGE TOTAL BENEFITS	–	–	–	$152	$730
ANNUAL COMPENSATION & BENEFIT					
AVERAGE	$5,591	$9,276	$11,295	$13,327	$13,231
NUMBER OF RESPONDENTS	172	123	35	40	39

– Not enough responses to provide meaningful data

16
PART-TIME ORGANISTS

Employment Profile

The position of church organist is a rare one, and few individuals are involved as a full-time staff member in this role. On part-time bases, organists are still a small group, though the group is larger than part-time pastors. Part-time organists are mostly female, and have been employed as such for about eight years. Approximately three-quarters of the part-time organists serve in smaller churches with church attendance less than 300 and church income less than $500,000. The statistical profile of organists is as follows:

	FULL-TIME	PART-TIME
Ordained	–	0%
Average years employed	–	8
Male	–	21%
Female	–	79%
Self-employed (receives 1099)	–	3%
Church employee (receives W-2)	–	97%
High school diploma	–	23%
Associate's degree	–	6%
Bachelor's degree	–	54%
Master's degree	–	11%
Doctorate	–	6%
Number of respondents	2	78

Total Compensation plus Benefits Package Analysis

The analysis below is based upon the tables found in this chapter. The tables present compensation data for organists who serve part-time, and are grouped according to worship attendance and church income. In this way, the part-time organist's compensation can be analyzed and compared from two useful perspectives. Note that base salary is shown both hourly and annually, while annual amounts are shown for the rest of the compensation package. The total compensation plus benefits package includes the base salary, housing and/or parsonage allowance, retirement contribution, life and health insurance payments, and educational funds. For an explanation of blanks, please see chapter 1.

98% percent of the organists participating in this survey worked at their church on a part-time basis. Very few receive fringe benefits as retirement, health insurance, auto allowance, and funds for continuing education. However, about one-third receives paid vacation.

COMPENSATION PLUS BENEFITS

Base salary	99%
Housing	0%
Parsonage	0%
Retirement	1%
Life insurance	0%
Health insurance	3%
Paid vacation	35%
Auto reimbursement	4%
Continuing education	1%

KEY POINTS

⮑ **Chuch worship attendance and income have direct influence upon the compensation and benefits package of the part-time organist.** As the church size increases, compensation for part-time organists increases. The rate of increase is almost double as the attendance grows from 100 or less to 101-300 and from 101-300 to 300-500. *See Tables 16-1 and 16-2.*

Note: There were not enought respondents to provide meaningful data to determine the national average compensation and benefits packages for full-time organists.

TABLE 16-1: COMPENSATION OF PART-TIME ORGANIST BY WORSHIP ATTENDANCE

CHARACTERISTICS	WORSHIP ATTENDANCE					
	100 or less	101 - 300	301 - 500	501 - 750	751 - 1,000	Over 1,000
AVERAGE SUNDAY AM WORSHIP ATTENDANCE	77	172	424	–	–	–
AVERAGE CHURCH INCOME	$145,048	$329,767	$790,384	–	–	–
AVERAGE # of YEARS EMPLOYED	7	9	5	–	–	–
AVERAGE # of WEEKS OF PAID VACATION	–	3	–	–	–	–
% COLLEGE GRADUATE OR HIGHER	88%	63%	82%	–	–	–
% WHO RECEIVE AUTO REIMBURSEMENT	–	8%	–	–	–	–
% ORDAINED	–	–	–	–	–	–
AVERAGE % SALARY INCREASE THIS YEAR	–	4%	4%	–	–	–
HOURLY RATES						
AVERAGE BASE RATE	$8.82	$10.00	$15.68	–	–	–
ANNUAL COMPENSATION						
AVERAGE BASE SALARY:	$3,776	$7,098	$13,029	–	–	–
AVERAGE HOUSING:	–	–	–	–	–	–
AVERAGE PARSONAGE:	–	–	–	–	–	–
AVERAGE TOTAL COMPENSATION	$3,776	$7,098	$13,029	–	–	–
ANNUAL BENEFITS						
AVERAGE RETIREMENT	–	–	$142	–	–	–
AVERAGE LIFE INSURANCE	–	–	–	–	–	–
AVERAGE HEALTH INSURANCE	–	$140	$346	–	–	–
AVERAGE CONTINUING EDUCATION	–	–	–	–	–	–
AVERAGE TOTAL BENEFITS	–	$140	$502	–	–	–
ANNUAL COMPENSATION & BENEFIT						
AVERAGE	$3,776	$7,237	$13,531	–	–	–
NUMBER OF RESPONDENTS	16	43	13	2	3	0

– Not enough responses to provide meaningful data

TABLE 16-2: COMPENSATION OF PART-TIME ORGANIST BY CHURCH INCOME

	CHURCH INCOME				
CHARACTERISTICS	$250 K & Under	$251 - $500K	$501 - $750K	$751K - $1M	Over $1 Million
AVERAGE SUNDAY AM WORSHIP ATTENDANCE	107	207	–	–	543
AVERAGE CHURCH INCOME	$170,619	$357,190	–	–	$1,504,088
AVERAGE # of YEARS EMPLOYED	8	8	–	–	–
AVERAGE # of WEEKS OF PAID VACATION	2		–	–	–
% COLLEGE GRADUATE OR HIGHER	53%	79%	–	–	–
% WHO RECEIVE AUTO REIMBURSEMENT	–	6%	–	–	–
% ORDAINED	–	–	–	–	–
AVERAGE % SALARY INCREASE THIS YEAR	6%	3%	–	–	–
HOURLY RATES					
AVERAGE BASE RATE	$7.22	$10.27	–	–	$16.86
ANNUAL COMPENSATION	$250 K & Under	$251 - $500K	$501 - $750K	$751K - $1M	Over $1 Million
AVERAGE BASE SALARY:	$4,266	$7,935	–	–	$12,986
AVERAGE HOUSING:	–	–	–	–	–
AVERAGE PARSONAGE:	–	–	–	–	–
AVERAGE TOTAL COMPENSATION	$4,266	$7,935	–	–	$12,986
ANNUAL BENEFITS					
AVERAGE RETIREMENT	–	–	–	–	–
AVERAGE LIFE INSURANCE	–	–	–	–	–
AVERAGE HEALTH INSURANCE	$188	–	–	–	–
AVERAGE CONTINUING EDUCATION	–	–	–	–	–
AVERAGE TOTAL BENEFITS	$188	–	–	–	–
ANNUAL COMPENSATION & BENEFIT					
AVERAGE	$4,454	$7,935	–	–	$12,986
NUMBER OF RESPONDENTS	32	25	7	4	9

– Not enough responses to provide meaningful data

17

STATISTICAL ABSTRACT OF PARTICIPATING CHURCHES

In addition to the individual compensation surveys, many of the participating churches also completed a congregational profile. That information is presented below. Data is presented according to Sunday AM worship attendance. Six size categories are portrayed. Second, attendance and income trends are presented according to both church size and setting.

TABLE 17-1: STATISTICAL ABSTRACT OF PARTICIPATING CHURCHES

KEY FINDINGS

On average, 46% of the church budget is devoted to salaries.

About 33% of churches provide additional salary to their ordained staff members to assist them with their social security payments. Of those churches that do help, 61% pay one-half of the social security tax while 33% pays all of it.

Eighty-four percent of the participating churches reimburse the professional expenses of their ordained employees.

The majority of churches (92%) require a full accounting of professional expenses including date, purpose, location, and amount of expense before a reimbursement is made.

Slightly less than half (44%) of all congregations experienced an increase in attendance over the past year. A majority of congregations with an attendance over 750 reported growth.

Forty-three percent of the participating churches reported that their income exceeded expenses in the past year.

TABLE 17-2: CONGREGATIONAL PROFILE BY CHURCH WORSHIP ATTENDANCE

	ALL CHURCHES n=1295	WORSHIP ATTENDANCE					
		100 or less	101 - 300	301 - 500	501 - 750	751 - 1,000	Over 1,000
AVERAGE WORSHIP ATTENDANCE	475	68	189	407	617	881	2,107
AVERAGE TOTAL INCOME	$861,170	$116,635	$343,640	$778,812	$1,243,081	$1,767,743	$3,560,029
AVERAGE PERCENTAGE COMPENSATION IS OF TOTAL CHURCH BUDGET	46%	46%	45%	46%	47%	47%	47%
AVERAGE NUMBER OF ORDAINED STAFF							
FULL TIME	2	1	1	2	3	4	7
PART TIME	0	0	0	0	0	1	1
AVERAGE NUMBER OF NON-ORDAINED STAFF							
FULL TIME	3	0	1	3	5	7	16
PART TIME	5	1	3	5	8	8	19
PERCENTAGE CONTRIBUTES TO SOCIAL SECURITY PAYMENTS OF ORDAINED STAFF	33%	27%	34%	41%	42%	31%	25%
CONTRIBUTION AMONG THOSE WHO RECEIVE							
PAYS ALL	33%	30%	29%	37%	31%	26%	44%
PAYS HALF	61%	59%	62%	56%	62%	71%	52%
PERCENTAGE REIMBURSES PROFESSIONAL EXPENSES	84%	77%	85%	88%	93%	86%	79%
PERCENTAGE CHURCH REIMBURSES THE PASTOR EACH YEAR	65%	56%	67%	69%	75%	71%	63%
PERCENTAGE REQUIRES A FULL ACCOUNTING SUCH AS DATE, PURPOSE, LOCATION, AND AMOUNT OF REIMBURSEMENT EXPENSES	92%	86%	92%	95%	90%	98%	97%

TABLE 17-3: ATTENDANCE AND INCOME TRENDS BY CHURCH SIZE

ATTENDANCE TREND OVER THE PAST YEAR	DECLINE	STABLE	INCREASE
ALL CHURCHES (1,275)	14%	42%	44%
100 OR LESS (281)	21%	47%	32%
101 - 300 (465)	17%	44%	39%
301 - 500 (186)	10%	45%	45%
501 - 750 (117)	10%	39%	51%
751 - 1,000 (73)	5%	32%	63%
OVER 1,000 (131)	5%	27%	68%

CHURCH FINANCIAL TREND OVER THE PAST YEAR	BELOW EXPENSES	MEETS EXPENSES	EXCEEDS EXPENSES
ALL CHURCHES (1,283)	19%	38%	43%
100 OR LESS (280)	31%	39%	29%
101 - 300 (467)	19%	41%	39%
301 - 500 (188)	14%	36%	50%
501 - 750 (118)	19%	33%	47%
751 - 1,000 (73)	15%	29%	56%
OVER 1,000 (131)	7%	34%	59%

TABLE 17-4: ATTENDANCE AND INCOME TRENDS BY GEOGRAPHICAL SETTING

ATTENDANCE TREND OVER THE PAST YEAR	DECLINE	STABLE	INCREASE
ALL CHURCHES (1,275)	14%	42%	44%
METROPOLITAN CITY (219)	16%	43%	41%
SUBURB OF A LARGE CITY (432)	14%	41%	45%
SMALL TOWN OR RURAL CITY (535)	13%	41%	46%
FARMING AREA (76)	18%	45%	37%
CHURCH FINANCIAL TREND OVER THE PAST YEAR	BELOW EXPENSES	MEETS EXPENSES	EXCEEDS EXPENSES
ALL CHURCHES (1,283)	19%	38%	43%
METROPOLITAN CITY (223)	21%	40%	39%
SUBURB OF A LARGE CITY (434)	21%	34%	45%
SMALL TOWN OR RURAL CITY (536)	19%	40%	42%
FARMING AREA (77)	18%	43%	39%

TAX LAW & COMPENSATION PLANNING

Welcome to the Special Section on Tax Law and Compensation Planning. No compensation planning process is complete until several key tax issues have been addressed and dealt with. Compensation planning for clergy and other church staff presents several unique tax issues that are not well understood by many church leaders and their advisers. This special section clears away the confusion and presents the key considerations to review while doing compensation planning.

In adopting a year 2007 compensation packages for your ministers and lay staff members, review these possible components of the compensation package.

1. SALARY. The most basic component of church staff compensation is salary. There are two important considerations to keep in mind with respect to staff salaries—the amount of the salary, and the use of "salary reduction agreements." These two issues will be discussed separately.

a. Amount. Staff salaries ordinarily are set by the church board. Churches generally may pay any amount they wish, with one important exception—if a church pays unreasonably high compensation to a pastor or other employee there are two possible consequences:

(1) Loss of tax-exempt status. In order for a church or any other charity to maintain its tax-exempt status it must meet a number of conditions. One condition is that it cannot pay unreasonably high compensation to any person. There are two considerations to note. First, very few charities have lost their exempt status for paying unreasonable compensation. The IRS has been very reluctant to impose this remedy. Second, the law does not define what amount of compensation is unreasonable, and neither the IRS nor the courts have provided much clarification.

> **Example.** *A federal appeals court concluded that combined annual income of $115,680 paid by a religious organization to its founder and his wife was **not** excessive.*

> **Example.** *A court ruled that maximum reasonable compensation for a prominent televangelist was $133,100 in 1984, $146,410 in 1985, $161,051 in 1986, and $177,156 in 1987. The court based its conclusions on a comparison of the salaries of other nonprofit officers in the state.*

(2) Intermediate sanctions. The IRS can assess substantial excise taxes called "intermediate sanctions" against "disqualified persons" who are paid an "excess benefit" by a church or other charity. A disqualified person is any officer or director, or a relative of such a person. An excess benefit is compensation and fringe benefits in excess of what the IRS deems "reasonable." Note that the IRS still can revoke the exempt status of any charity that pays excessive compensation to an employee. However, it is more likely that excessive compensation will result in intermediate sanctions rather than loss of exempt status. To illustrate, why should a major university lose its tax-exempt status because it pays excessive compensation to its head football coach?

The intermediate sanctions the IRS can impose include the following:

- **Tax on disqualified persons.** A disqualified person who benefits from an excess benefit transaction is subject to an excise tax equal to 25 percent of the amount of the "excess benefit" (the amount by which actual compensation exceeds the fair market value of services rendered). This tax is assessed against the disqualified person directly, not his or her employer.

- **Additional tax on disqualified persons.** If a disqualified person fails to "correct" the excess benefit by the time the IRS assesses the 25 percent tax, then the IRS can assess an additional tax of up to 200 percent of the excess benefit. The law specifies that a disqualified person can "correct" the excess benefit transaction by "undoing the excess benefit to the extent possible, and taking any additional measures necessary to place the organization in a financial position not worse than that in which it would be if the disqualified person were dealing under the highest fiduciary standards."

■ **Tax on organization managers.** If the IRS assesses the 25 percent tax against a disqualified person, it is permitted to impose an additional 10 percent tax (up to a maximum of $10,000) on any "organization manager" who participates in an excess benefit transaction knowing it is such a transaction, unless the manager's participation "is not willful and is due to reasonable cause." A "manager" is an officer, director, or trustee. IRS regulations clarify that the managers collectively cannot be liable for more than $10,000 for any one transaction.

>**Key point**< The intermediate sanctions law imposes an excise tax on members of a church's governing board who vote for a compensation package that the IRS determines to be excessive. This makes it essential for board members to carefully review the reasonableness of compensation packages.

Charities, disqualified persons, and governing boards may rely on a "presumption of reasonableness" with respect to a compensation arrangement if it was approved by a board of directors (or committee of the board) that: (1) was composed entirely of individuals unrelated to and not subject to the control of the disqualified person involved in the arrangement; (2) obtained and relied upon objective "comparability" information, such as (a) compensation paid by similar organizations, both taxable and tax-exempt, for comparable positions, (b) independent compensation surveys by nationally recognized independent firms, or (c) actual written offers from similar institutions competing for the services of the disqualified person; and (3) adequately documented the basis for its decision.

>**Key point**< The law creates a presumption that a minister's compensation package is reasonable if approved by a church board that relied upon objective "comparability" information, including independent compensation surveys by nationally recognized independent firms. One of the more comprehensive compensation surveys for church workers is this text. This means that most ministers will be able to use this text to establish the presumption of reasonableness. But it also suggests that the IRS may rely on the data in this text in any attempt to impose intermediate sanctions against ministers.

IRS regulations clarify that "revenue based pay" arrangements in which an employee's compensation is based on a percentage of the employer's total revenues do not automatically result in an excess benefit transaction triggering intermediate sanctions. Rather, "all relevant facts and circumstances" must be considered.

Caution. In a series of rulings published in 2004 the IRS assessed intermediate sanctions against a pastor as a result of excess benefits paid to him and members of his family by his church. The IRS concluded that taxable compensation and benefits a church pays to a disqualified person (any church officer, and members of his or her family), that are not reported as taxable income to the recipient, constitute "automatic excess benefits" that trigger intermediate sanctions regardless of the amount involved. The IRS concluded that the following transactions resulted in excess benefits to the pastor because they were not reported as taxable income: (1) personal use of church property (vehicles, cell phones, credit cards, computers, etc.) by the pastor and members of his family; (2) reimbursements of personal expenses; and (3) nonaccountable reimbursements of business expenses (*i.e.,* reimbursements of expenses that were not supported by adequate documentation of the business purpose of each expense). Since these taxable benefits were not reported as taxable income, they amounted to "automatic" excess benefits resulting in intermediate sanctions. This is a stunning interpretation of the tax code and regulations that directly affects the compensation practices of every church, and exposes some church staff members to intermediate sanctions.

Recommendation. *Churches that pay a minister (or any staff member) significantly more than the highest 25% for comparable positions should obtain a legal opinion from an experienced tax attorney confirming that the amount paid is not "unreasonable" and will not expose the employee or the board to intermediate sanctions*

Tax savings tip. *Ministers and other church staff members should carefully review their W-2 or 1099 to be sure that it does not report more income than was actually received. If an error was made, the church should issue a corrected tax form (Form W-2c for an employee, or a "corrected" Form 1099 for a self-employed worker).*

b. Salary reduction agreements. Many churches have established "salary reduction agreements" to handle certain staff expenses. The objective is to reduce a worker's taxable income since only the income remaining after the various "reductions" is reported on the worker's W-2 or 1099 form at the end of the year. It is important for churches to understand that they cannot reduce a worker's taxable income through salary reductions unless specifically allowed by law.

Here are three ways that taxable income can be reduced through salary reduction agreements:

(1) Tax-sheltered annuity contributions. Salary reduction agreements can be used to contribute to a tax-sheltered annuity (sometimes called a "403(b) annuity"), if the salary reductions meet certain conditions.

(2) "Cafeteria plans." Salary reduction agreements also can be used to fund "cafeteria plans" (including "flexible spending arrangements") if several conditions are met. A cafeteria plan is a written plan established by an employer that allows employees to choose between cash and a "menu" of nontaxable benefits specified by law (including employer-provided medical insurance premiums, group-term life insurance, and dependent care).

(3) Housing allowances. A church can designate a portion of a minister's salary as a housing allowance, and the amount so designated is not subject to income tax if certain conditions are met. Housing allowances are addressed in detail just below.

Observation. *In some cases "salary reductions" will not accomplish the goal of reducing a minister's taxable income. The income tax regulations prohibit the widespread practice of funding "accountable" reimbursement arrangements through salary reductions. This topic is addressed later in this chapter.*

>**Key point**< Can a church compensate a pastor solely through a housing allowance and other fringe benefits? Yes it can, but the church must report these benefits as taxable income on the pastor's W-2 form to the extent that they represent taxable income. As noted below, a housing allowance is nontaxable for income tax reporting purposes only if certain conditions and limits are met. One of these is that the nontaxable amount of a housing allowance for a pastor who owns a home cannot exceed the home's fair rental value, including utilities. In most cases, designating a housing allowance in excess of the fair rental value of the pastor's home will result in no tax benefit. The same is true for any taxable fringe benefit.

➲ Recommended Resources.

For more detailed information on salaries for church staff members,
see chapter 4 in the *Church & Clergy Tax Guide*.

2. HOUSING ALLOWANCES. The most important tax benefit available to ministers who own or rent their homes is the housing allowance. Ministers who own their home do not pay federal income taxes on the amount of their compensation that their employing church designates in advance as a housing allowance, to the extent that the allowance represents compensation for ministerial services, is used to pay housing expenses, and does not exceed the annual fair rental value of the home (furnished, plus utilities). Housing-related expenses include mortgage payments, utilities, repairs, furnishings, insurance, property taxes, additions, and maintenance.

Ministers who rent a home or apartment do not pay federal income taxes on the amount of their compensation that their employing church designates in advance as a housing allowance to the extent that the allowance represents compensation for ministerial services and is used to pay rental expenses such as rent, furnishings, utilities, and insurance.

Unfortunately, many churches fail to designate a portion of a minister's compensation as a housing allowance. This deprives their minister of an important tax benefit.

Ministers who live in a church-owned parsonage that is provided "rent-free" as compensation for ministerial services do not include the annual fair rental value of the parsonage as income in computing their federal income taxes. The annual fair rental value is not "deducted" from the minister's income. Rather, it is not reported as additional income anywhere on Form 1040 (as it generally would be by non-clergy workers).

Ministers who live in a church-provided parsonage do not pay federal income taxes on the amount of their compensation that their employing church designates in advance as a parsonage allowance, to the extent that the allowance represents compensation for ministerial services and is used to pay parsonage-related expenses such as utilities, repairs, and furnishings.

Tax savings tip. *Ministers who live in church parsonages, and who incur any out-of-pocket expenses in maintaining the parsonage (such as utilities, property taxes, insurance, furnishings, or lawn care) should ask their employing church to designate a portion of their annual compensation in advance as a "parsonage allowance." Such an allowance is not included on the minister's W-2 or 1099 at the end of the year and is nontaxable in computing federal income taxes to the extent the minister incurs housing expenses of at least that amount. This is a very important tax benefit for ministers living in church-provided parsonages. Many ministers and church boards are not aware of this benefit, or are not taking advantage of it.*

Note that these exclusions are for federal income tax purposes only. Ministers cannot exclude the fair rental value of a parsonage or a housing allowance when computing their self-employment (Social Security) taxes.

Recommendation. *Be sure that the designation of a housing or parsonage allowance for year 2007 is on the agenda of the church board for one of its final meetings in 2006. The designation should be an official action of the board or congregation, and it should be duly recorded in the minutes of the meeting. The IRS also recognizes designations included in employment contracts and budget line items—assuming in each case that the designation was duly adopted by the church board (or the congregation in a business meeting). Also, if the minister is a new hire, be sure the church designates a housing allowance prior to the date he or she begins working.*

How much should a church board or congregation designate as a housing allowance? Many churches base the allowance on their minister's estimate of actual housing expenses for the new year. The church provides the minister with a form on which anticipated housing expenses for the new year are reported. For ministers who own their homes, the form asks for projected expenses in the following categories: down payment, mortgage payments, property taxes, property insurance, utilities, furnishings and appliances, repairs and improvements, maintenance, and miscellaneous. Many churches designate an allowance in excess of the anticipated expenses itemized by the minister. Basing the allowance solely on a minister's actual expenses will penalize the minister if housing expenses in fact turn out to be higher than expected. In other words, the allowance should take into account unexpected housing costs or inaccurate projections of expenses.

Recommendation. *Plan a mid-year review of the housing allowance to make sure that the designated amount is sufficient to cover actual expenses. If a pastor's expenses will exceed the allowance, then the church may amend the allowance. But any amendment will only operate prospectively.*

Observation. *The compensation survey summarized over the next several chapters reveals that housing allowances are claimed by several associate ministers, administrators, music directors, secretaries, and custodians. However, it is important to note that the housing allowance is available only if two conditions are met: (1) the recipient is a minister and (2) the allowance is provided as compensation for services performed in the exercise of ministry. In many cases, these conditions will not be satisfied by administrators, music directors, secretaries, and custodians. See chapter 3 of Richard Hammar's annual* **Church & Clergy Tax Guide** *(available from the publisher of this text) for more information.*

⮑ Recommended Resources.

For more detailed information about tax law and housing allowances,
see chapter 6 in the *Church & Clergy Tax Guide*.

3. EQUITY ALLOWANCES. Ministers who live in church-owned parsonages are denied one very important benefit of home ownership—the opportunity to accumulate "equity" in a home over the course of many years. Many ministers who have lived in parsonages during much of their active ministry often face retirement without housing. Their fellow ministers who purchased a home early in their ministry often can look forward to retirement with a home that is either substantially or completely debt-free. To avoid the potential hardship often suffered by a minister who lives in a parsonage, some churches increase their minister's compensation by an amount that is sometimes referred to as an "equity allowance." The idea is to provide the minister with the equivalent of equity in a home. This is an excellent idea that should be considered by any church having one or more ministers living in church-provided housing. Of course, for the concept to work properly, the equity allowance should not be accessible by the minister until retirement. Therefore, some churches choose to place the allowance directly in a minister's tax-sheltered retirement account.

Recommendation. *Equity allowances should also be considered by a church whose minister rents a home.*

⊃ Recommended Resources.

For more detailed information about tax law and equity allowances,
see chapter 6, section A.7, in the *Church & Clergy Tax Guide.*

4. ACCOUNTABLE BUSINESS EXPENSE REIMBURSEMENT POLICY. One of the most important components of church staff compensation packages is an "accountable" business expense reimbursement arrangement. This benefit is available to both ministers and lay staff members alike. Under such an arrangement a church (1) reimburses only those business expenses that are properly substantiated within a reasonable time as to date, amount, place, and business purpose, and (2) requires any excess reimbursements (in excess of substantiated expenses) to be returned to the church. Churches should seriously consider adopting an accountable reimbursement policy for reimbursing staff business expenses. Such a policy has the following advantages:

- Church staff report their business expenses to the church rather than to the IRS.

- Church staff who report their income taxes as employees, or who report as self-employed and who are reclassified as employees by the IRS in an audit, avoid the limitations on the deductibility of employee business expenses. These limitations include (1) the elimination of any deduction if the worker cannot itemize deductions on Schedule A (most taxpayers cannot), and (2) the deductibility of business expenses on Schedule A as an itemized expense only to the extent that these expenses exceed 2% of the worker's adjusted gross income.

- The so-called *Deason* allocation rule is avoided. Under this rule, ministers must reduce their business expense deduction by the percentage of their total compensation that consists of a tax-exempt housing allowance.

- The "50% limitation" that applies to the deductibility of business meals and entertainment expenses is avoided. Unless these expenses are reimbursed by an employer under an accountable plan, only 50% of them are deductible by either employees or self-employed workers.

- Church staff who report their income taxes as self-employed avoid the risk of being reclassified as an employee by the IRS in an audit and assessed additional taxes.

Observation. *The compensation survey summarized over the next several chapters reveals that many churches provide automobile allowances to their ministers and lay staff. In many cases, a church will simply provide a fixed dollar amount every month to a worker (for example, $300), and require no substantiation of business miles or a return of any "excess reimbursements" (in excess of substantiated business miles). This is referred to as a "nonaccountable"* *reimbursement arrangement. What are the tax consequences of such an arrangement? The allowances must be added to the worker's W-2 or 1099 at the end of the year, and the worker can claim a business deduction on Schedule A (if an employee) or on Schedule C (if self-employed). If a worker is an employee with insufficient itemized deductions to use Schedule A, there is no deduction available for business expenses even though the full amount of the monthly allowances are added to taxable income. This is a very unfortunate tax result that can be avoided completely through an accountable reimbursement arrangement. For a sample board resolution adopting an accountable business expense reimbursement arrangement, see chapter 7 of Richard Hammar's annual* **Church & Clergy Tax Guide.**

Example. *A church pays its senior pastor an annual salary of $45,000 this year. In addition, it provides the pastor with a monthly car allowance of $400. This is an example of a nonaccountable reimbursement arrangement. Assume that the church treasurer reports none of these reimbursements as taxable income on the pastor's Form W-2 since she assumes that the pastor had "at least" $4,800 in expenses associated with the business use of his car and so there was no need to report the nonaccountable reimbursements as taxable income. This assumption not only is incorrect, but it also converts the nonaccountable reimbursements into an "automatic" excess benefit exposing the pastor to intermediate sanctions, as noted previously in this chapter.*

The income tax regulations prohibit the funding of accountable reimbursement arrangements through salary reductions.

Example. *Assume that a church pays Pastor Gary $500 each week, and also agrees to reimburse his substantiated business expenses for each month out of the first weekly payroll check for the following month. Assume further that Pastor Gary substantiated $300 of business expenses for January. The church issued Pastor Gary his customary check of $500 for the first week of February, but only $200 of this check represents taxable salary while the remaining $300 represents a nontaxable reimbursement under an accountable plan. Only the $200 salary component of this check is included on Pastor Gary's W-2 (or 1099) form at the end of the year. This arrangement was once common, and still is practiced by some churches. The income tax regulations do not prohibit the funding of business expense reimbursements out of salary reductions. Rather, a church's reimbursements under such arrangements cannot be "accountable." This means that a church cannot reduce W-2 income by reducing an employee's salary to pay for business expense reimbursements. In our example, the full $500 paycheck must be accumulated to Pastor Gary's W-2.*

>**Key point**< Many churches set aside a certain amount each year to cover an employee's total compensation. For ministers, this amount often includes salary, housing allowance, fringe benefits, and an amount for the reimbursement of business expenses. To illustrate, a church board determines in December of 2006 that Pastor Ted's compensation package for 2007 will consist of salary ($30,000), housing allowance ($10,000), fringe benefits ($5,000), and business expense reimbursements ($3,000). This is what is sometimes called a salary "restructuring" arrangement. Are such arrangements treated as salary reductions, meaning that the entire $3,000 must be accumulated to Pastor Ted's W-2 income? Not necessarily. A possible basis exists for not reporting the $3,000 as taxable income to Pastor Ted if all of the following conditions are met: (1) the $3,000 is used to reimburse Pastor Ted for business expenses only if the substantiation requirements of an accountable arrangement are met; (2) the salary "restructuring" occurs prior to the start of the year; (3) any undistributed portion of the $3,000 is not given to Pastor Ted at the end of the year; and (4) the church adopts two resolutions—a "compensation" resolution consisting of salary, housing, and fringe benefits, and a "business expense" resolution consisting of the $3,000 reimbursement amount. If the IRS audits Pastor Ted and asks to see the church resolution specifying his compensation, the church would produce the first resolution. This is an aggressive position that may be rejected by the IRS in an audit. No court has addressed the issue.

➲ Recommended Resources.

For more detailed information about tax law and business expense
reimbursement policies, see chapter 7, section E, in the *Church & Clergy Tax Guide.*

5. TRAVEL EXPENSES OF A SPOUSE. A church should decide if it will be paying for any of the travel expenses of a spouse accompanying a minister or other staff member on a business trip. Reimbursing these expenses represents a significant benefit. Unfortunately, there is much confusion regarding the correct reporting of such reimbursements for tax purposes. If the spouse's presence on the trip serves a legitimate business purpose, and the spouse's travel expenses are reimbursed by the church under an accountable arrangement (described above) then the reimbursements represent a nontaxable fringe benefit. If these two requirements are not met, the reimbursements represent taxable income to the minister or staff member.

Caution. If either of these conditions is not met, then a church's reimbursement of a nonemployee spouse's travel expenses will represent taxable income to the minister or other staff member. The same applies to children who accompany a minister or staff member on a business trip. Further, the IRS may assert that the church's failure to report the reimbursement of the spouse's expenses as taxable income to the minister makes the reimbursement an "automatic" excess benefit triggering intermediate sanctions, as noted previously in this chapter.

> **Tax savings tip.** *If a church does not reimburse the travel expenses of a pastor's spouse who accompanies the pastor on a business trip, then the spouse may be able to deduct travel expenses as a charitable contribution (assuming that the spouse's presence on the trip serves a legitimate "business" purpose).*

➲ Recommended Resources.

For more detailed information about tax law and the travel expense of a spouse,
see see chapter 7, section C.2, in the *Church & Clergy Tax Guide.*

6. CHURCH-OWNED VEHICLES. Churches should consider the advantages of acquiring an automobile for staff members' church-related travel. Here's why. If a church purchases a car, and the church board adopts a resolution restricting use of the car to church-related activities, then the worker reports no income or deductions, and better yet, there are no accountings, reimbursements, allowances, or recordkeeping requirements. This assumes that the car is in fact used exclusively for church-related purposes, and the strict conditions specified in the income tax regulations are satisfied.

Commuting is always considered to be personal use of a car, and so this procedure would not be available if a church allowed a worker to commute to work in a church-owned vehicle. Fortunately, the income tax regulations permit certain church employees who use a church-owned vehicle exclusively for business purposes except for commuting to receive all of the benefits associated with business use of a church-owned vehicle, if certain additional conditions are met.

Unfortunately, most churches that provide a staff member with a car do not consider either of these alternatives. Rather, they simply transfer the car to the individual and impose no limitations on personal use. This arrangement results in taxable income to the staff member, whether the staff member is a minister or a lay employee.

➲ Recommended Resources.

For more detailed information about tax law and church owned vehicles,
see chapter 4, section B.8, in the *Church & Clergy Tax Guide.*

7. SELF-EMPLOYMENT TAX. There is one provision in the tax code that has caused more confusion for ministers and church treasurers than any other, and it is this: Ministers are always treated as self-employed for Social Security with regard to services they perform in the exercise of their ministry. This is true even if they are employees for federal income tax reporting purposes. This is sometimes referred to as the "dual tax status" of ministers.

Social Security benefits are financed through two tax systems. Employers and employees each pay "Social Security" and "Medicare" (sometimes collectively referred to as "FICA") taxes which for 2007 amount to 7.65% of an employee's taxable wages (a total tax of 15.3%) up to a specified amount. Self-employed persons pay the "self-employment tax," which for 2007 is 15.3% of net self-employment earnings up to a specified amount. Note that self-employed workers are responsible for paying their entire Social Security tax liability, while employees pay only half (their employer pays the other half).

>**Key point**< Ministers always are treated as self-employed for Social Security with respect to services performed in the exercise of their ministry, and so they do not pay "Social Security" and "Medicare" taxes. Rather, they pay the "self-employment tax" with respect to church compensation, unless they have filed a timely application for exemption from Social Security taxes (and received back a copy of their exemption application from the IRS marked "approved"). As a result, ministers must be familiar with the self-employment tax rules. So must lay church employees who work for a church that filed a timely exemption from Social Security coverage (Form 8274), since they are considered self-employed for Social Security.

>**Key point**< Many churches pay some or all of their pastor's self-employment taxes. This is perfectly appropriate. After all, churches pay half of a non-minister employee's Social Security and Medicare taxes, so why shouldn't it do the same for its pastor? Research conducted by *Church Law & Tax Report* reveals that in 2006 about one-third (32%) of churches paid some or all of their senior pastor's self-employment taxes. Of those churches that did, 58% paid one-half of the self-employment tax, while 35% paid all of it. Any portion paid by the church is a taxable fringe benefit that must be reported as additional wages on the pastor's W-2 or 1099 form, and Form 1040. It also should be reported as additional income by the pastor in computing self-employment taxes.

>**Key point**< Housing allowances and the fair rental value of parsonages are includable in self-employment earnings for Social Security purposes.

Caution. Many churches withhold the employee's share of Social Security and Medicare taxes from ministers' compensation, and then pay the employer's share. In other words, they treat their minister as an employee for Social Security. This is understandable, especially when the church treats the minister as an employee for purposes of federal income taxation. But, it is always incorrect for a church to treat a minister as an employee for Social Security.

Ministers may exempt themselves from self-employment taxes with respect to services performed in the exercise of ministry if several requirements are met. Among other things, the exemption must be filed by the due date of a minister's federal tax return (Form 1040) for the second year in which he or she had net self-employment earnings of $400 or more, any part of which derived from the performance of ministerial duties. In most cases, this means the form is due by April 15 of the third year of ministry. Also, the minister must be opposed on the basis of religious convictions to accepting Social Security benefits.

As a self-employed person for Social Security, a minister computes self-employment taxes on Schedule SE of Form 1040.

➲ Recommended Resources.

For more detailed information about tax law and self-employment tax,
see chapter 9 in the *Church & Clergy Tax Guide*.

8. INSURANCE. Churches often provide ministers with life, health, or disability insurance coverage and pay all of the premiums for such coverage. In some cases, churches make the same benefits available to lay staff members. The income tax regulations specify that the gross income of an *employee* does not include

- contributions which his employer makes to an accident or health plan for compensation (through insurance or otherwise) to the employee for personal injuries or sickness incurred by him, his spouse, or his dependents . . . . The employer may contribute to an accident or health plan by paying the premium (or a portion of the premium) on a policy of accident or health insurance covering one or more of his employees, or by contributing to a separate trust or fund . . . .

The exclusion of employer-paid health insurance premiums from the taxable income of employees is one of the main reasons why ministers and other staff members often are better off reporting their income taxes as employees. This important benefit is not available to workers who report their income taxes as self-employed. A church wishing to make this benefit available to its ministers (or other employees) should adopt a plan in an appropriate board resolution. Plans that benefit only ministers are exempted from the "nondiscrimination" rules that apply to most of these kinds of plans.

> **Observation.** *The compensation survey data summarized over the next several chapters reveal that many churches provide ministers with health insurance. A smaller percentage of churches provide these benefits to lay staff members. Such discrimination by church employers ordinarily does not violate federal law.*

The cost of group term life insurance bought by an employer for its employees ordinarily is not taxable to the employees so long as the amount of coverage does not exceed $50,000 per employee. Generally, life insurance can qualify as group term life insurance only if it is available to at least ten full-time employees. However, there are some exceptions to this rule. For example, the ten full-time employee rule does not apply if (1) an employer provides the insurance to all full-time employees who provide satisfactory evidence of insurability, (2) insurance coverage is based on a uniform percentage of pay, and (3) evidence of insurability is limited to a medical questionnaire completed by the employee that does not require a physical examination.

Other kinds of insurance premiums paid by the church on behalf of a minister or lay church employee ordinarily represent taxable income. For example, the cost of premiums on a whole life or universal life insurance policy paid by a church on the life of its minister (and naming the minister's spouse and children as beneficiaries) ordinarily must be reported as income to the minister.

⊃ Recommended Resources.

For more detailed information about tax law and insurance,
see chapter 5 in the *Church & Clergy Tax Guide*.

9. RETIREMENT ACCOUNTS. Most ministers (and some lay staff members) participate in some form of retirement plan. Such plans often are sponsored either by the local church, or by a denomination or agency with which the church is affiliated. Church workers covered by certain kinds of plans can choose to have part of their pay set aside each year (through "salary reductions") in the retirement fund, rather than receiving it as income. Amounts set aside by the employing church under these plans may be excludable from gross income for tax purposes. These amounts are sometimes called "elective deferrals" because the employee elects to set aside the money, and tax on the money is deferred until it is taken out of the account. This option is available to ministers or lay workers who are covered by tax-sheltered annuities ("403(b) plans"), simplified employee pensions (SEPs), and certain other plans.

Payments made by an employing church toward an employee's tax-sheltered annuity, SEP, and certain other plans, and funded out of church funds rather than through a reduction in an employee's compensation, may also be excluded from the employee's gross income for tax purposes under certain circumstances. There are limits on how much an employee can elect to contribute into such plans, and on how much the employing church can contribute out of its own funds. Of course, ministers and lay workers (whether employees or self-employed for income tax purposes) can also contribute to an IRA.

> **Recommendation.** *If a church has not established or contributed to a retirement plan for its staff members, then it should consider doing so or at least ensuring that staff members are participating in an adequate alternative (particularly in the case of ministers who have exempted themselves from Social Security coverage). Further, if staff members are participating in a retirement plan, then now is a good time to determine how contributions to the plan in 2007 will be funded (i.e., through employee contributions, salary reductions, or church contributions) and in what amounts.*

>**Key point**< Churches that have not adequately contributed to their minister's retirement, or that would like to make contributions in excess of applicable limits, should consider the possible advantages of a "rabbi trust." A church's contributions to such a trust will not be included in a minister's current taxable income, and income generated by the trust is tax-deferred. Further, a church ordinarily can contribute more toward a rabbi trust than to most other kinds of retirement program. This is very attractive for churches whose minister is approaching retirement with inadequate retirement savings.

➲ Recommended Resources.

For more detailed information about tax law and retirement accounts,
see chapter 10 in the *Church & Clergy Tax Guide*

10. WORKS MADE FOR HIRE. It is common for church employees to compose music or write books or articles in their church office during office hours. What is often not understood is that such persons do not necessarily own the copyright to the works they create. While the one who creates a work generally is its author and the initial owner of the copyright in the work, section 201(b) of the Copyright Act specifies that "in the case of a work made for hire, the employer or other person for whom the work was prepared is considered the author . . . and, unless the parties have expressly agreed otherwise in a written instrument signed by them, owns all of the rights comprised in the copyright."

The copyright law defines "work made for hire" as "a work prepared by an employee within the scope of his or her employment." There are two requirements that must be met: (1) the person creating the work is an employee, and (2) the employee created the work within the scope of his or her employment. Whether or not one is an employee will depend on the same factors used in determining whether one is an employee or self-employed for federal income tax reporting purposes (see chapter 2 of Richard Hammar's annual *Church & Clergy Tax Guide*). However, the courts have been very liberal in finding employee status in this context, so it is possible that a court would conclude that a work is a work made for hire even though the author reports federal income taxes as a self-employed person.

The second requirement is that the work must have been created within the scope of employment. This requirement generally means that the work was created during regular working hours, on the employer's premises, using the employer's staff and equipment. This is often a difficult standard to apply. As a result, it is desirable for church employees to discuss this issue with the church leadership to avoid any potential misunderstandings. Section 201(a), quoted above, allows an employer and employee to agree in writing that copyright ownership in works created by the employee within the scope of employment belongs to the employee. This should be a matter for consideration by any church having a minister or other staff member who creates literary or musical works during office hours, on church premises, using church staff and church equipment (e.g., computers, printers, paper, library, secretaries, dictation equipment).

If a church transfers the copyright in a work made for hire to an employee, this may be viewed by the IRS as "private inurement" of the church's resources to an individual. If so, this could jeopardize the church's tax-exempt status. Neither the IRS nor any court has addressed the tax consequences of such an arrangement to a church. Here are some options:

(1) The church transfers copyright ownership to the staff member. This may constitute private inurement. When a church employee writes a book during office hours at the church, using church equipment, supplies, and personnel, the copyright in the work belongs to the church. If the church chooses to renounce its legal rights in the book, and transfers the copyright back to the employee, then it is relinquishing a potentially valuable asset that may produce royalty income for several years. Few if any churches would attempt to "value" the copyright and report it as additional taxable compensation to the employee, and as a result it is hard to avoid the conclusion that such arrangements result in inurement of the church's assets to a private individual. The legal effect is to jeopardize the church's tax-exempt status. While this risk may be remote, the consequences would be so undesirable that it should be taken seriously.

>**Key point**< Staff members who retain ownership of a work made for hire because of a written transfer signed by the church may be subject to intermediate sanctions (discussed above). Since the church is the legal owner of the copyright in a work made for hire, it is legally entitled to any income generated from sales of the work. By letting the writer or

SPECIAL SECTION—TAX LAW & COMPENSATION PLANNING

composer retain the copyright, and all rights to royalties, the church in effect is paying compensation to that person in this amount. If the work generates substantial income, then this may trigger intermediate sanctions.

(2) The church retains the copyright. The risk of inurement can be minimized or even avoided if the church retains the copyright in works made for hire, and pays a bonus or some other form of taxable compensation that is added to the author's W-2 at the end of the year. This arrangement will not jeopardize the church's tax-exempt status.

(3) The church urges employees to do "outside work" at home. Do you have a writer or composer on staff at your church? If so, it is possible that this person is doing some writing or composing on church premises, using church equipment, during office hours. One way to avoid the problems associated with work made for hire status is to encourage staff members to do all their personal writing and composing at home. Tell staff members that (1) if they do any writing or composing at church during office hours, their works may be works made for hire; (2) the church owns the copyright in such works; and (3) the church can transfer copyright to the writer or composer, but this may constitute "inurement" of the church's assets to a private individual, jeopardizing the church's tax-exempt status. By urging staff members to do all their personal writing and composing at home the church will also avoid the difficult question of whether works that are written partly at home and partly at the office are works made for hire.

(4) Sermons. It is likely that the courts would consider sermons to be works made for hire, no matter where or when they are written, since they constitute the primary reason that most pastors are hired and therefore represent the essence of the employment relationship.

⟳ Recommended Resources.

For more detailed information about tax law and works made for hire,
see Richard Hammar's *Church Guide to Copyright Law.*

11. QUALIFIED TUITION REDUCTIONS ("QTRs"). Many churches operate elementary or secondary schools, and charge reduced tuition to certain school employees. For example, assume that a church operates an elementary school, charges annual tuition of $2,000, but only charges tuition of $500 for the children of school employees and charges no tuition at all for the child of Pastor Eric (the church's senior minister and president of the school). Such "tuition reductions" are perfectly appropriate. Further, section 117(d) of the federal tax code specifies that they will not result in taxable income to the school employees. In other words, a $500 annual tuition reduction awarded to a school employee whose child attends the school need not be reported as income (on the employee's W-2 or Form 1040). This obviously can be a significant benefit to school employees.

However, section 117(d) also provides that "highly compensated employees" cannot exclude qualified tuition reductions from their income unless the same benefit is available on substantially similar terms to other employees. The term "highly compensated employee" is defined to include any employee who was paid compensation for the previous year in excess of a specified amount. For 2006, the amount was $100,000. The amount for 2007 was not available at the time of publication of this text.

If in the example cited above Pastor Eric was paid more than $100,000 for the previous year, then the church would have to include $2,000 (the entire amount of the tuition reduction) in Pastor Eric's reportable income since he is a highly compensated employee and the benefit available to him is not available on substantially similar terms to other employees. However, this will not affect other school employees who are not "highly compensated." They will be able to exclude tuition reductions from their income.

>**Key point**< The IRS has ruled that tuition reductions are tax-free only for school employees, and so if a church operates a private school only employees who perform duties on behalf of the school qualify for this benefit. If the school offers tuition reductions to church employees who perform no duties for the school, these reductions are a taxable fringe benefit.

➲ Recommended Resources.

For more detailed information about tax law and QTRs,
see chapter 5, section K.5, in the *Church & Clergy Tax Guide*

12. LOANS TO MINISTERS. Churches often make loans to ministers to enable a minister to pay for housing or some other major purchase. In some cases the church charges no interest or a low rate far below the prevailing market rate of interest. These loans can create problems for a number of reasons. Consider the following.

■ Many state nonprofit corporation laws prohibit loans to officers and directors. No church should consider making any loan (even at a reasonable rate of interest) to a minister who is an officer or director of the church without first confirming that such loans are permissible under state law.

■ No-interest or low-interest loans to ministers may be viewed as "inurement" of the church's income to a minister. As noted above, this can potentially jeopardize the church's tax-exempt status.

■ For loans of $10,000 or more (or for loans of lower amounts where an intent to avoid taxes exists), a church must value the benefit to a minister of receiving a no-interest or low-interest loan and add this amount to the minister's reportable income. This is a complex calculation that is beyond the scope of this book. The point is this—even if loans to ministers are allowed under your state's nonprofit corporation law, the church must recognize that no-interest and low-interest loans of $10,000 or more will result in income to a minister that must be valued and reported (on the minister's W-2 or 1099-MISC, and Form 1040). Failure to do so could result in prohibited "inurement" of the church's income to a private individual, jeopardizing the church's tax-exempt status.

Observation. *Sadly, some ministers and lay workers never fully repay a loan made to them by their church. The forgiveness of debt ordinarily represents taxable income to the debtor. As a result, if a church makes a loan to a minister or other staff member and the debt is later forgiven by the church, taxable income is generated in the amount of the forgiven debt.*

➲ Recommended Resources.

For more detailed information about tax law and loans to ministers,
see chapter 4, section B.9, in the *Church & Clergy Tax Guide*

13. VOLUNTARY WITHHOLDING. Ministers' compensation is exempt from income tax withholding whether a minister reports income taxes as an employee or as self-employed. While it is true that the tax code requires *every* employer, including churches and religious organizations, to withhold federal income taxes from employee wages, there are some exceptions to this rule. One exception is wages paid for "services performed by a duly ordained, commissioned, or licensed minister of a church in the exercise of his ministry." Therefore, a church need not withhold income taxes from the salary of a minister who is an employee for income tax reporting purposes. Further, since the withholding requirements only apply to the wages of *employees,* a church should not "withhold" taxes from the compensation of a minister (or any other worker, such as a part-time custodian) who reports his or her income taxes as a *self-employed* person.

The IRS maintains that a church and a minister-employee may agree voluntarily that federal income taxes be withheld from the minister's wages, but this is not required. Some ministers find voluntary withholding attractive since it eliminates the guesswork, quarterly reports, and penalties associated with the estimated tax procedure (which applies automatically if voluntary withholding is not elected). A minister-employee who elects to enter into a voluntary withholding arrangement with his or her church need only file a completed Form W-4 (employee's withholding allowance certificate) with the church. The filing of this form is deemed to be a request for voluntary withholding. Voluntary withholding arrangements can be terminated unilaterally by either a minister or the church, or by mutual consent. Alternatively, a minister can stipulate that the voluntary withholding arrangement will terminate on a specified date. In such a case, the minister must give the church a signed statement setting forth the date on which the voluntary withholding is to terminate; the minister's name and address; and a statement that he wishes to enter into a voluntary withholding arrangement with his or her employer. This statement must be attached to a completed Form W-4. The voluntary withholding arrangement will terminate automatically on the date specified.

But what about a minister's self-employment taxes? Ministers who have not exempted themselves from Social Security coverage are required to pay the self-employment tax (Social Security tax for self-employed persons). Can a church "withhold" the self-employment tax from a minister-employee's wages? The answer is yes. IRS Publication 517 ("Social Security and Other Information for Members of the Clergy") states that "if you perform your services as an employee of the church (under the common law rules), you may be able to enter into a voluntary withholding agreement with your employer, the church, to cover any income *and self-employment tax* that may be due." A church whose minister has elected voluntary withholding (and who is not exempt from Social Security taxes) simply withholds an additional amount from each paycheck to cover the minister's estimated self-employment tax liability for the year. The additional amount withheld to cover self-employment taxes must be reported (on the minister's W-2 form and the church's 941 forms) as additional income tax withheld, and not as "Social Security taxes" (or "FICA" taxes). The minister should amend his or her W-4 (withholding allowance certificate) by inserting on line 6 the additional amount of tax to be withheld. The excess income tax withheld is a credit against tax that the minister claims on his or her federal income tax return, and it in effect is applied against the minister's self-employment tax liability. Further, it is considered to be a timely payment of the minister's self-employment tax obligation, and so no penalties for late payment of the quarterly estimates will apply.

> **Recommendation.** *Churches should apprise ministers that they may enter into a voluntary withholding arrangement. For many ministers, such an arrangement will be preferable to the estimated tax procedure. This procedure requires ministers to estimate their income tax and self-employment tax liability for the year 2007 prior to April 15, 2007, and then to pay one-fourth of the total estimated tax liability on or by April 15, June 15, September 15, and the following January 15. These quarterly payments are accompanied by a "payment voucher" that is contained in IRS Form 1040-ES. Some ministers find the estimated tax procedure inconvenient and undesirable (it is often hard to budget for the quarterly payments).*

⮞ Recommended Resources.

For more detailed information about tax law and voluntary withholding,
see chapter 1, section D, in the *Church & Clergy Tax Guide*

14. SPECIAL OCCASION GIFTS. It is common for ministers (and in some cases lay workers) to receive special occasion gifts during the course of the year. Examples include Christmas, birthday, and anniversary gifts. Churches and church staff members often do not understand how to report these payments for federal tax purposes. The general rule is this—if the "gifts" are funded through members' contributions to the church (i.e., the contributions are entered or recorded in the church's books as cash received and the members are given charitable contribution credit) then the distribution to the minister or lay worker should be reported as taxable compensation and included on his or her W-2 or 1099 and Form 1040. The same rule applies to special occasion "gifts" made to a minister or lay worker by the church out of the general fund. Members who contribute to special occasion offerings may deduct their contributions if (1) the contributions are to the church and are entered or recorded in the church's books as cash received, and (2) they are able to itemize deductions on Schedule A (Form 1040). Churches should be prepared to include such "gifts" to a minister or lay worker on his or her

W-2 or 1099-MISC. Of course, members are free to make personal gifts to ministers and lay staff members, such as a card at Christmas accompanied by a check or cash. Such payments may be tax-free gifts to the recipient (though they are not deductible by the donor). These same rules apply to other kinds of special occasion gifts as well.

It is common for churches to make generous retirement gifts to retiring ministers (and in some cases lay workers). Do these gifts represent taxable income to the recipient? To the extent that the recipient is an employee (or would be classified as an employee by the IRS), there is little doubt that the "gift" would constitute taxable income since section 102(c) of the tax code specifies that "any amount transferred by or for an employer to or for the benefit of an employee" is not excludable from taxable income by the employee as a gift, other than certain employee achievement awards and insignificant holiday gifts. This conclusion is reinforced by the narrow definition of the term *gift*. The Supreme Court has noted that "a gift . . . proceeds from a detached and disinterested generosity . . . out of affection, respect, admiration, charity, or like impulses . . . . The most critical consideration . . . is the transferor's intention." *Commissioner v. Duberstein, 363 U.S. 278, 285 (1960)*. The Court also observed that "it doubtless is the exceptional payment by an employer to an employee that amounts to a gift," and that the church's characterization of the distribution as a "gift" is "not determinative—there must be an objective inquiry as to whether what is called a gift amounts to it in reality."

>**Key point**< Intermediate sanctions, discussed earlier in this chapter, may apply to a retirement gift that results in unreasonable compensation to the recipient, or that is not reported as taxable income regardless of the amount involved. Church leaders must be sure to consider this possibility before finalizing such a gift.

➲ Recommended Resources.

For more detailed information about tax law and special occasion gifts,
see chapter 4, section B.2, in the *Church & Clergy Tax Guide*.

15. BARGAIN SALES. Occasionally, a church will sell property to a staff member at a price that is below market value. To illustrate, some churches "sell" a parsonage to a retiring minister at a price well below the property's fair market value. Other churches may sell a car or other church-owned vehicle to a minister at a below-market price. The important consideration with such "bargain sales" is this—the "bargain" element (i.e., the difference between the sales price charged by the church and the property's market value) must be reported as income to the minister on his or her W-2 or 1099-MISC and Form 1040. Churches should consider thoroughly the tax consequences of such sales before approving them.

➲ Recommended Resources.

For more detailed information about tax law and bargain sales,
see chapter 8, section B.4, in the *Church & Clergy Tax Guide*.

16. DIRECTOR IMMUNITY. Most states have adopted laws that provide *uncompensated* officers and directors of most charitable organizations (including churches) with limited immunity from legal liability. The federal Volunteer Protection Act provides similar protection as a matter of federal law. The immunity provided under state and federal law only applies to uncompensated officers and directors. What does this have to do with compensation planning? Simply this—churches should consider adopting an appropriate resolution clarifying that a minister's annual compensation package is for ministerial duties rendered to the church, *and is not for any duties on the church board*. Like any other church officer or director, the minister serves without compensation. Such a provision, if adopted, might qualify the minister for protection under the legal immunity law. It is worth considering.

➲ Recommended Resources.

For more detailed information about tax law and director immunity,
see section 6-08 in *Pastor, Church & Law* (3rd ed. 2000).

17. DISCRETIONARY FUNDS. It is a fairly common practice for a church to set aside a sum of money in a "discretionary fund" and give the senior minister the sole authority to distribute the money in the fund. In some cases, the minister has no instructions regarding permissible distributions. In other cases, the church establishes guidelines, but these often are oral and ambiguous. Many churches are unaware of the tax consequences of such arrangements. To the extent the minister has the authority to use any portion of the discretionary fund for his or her own personal use, then the entire fund must be reported as taxable income to the minister in the year it is funded. This is so even if the minister does not personally benefit from the fund. The mere fact that the minister *could* personally benefit from the fund is enough for the fund to constitute taxable income. The basis for this result is the "constructive receipt" rule, which is explained in the income tax regulations as follows:

> ■ Income although not actually reduced to a taxpayer's possession is constructively received by him in the taxable year during which it is credited to his account, set apart for him, or otherwise made available so that he may draw upon it at any time, or so that he could have drawn upon it during the taxable year if notice of intention to withdraw had been given. However, income is not constructively received if the taxpayer's control of its receipt is subject to substantial limitations or restrictions.

For a discretionary fund to constitute taxable income to a minister, it is essential that the minister have the authority to "draw upon it at any time" for his or her own personal use. This means that the fund was established without any express prohibition against personal distributions. On the other hand, if a discretionary fund is set up by a board resolution that absolutely prohibits any distribution of the fund for the minister's personal use, then the constructive receipt rule is avoided. In the words of the regulation, "income is not constructively received if the taxpayer's control of its receipt is subject to substantial limitations or restrictions." Accordingly, in order to avoid the reporting of the entire discretionary fund as taxable income to the minister, it is essential that the fund be established by means of a board or congregational resolution that absolutely prohibits any use of the fund by the minister for personal purposes. Further, the resolution should specify that the fund may be distributed by the minister only for needs or projects that are consistent with the church's exempt purposes (as set forth in the church's charter). For accountability purposes, a member of the church board should review all distributions from the discretionary fund to be sure that these requirements are met.

⊃ Recommended Resources.

For more detailed information about tax law and discretionary funds,
see chapter 4, section B.13, in the *Church & Clergy Tax Guide*.

18. SEVERANCE PAY. Many churches have entered into severance pay arrangements with a pastor or other staff member. Such arrangements can occur when a pastor or staff member is dismissed, retires, or voluntarily resigns. Church treasurers must determine whether severance pay is taxable so that it can be properly reported (on a W-2 and the church's 941 forms). Also, taxes must be withheld from severance pay that is paid to nonminister employees (and ministers who have elected voluntary withholding). Failure to properly report severance pay can result in substantial penalties for both a church and the recipient.

In most cases severance pay represents taxable income to the recipient. There is one exception that will apply in some cases. The tax code excludes from taxable income "the amount of any damages received (whether by suit or agreement and whether as lump sums or as periodic payments) *on account of personal injuries or sickness.*" According to this provision, severance pay that is intended to settle personal injury claims may be nontaxable. The words "personal injuries" are defined broadly by the IRS and the courts, and include potential or threatened lawsuits based on discrimination and harassment.

>**Key point**< The Tax Court has noted that "payments for terminating and canceling employment contracts are not payments for personal injuries."

>**Key point**< The tax code specifies that the term "personal injury" does not include emotional distress.

Here are some factors to consider (based on actual cases) in deciding whether a severance payment made to a former worker represents taxable compensation or nontaxable damages in settlement of a personal injury claim: (1) An amount paid to a former employee "to reward her for her past services and to make her severance as amicable as possible" is taxable compensation. (2) An amount paid to a former employee under a severance agreement that contains no reference to a specific discrimination or other personal injury claim is taxable compensation. (3) If an employer pays a former employee severance pay, and reports the severance pay on a W-2 (or 1099), this is strong evidence that the amount represents taxable compensation. (4) If an employer continues one or more employee benefits (such as health insurance) as part of a severance agreement, this suggests that any amount payable under the agreement represents taxable compensation. (5) If an employer withholds taxes from amounts paid under a severance agreement, this "is a significant factor" in classifying the payments as taxable income. Of course, this factor will not be relevant in the case of ministers whose wages are not subject to withholding (unless they elect voluntary withholding). (6) Referring to a payment as "severance pay" indicates that it is taxable compensation rather than nontaxable damages in settlement of a personal injury claim. (7) Severance pay based on a former employee's salary (such as one year's salary) is more likely to be viewed as taxable compensation rather than nontaxable damages in settlement of a personal injury claim. (8) To be nontaxable, severance pay must represent "damages" received in settlement of a personal injury claim. The IRS has noted that this language requires more than a settlement agreement in which a former employee "waives" any discrimination or other personal injury claims he or she may have against an employer. If the employee "never filed a lawsuit or any other type of claim against [the employer] . . . the payment cannot be characterized as damages for personal injuries" since "there is no indication that personal injuries actually exist."

➲ Recommended Resources.

For more detailed information about tax law and severance pay,
see chapter 8, section B.17, in the *Church & Clergy Tax Guide*.

19. INCOME "SPLITTING." Some ministers have attempted to "split" their church income with their spouse. This often is done to qualify the spouse for Social Security or other benefits or to avoid the Social Security "annual earnings test" (which reduces Social Security benefits to retired workers who are under "full retirement age" who earn more than an amount prescribed by law). For income splitting arrangements to work, the courts have required proof that the spouse is in fact an employee of the church. This means that the spouse performs meaningful services on behalf of the church. The courts have pointed to a number of factors indicating that a spouse is *not* an employee: (1) The spouse did not receive a paycheck. (2) The spouse was not employed elsewhere. (3) The spouse's "compensation" was designed to provide a tax benefit (such as an IRA contribution), and lacked any economic reality. (4) Neither the church nor the minister documented any of the services the spouse performed. (5) Neither the church nor the minister could explain how the spouse's "salary" was determined. (6) There was no employment contract between the church and the minister's spouse. (7) No taxes were withheld from the spouse's "salary." (8) The spouse's income was not reported on the church's employment tax returns (Forms 941). (9) There was no evidence that wages were actually paid to the spouse, or that any employment contract existed, or that the spouse was treated as an employee.

The courts generally have been skeptical of attempts by taxpayers to shift income to a spouse. The message is clear—ministers should not attempt to obtain tax benefits by shifting income to a spouse unless there is economic reality to the arrangement.

➲ Recommended Resources.

For more detailed information about tax law and income "splitting,"
see chapter 4, section H, in the *Church & Clergy Tax Guide*.

In order to simplify your examination of the tax issues related to compensation planning, use the checklist below which summarizes the recommendations within each category.

COMPENSATION CHECKLIST FOR 2007

ITEM	RECOMMENDATION
SALARY	■ avoid unreasonable compensation ■ avoid use of salary reductions that are not recognized by federal tax law
HOUSING ALLOWANCE	■ for ministers who own or rent their home, designate a portion of their compensation as a housing allowance prior to December 31 for the next year ■ for ministers who live in a church-owned parsonage, designate a portion of their compensation as a parsonage allowance (if they will incur any housing expenses) prior to December 31 for the next year
EQUITY ALLOWANCE	■ consider contributing to a tax-sheltered investment (such as a retirement fund) for ministers who live in church-owned parsonage, to compensate for their inability to accumulate equity in a home
ACCOUNTABLE BUSINESS EXPENSE REIMBURSEMENT ARRANGEMENT	■ adopt an accountable business expense reimbursement arrangement by reimbursing only those business expenses that are adequately substantiated, and by requiring any excess reimbursements to be returned
TRAVEL EXPENSES OF A SPOUSE	■ reimburse a spouse's travel expenses incurred in accompanying a minister or lay employee on a business trip if the spouse's presence serves a legitimate business purpose and the expenses are duly substantiated (if these requirements are not met, then the church's reimbursements represent taxable income to the minister or lay employee)
CHURCH-OWNED VEHICLES	■ avoid allowing minister or lay employee unrestricted personal use of a church-owned car (such usage must be valued and reported as taxable income) ■ consider adopting a policy limiting the use of the car to business purposes and requiring it to be kept on church property (this avoids most recordkeeping requirements and does not result in any income to the minister) ■ an alternative is to limit use of the car to business purposes except for commuting to and from work (if the commuting is required for security reasons); each round trip commute represents $3 of reportable income
SELF-EMPLOYMENT TAX PAID BY CHURCH	■ all ministers are self-employed for Social Security purposes with respect to their church work; this means they pay the self-employment tax rather than FICA taxes ■ some churches pay a portion of a minister's self-employment tax (as they pay a portion of a nonminister employee's FICA taxes), such payments represent taxable income ■ nonminister employees of churches that waived payment of FICA taxes by filing a timely Form 8274 are treated as self-employed for Social Security purposes—churches may want to pay a portion of the self-employment taxes owed by these workers if the do so for ministers

COMPENSATION CHECKLIST FOR 2007

ITEM	RECOMMENDATION
INSURANCE	■ consider paying health insurance premiums for ministers and lay employees (a tax-free fringe benefit for employees) ■ consider paying premiums for up to $50,000 of group term life insurance (a tax-free fringe benefit for employees)
RETIREMENT ACCOUNTS	■ consider contributing toward a tax-sheltered retirement plan
WORKS MADE FOR HIRE	■ urge staff members to write books and articles
QUALIFIED TUITION REDUCTIONS	■ consider tuition discounts for ministers and lay employees whose children attend church-operated schools or preschools (they may be a tax-free fringe benefit)
LOANS TO MINISTERS	■ avoid making any low or no interest loan to ministers ■ avoid making any loan to ministers at market rates unless permitted by state nonprofit corporation law
VOLUNTARY WITHHOLDING	■ ministers and lay workers who report their income taxes as employees should consider entering into a voluntary withholding arrangement with the church (can avoid the quarterly estimated tax procedure); be sure to provide for the withholding of self-employment taxes too, but classify these extra withholdings as additional income taxes
SPECIAL OCCASION GIFTS	■ special occasion gifts to ministers and lay employees that are processed through the church's books, and for which contribution credit is given to donors, are taxable income to the minister or lay employee
BARGAIN SALES	■ any property sold to a minister or lay employee at less than fair market value will result in taxable income (the amount by which the fair market value exceeds the sales price)
DIRECTOR IMMUNITY	■ consider adopting a board resolution certifying that all church board members, including the senior minister, serve without compensation (this may qualify the minister for the limited immunity the law provides to uncompensated directors of nonprofit organizations)
DISCRETIONARY FUNDS	■ avoid them unless (1) the minister cannot use the fund for his or her own personal use, (2) the fund may be distributed only for purposes consistent with the church's exempt purposes, and (3) a board member reviews all distributions to ensure compliance with these limits
SEVERANCE PAY	■ severance pay is perfectly appropriate, but be sure that it is reported as additional taxable income unless it represents payment *on account of personal injuries or sickness*
INCOME "SPLITTING"	■ do not attempt to shift a portion of a minister's compensation to his or her spouse for tax savings purposes, unless there is "economic reality" to the arrangement (the spouse performs services that otherwise would be compensated, and receives a reasonable rate of compensation)

APPENDICES

APPENDIX 1

TEN YEAR COMPENSATION TREND*

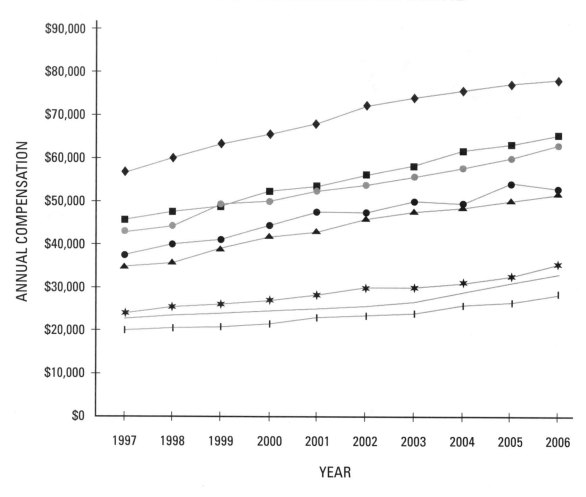

* No historical data is available for Adult Ministry
Director or Children's/Preschool Director.

**National averages for Pastor include data for both
Senior and Solo Pastors.

♦ Pastor**
■ Associate Pastor
▲ Youth Pastor
● Music Director
● Administrator
★ Bookkeeper
+ Secretary
— Custodian

APPENDIX 2

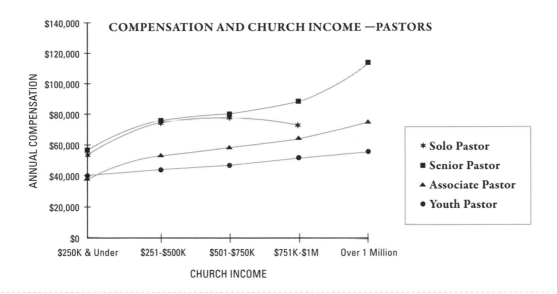

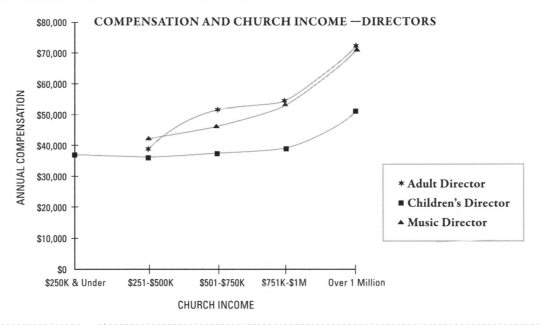

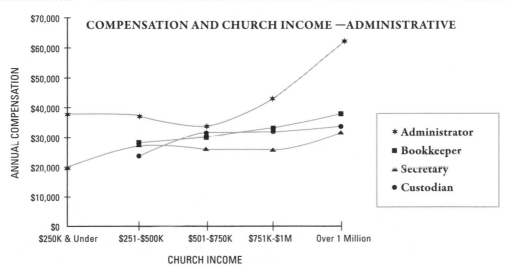

APPENDIX 3

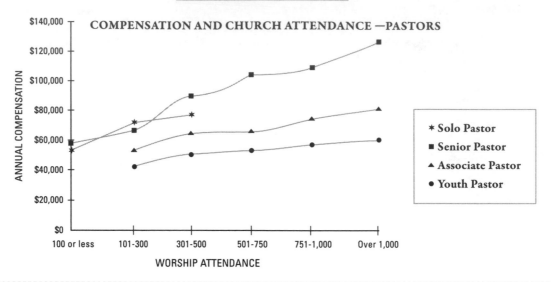

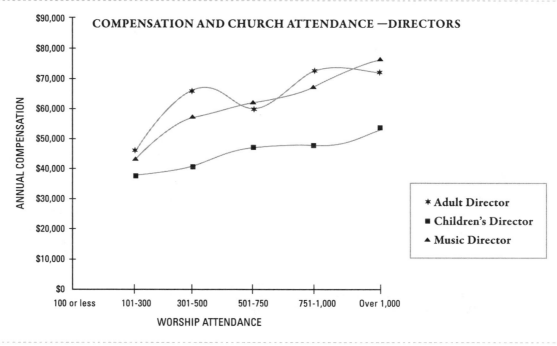

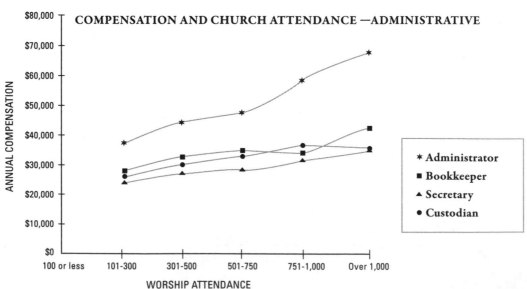

APPENDIX 4

COMPENSATION AND EDUCATION —PASTORS

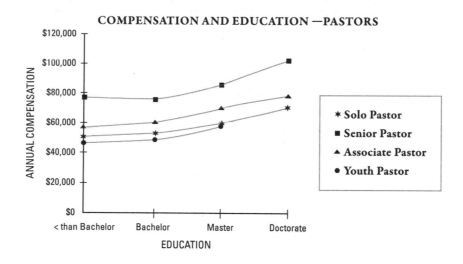

COMPENSATION AND EDUCATION —DIRECTORS

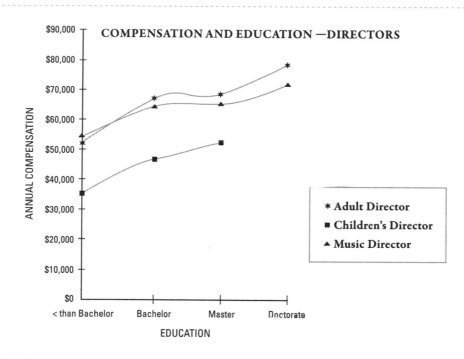

COMPENSATION AND EDUCATION —ADMINISTRATIVE

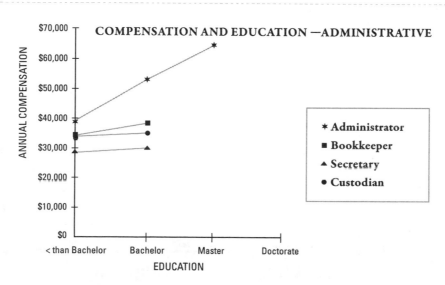

A TAX & CHURCH REFERENCE GUIDE TO USE YEAR ROUND

You'll find easy-to-understand charts and real-life illustrations, which not only make this a guide for the tax season, but also one that you can use throughout the year!

Q&A: For how many years can the IRS question or audit my income tax returns? Consider the following three rules:

1. Three Years. In general, the IRS may audit your returns, to assess any additional taxes, within three years from the date the return is filed (or within three years from the due date of the return, if later).

EXAMPLE: *Pastor W files his 2002 tax return on April 10, 2003. The IRS ordinarily may audit Pastor W's 2002 return only if they do so by April 15, 2006.*

2. Six Years. The three-year period during which the IRS may audit your returns is expanded to six years if you omit from gross income an amount greater than 25% of the amount reported on your return.

3. No Limit. The IRS can audit returns without any time limitation in any of the following situations: (a) a false or fraudulent return is filed with the intent to evade tax; (b) a taxpayer engages in a willful attempt in any manner to defeat or evade tax; or (c) a failure to file a tax return.

DID YOU KNOW?

Ministers have a 'dual tax status.'

"While most ministers are employees for federal income tax reporting purposes, they all are self-employed for social security purposes (with respect to services they perform in the exercise of their ministry). This means that ministers are not subject to 'social security' and 'Medicare' taxes, even though they report their income taxes as employees and receive a W-2 from their church. Rather, they pay the 'self-employment tax.'"

—Chapter 2

Unlike other tax publications that lose their relevance on April 15th, this volume serves a unique purpose— to have direct and immediate relevance to ministers, churches, and their advisers *throughout the year*. You'll learn how to understand the tax laws and how they apply to you, how to correctly report your federal income taxes and social security taxes, understand relevant exemptions, and reduce your tax liability as much as possible. It's designed to be a resource for ministers and also church treasurers, board members, bookkeepers, attorneys, CPAs, and tax practitioners.

Entire chapters are devoted to the items that you have the most questions about, including:

- Tax changes from 2006
- Charitable contributions
- Clergy retirement plans
- Social security
- Church reporting requirements
- Housing allowances
- Business expense reimbursement

2007 Church & Clergy Tax Guide book
ITEM #L107
$29.95

RELATED TAX GUIDE RESOURCES

**2007 Church & Clergy Tax Guide
in Adobe Acrobat format** on *CD*.

This CD features the entire *2007 Church & Clergy Tax Guide* book in Adobe Acrobat format, searchable by keyword. Includes an interactive Table of Contents and web links.

ITEM #L107C   **$29.95**

Federal Reporting Requirements for Churches;
2007 Tax Resources *Audio CD*.

This audio CD covers all topics related to filing federal tax forms, including: W-2, W3, 941, 1099 and 1096 forms. Plus it provides a review of church staff tax reporting status, help for setting up and maintaining a business expense plan for the coming year, and an update on housing and parsonage allowances for clergy.

ITEM #L213   **$9.95**

Clergy Filing Procedures;
2007 Tax Resources *Audio CD*.

This audio CD presents a step-by-step explanation of how to complete your tax forms. It includes rules for filing both as an employee and as self-employed.

ITEM #L214   **$9.95**

Update for Church Treasurers;
2007 Tax Resources *Audio CD*.

This audio CD summarizes the key legal and tax developments of the past year, plus alerts you to other pending changes.

ITEM #L215   **$9.95**

SPECIAL OFFER

2007 Church & Clergy Tax Guide *book, Adobe Acrobat format on CD*, plus the three **Tax Resources** *Audio CDs*

ITEM #L927S
$79.95

2007 CHURCH & CLERGY TAX GUIDE

PRICING INFORMATION & COMBINATION OFFERS:

ITEM #L107: **2007 Church & Clergy Tax Guide** *book* **$29.95**

ITEM #L107C: **2007 Church & Clergy Tax Guide** in *Adobe Acrobat PDF format on CD* **$29.95**

ITEM #L107S: **2007 Church & Clergy Tax Guide** *book* plus the *Adobe Acrobat PDF format on CD* **$54.95**
(a savings of 12% when you buy both)

ITEM #L927: **2007 Church & Clergy Tax Guide** *book*, plus the three **Tax Resources** *Audio CDs* $ **54.95**
(a savings of 10% when you buy all four items together!)

ITEM #L927S: **2007 Church & Clergy Tax Guide** *book, Adobe Acrobat PDF format on CD*,
plus the three **Tax Resources** *Audio CDs* **$79.95** *SPECIAL OFFER*
(a savings of 14% when you buy all tax resources together)

ITEM #L213: **Federal Reporting Requirements for Churches**; 2007 Tax Resources *Audio CD* **$9.95**

ITEM #L214: **Clergy Filing Procedures**; 2007 Tax Resources *Audio CD* **$9.95**

ITEM #L215: **Update for Church Treasurers**; 2007 Tax Resources *Audio CD* **$9.95**

QUESTIONS YOU ASK

"Would a volunteer youth pastor with no ministerial credentials be considered a 'minister' for purposes of the clergy-penitent privilege? Would such a person be eligible to perform marriage ceremonies? What about eligibility for a housing allowance under federal tax law?"

—answer found on page 25
Pastor, Church & Law,
Third Edition

A LEGAL ENCYCLOPEDIA AT YOUR FINGERTIPS!

DID YOU KNOW?

"Churches do not have to tolerate persons who disrupt religious services. Church leaders can ask a court to issue an order barring the disruptive person from the church's premises. If the person violates the order, he or she may be removed from church premises by the police, and may be found to be in contempt of court."

—page 471
Pastor, Church & Law,
Third Edition

No other resource can compare in scope and depth of this volume, often considered the "encyclopedia of legal information" for churches. This extensive, 1,000-page, third-edition volume is used as a textbook in seminary classrooms and is an often-referred-to legal resource for clergy, board members, and church officers. Billy Graham has commented,*"Pastor, Church & Law* ought to be studied by every pastor and other church leader in America." Fourteen lengthy chapters include interesting and detailed legal information including:

- Definition of terms and legal status of positions like Pastor, Clergy and Minister
- Civil court's review of clergy selection and clergy termination disputes
- Clergy exemption from military and jury duty
- Clergy-penitent privilege regarding marriage counseling and spiritual advice
- Election, appointment and authority of Officers, Directors and Trustees
- Disciplining and dismissing church members
- Church property, expansion and zoning laws
- Significant First Amendment issues as they relate to the church

To view the entire table of contents in detail, visit ChurchLawTodayStore.com

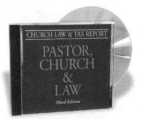

QUICK & EASY UPDATES ON THE
CRITICAL ISSUES THAT CONTINUALLY CONCERN THE CHURCH.
Church Law Special Reports

THESE SHORT LEGAL BRIEFS HELP YOU BECOME AN EXPERT QUICKLY!

▶ Personal Liability of Members of an Unincorporated Church
This special report reviews illustrative court decisions that led to some states holding members of unincorporated churches personally liable for the actions of other church members in the course of church work, as well as for contracts and liabilities of the church. Additionally, you'll find guidance on how to minimize or eliminate this risk.
ITEM #L801 **$9.95**

▶ Personal Liability of Church Officers for Uncollected or Unpaid Payroll Taxes
This special report summarizes two cases where the IRS has assessed a penalty against a church officer for willfully withholding payroll taxes. Also addressed are three important developments that make it more difficult for the IRS to be able to assert these penalties in some situations.
ITEM #L802 **$9.95**

▶ Can Church Members Examine Church Records?
This special report discusses how much legal authority church members have to inspect church records, including: financial records, membership lists, corporate documents, board and member meeting minutes, tax records and more.
ITEM #L803 **$9.95**

▶ Are Your Church's Board Members at Legal Risk?
This special report summarizes several different theories of liability, along with a description of immunity laws that provide uncompensated officers and directors with limited protection in most states.
ITEM #L804 **$9.95**

▶ Does Unrelated Business Income Tax Affect Your Church?
This special report explains the background and application of tax on the net income generated by tax-exempt organizations from unrelated business or trade that applies to churches.
ITEM #L805 **$9.95**

▶ Foxes in God's Storehouse
This special report combines statistical data about how often church embezzlement occurs with action steps for how to reduce the probability of it happening at your church.
ITEM #L806 **$9.95**

▶ Safety & Legal Issues for Church Vans and Buses
This special report reviews the legal risks of using the church's 15-passenger vans and buses to transport groups of people on trips.
ITEM #L807 **$9.95**

▶ Adopting a Church Cell Phone Policy
This special report helps you develop a new church cell phone policy based on relevant court cases involving accidents in which staff were driving and using their phones. The report also includes a sample church policy.
ITEM #L808 **$9.95**

▶ Is Your Church Violating the Fair Labor Standards Act?
This special report familiarizes you with the requirements, issued by the Department of Labor on 8/23/04 re-defining "exempt" vs. "non-exempt" employees, and how they apply specifically to churches.
ITEM #L809 **$9.95**

▶ Purchasing Church Insurance: What Church Leaders Need to Know
This special report walks you through questions to help you decide whether or not your church needs insurance and what kind, optimal coverage amount, where to obtain the coverage, and more.
ITEM #L810 **$9.95**

▶ Religious Land Use and Institutionalized Act
This special report tackles the religious freedom of churches in the context of state and local zoning laws, plus the freedoms of religious exercise for persons who are institutionalized.
ITEM #L811 **$9.95**

DID YOU KNOW?

"Many churches own 15-passenger vans, and most use them exclusively to transport children and adults on church-approved trips. Few church leaders are aware that these vans are designed to transport cargo, not people..."

— *Safety & Legal Issues for Church Vans and Buses* Special Report: Item #L807

Special Reports

YOUR CHOICE
$9.95 EACH

ANSWERS TO ALL YOUR EMPLOYMENT LAW QUESTIONS

COMPLETE COVERAGE OF ALL IMPORTANT EMPLOYMENT ISSUES FOR CHURCHES

Have you ever wondered if your hiring and firing practices are fair? Legal? This comprehensive book provides practical advice and realistic examples of one of the most problematic areas facing churches today. Learn all you need to know about employment laws and how they differ in application for churches in comparison to regular businesses. Every church needs this vital and expansive reference tool in its library!

Topics include:
- Affirmative Action
- Age discrimination
- AIDS
- Americans with Disabilities Act
- Employee discipline
- Hiring
- Fair Labor Standards
- Family Leave Act
- Firing
- Immigration Law
- National Labor Relations Act
- Reference checks
- Religious discrimination
- Sexual Harassment
- Smoking
- Title VII of Civil Rights Act of 1984
- Veteran's Reemployment Rights
- Worker's Compensation

The Church Guide to Employment Law
ITEM #L307
$14.95

Edited by Betty Childs
Production coordination by Nan Jernigan
Designed by Irwin Glusker with Kristen Reilly and Sara Burris
Composition by Maple-Vail Book Manufacturing Co.
Paper supplied by S. D. Warren Co.
Color separations by Offset Separations Corp., New York
Printed by Case-Hoyt

Library of Congress Cataloging in Publication Data
Main entry under title:

The Search for Alexander.

  Bibliography: p.
  1. Greece, Modern — Antiquities — Exhibitions.
2. Alexander the Great, 356–323 B.C. — Exhibitions.
I. United States. National Gallery of Art.
II. Yalouris, Nikolaos, 1917–   III. Andronicos,
Manolis, 1919–   IV. Rhomiopoulou, Katerina.
DF11.3.W37S4   938'.08   80-21569
ISBN 0-8212-1108-0
ISBN 0-8212-1117-X (pbk.)

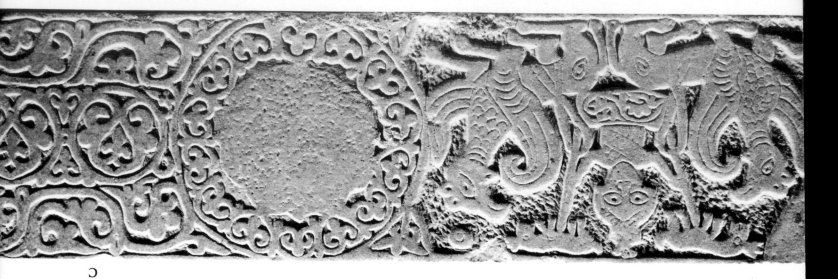

C

D

HISTOIRE ANCIENNE.

ALEXANDRE ET DIOGÈNE.

Le Sage qui soignait dans le simple appareil
D'un rayon fumant sa bouffarde,
Dit au héros qui le regarde
Éloigne-toi de mon soleil!

B